D0146123

Introduction
to
Learning
Disabilities

Introduction
to
Learning
Disabilities

second edition

Daniel P. Hallahan
James M. Kauffman
John Wills Lloyd
University of Virginia

Prentice-Hall, Inc., Englewood Cliffs, New Jersey 07632

Library of Congress Cataloging in Publication Data

HALLAHAN, DANIEL P.
  Introduction to learning disabilities.

  Bibliography: p.
  Includes index
  1. Learning disabilities.   I. Kauffman, James M.
  II. Lloyd, John W.   III. Title,
LC4704.H34 1985   371.9   84-19341
ISBN 0-13-485541-8

Editorial/production supervision and
  interior design: Dee Josephson
Photo Research: Rhoda Sidney
Cover design: Joe Curcro
Manufacturing buyer: Barbara Kelly Kittle
Cover photos: Top: Sybil Shelton/Peter Arnold
            Bottom left: Christopher Morrow, Stock/Boston
            Bottom right: Sybil Shelton/Peter Arnold

Printed in the United States of America

10 9 8 7 6 5 4 3 2 1

ISBN 0-13-485541-8   01

Prentice-Hall International, Inc., *London*
Prentice-Hall of Australia Pty. Limited, *Sydney*
Editora Prentice-Hall do Brasil, Ltda., *Rio de Janeiro*
Prentice-Hall Canada, Inc., *Toronto*
Prentice-Hall Hispanoamericana, S.A., *Mexico*
Prentice-Hall of India Private Limited, *New Delhi*
Prentice-Hall of Japan, Inc., *Tokyo*
Prentice-Hall of Southeast Asia Pte. Ltd., *Singapore*
Whitehall Books Limited, *Wellington, New Zealand*

Contents

Preface

OVERVIEW

This book is a thorough introduction to the field of learning disabilities. It covers the basic characteristics, causes, educational approaches, theories and issues pertaining to the learning disabled. It has been our goal to prepare a highly readable text that presents clear, comprehensible, and practical information about the field of learning disabilities. Our primary intent has been to write a practitioner-oriented book; at the same time we have tried to present the basic concepts of the field in a well-grounded context of research and theory. The text is designed for the first course in an undergraduate or graduate student's sequence of study in the area of learning disabilities.

We have organized the book in what, we believe, the reader and instructor will find a consistent and logical manner. We proceed from an introductory chapter dealing with definition, prevalence, and history to chapters concerned with major behavioral characteristics (perceptual disabilities, cognitive disabilities, attention disabilities and hyperactivity) to chapters concerned with disabilities in academic subject areas (oral and written language, reading, and arithmetic) to a final chapter on some of the most critical issues facing the field today.

KEY REVISION POINTS

Our major goal in this second edition has been to write a text that is more introductory in nature than the first edition. In order to meet this objective, we have written with the introductory student in mind, e.g., the level is now appropriate for undergraduate as well as graduate students, unfamiliar terms are well defined, numerous examples are provided for key concepts, the organization is as consistent as possible across chapters. In addition, we have added a feature of using boxes to provide examples of some of the key concepts in the text, present teaching tips derived from material contained in the book, and arouse readers' interest. Also, we have striven for a more balanced coverage of the major theoretical approaches to learning disabilities. Whereas the first edition was quite behavioral in focus, the second edition gives extensive treatment to the major theoretical models used by practitioners in the field of learning disabilities today—process training, cognitive training, behaviorism, and direct instruction.

Besides extensively rewriting and updating several of the chapters of the first edition, we have written five chapters that are essentially new chapters. In keeping with the most current thinking in special education, in general, and learning disabilities, in particular, we have included a chapter—Cognitive Disabilities—that focuses on recently developed techniques that fall under the general rubric of cognitive behavior modification. Other chapters that are essentially new are Spoken Language Disabilities, Reading Disabilities, Writing Disabilities, and Arithmetic and Mathematics Disabilities. These chapters, focusing on academic areas, were written to give the second edition a broader and more practical perspective. This coverage of academic content areas should be particularly appealing to those instructors who like a blend of characteristics and methods in their introductory course.

ACKNOWLEDGMENTS

We would like to thank several individuals for their help in the preparation of this book. We are indebted to students at the University of Virginia for their help with literature searches and proofreading: Mary Beirne-Smith, Susan Hart-Hester, Kathleen J. Marshall (now an Assistant Professor at Southern Illinois University), Clayton Keller, Donna Murphy, Regina Sapona, and Ruth Williams. In addition, we are grateful to Betsy Talbott for her writing of first drafts of summaries for chapters 2–9. We also thank Karen Dwier for her typing of some of the manuscript.

DPH
JMK
JWL

Introduction
to
Learning
Disabilities

Introduction

Today people from nearly every walk of life recognize the term *learning disability*. Teachers, students, and parents use it frequently and with apparent understanding. Learning disability is a separate category in the special education literature, a handicapping condition defined by federal and state laws, and a specialization for which teachers in many states must obtain certification. Although the term has gained almost universal acceptance among educators and the general public in the United States and many foreign countries since its inception in the early 1960s, the precise definition of learning disability is still being debated. Ironically, though even the most illiterate student of education is likely to know the term, even the most literate scholar is likely to have difficulty explaining exactly what a learning disability is.

The concepts underlying the term *learning disability* are not modern inventions or recent insights (Hallahan & Cruickshank, 1973; Hallahan & Kauffman, 1977; Mann, 1979; Wiederholt, 1974). Nevertheless, the term itself and popular interest in what it means are relatively new. Learning disability is the category within special education that has experienced by far the fastest growth and expansion during the past two decades. Capturing the interest and attention of professionals and laypersons alike, this burgeoning sphere of work and study has quickly gathered into its ranks individuals from a wide variety of backgrounds. Professionals from every sector of special education and disciplines related to special education—general educators, physical educators, neurologists, ophthalmologists, optometrists, pediatricians, physical therapists, psychologists, and a host of others—have all taken an active interest in the "learning disabilities explosion."

While this ground swell of interest has resulted in the rapid formation of professional and parent groups and services for children, it has not been without its problems. When so many individuals from diverse backgrounds attempt to combine their energies, a certain amount of confusion is inevitable. Considering the diversity of professionals who were instrumental in developing the field of learning disabilities, one should not be surprised that a variety of "official" definitions have been written.

Neither should one be surprised that disagreements have been voiced about the percentage of the population that should be classified as having a learning disability or about the strategies that are most appropriate for dealing with the problem. The case described in Box 1.1 illustrates the puzzling characteristics of children who may be considered learning disabled and the possible confusions that often arise during assessment for special education.

Box 1.1
JON: A CHILD WITH MANY LABELS

The case of Jon illustrates the problems learning disabled (LD) children *may* present. It does not illustrate *all* the types of problems such children may show. Neither does it illustrate the *typical* problems of LD children. It is presented here to illustrate the *diversity* of problems a child may show before being labeled LD and the confusion that frequently arises in deciding which of many possible disability labels fits the child best.

At the time of referral by his parents to this particular school district, Jon was age 6 and had already undergone extensive psychological evaluations. His parents, both professionals, had early noted severe lags in Jon's motor, language, and social development. Jon did not sit alone until age 11 months and began walking only at the age of 24 months. Presently, at age 7, Jon still has an unusually labored gait and trouble with most gross-motor movements such as running and climbing. Fine-motor problems prevent his being able to dress himself independently. In addition, Jon has considerable difficulty printing his name.

Language development was similarly delayed, particularly with regard to comprehension of language and meaningful communication of ideas. Jon spoke his first words at a normal age; however, response to simple commands did not develop until the age of 4. Until age 6, Jon's oral expression consisted predominantly of bizarre forms of echolalia such as repetition of lines heard on TV game shows or direct quotes from printed labels or written text. Jon was, and to some degree still is, unable to express his feelings in words, particularly when he is in a state of excitement or anxiety. In addition to poor communication patterns, Jon has many difficulties differentiating socially appropriate behaviors in various situations.

Jon's behavior problems are not the traditional problems associated with disruptive or destructive behaviors. Rather his behavior seems to be more a result of not understanding that specific actions are appropriate only within certain situations. For example, calling his sister disparaging names when she does not comply with his wishes is typical of children his age, but Jon uses these same expressions when he is upset with his teachers. He also has trouble distinguishing other normal everyday home behaviors from appropriate public behaviors. The inability to communicate with others has, to some degree, led Jon to solve problems with peers physically rather than verbally. An additional characteristic of Jon's social behavior is his tendency to isolate himself from other people the majority of the time, with the exception of his immediate family and some other adults.

Jon also has several highly unusual strengths. Not long after his parents became worried about his oral-language development, they noted that Jon was reading children's books aloud to himself. He began this at the age of 3 with no previous instruction. At age 5, Jon not only read adult-level books aloud but would laugh appropriately at the humorous sections. This led most observers to believe Jon was not only word calling but also comprehending what he read. This unusual talent became quite reinforcing to him and was often used as a mechanism to isolate himself from groups of peers or adults. Other unusual abilities include Jon's skill in using a typewriter to communicate with others. He also has an uncanny way of remembering persons' names, important dates, and the proper spelling of most words. . . .

For several years, Jon has undergone numerous and extensive psychological and neurological examinations. These examinations have resulted in his being labeled with a multitude of handicapping conditions. Over the years the conditions exhibited by Jon have been diagnosed as aphasic, autisticlike, dull-normal to neurologically dysfunctioned, speech and language disordered, perceptually handicapped, minimal brain dysfunction, emotionally unstable, and severely learning disabled. . . .

Although Jon has had several diagnostic labels applied to him by various psychologists and therapists in the past, for our purposes Jon qualifies as a child experiencing specific learning disabilities. The data . . . qualify him on the basis of oral-expression delay and normal intelligence. In addition to the language problem, Jon experiences motor and socialization difficulties. Results of vision and hearing screening by private physicians indicate that with correction Jon's vision is normal and his hearing is also well within normal ranges.

Source: S. C. Larsen & M. S. Poplin, *Methods for Educating the Handicapped: An Individualized Education Program Approach* (Boston: Allyn & Bacon; 1980), pp. 408–418.

Although the field of learning disabilities continues to have its problems, disagreements, and confusions, we believe it is a comprehensible field, one in which solutions, agreement, and clarity are possible. In this first chapter we will sketch the historical roots of the field, present current definitions, discuss the prevalence of learning disability, summarize causal factors, and outline conceptual approaches to intervention. In the last chapter we will return to the issues of definition and prevalence because they remain points of piquant controversy.

HISTORICAL ROOTS

One of the primary reasons for the current confusion in the field of learning disabilities with regard to such basic considerations as definition and classification is the field's rather unique evolution. Other special education professionals have traditionally developed their practices, for the most part, from a common source. Concern for the special educational needs of the mentally retarded, emotionally disturbed, deaf, and blind, for example, came about primarily through the physicians' treatment of children with these handicaps. Medical personnel, in other words, were the first professionals to be confronted with the problems of children now served under the auspices of special education. Once a group of children was defined as deviant by the medical profession, a distinct sphere of special education, with its own techniques and philosophy, was created by educators to address the learning problems of those children. Because the medical profession had a long history of established procedures, most areas of exceptionality could be built upon a common foundation of ideas and directions.

In contrast, the development of learning disabilities as a field of special education did not follow the usual course. Although the medical profession was involved in the initial identification of learning-disabled children, the field of learning disabilities, unlike other sectors of special education, lacked the "advantage" of developing within a unified framework of thinking. Instead, the concepts, ideas, and directions of this "new" field were, and continue to be, fostered almost exclusively within widely varied educational circles. Undoubtedly, in the best of all possible worlds, a field of special education would have been established by the educational profession, but unfortunately the educational profession of the early 1960s was not prepared to accept the challenge of developing this new area of exceptionality. Instead, special education began to assert itself as an entity apart from general education and, especially, from medicine. Because of the rapid expansion of both federal legislation and university training programs, special education was beginning to flex its muscles as a national power. Out of this professional and legal flux of the early 1960s the specialty of learning disabilities *presumably* was formed.

Within this historical context of educational instability, learning disabilities has become known as the avant-garde field of specialization. The field itself was to be the prototype of all that should be "good" about any aspect of special education. With a zeal characteristic of any new movement, the people in learning disabilities tended to discard associations with the past and sever their ties with other divisions of special education. This isolationist tendency doubtless was the single most significant cause of today's confusion regarding definition and terminology. Because existing terminology belonged to the past, the "young" field of learning disabilities in its quest for new frontiers created for itself the task of reclassification.

Despite the efforts of learning disabilities specialists to foster a trend of separatism, however, our basic tenet is that the present-day field of learning disabilities has its roots firmly planted in both the area of emotional disturbance and, particularly, the area of mental retardation (this idea has been further developed elsewhere; Cruickshank & Hallahan, 1973; Hallahan & Cruickshank, 1973). In fact, the theoretical rationale and many of the teaching methods now advocated by learning disabilities teachers have a long history in the areas of emotional disturbance and mental retardation. Although few teachers today are aware of it, the methods and concepts they believe are under the exclusive domain of learning disabilities actually have an established precedent in the area of mental retardation.

The situation is most unfortunate. Not only have the truly pioneering efforts of previous theoreticians and practitioners gone unrecognized, but ignorance of these historical roots has contributed significantly to the myriad present-day misunderstandings about the definition of learning disabilities as well. In the hope of bringing some clarity to the issues of definition, prevalence, and conceptual approaches, we offer the following historical perspective on the field, from early work with brain-injured soldiers to recent changes in professional organizations. We do not present here all the significant persons and events that could be cited, but we do trace the *major* lines of development with regard to the basic orientation and definition of the field. (For more detailed analyses of historical background, see Hallahan & Cruickshank, 1973, chap. 3; Mann, 1979; Wiederholt, 1974.)

Early Work with the Brain Injured

Kurt Goldstein was one of the foremost behavioral scientists to take advantage of the opportunity to study the physical disabilities of soldiers suffering from head wounds incurred during World War I. Much of what Goldstein learned about his brain-injured soldiers, whom he referred to as "traumatic dements," formed the basis of his now classic work *The Organism* (Goldstein, 1939), which dealt with broad issues of human development. Although Goldstein did not have at his disposal today's methods of rigorous experimentation, he studied the behavior of the soldiers within a clinical framework. Through careful observation, he was able to identify the following five behavioral characteristics in his patients: forced responsiveness to stimuli, figure-background confusion, hyperactivity, meticulosity, and catastrophic reaction.

With regard to forced responsiveness to stimuli, Goldstein noted that his patients seemed driven to respond to all salient objects in their surroundings. They were easily distracted by other people and objects in their environment. While awareness of events in the immediate environment can be considered critical to one's well-being, the extent to which Goldstein's patients spent their time on these activities made their behavior truly pathological. Reacting indiscriminately to various stimuli, they seemed unable to distinguish the essential from the inessential.

Figure-background confusion can be viewed as a special case of forced responsiveness to stimuli. Because Goldstein was a disciple of the German school of Gestalt psychology, he was interested in the perception of form and the perceptual figure-ground relationships of his patients. Whereas normal readers are able to perceive this book, as they are reading it, as a figure distinct from the background of the desk on which it may rest, and whereas they also are able to focus their attention on a word or on a simple group of words in the midst of the hundreds of words on the facing page, Goldstein's patients would have had great difficulty with the activity of reading. Unable to inhibit response to any stimuli, they would react nearly equally to "background" and "figure" stimuli alike. Such behavior impeded their ability to form essential figure-background relationships.

Another possible manifestation of their overresponsiveness to stimuli was their extreme motor activity. Again, the frequency and apparent aimlessness of their movement distinguished it as hyperactivity rather than productive exploration of the environment.

According to Goldstein, the other two characteristics—meticulosity and catastrophic reaction—were intimately interwoven, with the former used as a defense against the latter. Catastrophic reaction, hypothesized Goldstein, resulted from the chaotic existence of living in a world of bizarre perceptions, wherein the soldiers frequently lost contact with reality and experienced a total emotional breakdown analogous to a severe temper tantrum. Goldstein posited that the meticulous life-style of these brain-injured individuals was a defensive ploy to prevent catastrophic reactions from occurring. When the soldiers became very rigid in their everyday living habits, when they spent a great deal of effort in structuring their time schedules and the objects in their environment, they merely were protecting themselves from a damaging break in routine. Without such a self-imposed structure, the soldiers presumably would be at the mercy of their own gross misperceptions.

These germinal investigations of Goldstein laid the foundation for the two most important figures in the evolution of the field of learning disabilities: Alfred Strauss and Heinz Werner. Strauss, a neuropsychiatrist and associate professor at the University of Heidelberg, and Werner, a developmental psychologist and associate professor at the University of Hamburg, emigrated from Germany to the United States after Hitler's rise to power. Both subsequently continued their work at the Wayne County Training School in Northville, Michigan. Though each man successfully pursued lines of research and practice peculiar to his own interests (Werner, for example, with his *Comparative Psychology of Mental Development* [1948], became one of the leading theorists of developmental psychology), their many years of collaboration contributed to the chain of events that eventually led to the field of learning disabilities as we know it today.

Through a series of investigations with purportedly brain-injured, mentally retarded children (Strauss & Werner, 1942; Werner & Strauss, 1939; 1940; 1941), Werner and Strauss replicated the results that Goldstein had reported with brain-injured adults. In particular, they found that the retarded children whom they classified as brain injured (*exogenous* mentally retarded) displayed more forced responsiveness to stimuli than the retarded children who revealed no indication of brain injury (*endogenous* mentally retarded).

This work of Werner and Strauss did not go without criticism. Specifically, the procedures they used to form their exogenous and endogenous groups were attacked as being inappropriate (Sarason, 1949). One way in which an individual could be classified as exogenous (brain injured) was on the basis of behavior alone. Even if no direct evidence of a lesion was obtained through neurological tests and there was no indication of brain damage in the medical history of the individual (e.g., abnormal birth), a child was classified as exogenous if he or she displayed behavior clinically observed to occur in brain-damaged individuals. Although Werner and Strauss could be faulted on the grounds of having formed their exogenous group on other than stringent neurological evidence, the case against them would not have been so damaging had they used, for classification purposes, behaviors other than those on which they eventually were to compare the exogenous and endogenous subjects (e.g., forced responsiveness to stimuli). Circular logic is evident in their comparing in experimental tests the two groups—exogenous and endogenous—on behaviors used to place the children differentially into one or the other group in the first place.

While these criticisms certainly weaken the inference drawn by Werner and Strauss that brain damage is a *cause* of distractibility and hyperactivity, they do not negate the fact that these two researchers did find evidence of a sizable subgroup of retarded children who did exhibit a forced responsiveness to stimuli. It is important to point out here that up until this time mental retardation was perceived as a relatively homogeneous state. All retarded people were considered to be alike, and consequently no differential or individual educational or psychological programming was initiated on their behalf. Because it dispelled the long-standing notion that there were no individual differences among the retarded, the work of Werner and Strauss had revolutionary impact.

Their concern for taking heed of individual differences prompted Werner and Strauss to make educational recommendations for their exogenous children. Significant studies that initiated these recommendations were those of Strauss and Kephart (1939) and Kephart and Strauss (1940), who found that after admission to Wayne County Training School, the IQs of the endogenous children increased over the years, whereas those of the exogenous declined. Concluding that the institutional regime was inappropriate for the exogenous group, Werner and Strauss (1940) and Strauss (1943) recommended an educational program to combat the major deviant psychological characteristics of the exogenous group. Keeping in mind the tendency in these children to overreact to stimuli in the environment, they suggested a diminution of inessential stimuli in favor of an increase in saliency of materials essential to learning.

These experimental investigations of Werner and Strauss, together with subsequent papers dealing with educational practices, provided the basis for the now classic volumes—*Psychopathology and Education of the Brain-Injured Child* (Strauss & Lehtinen, 1947) and *Psychopathology and Education of the Brain-Injured Child: Progress in Theory and Clinic* (Vol. 2) (Strauss & Kephart, 1955). Both volumes, but especially the first, became the educational handbook for teachers of mentally retarded and brain-injured children. The educational techniques detailed by Strauss and Lehtinen for the brain-injured, mentally retarded child are still espoused in present-day methods books for the learning-disabled child.

To evaluate adequately the impact of research begun by Werner and Strauss would be difficult indeed. Not only did they provide a most crucial link (in terms of influencing people and future events) in the evolution of the field eventually called "learning disabilities," but they also proposed a notable conceptual frame of reference with regard to the role of psychological diagnosis in education. Basing educational recommendations on the *particular* behavioral pathology of the child, they advocated educational programming that has the same orientation as "prescriptive teaching" (Peter, 1965)—a term that was practically the byword of contemporary professionals in the field of learning disabilities. The concept of diagnosing strengths and weaknesses and then constructing an educational prescription on

this diagnostic information became a core strategy of the field.

Work with Cerebral-Palsied and Hyperactive Children

Under the influence of Werner and Strauss, the Wayne County Training School was on the "cutting edge" of research and practice. The institution therefore attracted numerous young scholars launching their careers. Consequently, in addition to creating research and educational concepts, Werner and Strauss influenced the eventual development of the field of learning disabilities because of the effect their ideas had on other individuals with whom they were in close professional contact.

One such individual was William Cruickshank. Though Cruickshank has been recognized for many years as a leader in the field of special education, perhaps his most significant work in terms of the evolution of learning disabilities has gone relatively unrecognized by special education professionals. In 1957, he published the results of a major study in which he replicated the work of Werner and Strauss, and Goldstein before them, with cerebral-palsied children of near-normal, normal, and above-normal intelligence (Cruickshank, Bice, & Wallen, 1957). This study formed a conceptual bridge between lowered and normal intelligence. Finding that cerebral-palsied children of normal intelligence exhibited poor figure-ground relationships, presumably because of distractibility, just as did the exogenous mentally retarded children of Werner and Strauss, Cruickshank facilitated the historically necessary transfer of concern to children of normal intelligence.

Cruickshank's research project with cerebral-palsied children is significant because it was the first major extension of the research of Werner and Strauss to children with normal intelligence, and his Montgomery County

(Maryland) Project is important because it was the first formalized attempt to implement the educational recommendations of Werner and Strauss with children of normal intelligence (see Cruickshank, 1976). In the late 1950s, Cruickshank initiated a demonstration-pilot study that culminated in *A Teaching Method for Brain-Injured and Hyperactive Children* (Cruickshank, Bentzen, Ratzeburg, & Tannhauser, 1961). In this project, Cruickshank and his colleagues included children who ranged in tested IQ from educable retarded to normal, and extended the principles of a highly structured program within a classroom devoid of distracting stimuli.

Although the details of the Montgomery County Project will not be discussed until a later chapter, it is important to note here that many of the children included in the project classrooms would otherwise have been placed in classes for the emotionally disturbed or the educable mentally retarded. More importantly, from the extensive case histories of the children, it is also apparent that many of them would today be placed in programs for the learning disabled. The study thus serves as a link among the fields of educable mental retardation, emotional disturbance, and learning disabilities.

As the following passage reveals, among the greatest problems encountered by individuals associated with the Montgomery County Project were those of terminology and classification.

> The authors of this study and the members of the Diagnostic Team struggled for many hours to obtain a meeting of the minds regarding definitions. They were hindered by the stereotypes of the several professions and by the literature which employed such terms as *brain injury, brain damage,* and *brain disorder.* The traditional medical classifications of cerebral palsy, aphasia, epilepsy, and others, and the literature pertaining to each, carry further implications for definitions and contain somewhat different definitions.

The children about whom this monograph is concerned are those who are defined as hyperactive, with or without diagnosis of brain damage. Specific brain injury is difficult to delineate in every instance. While neurological examination and pediatric history in over half the cases supported the fact that brain injury was undoubtedly present, the Diagnostic Team members were frequently reluctant to agree that brain injury or other form of central nervous system disorder did actually exist. The diagnostic and clinical data accumulated on the individual children, however, fell into a pattern or "clustering" which made it possible to describe the children in terms of behavioral and learning disorders. A group decision to include a child in the study was made on this basis.

Thus, children who demonstrated hyperactivity, dissociative tendencies, perseveration, figure-background reversals, and angulation problems in combination or as separate psychological characteristics; children who indicated traditional organic characteristics in pattern and scatter analysis on intelligence tests; and children who demonstrated these characteristics in appropriate ways in pediatric examinations, in neurological, audiological, and psychiatric examinations, as well as in the psychological examinations, were included in the group. Hyperactivity, in traditional terms, often applies to those children who are characterized by emotional disturbances and gross manifestations of behavior disorders. While some children in the population of the current study were characterized by these factors, hyperactivity is herein defined to include much more subtle deviations in behavior, and is more specifically considered to be related to matters of short attention span, visual and auditory distractibility, and disturbances in perception leading to dissociative tendencies.* (Cruickshank et al., 1961, pp. 9–10)

The Montgomery County Project thereby provided a rationale for employing Werner and Strauss's concepts with children of normal intelligence. In fact, by including children who

---

* W. M. Cruickshank, F. A. Bentzen, F. H. Ratzeburg, & M. T. Tannhauser, *A Teaching Method for Brain-Injured and Hyperactive Children* (Syracuse, N.Y.: Syracuse University Press, 1961), pp. 9–10. Reprinted by permission.

tested as retarded in the same classroom with children who tested as normal, Cruickshank was one of the first educators to recognize that differential grouping of children should be based on information other than IQ levels. The mental age rather than the IQ of the child, and important behavioral characteristics (e.g., hyperactivity and figure-background problems), should be the primary criteria used for educational grouping. This concern for the specific behavioral characteristics of the nonlearning child was no doubt generated by the work of Werner and Strauss and is a central theme of learning disabilities today.

Work with Slow Learners and Development of the ITPA

At about the same time as Cruickshank's publication of results of the Montgomery County Project, two other contributions destined to be significant to the development of the field of learning disabilities were made by former staff members of the Wayne County Training School—Newell Kephart's *The Slow Learner in the Classroom* (1960; 2nd ed., 1971) and S. A. Kirk, J. J. McCarthy, and W. D. Kirk's *Illinois Test of Psycholinguistic Abilities* (1961: rev. ed., 1968).

Whereas Cruickshank elaborated upon Werner's and Strauss's and Strauss and Lehtinen's concepts of reduced environmental stimuli and structured educational programming, Kephart emphasized perceptual-motor training. Kephart's *Slow Learner*, in which he provided numerous techniques for teachers to use in training the perceptual-motor skills of "slow-learning" children (soon to be referred to as "learning disabled"), quickly became a classic methods book. Primarily because of the work of such individuals as Kephart, and to a lesser extent Cruickshank, the field of learning disabilities has a perceptual-motor orientation. Owing to the assumption, first advocated by

Werner and Strauss and later emphasized by Kephart, that perceptual and perceptual-motor development form the basis for later conceptual learning, many educational tests, materials, and programs for the learning disabled are perceptual-motor in nature rather than oriented toward other aspects of development, such as language (Hallahan & Cruickshank, 1973).

One individual who did give some visibility to the language disabilities of learning-disabled children was Samuel Kirk. After many years of work and experimentation with retarded children, Kirk and his colleagues published the experimental edition of the *Illinois Test of Psycholinguistic Abilities* (Kirk, McCarthy, & Kirk, 1961). Built upon the communications model of C. E. Osgood (1957), the ITPA considers (1) channels of communication (auditory-vocal and visual-motor); (2) psycholinguistic processes (reception, organization, and expression); and (3) levels of organization (representational and automatic). Each of the various subtests of the ITPA fits within the three dimensions of the Osgood model.

The ITPA was significant in furthering the concept of differential abilities inherent in contemporary learning disability literature. This instrument was devised with the intent of enabling a teacher to construct a blueprint of the child's particular strengths and weaknesses before structuring his/her educational program. The uniqueness of the ITPA is its educational orientation; subsequent pamphlets and manuals drawing on the test offer specific educational recommendations for disabilities in specific skill areas (Bush & Giles, 1969; Karnes, 1968; Kirk & Kirk, 1971). While research has offered only partial support for the basic rationale of the ITPA (Hallahan & Cruickshank, 1973), the educational focus of the test, as well as its attempt to assess different areas of ability, has made its construction an extremely important historical event in the field of learning disabilities. The ITPA provided another rationale for the concern for differential abilities and held the promise of an instrument for assessing these various abilities.

Formation of Professional and Parent Associations

One should note that by the early 1960s professional literature was beginning to reflect a new concern for the child of average intelligence with learning problems—the same learning problems evidenced by a sizable proportion of mentally retarded children. The formation of a parent organization, the Association for Children with Learning Disabilities (ACLD), in 1963, coupled with the creation a few years later of a Division for Children with Learning Disabilities (DCLD) within the professional organization known as the Council for Exceptional Children (CEC), provided formal confirmation of this new field of special education.

The actual acceptance of the term *learning disabilities* was the result of a meeting of parents in Chicago in 1963. Until that time, concerned parents were confused by the professional literature, which was using interchangeably some two or three dozen terms (e.g., dyslexia, reading disabilities, perceptual handicaps, minimal brain injury). Because of this confusion, they were unable to mount a concerted effort on behalf of their children, despite the fact that in the early 1960s the impact of parent organizations on legislation for services, research, and professional training was perhaps at its height, and parent groups representing other areas of special education had scored many victories for their children. The parents at this meeting pressed for a suitable label for their children, and in his address to the group Samuel Kirk suggested that the term should be educationally rather than etiologically based. Kirk's term, learning disabilities, was accepted, and the Association for Children

with Learning Disabilities was formally established the following year (see Kirk, 1976).

Though the formation of ACLD provided a rallying point for parents of children who had been denied services, the orientation of the group has been a factor in the current confusion regarding the definition of learning disabilities. Perhaps fearful of the stigma attached to the retarded, ACLD has tended to dissociate itself from the area of mental retardation. The result has been that the shared characteristics of retarded and learning-disabled children and the similarities in services and educational programming for the two groups—the heritage of the field of learning disabilities—have been ignored. This zeal to create a separate category with no conceptual ties to other areas of special education has been a primary factor in the rampant confusion regarding the definition of learning disabilities.

By 1975, when the Education of All Handicapped Children Act (Public Law 94-142) was passed, learning disability had become firmly entrenched as a separate special education category. PL 94-142 was framed to meet the needs of *all* handicapped children for special education, and learning-disabled children were included in the law and the accompanying rules and regulations. Today the learning disabled constitute the largest and fastest growing category of exceptional children in American schools.

Changes in Professional and Parent Organizations

During the early 1980s, changes were made in the names of the ACLD and DCLD, reflecting the realization that adults as well as children have learning disabilities: the ACLD became the Association for Children and Adults with Learning Disabilities; the DCLD became simply the Council for Learning Disabilities (CLD). The inclusion of *adults* in the name of the Association and the removal of the word *children* from the name of the Council were actions taken in response to the argument by advocates for the handicapped that learning disabilities occur in individuals of all ages. By the late 1970s, a major trend in the field was the development of special programs for the learning disabled in high schools. Moreover, several new organizations serving adults with learning disabilities have been founded in recent years.

Besides the change in its name, one of the primary organizations concerned with the learning disabled changed its affiliation: CLD seceded from the Council for Exceptional Children. The overwhelming majority of the members of CLD voted to become a completely separate, independent organization, reflecting the strength of learning disabilities as a distinct category of exceptionality and the desire of many professionals to determine their own destiny outside their parent Council. Shortly after the secession of CLD, a new division of CEC, the Division for Learning Disabilities (DLD), was organized.

In 1977, under the leadership of William M. Cruickshank, the International Association for Research in Learning Disabilities (IARLD) was founded. This association links scholars from many countries—through newsletters, monographs, and conferences—who are investigating the nature of learning disabilities and their treatment.

Some of the *major* events and individual contributions related to the development of the field of learning disabilities are shown in Figure 1.1. Other events and people obviously could have been included; only the basic framework has been outlined. The main conclusion to be drawn from Figure 1.1, specified in the section labeled "Identification of Population," is that the field of learning disabilities evolved from a preoccupation with the mentally retarded to a concern for children—and later adults—of

normal intelligence. The point to be emphasized is that the brain-injured adults of Goldstein; the exogenous retarded children of Werner and Strauss; the brain-injured children of normal intelligence of Cruickshank; the slow learners, "minimally brain-injured," emotionally disturbed, or hyperactive children with normal intelligence of Cruickshank, Kephart, and Kirk; and the learning-disabled children and adults of the present day all have a great deal in common with regard to psychological and behavioral characteristics. The individuals in each of these groups have evidenced problems in functioning in specific areas of ability. Our historical review of the development of the field should help you understand why the definition of learning disability is a controversial issue today and why the inclusion of certain terms, especially those related to brain injury or neurological dysfunction, is a particularly controversial matter.

DEFINITION

Many definitions of learning disability have been suggested during the past 20 years. As our historical review has indicated, the legacy of the field is a confusing array of terms. Consequently arguments about definitions tend to be arguments about the appropriateness of the inclusion of certain terms, particularly those referring to psychological processes or manifestations of brain injury.

The two definitions currently receiving the widest acceptance are the definition used in PL 94-142 and the one adopted by the National Joint Committee for Learning Disabilities. These definitions may at first reading seem to differ only slightly. Each, however, has its advocates and critics, and as you study the field of learning disabilities in greater depth, the differences between these definitions will become more obvious.

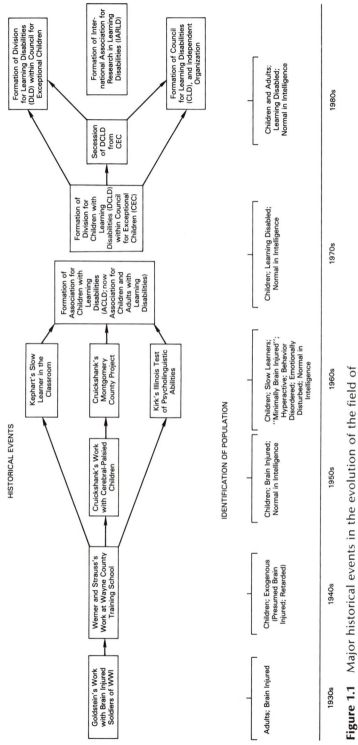

Figure 1.1 Major historical events in the evolution of the field of learning disabilities.

13

The Public Law 94-142 Definition

The PL 94-142 definition, which is nearly identical to one developed in 1967 by the National Advisory Committee on Handicapped Children, reads as follows:

> Specific learning disability means a disorder in one or more of the basic psychological processes involved in understanding or in using language, spoken or written, which disorder may manifest itself in imperfect ability to listen, think, speak, read, write, spell, or do mathematical calculations. The term includes such conditions as perceptual handicaps, brain injury, minimal brain dysfunction, dyslexia, and developmental aphasia. The term does not include children who have learning problems which are primarily the result of visual, hearing, or motor handicaps, of mental retardation, of emotional disturbance, or environmental, cultural, or economic disadvantage.

This definition, besides being the one under which federal programs are administered, has been adopted by most states. Although it is "official" in the sense that it has legal status, it has been criticized for a variety of reasons. Chief among them are: (1) some of the concepts and terms included in the definition (e.g., *minimal brain dysfunction*) are obsolete (Kauffman & Hallahan, 1979); and (2) the specific exclusion of disabilities presumed to be caused by environmental disadvantage, mental retardation, and emotional disturbance is not completely rational (Hallahan & Bryan, 1981; Kauffman & Hallahan, 1979; Lloyd, Hallahan, & Kauffman, 1980).

The National Joint Committee for Learning Disabilities Definition

In 1981, the National Joint Committee for Learning Disabilities (NJCLD) issued an alternative definition. The NJCLD was comprised of representatives from the American Speech-Language-Hearing Association (ASHA), the Association for Children and Adults with Learning Disabilities (ACLD), the Council for Learning Disabilities (CLD), the Division for Children with Communication Disorders (DCCD), the International Reading Association (IRA), and the Orton Dyslexia Society. The definition stated:

> Learning disabilities is a generic term that refers to a heterogeneous group of disorders manifested by significant difficulties in the acquisition and use of listening, speaking, reading, writing, reasoning or mathematical abilities. These disorders are intrinsic to the individual and presumed to be due to central nervous system dysfunction. Even though a learning disability may occur concomitantly with other handicapping conditions (e.g., sensory impairment, mental retardation, social and emotional disturbance) or environmental influences (e.g., cultural differences, insufficient-inappropriate instruction, psychogenic factors), it is not the direct result of those conditions or influences. (Hammill, Leigh, McNutt, & Larsen, 1981, p. 336)

According to Hammill et al. (1981), the NJCLD felt its definition had the following advantages over the PL 94-142 definition: (1) it is not concerned exclusively with children; (2) it avoids the phrase *basic psychological processes*, which has generated much confusion and debate; (3) spelling is not included as a specific disorder because it is logically subsumed under other areas of function, especially written language; (4) it avoids mentioning ill-defined conditions (e.g., *perceptual handicaps, dyslexia, minimal brain dysfunction*), which have caused much confusion; and (5) it clearly states that learning disabilities may occur concomitantly with other handicapping conditions.

Though the member organizations participating in the NJCLD have given formal approval or endorsement to the new definition, the PL 94-142 definition remains the only one with legal status. The NJCLD readily admits that its definition is not perfect and is likely to be modified or replaced. Also the NJCLD definition contains the presumption that learning disabilities are due to central nervous system dysfunction, a presumption that many believe is not justified by research on the causes of learning disabilities.

The controversies surrounding definition are discussed in more detail in the last chapter. Here it is sufficient to point out the dissatisfaction of many writers and scholars with the current federal definition and the lack of legal status for the NJCLD definition. The important commonalities in the two definitions are these: Learning-disabled children

1 have significant problems in learning academic skills (i.e., do not achieve at a level commensurate with their intelligence);

2 do not exhibit academic problems as a direct result of other handicapping conditions.

A discrepancy between academic achievement and intellectual ability is the central feature of all definitions of learning disability—the child is not learning as expected or predicted at school. This concept of discrepancy plays a key role in the issue of the prevalence of learning disabilities.

PREVALENCE

If the definition of something is vague, quantifying it will obviously be very difficult. Since the definition of learning disability is imprecise, it follows as a logical consequence that the prevalence of learning disability is impossible to determine with much accuracy. Prevalence, like definition, is a controversial topic in the field, one to which we shall return in the final chapter of this book.

Estimates of the prevalence of learning disability have ranged from 1% to 30% of the school-age population. Special Education Pro-

grams (SEP), a unit in the U.S. Department of Education, for a number of years used an estimate of 3.0%. Today, however, SEP publishes a *range* of estimated prevalence rates for each category of special education, the range being 1.0–3.0% for learning disability. Nevertheless, over 3.0% of the school population is now considered learning disabled according to SEP.

Studies of the number of children receiving special education under the category of learning disability reveal dramatic growth during the 1980s. Today nearly 2 million children in the United States are provided special education under the category of learning disability. The General Accounting Office (1981) reported that for the 1980–1981 school year learning-disabled children constituted over 50% of all handicapped children served in 2 states, and over 40% in 12 other states. It is significant that while the percentage of the child population labeled learning disabled has been increasing dramatically, the percentage labeled mentally retarded has been declining (General Accounting Office, 1981; *Report on Education Research*, 1983).

These figures, plus studies by Algozzine and Ysseldyke (1983) and Shepard, Smith, and Vojir (1983), indicate serious problems in the identification of children for special education services. The identification of learning-disabled children has increased so rapidly and the number identified has reached such a high level that some education officials are concerned that the situation may have gotten out of hand (*Report on Education Research*, 1983). Many of the children identified as learning disabled do not exhibit the characteristics specified in the PL 94-142 definition (Shepard et al., 1983; Algozzine & Ysseldyke, 1983). Apparently the clinicians who make the judgments that certain children are learning disabled often do not agree on the distinguishing characteristics of learning disabilities. Moreover, some children who exhibit the characteristics specified in the

PL 94-142 definitions of mentally retarded and emotionally disturbed children are given the label "learning disabled" because it is less stigmatizing or more acceptable to parents.

One of the key elements in definitions and prevalence estimates of learning disabilities is *discrepancy* between the child's actual achievement and expected achievement based on the child's intelligence. That is, according to most criteria for labeling a child "learning disabled," the child must not merely exhibit educational retardation compared to other children of the same chronological age, but must also show a lag in achievement based on mental age. Typically a child's mental age is determined statistically on the basis of distributions of scores on an intelligence test. Mental age can be approximated, however, by the formula: $IQ/100 \times$ chronological age = mental age. Thus the mental age of a 10-year-old child with an IQ of 90 is approximately $90/100 \times 10$ years = 9 years. The academic achievement of this hypothetical child would be compared to that of average 9-year-old children, not average 10-year-olds, in determining the extent of her or his academic retardation.

How large a discrepancy between expected achievement and actual achievement is necessary before a child is considered LD? Federal guidelines do not answer this question, nor do any of the generally accepted definitions. Definitions suggest that the child's problems must be "severe" or "significant," but no specific achievement-ability discrepancy is set. Obviously the answer to this question is arbitrary, but how it is answered has implications for prevalence estimates. The larger the discrepancy required for identifying a child as learning disabled, the smaller the number of children who will be identified—at least in theory. Moreover, the size of the discrepancy for any child will vary according to the specific achievement and intelligence tests that are administered.

To some extent the discrepancy question is a moot point. Various researchers have documented the fact that school personnel do not use clear and consistent criteria for determining that a "significant" or "severe" discrepancy exists before they label children learning disabled (Algozzine & Ysseldyke, 1983; Perlmutter & Parus, 1983; Shepard et al., 1983; Ysseldyke et al., 1983). The question of prevalence of learning disabilities, therefore, is not answerable definitively. At present, between 3% and 4% of the school-age population is identified as learning disabled. Many educators would argue that 3% is a reasonable estimate of the prevalence of learning disabilities.

CAUSES OF LEARNING DISABILITIES

The history of the field of learning disabilities suggests that brain injury or neurological dysfunction is the known or presumed cause of learning-disabled children's problems. Moreover, the NJCLD definition states, and the PL 94-142 definition hints, that learning disabilities are intrinsic to the individual and due to neurological dysfunction. But what actually is *known* about why children are learning disabled? The answer to this question is "very little!"

Research has shown that a wide variety of factors *can* cause a child to have a learning disability, but the same body of research shows clearly that not one of these factors is *necessarily* involved in any given case. The same factors, that *can* cause a learning disability can cause other handicapping conditions, such as mental retardation or emotional disturbance. Brain damage or neurological dysfunction is only a *presumed* cause in most cases of learning disability; the actual cause typically cannot be pinpointed (Hallahan & Cruickshank, 1973; Kauffman & Hallahan, 1979; Whalen, 1983).

Definitions of learning disability suggest that the cause is presumed to be neurological because no other explanation for the problem is readily available.

Many possible causes of learning disabilities have been suggested. Among them are:

genetic factors;

brain injury (due to physical trauma or lack of oxygen before, during, or soon after birth);

biochemicals that are missing (e.g., chemicals necessary for proper functioning of the central nervous system);

biochemicals that are present (e.g., food additives, such as dyes, or food substances, such as sugars);

environmental factors, such as lead or fluorescent lighting;

psychological or social influences, such as cultural differences or disadvantages, inadequate instruction, or poor parenting.

Some of these potential causal factors are intrinsic, some are extrinsic to the individual. None has been shown to be the primary cause of learning disabilities. Each is known to be able to produce a variety of effects ranging from mild disorders to severe disabilities. The relationship between these factors and handicapping conditions is diagrammed in Figure 1.2. Our point here is simply that while many factors *can* cause a learning disability, these same factors can cause a variety of other disabilities, and the cause of a particular child's disability is very seldom identifiable with cer-

Figure 1.2 Causal factors related to learning disabilities and other disorders. Any one of several extrinsic, intrinsic, or unknown factors can cause a child to be learning disabled (LD), mentally retarded (MR), or emotionally disturbed (ED). Typically, the causal factors in a given case cannot be pinpointed. The causal factors tend to be interrelated, as do the disabilities.

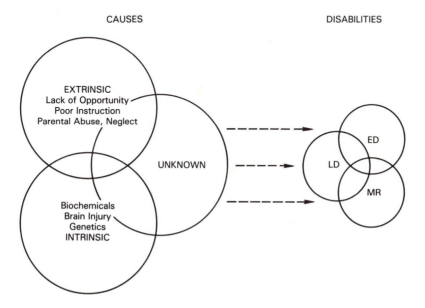

tainty. Learning disability, emotional disturbance, and mental retardation are closely related conditions in terms of their causal factors as well as their distinguishing characteristics. In the following chapters on specific disabilities we discuss causal factors in more detail when appropriate.

CONCEPTUAL MODELS OF INTERVENTION

Regardless of controversies about the definition and causes of learning disabilities and estimates of their prevalence, schools must attempt to identify all learning-disabled children and devise plans for educating them. In fulfilling this obligation to educate handicapped children, local schools must deal with legal, administrative, and theoretical models of intervention in the child's disabilities.

Legal Models

Federal law (PL 94-142) requires that each state and locality have plans to ensure that every handicapped child is identified and provided a free and appropriate education. Local schools must establish programs that comply with both federal and state laws. Today most states have laws regarding the education of handicapped children that closely parallel federal law. Consequently, we outline here only the essential requirements of the federal law.

PL 94-142 is designed to protect the right of handicapped children to an appropriate education and the right of parents to reasonable participation in decisions about their handicapped children's education. The following is a brief description of the major requirements of the law. For a detailed discussion of many of the law's requirements and appropriate teachers' responses to them, especially the requirements

for individualized educational planning, see Larsen and Poplin (1980) and Smith (1981).

Identification   Extensive efforts must be made to screen and identify all handicapped children. In the case of learning-disabled children, this typically means encouraging teachers to refer for evaluation any children in their classes who they think may have a learning disability. Some school systems routinely make comparisons of children's achievement test scores and IQs to screen students for learning disabilities.

Nondiscriminatory Evaluation   The child who is referred for evaluation must be evaluated in each area of suspected disability. The evaluation must not be biased by the child's language or cultural background or by his or her handicaps. The evaluation must be carried out by a multidisciplinary team, and no single evaluation procedure may be used as the sole criterion for identification, placement, or planning.

Confidentiality   The results of the evaluation must be kept confidential, as must information regarding placement of the child in special education. Parents and guardians have the right of access to the school's records regarding their children.

Due Process   Before a child can be evaluated, labeled, or placed in special education, the parents or guardians must give their informed consent. If they disagree with the school's decision on any of these matters, they have the right to a due process hearing before an impartial hearing officer. The school must make reasonable efforts to consult the child's parents or guardians at each stage of evaluation, planning, and placement. If the parents or guardians cannot be located or are unknown, then the school must find a surrogate parent to serve as an advocate for the child.

Individual Education Plan (IEP) A written individualized plan must be on file for each handicapped child who is receiving special education. The plan must state the child's present level of functioning, long-term and short-term goals, the specific services to be provided, when the services will be initiated, and how the services will be evaluated. For an example of an IEP, see Box 1.2.

Box 1.2
AN INDIVIDUAL EDUCATION PLAN

PL 94-142 requires that each child receiving special education services have an individual education plan. Local school systems are responsible for devising their own forms or formats for writing IEPs. Consequently, the appearance, organization, and amount of detail found in IEPs vary widely, although all IEPs must by law contain certain elements. The sample IEP we present here on pages 20 and 21 is, in our opinion, adequate, but it should not be taken as an example of the way an IEP must or should be written. For extensive discussion of IEPs, see Larsen and Poplin (1980).

Least Restrictive Environment (LRE) When special education is provided, it must be provided in the least restrictive environment that is consistent with the child's educational needs. In the case of learning-disabled children, this typically means that if the child's needs can be met without removing the child from the regular classroom, then he or she will not be placed in a special class.

Related Services The child who is provided with special education must also be provided related services that are necessary if he or she is to benefit from special education. Related services include such things as transportation, occupational or physical therapy, speech or language therapy, adapted physical education, and diagnostic medical or counseling services.

Full Educational Service at No Cost to Parents The special education given to children who are identified as learning disabled must be provided by the public school at no cost to the parents or guardians.

Legal models of intervention place large responsibilities on school personnel, including teachers. The teacher, whether a regular classroom teacher or a special educator, may be called upon to participate in any of the following:

referral of children for evaluation;

evaluation of children's specific academic abilities and disabilities;

an interdisciplinary conference to determine the child's eligibility for special education;

a conference (possibly including the child and the parents, as well as other professionals) to write an individual education plan, including the need for related services, and to determine the least restrictive environment in which the child's needs can be met;

communication with parents or guardians regarding the school's response to the child's needs;

impartial due process hearings regarding the appropriateness of the school's response to the child's needs and the parents' opinions.

Clearly the demands of current legal models of intervention require the highest level of pro-

Confidential Information

INDIVIDUALIZED EDUCATION PROGRAM

School Year 1983-84

Name _Jonathan Gould_ DOB _8/4/74_ School _Greenway_ Grade _3_

Handicapping condition _Learning Disability_ Date of IEP meeting _11/8/93_ M-D-Y Notification to parent _10/21/83_ M-D-Y

Initiation and anticipated duration of services _11/83_ M-Y to _6/84_ M-Y Eligibility/Triennial _10/14/83_ M-D-Y Plan to be reviewed no later than _11/84_ M-Y

Educational/Vocational Program

Special Education Services

Work with LD resource teacher

Regular Education Services

regular third grade

Total Amount _____ Times/Wk. _5_ Hrs./Day _1_   Total Amount _____ Times/Wk. _5_ Hrs./Day _5_

Related Services

Type	Amount
Speech/language therapy	_20 min. twice/wk._

Physical Education

Adapted Class   Amount _____

Regular Class   Amount _as scheduled_

Transportation

Special _____   Regular _✓_

Current Level of Performance

Reading: 2' level
poor word attack skills; trouble reading sight words
Math: at grade level
Language Arts: difficulty writing sentences
and difficulty spelling
Work Habits: needs frequent reminders to stay
on task; problems completing daily class
assignments and homework

Participants in Plan Development

Name	Title
Mr. & Mrs. W. Gould	_parents_
Sandra Wright	_3rd grade teacher_
Marcia Garten	_LD resource teacher_
John Adams	_principal_

For High School Students ONLY (to be initially completed at 9th grade IEP meeting and reviewed annually).

This student is a candidate for: High School Diploma _____ ; Special Ed. Certificate _____ ; GED Equivalency Diploma _____

Is the Minimum Competency Test to be administered this school year? Yes _____ No _____ If yes, attach addendum.

White: Confidential Folder   Yellow: Parent Copy

School Year 1983-84

ANNUAL GOAL: The student _Jonathan Gould_ will: successfully complete the 3' level of his classroom reading series

SHORT TERM OBJECTIVES	Grading Periods	PROGRESS REPORTS COMMENTS
Objective: When asked to read a list of 30 words from his classroom reader, Jonathan will read them with 85% accuracy. Beginning Skill Level: reading at 1² level Date Initiated 11/15/83	1.	
	2. 12/83	P
	3. 3/84	P - needs help with Dolch words
	4.	
Objective: Given a set of 50 one-syllable words, with perfect letter-sound correspondence, Jonathan will read and spell the words with 85% accuracy. Beginning Skill Level: able to read CVC words - short a & short i Date Initiated 11/15/83	1.	
	2. 12/83	P - confuses short e and short i sounds
	3. 3/84	M/R - review with two-syllable words
	4.	
Objective: Given 30 one-syllable words with long vowel sounds, Jonathan will read and spell them with 90% accuracy. Beginning Skill Level: able to read words with silent e Date Initiated 2/84	1.	
	2.	
	3. 3/84	D- trouble spelling words, esp. with long a P- able to read words
	4.	
Objective: When given 10 words from his spelling book (3'), Jonathan will write sentences (5 words or more) with correct verb tense and 90% accuracy in spelling. Beginning Skill Level: able to write 3 word sentences with assistance from teacher Date Initiated 11/15/83	1.	
	2. 12/83	D- great difficulty generating sentences
	3. 3/84	M/R
	4.	

Evaluation Procedures: Annual goals will be evaluated during the annual review. Short term objectives will be monitored at each nine week marking period. Beginning skill level indicates the student's performance prior to instruction.

Progress Key: No mark—Objective not initiated   P—Progressing on the Objective   D—Having difficulty with the objective (comment to describe difficulty)
                         M—Objective mastered   M/R—Objective mastered, but needs review to maintain mastery

White: Confidential Folder   Yellow: Parent Progress Report   Pink: Teacher Working Copy   Goldenrod: Parent Original

Abigail Heyman, Archive Pictures, Inc.

Federal law guaranteed the rights of learning disabled children to free appropriate education and to education in the least restrictive environment. Their parents have rights in information about their child's disabilities and to participation in decision making about his/her education.

fessional conduct on the part of teachers and administrators. The laws and regulations that are necessary to protect the rights of children and their parents can present serious dilemmas for school personnel involved in special education. For example, teachers may be caught between serving the interests of children and their parents and conforming to pressure from school administrators, or between following their own best judgment about what to teach and conforming to the wishes of parents or the dictates of a prescribed curriculum (Bateman, 1982).

Administrative Models

Learning-disabled children perhaps receive special education in normal or nearly normal school settings more frequently than students in any other category of special education. This may be due to the fact that LD students' prob-

lems tend to center on academic retardation—and academic instruction is the stock-in-trade of the regular classroom teacher, the focus of traditional schooling. Administrative plans for offering special education to the learning disabled run the gamut from consultation of the child's regular classroom teacher with a special educator to full-time placement of the child in a residential school. Services to the learning disabled tend to be concentrated, however, in the least restrictive alternatives, i.e., plans involving placement of the child in the regular classroom for all or most of the day.

The range of administrative arrangements for service to LD children may be summarized as follows, beginning with the least restrictive and ending with the most restrictive environment:

A *consultant teacher* confers with the regular classroom teacher and advises on educational methods and materials.

Donald Dietz, Stock, Boston

Teachers choose teaching techniques based on their interpretation and evaluation of alternative theoretical models.

An *itinerant* special education teacher serving two or more schools periodically (perhaps once or twice weekly) works with LD children individually or in small groups and advises the regular classroom teacher.

A *resource teacher*, trained as a special educator and assigned permanently to the school, works daily (perhaps 1 or 2 hours) with the LD child individually or in a small group and advises the regular classroom teacher.

The LD child is placed temporarily (perhaps 2 to 3 weeks) in a *diagnostic-prescriptive center* where his or her special abilities and disabilities are assessed, teaching procedures are used on a trial basis, and a teaching "prescription" is written for a regular classroom teacher or special educator to follow.

The LD child is placed in a *special self-contained class* and taught by a special education teacher, usually with a group of 10 to 15 other LD children.

The LD child is placed in a special *day school* or a special *residential school* for the learning disabled.

We caution here that although this listing of administrative plans for service is in a logical order of least to most restrictive for LD chil-dren, in general, the type of placement that is least restrictive for a given child depends on the severity of her or his problems. As Cruickshank (1977) noted, greater physical restriction can mean less psychological restriction for some handicapped children. From a legal point of view, Bateman and Herr (1981) note that the least restrictive environment for a child can be determined *only* after one has determined that the child can in fact receive an *appropriate* education in two or more different settings. That is, one must first arrive at a conclusion regarding the educational services that are appropriate for the child, and only then consider the least restrictive environment in which the child can be given those services.

Theoretical Models

Teachers are always guided, knowingly or unknowingly, by a theory about how children learn and what they should be taught. When they simply follow curriculum guides or give children textbooks, workbooks, or ditto materials that are handy, teachers are implicitly adopting the theory of the curriculum designer or the author of the instructional materials. Unless they are aware of the theory by which they are guided, teachers are not able to make adequate decisions about the appropriateness of specific instructional strategies and materials.

Theoretical models are a point of controversy in the learning disabilities literature and in the training of teachers. You may find it useful to keep in mind as you approach the other chapters that interventions in learning disabilities have been guided by a variety of theoretical perspectives. The major points of view can be summarized briefly as follows.

Process Training Theories   Proponents of process training assume that the primary problem of learning-disabled children is that they have deficits in their abilities to perceive and interpret stimuli, i.e., they have psychological *processing* problems. For example, a child may not learn to read because of difficulties in perceiving and integrating (processing) visual information; therefore intervention should include training in the process of visual perception before the child is presented with reading tasks. Process training may include training in visual perception, auditory perception, motor learning, or any combination of these processes that are assumed to underlie academic learning. The assumption is that if the basic processing problems are remediated, then academic learning will be made much easier; academic instruction before the basic processing problems are remediated will be fruitless.

Cognitive Theory   Learning disabilities may be conceptualized as thinking disabilities or problems in processing information. Accordingly, one approach to intervention is to assess how children use, misuse, or fail to use information in problem solving. The assumption here is that children fail at academic tasks not so much because they misperceive stimuli as because they have not developed thinking or problem-solving skills—they do not know how to select information, remember it, connect new information to old, and use efficient strategies for learning. Once the child's *cognitive* problems have been identified, intervention consists of teaching the child thinking skills or cognitive strategies. The child should then be able to use these strategies to solve many types of academic problems.

Behavioral Theory   Behavioral psychology provides the basis for behavioral theories of learning disabilities. The learning of any child, LD or normal, is assumed to be a function of the consequences of behavior. Thus the basic problem of LD children is that they have not been provided effective reinforcing consequences for performing appropriate academic tasks. Intervention therefore consists of presenting educational tasks at which the child can be successful, and that are successive approximations of a behavioral objective, and then reinforcing acceptable performance.

Theory of Direct Instruction   One theory of instruction is that all children will learn if they are given the right kind of examples of concepts, as long as they have learned the necessary prerequisite skills. This theory emphasizes a logical analysis of the concept to be taught rather than an analysis of the characteristics of the learner. The problem of any child, LD or normal, who has not learned a concept is that her or his teacher has not offered appropriate instruction—i.e., has not presented tasks in a sequence that removes the possibility of the child's learning an erroneous concept. Normal children learn from instruction that is not planned and executed with great precision, but LD children do not learn unless they are instructed more carefully.

Teachers and researchers do not always use one of these theoretical models to the exclusion of the others. Although they may be guided primarily by one point of view, they often employ concepts from more than one theory.

SUMMARY

Learning disability is a term that is widely known but not well understood. The historical roots of the term are found in work with adults and children who were known or presumed to have brain damage or were mentally retarded, slow learners, emotionally disturbed, or hyperactive. Numerous disciplines and professional groups have contributed to the concept of learning disability, leading to confusion about definition and terminology.

The term *learning disability* was coined in the early 1960s, when parents organized to lobby for services for their children who were having extreme difficulty in school but were not then considered mentally retarded or handicapped in any other way. The field of learning disabilities is nevertheless connected historically and logically to other areas of special education, particularly special education for the mentally retarded and the emotionally disturbed.

The two definitions of learning disability that have received widest acceptance are the definition used in PL 94-142 and the one adopted by the National Joint Committee for Learning Disabilities. The common features of definitions of learning disabilities are that LD children have significant problems in learning academic skills (i.e., show a discrepancy between their actual academic achievement and their expected achievement based on their mental age) and do not exhibit these problems as a direct result of other handicapping conditions. The prevalence of learning disabilities is difficult to determine with much accuracy. Current estimates range from 1% to 3% of the school-age population, although over 3% of school-age children in the United States were receiving special education under the learning disabilities category in 1984.

The potential causes of learning disabilities are many and include genetic, neurological, environmental, and psychological factors. All the factors that can cause learning disabilities can also cause other handicapping conditions, and in most cases the specific cause of a child's learning disability cannot be determined.

Conceptual models of intervention in learning disabilities include legal, administrative, and theoretical models. PL 94-142 provides the basis for legal concepts of appropriate intervention. Administrative concepts of intervention range from special educators' consultation with regular classroom teachers regarding methods and materials for teaching LD children in the regular class to placement of LD children in full-time residential schools. Theories that guide teachers' instructional decisions may be related to process training, cognitive strategy training, behavioral intervention, or direct instruction.

REFERENCES

ALGOZZINE, B., & YSSELDYKE, J. (1983). Learning disabilities as a subset of school failure: The oversophistication of a concept. *Exceptional Children, 50,* 242–246.

BATEMAN, B. (1982). Legal and ethical dilemmas of special educators. *Exceptional Education Quarterly, 2*(4), 57–67.

BATEMAN, B., & HERR, C. (1981). Law and special education. In J. M. Kauffman & D. P. Hallahan (Eds.), *Handbook of special education* (pp. 330–360). Englewood Cliffs, NJ: Prentice-Hall.

BUSH, W. J., & GILES, M. T. (1969). *Aids to psycholinguistic teaching.* Columbus, OH: Charles E. Merrill.

CRUICKSHANK, W. M. (1976). William M. Cruickshank. In J. M. Kauffman & D. P. Hallahan (Eds.), *Teaching children with learning disabilities: Personal perspectives* (pp. 94–127). Columbus, OH: Charles E. Merrill.

CRUICKSHANK, W. M. (1977). Guest editorial. *Journal of Learning Disabilities, 10,* 193–194.

CRUICKSHANK, W. M., BENTZEN, F. A., RATZEBURG, F. H., & TANNHAUSER, M. T. (1961). *A teaching method for brain-injured and hyperactive children.* Syracuse, NY: Syracuse University Press.

CRUICKSHANK, W. M., BICE, H. V., & WALLEN, N. E. (1957). *Perception and cerebral palsy.* Syracuse, NY: Syracuse University Press.

CRUICKSHANK, W. M., & HALLAHAN, D. P. (1973). Alfred A. Strauss: Pioneer in learning disabilities. *Exceptional Children, 39,* 321–327.

General Accounting Office (1981). *Disparities still exist in who gets special education.* Report to the Chairman, Subcommittee on Select Education, Committee on Education and Labor, House of Representatives of the United States. Gaithersburg, MD: GAO.

GOLDSTEIN, K. (1939). *The organism.* New York: American Book.

HALLAHAN, D. P., & BRYAN, T. H. (1981). Learning disabilities. In J. M. Kauffman & D. P. Hallahan (Eds.), *Handbook of special education* (pp. 141–164). Englewood Cliffs, NJ: Prentice-Hall.

HALLAHAN, D. P., & CRUICKSHANK, W. M. (1973). *Psychoeducational foundations of learning disabilities.* Englewood Cliffs, NJ: Prentice-Hall.

HALLAHAN, D. P., & KAUFFMAN, J. M. (1977). Categories, labels, behavioral characteristics: ED, LD, and EMR reconsidered. *Journal of Special Education, 11,* 139–149.

HAMMILL, D. D., LEIGH, J. E., MCNUTT, G., & LARSEN, S. C. (1981). A new definition of learning disabilities. *Learning Disability Quarterly, 4,* 336–342.

KARNES, M. B. (1968). *Helping young children develop language skills.* Reston, VA: Council for Exceptional Children.

KAUFFMAN, J. M., & HALLAHAN, D. P. (1979). Learning disability and hyperactivity (with comments on minimal brain dysfunction). In B. B. Lahey & A. E. Kazdin (Eds.), *Advances in clinical child psychology,* Vol. 2 (pp. 71–105). New York: Plenum.

KEPHART, N. C. (1960). *The slow learner in the classroom.* Columbus, OH: Charles E. Merrill.

KEPHART, N. C. (1971). *The slow learner in the classroom* (2nd ed.). Columbus, OH: Charles E. Merrill.

KEPHART, N. C., & STRAUSS, A. A. (1940). A clinical factor influencing variations in IQ. *American Journal of Orthopsychiatry, 10,* 345–350.

KIRK, S. A. (1976). Samuel A. Kirk. In J. M. Kauffman & D. P. Hallahan (Eds.), *Teaching children with learning disabilities: Personal perspectives* (pp. 238–269). Columbus, OH: Charles E. Merrill.

KIRK, S. A., & KIRK, W. D. (1971). *Psycholinguistic learning disabilities: Diagnosis and remediation.* Urbana, IL: University of Illinois Press.

KIRK, S. A., MCCARTHY, J. J., & KIRK, W. D. (1961). *Illinois Test of Psycholinguistic Abilities* (Experimental ed.). Urbana, IL: University of Illinois Press.

KIRK, S. A., MCCARTHY, J. J., & KIRK, W. D. (1968). *Illinois Test of Psycholinguistic Abilities* (Rev. ed.). Urbana, IL: University of Illinois Press.

LARSEN, S. C., & POPLIN, M. S. (1980). *Methods for educating the handicapped: An individualized education program approach.* Boston: Allyn & Bacon.

LLOYD, J. W., HALLAHAN, D. P., & KAUFFMAN, J. M. (1980). Learning disabilities: Selected topics. In L. Mann & D. A. Sabatino (Eds.), *The fourth review of special education* (pp. 35–60). New York: Grune & Stratton.

MANN, L. (1979). *On the trail of process.* New York: Grune & Stratton.

OSGOOD, C. E. (1957). A behavioristic analysis of perception and language as cognitive phenomena. In J. S. Bruner (Ed.), *Contemporary approaches to cognition* (pp. 75–118). Cambridge, MA: Harvard University Press.

PERLMUTTER, B. F., & PARUS, M. V. (1983). Identifying children with learning disabilities: A comparison of diagnostic procedures across school districts. *Learning Disability Quarterly, 6,* 321–328.

PETER, L. J. (1965). *Prescriptive teaching.* New York: McGraw-Hill.

Report on Education Research (July 6, 1983). Number of handicapped students leveling off, ED official says. *15*(14), 5–6.

SARASON, S. B. (1949). *Psychological problems in mental deficiency.* New York: Harper.

SHEPARD, L. A., SMITH, M. L., & VOJIR, C. P. (1983). Characteristics of pupils identified as learning disabled. *American Educational Research Journal, 20,* 309–331.

SMITH, D. D. (1981). *Teaching the learning disabled.* Englewood Cliffs, NJ: Prentice-Hall.

STRAUSS, A. A. (1943). Diagnosis and education of the cripple-brained, deficient child. *Journal of Exceptional Children, 9,* 163–168.

STRAUSS, A. A., & KEPHART, N. C. (1939). *Rate of mental growth in a constant environment among higher grade moron and borderline children.* Paper presented at the meeting of the American Association on Mental Deficiency.

STRAUSS, A. A., & KEPHART, N. C. (1955). *Psychopathology and education of the brain-injured child.* Vol. 2: *Progress in theory and clinic.* New York: Grune & Stratton.

STRAUSS, A. A., & LEHTINEN, L. E. (1947). *Psychopathology and education of the brain-injured child.* New York: Grune & Stratton.

STRAUSS, A. A., & WERNER, H. (1942). Disorders of conceptual thinking in the brain-injured child. *Journal of Nervous and Mental Disease, 96,* 153–172.

WERNER, H. (1948). *Comparative psychology of mental development.* New York: International Universities Press.

WERNER, H., & STRAUSS, A. A. (1939). Types of visuo-motor activity in their relation to low and high performance ages. *Proceedings of the American Association on Mental Deficiency, 44,* 163–168.

WERNER, H., & STRAUSS, A. A. (1940). Causal factors in low performance. *American Journal of Mental Deficiency, 45,* 213–218.

WERNER, H., & STRAUSS, A. A. (1941). Pathology of figure-background relation in the child. *Journal of Abnormal and Social Psychology, 36,* 236–248.

WHALEN, C. K. (1983). Hyperactivity, learning problems, and attention deficit disorders. In T. H. Ollendick & M. Hersen (Eds.), *Handbook of child psychopathology* (pp. 151–199). New York: Plenum.

WIEDERHOLT, J. L. (1974). Historical perspectives on the education of the learning disabled. In L. Mann & D. Sabatino (Eds.), *The second review of special education* (pp. 103–152). Philadelphia: Journal of Special Education Press.

YSSELDYKE, J. E., THURLOW, M., GRADEN, J., WESSON, C., ALGOZZINE, B., & DENO, S. (1983). Generalizations from five years of research on assessment and decision making: The University of Minnesota Institute. *Exceptional Education Quarterly, 4* (1), 75–93.

Nov. 20, 1981

Joan prth bay

Sleq over at hows
I ate Saget anb
plab tresher hut.

Perceptual Disabilities

Perception refers to an individual's ability to process stimuli meaningfully, to organize and interpret sensory information. While there are many senses (such as sight, hearing, smell, taste, and touch), in this chapter we will discuss perceptual disabilities that are visual, visual-motor, tactual (touch), and kinesthetic (movement) in nature. These four disabilities are treated together because of the close link among them. Many activities we engage in involve all four of these areas, and educational programming for any one of them almost always includes activities for the others. Smell and taste are not included in this chapter, or in the book, because they are not important for the field of learning disabilities. Auditory perceptual problems are discussed in Chapter 6 because of their relevance to oral-language disabilities.

VISUAL PERCEPTUAL DISABILITIES

Not all children identified as learning disabled have visual perceptual problems. To the reader for whom this text is the first exposure to the field of learning disabilities, the above statement will probably seem logical. We have chosen to begin this chapter with such an assertion, however, in order to alert the introductory student to one of the most common misconceptions in the area of learning disabilities. Though it should be obvious that children can have learning problems for a variety of reasons, in some circles "learning disabilities" is synonymous with "visual perceptual disabilities." As was pointed out in Chapter 1, the fact that the field of learning disabilities evolved from the pioneering work of Werner and Strauss, whose primary interest was visual processes, has undoubtedly led to such concern for visual perceptual problems. One of the most frequently occurring modes of educational programming for learning-disabled children focuses on visual perceptual training activities.

In reaction to this strong emphasis on visual perceptual training, there has been since the early 1970s a growing movement to discount the existence of visual problems in favor of consideration of disabilities in other spheres of development—language, cognition, audition, for example. It is undeniably true that visual perceptual training programs as they are usually employed are of questionable benefit. Unfortunately, in their vociferous attack upon the efficacy of visual training, critics have implied that one should not be concerned about whether or not a child has a visual problem (e.g., Cohen 1969a, 1969b). On the other hand, in defense of their positions, advocates of visual training often sound *as if* they believe that all learning-disabled children have visual deficits.

The commonsense point of view holds that (1) not all children with learning problems have visual perceptual deficits, (2) some children with learning problems do have visual perceptual deficits, and (3) the remediation of visual perceptual disabilities may *help* in the remediation of the child's learning problems. (We will return to point (3) later in the chapter.)

The kinds of visual perceptual disabilities with which we are concerned in this chapter should be distinguished from the types of visual deficits that are most commonly associated with the blind and partially sighted, that is, deficits in visual acuity. The latter defects are caused by improper functioning of the sensory organ itself—the eye—due to malformation, injury, or disease. Examples of such visual deficits are myopia (nearsightedness) and hyperopia (farsightedness). Strabismus (cross-eye) and nystagmus (jerking eye movements) are further examples of problems that may be due to a functional problem of the eye. The visual perceptual problems addressed within the field of learning disabilities, however, are concerned with disabilities that occur despite the fact that a child has structurally sound eyes and adequate muscular control over them. Getman (1965) draws the distinction between problems associated with a defect in the sensory organ and problems due to a *perceptual* disability when he distinguishes between "sight" and "vision."

> Neither can vision and sight be equated. In the hope that this confusion can be terminated once and for all, time and space will be taken to define vision so all phrases in which it is used will be more meaningful and productive. Certainly, vision is usually related to the actions of the eye, and to the impact of light upon a retina. We must constantly remember that vision will not, and cannot, occur JUST BECAUSE light patterns are distributed across the retina. The eye is not a camera that takes pretty pictures which are then sent on to the brain for storage in a film locker. When light strikes the eye, there is *sight* response in the eye itself, but if the organism is to profit from this sight action, there must be an integration of this information with all other information systems before any interpretation of the light pattern is achieved. Vision is a very complex result of a very simple action in the light receptor end-organ. (p. 51)

Thus a child may have 20/20 visual acuity and still have a visual perceptual problem. It is not enough simply to administer a standard test of visual acuity such as a Snellen chart to a child experiencing learning problems in school. The child's ability to make perceptual judgments must also be assessed.

Children with learning problems may manifest numerous kinds of visual perceptual disabilities. Two of the most common will be discussed in this chapter: problems in form and position-in-space perception. These particular disabilities have been chosen because they are among the most frequently cited visual problems and are deemed by many to be influential in contributing to academic disabilities.

Analysis of Distinctive Features

Important to our understanding of visual perceptual problems is Eleanor Gibson's (1969) theory of perceptual learning. Much of what can be said about visual perceptual disabilities can be stated within the framework of Gibson's theory. She posits that as children develop perceptually, they learn to discriminate among stimuli on the basis of what have been termed *distinctive features*. That is, the child learns to distinguish objects by noting those particular features that are most salient in terms of defining the particular object being perceived. The child learns, for example, that a square is different from a circle because one has four corners and the other has no corners at all. The feature that distinguishes a square from a circle is the existence of corners. The discrimination between a square and a rectangle, however, is based upon the further distinctive feature of the relationship between the lengths of the four sides of the square and the lengths of the four sides of the rectangle.

Form Perception

Perhaps the most basic visual discrimination that the child makes is that of the perception of the property of form. Whether it be the differentiation of the letter *B* from *P* or the shape of a ball from a block, the ability to perceive the shape of objects and pictures is an important skill for the developing child to obtain. The child with poor form perception is at a distinct disadvantage when confronted with school-related activities. The printed materials the teacher presents to the child require the ability to discriminate among a variety of forms. Because visual stimuli are constantly being presented in the classroom, the child

must be an efficient perceiver of a variety of shapes. The inability to discriminate form can produce a chaotic and frustrating world for the child.

There is hardly an academic activity that does not require the child to engage in form perception. Consider, for example, the typical math problems presented. In the early stages of math instruction, the proverbial concrete aid of the pictures of three apples and two apples shown to the child with the statement, "If we have three apples and add two more apples, how many will we have?" will be of little benefit to the student unable to perceive the apples as individuals and groups. During the later stages of math, children will be able to perform computations in "their heads"; if they have visual perceptual problems, however, they will likely have difficulty with problems in written form. Children who have difficulty discriminating between a + and a − or a 7 and a 1 will have problems with their math worksheets.

The most obvious classroom activity requiring the child to discriminate forms is that of reading. The learning of the letters of the alphabet, syllables, and words will undoubtedly be impeded if there is difficulty in perceiving the form of the letters, syllables, and words. That the discrimination of letters is a crucial skill in the early stages of reading is evidenced by an extensive literature review conducted by Chall (1967). She concluded that the letter knowledge of young children is a better predictor of early reading ability than the various tests of intelligence and language ability. The work of Staats (Staats, Brewer, & Gross, 1970; Staats & Butterfield, 1965; Staats, Finley, Minke, & Wolf, 1964; Staats, Minke, Goodwin, & Landeen, 1967) also stresses the importance of letter discrimination, and his reading program (which will be discussed later in this chapter) emphasizes the training of letter discrimination. As Staats, Brewer, and Gross (1970) state:

However, in the area of reading learning, one very basic skill is the discrimination of letters. That is, the stimuli involved in reading letters are in the child's world of stimuli quite similar, even when generally considered (Staats, 1968). For example, if one trained a child to read the letter A mixed in with a group of pictures, it would be found that the child would also give the response A to *any* other letter presented. Some letters are even more similar and difficult to learn to discriminate. (p. 10)

Gibson (1969) conducted a series of investigations to determine which letters are more difficult to discriminate than others. She found that discrimination difficulty relates directly to the kinds and numbers of distinctive features of the letters. The chart in Figure 2.1 presents the distinctive-feature analysis for the capital letters of the alphabet. For example, the letter *W* is composed of two diagonal lines. It also possesses cyclic redundancy in that it is composed of the two forms *V* and *V*. It also has the property of symmetry. Letters that possess similar features are the most difficult to distinguish one from another. One would expect, for instance, that children would have a relatively harder time discriminating an *M* from an *N* and an *M* from a *W* than an *O* from an *N* or an *R* from an *M*. Gibson also found that letters containing diagonals were quite difficult. Letters differing only on the feature of curved versus straight (e.g., *P* and *F*), however, were easily differentiated.

Armed with the knowledge of the distinctive features of letters, classroom teachers can be more aware of the specific task demands they make of their pupils. For example, teachers should not be alarmed if in the early stages of learning letters a child has some initial difficulty in distinguishing among those that are composed of diagonal lines. Occasional mistakes with difficult letters should also be expected. It is the child who continues to have difficulty and who makes frequent errors on easily discriminable letters who should be given

Figure 2.1   Chart of distinctive features for a set of graphemes.
Source: E. J. Gibson, *Principles of Perceptual Learning and Development*, © 1969, p. 88. Reprinted by permission of Prentice-Hall, Inc.

Features	A	E	F	H	I	L	T	K	M	N	V	W	X	Y	Z	B	C	D	G	J	O	P	R	Q	S	U
Straight																										
horizontal	+	+	+	+		+	+								+	+										
vertical		+	+	+	+	+	+	+	+	+						+		+				+	+			
diagonal /	+							+	+		+	+	+	+	+											
diagonal \	+							+	+	+	+	+	+										+	+		
Curve																										
closed																+		+			+	+	+	+		
open V																				+						+
open H																	+		+						+	
Intersection	+	+	+	+			+	+					+			+						+	+	+		
Redundancy																										
cyclic change		+										+			+										+	
symmetry	+	+		+	+	+	+	+	+	+	+	+	+	+	+	+					+					+
Discontinuity																										
vertical	+		+	+	+		+	+	+	+			+									+	+			
horizontal		+	+			+	+							+												

extra attention. In the teaching process itself, awareness of the distinctive features of letters will enable teachers to focus their efforts on the most probable cause(s) for error. The child making errors in differentiating an *R* from a *P* can be instructed that the difference between the two letters is the addition of a diagonal line on the letter *R*. The child's attention can also be drawn to the crucial distinctive feature by highlighting the diagonal line with a bright color cue.

Position in Space

The ability to perceive the particular spatial orientation of stimuli in the environment has come to be known as "position-in-space" ability. Actually, position-in-space ability can be thought of as a more refined or particular kind of form perception ability. The child with this disability has problems with the relative position of stimuli.

The classic example of a position-in-space disability is that of the child who has a strong tendency to reverse letters or whole words while reading—for example, reading "ben" instead of "den" or "was" instead of "saw." At one time the reading disability literature contained many references to "reversal" problems and numerous case studies were discussed. There is no solid empirical basis for establishing the proportion of poor readers who exhibit reversals. Nonetheless, the general notion espoused today is that reversal problems occur in fewer children than was previously thought.

Some children do, of course, make reversals in reading, and a few of them make enough such errors to be considered to have position-in-space problems. Every teacher of the early elementary grades can attest to the fact that some children exhibit an inclination to reverse letters and words. It is the *severity* of the reversal problem that must be considered.

If it is relatively normal for children to con-fuse letters that may be reversed—*b* and *d*, *g* and *d*, *p* and *g*, and so forth—then when should the teacher become concerned? Gibson and her colleagues have performed experiments that provide the teacher with general guidelines regarding the relative frequency of reversals. Gibson, Gibson, Pick, and Osser (1962) conducted a classic study in which 12 variants were drawn for a number of artificial graphic forms. The letterlike forms were made to correspond closely to the distinctive features of actual letters. The standards (S column) along with their variants are presented in Figure 2.2, taken from Gibson (1963). There were four kinds of variations used. The lines of a form could be changed to curves or vice versa. The forms could be rotated to various degrees or reversed. The forms could be changed with regard to perspective, and they could undergo a topological change with regard to a break or close in lines.

Children aged 4 to 8 years were presented with a matching task. Given a standard figure, the child was required to find from among the variants at least one identical form among the figures that was the same as the standard. The results are shown in Figure 2.3. Relevant to our discussion here is the graph's indication that at early ages the reversal transformation is a difficult one. However, children's reversal errors drop markedly until by age 7 or 8 they are few in number. This study therefore provides an *indication* to the teacher that while in the very early grades children may have some initial reversal problems, by the second or third grade, reversal errors should occur infrequently, if at all.

Using Gibson's results, we would predict that because of the greater difficulty of reversal and rotation transformations relative to break and close transformations, the former would be more of a problem for the learning disabled than the latter. In fact, learning-disabled children are described more often as confusing

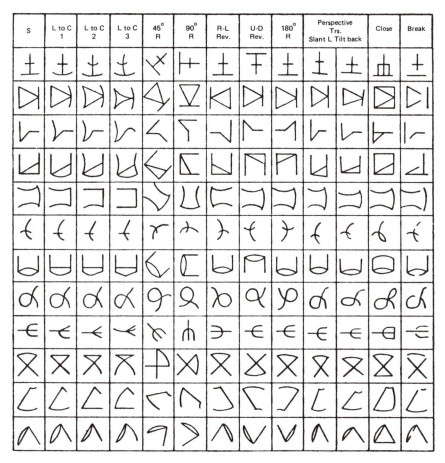

Figure 2.2 Artificial graphic forms and 12 variants. (Note: S is the standard. The 4 variations are: lines to curves [L to C]; rotation [45°, 90°, 180°] or reversal [right to left, up and down]; perspective changes; and break or close in lines.)
Source: E. J. Gibson, "Development of Perception: Discrimination of Depth Compared with Discrimination of Graphic Symbols." In J. C. Wright and J. Kagan (Eds.), *Basic Cognitive Processes in Children*, Monographs of the Society for Research in Child Development, 1963, Ser. No. 86, Vol. 28, No. 2, p. 17. Reprinted with permission.

such letters as *b* and *d* (reversal transformation) than such letters as *P* and *F* (closed versus break transformation).

With regard to the orientation of letters, the examples we have used thus far have been those in which the letters were left-right rever-

sals of each other: *b* and *d*. It is usually reported by teachers that left-right reversals are more frequent; however, there are also instances when children will confuse up-down reversals, for example, *p* and *b*. The research on normal children supports the teachers' observa-

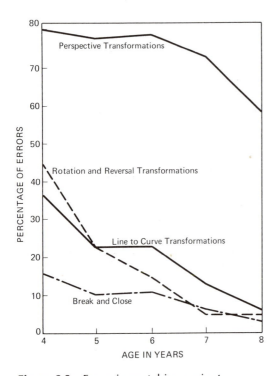

Figure 2.3 Errors in matching variants with standard graphic forms by type of variant and age of S.
Source: E. J. Gibson, "Development of Perception: Discrimination of Depth Compared with Discrimination of Graphic Symbols." In J. C. Wright and J. Kagan (Eds.), *Basic Cognitive Processes in Children*, Monographs of the Society for Research in Child Development, 1963, Ser. No. 86, Vol. 28, No. 2, p. 19. Reprinted with permission.

tions that left-right reversals are more frequent in the process of reading. Sekuler and Rosenblith (1964) and Huttenlocher (1967) found that whether the letters to be discriminated are aligned vertically or horizontally will make a difference in whether the left-right or up-down reversal is more confusing. When the letters are presented horizontally (as they are in reading), the left-right reversal (e.g., *b* and *d*) is more difficult than when the letters are presented vertically. Just the opposite is true for up-down reversible letters. Table 2.1 summarizes the results of the two studies. Pick and Pick (1970) speculate that the reason for this interaction between mode of presentation and difficulty of discrimination may be the scanning strategies of children:

> Why should there be an interaction of this type? A scanning hypothesis might be invoked. Suppose S scanned repeatedly across a pair of stimuli in the direction of their alignment, as in a TV scanner, registering only the number of elements present on each scan. Then left-right mirror images would register identically in horizontal alignment, and up-down mirror images would register identically in vertical alignment. (p. 801)

Whatever the exact reason, the results of these studies corroborate the reports of teachers that left-right reversals are more frequent than up-down reversals. Inasmuch as reading is a left-to-right activity rather than an up-and-down process, we would expect the left-right reversible letters to be harder to discriminate than the up-down reversibles (see Box 2.1).

Table 2.1   Reversible Letters Presented Horizontally or Vertically

Letters to Be Discriminated	Mode of Presentation	
	Resulting in More Errors	*Resulting in Fewer Errors*
b and d	b d	b d
b and p	b p	b p

Box 2.1
PRESENTATION OF REVERSIBLE LETTERS: A TEACHING TIP

Given the evidence that left-right reversals are more difficult to discriminate in reading from left to right than when the letters are presented one above the other, teachers may wish to incorporate this knowledge in their teaching techniques. The child who exhibits problems in differentiating *b* from *d* may be given a series of teacher-made training exercises in which the *b* and *d* are presented vertically on flash cards. After a number of successful discriminations with these presentations, the teacher could gradually align the *b* and *d* closer and closer to the horizontal on the flash card. After a series of exercises, the *b* and *d* would be aligned horizontally. For example see Fig. 2.4.

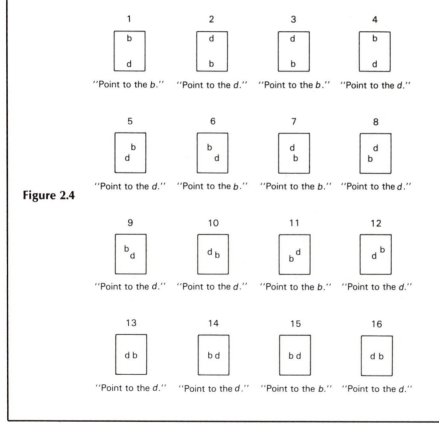

Figure 2.4

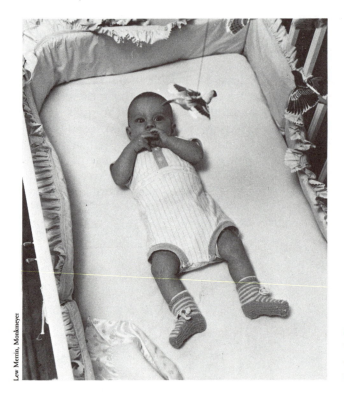

Lew Merrim, Monkmeyer

Current research indicates that visual perceptual skills begin to develop much easier than was once thought.

VISUAL-MOTOR, TACTUAL, AND KINESTHETIC DISABILITIES

We have included *visual-motor* (the coordination of the visual and motor systems), *tactual* (touch perception), and *kinesthetic* (sensations gained from moving one's body or a position of one's body) *disabilities* in one section because many authorities believe these three go hand in hand. Educational programming for one area almost always includes activities for the other areas. As with visual perception, interest in visual-motor, tactual, and kinesthetic development can be traced back to the early work of Werner and Strauss, who studied the visual perceptual and visual-motor problems of mentally retarded children. They believed that one of the behavioral symptoms of brain damage was faulty visual-motor coordination. They popularized the position that adequate concep-

tual development is dependent upon appropriate perceptual development. Among the most frequently recommended educational activities were those relating to the integration of visual and motor processes. Numerous suggestions were made for training visual-motor skills, not only for their own sake, but also for the betterment of visual perceptual abilities and, ultimately, higher-order conceptual abilities.

Visual-Motor Problems

The Perceptual-Motor Match The individual who did the most to further the idea that the coordination of the visual and motor systems is particularly difficult for the learning disabled was Newell Kephart. Kephart's own theoretical formulations and educational program are contained in *The Slow Learner in the Classroom* (Kephart, 1960/1971). The major theoretical construct Kephart espoused was that of the *perceptual-motor match*. Basically, the perceptual-motor match is concerned with the coordination of the eyes and the hands. The perceptual-motor match was considered by Kephart to be the foundation on which higher conceptual thinking is built.

There are two essential aspects of the perceptual-motor match: (1) motor development precedes visual development, and (2) kinesthetic sensation obtained from motor functioning acts as a feedback device for the monitoring of visual-motor activities. The following summarizes Kephart's conception of the perceptual-motor match:

> This process of establishing a perceptual-motor correspondence has been called the perceptual-motor match. It normally occurs in three stages best illustrated by the development of eye-hand coordination. In the first stage, the hand leads and generates most of the information. In this stage, the process is hand-eye, the hand leading and the visual information being matched to it. As this matching becomes more complete, the rapid, extensive nature of the visual data becomes apparent and the child learns to monitor and let kinesthesis control the response while he uses the visual data for more remote predictions. He has entered the second stage: eye-hand. Here the greatest reliance is upon vision, the hand being used only to confirm or to solve complex or confusing situations. Finally, the match is close enough that he can depend upon vision alone. He can explore with his eyes in the same way and get the same information as he originally did with his hand. This shift is possible because of a firm, accurate perceptual-motor match. The child has entered the third stage and become perceptual. (Kephart, 1975, pp. 65–66)

The most important element of the perceptual-motor match—the one Kephart emphasized over and over again—was his strong conviction that motor development precedes visual development. Because of this supposedly invariant ordering, Kephart maintained that meaning is gained from visual activity only if it can be matched with previously acquired motor experiences. If these prior motor learnings are deficient, then the child will be unable to achieve a perceptual-motor match. Such a child would be referred to as one who has a perceptual-motor disability. Kephart postulated that the education of the perceptual-motor–disabled child must proceed with the training of motoric development prior to the training of visual skills. In other words, the order of remediation is to correspond with the order of development—from motor to visual.

Visual Versus Motor Development Kephart's postulation that motor precedes visual development is by no means the only point of view within the field of child development, nor is it the dominant viewpoint today. Eleanor Gibson (1969), for example, postulates a different hierarchy of development. She posited that the child proceeds through three stages: (1) discrimination, (2) recognition, and (3) production. The first two stages are concerned with the visual modality, whereas the third—the combining of visual and motor processes—corresponds to Kephart's perceptual-motor match. Gibson's match, however, is in the opposite direction: visual development is prior to visual-motor coordination.

Gibson presented several research studies to support her contention that visual perception precedes motor and tactual development. The classic longitudinal study of White, Castle, and Held (1964) on visual-motor development, for example, found that at about 1 month of age infants begin following moving objects with their heads and eyes. Between the ages of 6 weeks and 2 months, the infant's tracking becomes more precise. When presented with an object at about 2 months of age, the infant first fixates the object and *then* hits it with a closed fist. Infants then enter a period of trial and error in which they attempt to reach for objects while glancing back and forth between the object and the hand until attaining what Gibson refers to as "top-level reaching" at about 5 months. The infant's first graspings of objects at about 4 months, it should be noted, are of a very gross nature. The study of White and his colleagues thus indicates that the first systematic exploration of the environment is made with the eyes and not the hands. Only after a period of some months does the infant's motor activity of reaching catch up with his or her visual tracking ability. Furthermore, the initial tactual contacts with objects are quite undifferentiated, and it is some time before the infant is capable of manipulating objects with his or her fingers and hands.

Gibson, as well as Pick and Pick (1970), reviewed numerous Soviet studies (Lavrent'eva & Ruzskaya, 1960; Tarakvanov & Zinchenko, 1960; Zaporozhets, 1965; Zinchenko, 1957; 1960; Zinchenko, Chzhi-tsin, & Tarakvanov, 1962; Zinchenko, Lomov, & Ruzskaya, 1959; Zinchenko & Ruzskaya, 1960a, 1960b) with children in early childhood that confirm the position that visual development advances more rapidly than tactual-motor ability. An example of the format of these experiments is giving children wooden forms of various shapes to explore either tactually or visually and then requiring them to recognize the same shape from among a number of choices presented either visually or tactually. The findings consistently reveal that visual-visual matching is the easiest and tactual-tactual the most difficult. The results of these studies argue strongly against the position of Kephart that motor development precedes visual development.

The Interaction of Visual and Motor Abilities Although the research evidence does not support Kephart's notion of the precedence of

Figure 2.5 The kitten carousel.
Source: R. Held & A. Hein, "Movement Produced Stimulation in the Development of Visually Guided Behavior," *Journal of Comparative and Physiological Psychology*, 1963, 56, 873. Copyright 1963 by the American Psychologial Association. Reprinted with permission.

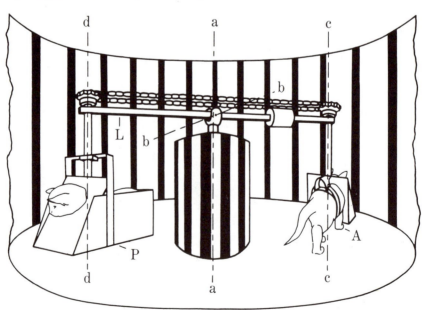

Russell Abraham, Stock Boston

The seemingly simple act of copying actually involves a number of cognitive skills.

motor development over vision, a number of sources can be used to justify his educational strategy of attempting to link the visual and motor domains. Thus Kephart's postulation of the importance of motor learning for visual development has a research foundation.

The classic study of Held and Hein (1963) emphasized the importance of motor movement for the development of visual-motor skills. Held and Hein placed two kittens in an apparatus pictured in Figure 2.5. The two animals were yoked so that whenever one cat walked around in a circle, the other cat was passively moved around in a gondola without the opportunity of locomotion. Thus one kitten saw the environment and walked in it, while the other one saw the very same environment but did *not* walk in it. On subsequent tests of a visual and visual-motor nature, the walking kitten was distinctly superior to the kitten deprived of motoric experiences.

That motor feedback is a significant factor in terms of the visual development of humans is also supported by a review of research by Wohlwill (1970). The conclusions were that

motoric and haptic (tactual) responses of the child serve a monitoring function in that they enable him to compare visual and motor input, and that on the basis of this match (similar to the perceptual-motor match of Kephart) visual judgments can be altered.

In terms of direct classroom application, Reese and Lipsitt (1970) reported the results of a study that indicates the usefulness of engendering motor responses in children. Hendrickson and Muehl (1962) trained kindergartners to push a lever in the opposite direction for the presentation of a *b* or *d* while also labeling the letters. The motor training facilitated discrimination of two potentially reversible letters.

While Kephart's contention that motor development precedes visual development is suspect, the position that visual and motor development can interact to aid one another is generally supported. The teacher who has a child with either a visual or a motor problem should thus attempt to train the child to combine the two sources of information (visual and motor). See Box 2.2 for a discussion of the visual-motor skills involved in copying.

Box 2.2
COPYING AS A CONCEPTUAL ACT

One of the most frequent concerns of the teacher in the early elementary grades is the child's ability to copy. The kindergartner who is unable to use a pencil and paper or crayon and paper to reproduce simple lines and geometric figures may be exhibiting a visual-motor deficit. Likewise, the child in the early elementary grades who cannot copy geometric forms or the letters of the alphabet, but who can visually discriminate among them, may have a visual-motor disability. On the other hand, a child who does poorly with paper and pencil or crayon and paper may actually have a conceptual rather than a perceptual problem. The ability to copy is a more complex activity than is at first apparent. Not only does the child have to perceive the to-be-copied figure accurately and then coordinate hand and eyes (an extremely complex phenomenon in itself), but he or she must also spatially organize and plan the drawing movements. This latter activity of building a spatial "layout" of the pattern before and during the construction of the figure is what differentiates copying from tracing. In the former task, the child is much more on his/her own in deciding how to organize the strokes of his or her pencil in order to obtain the final product of an accurate representation. In tracing, the child must merely coordinate eyes and hand to follow a prescribed path: the child is less concerned with how to organize his or her movements to reach an end product. Copying requires the child to be aware of the relationships of the component movements necessary to complete the drawing of the figure.

In copying an equilateral triangle whose sides are all 2 inches long, for example, Jimmy must consider a number of factors *both before and while he is drawing*. He will be greatly aided if he notes that: (1) the figure is composed basically of three lines; (2) the lines are of the same length; (3) the length of each of the lines is about 2 inches; (4) two of the lines are diagonal and one is horizontal; (5) there are three angles; (6) all of the angles are equal; and (7) each of the angles is 60 degrees (it is not necessary for the child to comprehend the numerical equivalent of 60 degrees, only its visual impression). If Jimmy is able to appreciate these relationships and adjust his drawing accordingly, he will produce a better copy than the child who can guide his/her hand visually just as well but is unable to organize and conceptualize the task requirements.

In this respect, then, copying activities can be conceived of as involving higher-level thought processes than has generally been assumed. Wedell (1973) has also noted that a child can fail copying tasks because of other than visual or visual-motor deficits. His model includes the kinds of organizational planning and decision-making components we just outlined. His research shows that tracing becomes progressively easier with age in comparison to copying. Between 3¾ years and 4½ years, tracing improves much more dramatically than does copying. These findings are consistent with the notion that copying involves abilities that are less readily influenced by mere practice. If copying involves certain cognitive processes, as we are suggesting, then it would be expected that improvement would be more gradual.

Tactual and Kinesthetic Problems

Closely related to visual-motor problems are tactual and kinesthetic problems. Tactual refers to the sensation of touch and kinesthetic refers to those bodily sensations gained when one moves. For instance, when a person moves an arm in a certain way, a certain sensation of movement is experienced; when the arm is moved in a different manner, a different sensation is obtained.

Kinesthetic and tactual disabilities are apparently not very widespread and therefore there has been relatively little study of them. A. Jean Ayres, however, has written frequently on the subject of tactual and kinesthetic deficiencies. She has referred, for instance, to the rather unusual cases of children who are described as tactually "defensive" (Ayres, 1975); the slightest stimulation of the skin is highly ir-

ritating for these children. She also believes that tactual discrimination abilities and kinesthetic abilities are quite often impaired in children who are apraxic, that is, children who do not have the ability to perform complex motor acts:

> Of the sensory systems involved in the apraxic child, the discriminative tactile system is the most consistently deficient, but kinesthesis or the perception of joint position and movement is not infrequently poor (Ayres, 1965, 1969, 1971, 1972). Postural responses are usually poorly developed, suggesting involvement of the vestibular and possibly other proprioceptive systems. (Ayres, 1975)

Body Image and Laterality   The writings of many learning disabilities theorists and practitioners posit a close relationship between visual-motor, tactual, and kinesthetic abilities and what have been termed *body image* and

Wedell (1973) offers the case of a child who has difficulty putting on a sweater as an example of a child who might be referred to as having poor body image.

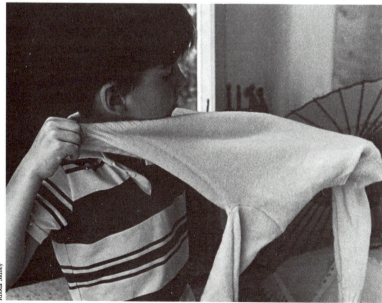

Rhoda Sidney

laterality. Body image is a rather vaguely defined construct that refers generally to an individual's awareness of his or her body in terms of the relationship of its parts and the relationship of the body to its spatial environment. The child with an inadequate body image, or body schema, is one who is likely to have difficulty in moving his/her limbs in an organized way and in judging where his/her body is in relation to other objects in the environment. Wedell (1973) offers the case of a child who has difficulty in putting on a sweater as an example of a child with a poor body image.

Children with visual-motor disabilities are also frequently described as lacking in laterality—the ability to detect the difference between the left and right side of one's own body. Asked to identify his/her right hand, for instance, the child with a laterality problem may become disoriented. Kephart (1960), among others, attributed a causal relationship between the ability to differentiate right from left on one's own body and orientation errors of left-right reversal in reading. His training for the child exhibiting reversals in reading thus emphasizes activities constructed for the purpose of teaching the distinction between the body's right and left side. There is no solid research to support Kephart's contention that laterality (left and right on the body) and directionality (left and right on stimuli outside of the body) are causally related (Naylor, 1980).

ASSESSMENT

Assessment of Visual Perception

When a child is referred to a school psychologist because he or she is exhibiting a reading disability, often one of the first areas to be assessed is that of visual perception. The school psychologist may choose to administer tests designed to look at the visual abilities of the child—for instance, Frostig's Developmental Test of Visual Perception or Colarusso and Hammill's Motor-Free Visual Perception Test (1972); or he or she may select tests that include certain items or subtests constructed to require the child to use his visual perceptual abilities—the Stanford-Binet or WISC tests, for example. It is, of course, essential that a number of measures be taken.

Many of the visual tests (such as Bender-Gestalt) or visual items on more general tests require the child to copy a figure or in some other way use both his or her motor and visual skills at the same time. We will deal more specifically with visual-motor abilities and their assessment in the next section; nevertheless, a word needs to be said here regarding the difference between visual perceptual and visual-motor problems. If a child copies a figure incorrectly, the teacher or psychologist cannot assume the child has a visual perceptual difficulty *or* a visual-motor problem. More information is needed. One technique that can be used was employed by Bortner and Birch (1962) in an experimental study. If a child copies a number of figures incorrectly, he or she can later be shown the correct figure as a standard to which he or she is to choose a match from choices, including a correct one and the incorrect copy. If a correct match can be made, then there is an indication that the problem is a visual-motor one. If the child chooses the incorrect copy as being identical to the standard, then there is evidence that there is a visual perceptual difficulty.

Assessment of Form Perception If the caution just stated regarding the difference between visual perceptual and visual-motor problems is kept in mind, many of the tests that require the child to draw or copy a figure can be indicative of form perception problems. The tester must be sure to ascertain that the problem is not a motor or visual-motor one. Examples of tests and subtests that require the child to draw a figure are the Bender-Gestalt, the Visual-Motor Coordination subtest from Frostig's Developmental Test of Visual Perception, the Draw-a-Design and Draw-a-Child subtests from the McCarthy Scales of Children's Abilities, and the Visual Achievement Forms from the Purdue Perceptual-Motor Survey.

Another way of looking at a child's visual discrimination ability, without involving any drawing by the child, is to analyze carefully how the child responds to items or subtests that require a response to visually presented material. For example, at the 4-year-old level there is a test on the Stanford-Binet entitled

Picture Vocabulary. The child is required to identify by name 14 out of 18 line drawings of familiar objects: airplane, telephone, horse, et cetera. If a child does poorly on this test, there are still any number of reasons why this may be so. There are some ways, however, in which one can attempt to find out what the chances are that the poor performance is due to poor visual discrimination. Consider the case study of Freddy in Box 2.3. Note how the psychologist uses a standardized test in a rather unorthodox manner in order to obtain a clearer picture of what the specific disability is.

The Visual Reception subtest of the Illinois

Box 2.3
FREDDY: A CASE STUDY

Freddy, aged 7 years, has been referred by his second-grade teacher to the school psychologist for evaluation. The teacher has observed that though Freddy seems to have a more than adequate vocabulary, he has a great deal of difficulty in reading. The school psychologist administers the Stanford-Binet IQ test* and obtains an overall IQ of 110. He is curious about Freddy's visual perceptual functioning, however, so he goes back and administers the Picture Vocabulary subtest of the Stanford-Binet. This would not normally be done because Freddy had passed all of the tests well beyond the 4-year-old level. The psychologist finds that Freddy has a very difficult time with the Picture Vocabulary; he is able to identify only 6 of the 18 pictured objects (14 are required in order to pass at the 4-year-old level). On the other hand, Freddy was quite capable of defining words on the Vocabulary test (orally administered) at the 8-year-old level; he did well enough, in fact, to get credit for the 8-year-old level even though he was only 7. Before concluding that Freddy might have a visual perceptual disability that caused him to do quite poorly on Picture Vocabulary compared to Vocabulary, the school psychologist did one more thing. To determine if Freddy might have a problem in recalling names of objects, the examiner *read* a definition of the objects from the Picture Vocabulary test without showing the pictures. On this kind of administration, Freddy was able to identify 16 of the 18 objects, indicating that he was able to recall their names. The school psychologist therefore concluded that it was *quite possible* that Freddy had a difficulty in visually discriminating objects that caused him to do poorly in naming pictures of objects.

The words *quite possible* are italicized in the preceding sentence because it is never wise to come to firm conclusions on the basis of a few instances of test behavior. In this example, further indications would need to be looked for on the Stanford-Binet and other tests. For instance, the examiner might wish to administer another test—Discrimination of Forms—from the Stanford-Binet. Again, this test is from the 4-year-old level, but because there is already some information suggesting that Freddy's ability to discriminate among foms is well below his chronological age of 7, it would be quite appropriate to administer it to him. The test requires the child to match a geometric figure—e.g., a circle, a square—with an identical one from among a number of alternatives. If Freddy were to do poorly on this 4-year-old-level test, then there would be an even stronger case that his problem was a visual perceptual disability.

* The items used in this example and others in this chapter are from the 1973 edition of the Stanford-Binet and not the Fourth Edition published in 1985.

Test of Psycholinguistic Abilities is yet another device that is often used to indicate the visual discrimination ability of children. Here the child is shown a picture of a familiar object (e.g., a dog) for 3 seconds. A card containing another dog plus a number of other figures is shown to the child and he is asked to find an object in it like the one in the original picture. The correct answer, of course, is the dog on the new card. On the early cards, the child must find choices that are of the same specific category, e.g., dogs, wagons, balls. On later cards, however, the matching becomes more difficult in that the child must match on the basis of the function of the object, even though there is no similarity in what the two objects look like. In fact, "look-alikes" are included as distracters among the alternatives. A stoplight is to be paired with a stop sign, and one of the alternatives is a picture of three pie plates attached to a stick that looks like a stoplight in a gross way. The child is thus required to obtain visual meaning from the pictures. Form perception problems would prohibit a child from performing well on the Visual Reception subtest. However, if a child were to do poorly only on this subtest and appropriately on other tests of visual perception (e.g., Bender-Gestalt, Discrimination of Forms test on the Stanford-Binet), one would *suspect* that the child had

adequate form discrimination but had problems in deciphering the conceptual meaning of pictures.

Assessment of Position-in-Space Ability
In considering potential perception-of-form disabilities, the possibility of an even more specific disability cannot be ruled out. The child, for instance, may be unable to match two squares on the Discrimination of Forms test of the Stanford-Binet because he/she cannot perceive the spatial orientation of the figures. For that child, the square may be perceived in a state of rotation.

There is one subtest in particular that has been designed to test the ability to appreciate the perceptual characteristic of position in space—the Position in Space subtest of Marianne Frostig's Developmental Test of Visual Perception. On this subtest the child is shown an object in a particular position. He or she is to choose the same object in the same position from among a number of choices of the same object in a variety of positions. Figure 2.6 is an example of one of the items from the Position in Space subtest.

Another test that could cause problems for the child with a position-in-space disability is the Patience: Rectangles test from the 5-year-

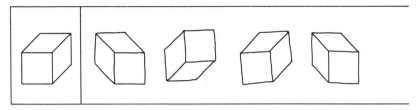

Figure 2.6   Example of one of the items from the Position in Space subtest of the Marianne Frostig Developmental Test of Visual Perception.
Source: Reproduced by special permission from *Marianne Frostig Developmental Test of Visual Perception* by Marianne Frostig in collaboration with Welty Lefever, Ph.D., and John R. B. Whittlesey, M. S., Copyright 1961, published by Consulting Psychologists Press Inc.

old-level of the Stanford-Binet. The tester presents two pieces of cardboard like those pictured in Figure 2.7. The child is then in-

Figure 2.7   The Patience: Rectangles test from the Stanford-Binet.
Source: The Stanford-Binet materials cited pertain to the 1973 edition and not to the Fourth Edition published in 1985. Reproduced by permission of The Riverside Publishing Co.

Child is required to make a rectangle

from two triangles placed before him.

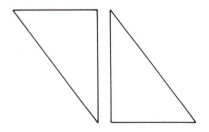

structed to put the two pieces together in order to make a rectangle. It is easy to see from Figure 2.7 that a child with an orientation problem could have difficulty on this task.

As with form perception, position-in-space ability should be assessed by looking for a number of different instances in which position-in-space perception is required for appropriate performance. Final diagnosis based on a single item is not appropriate. If a child frequently reverses letters while reading, that is a cue for the teacher, or the school psychologist, to look carefully to determine whether the child possesses a disability in visual perception of position in space.

Assessment of Visual-Motor Abilities

A number of different instruments and parts of tests have been designed specifically for the purpose of assessing a child's eye-hand coordination. The major distinction that the diagnostician must keep in mind when assessing eye-hand coordination is that a child can perform poorly on a pencil-and-paper task because he has primarily a visual problem, primarily a visual-motor problem, primarily a motor problem, or some combination of these. Cutler, Cicirelli, and Hirshoren (1973), for example, have investigated the performance of nursery-school children on a test of visual discrimination and one of visual-motor production. Little relationship was found between the results from the two tests, suggesting that children who might have problems on one might not have problems on the other.

One of the oldest and most established tests of eye-hand functioning is the Bender-Gestalt (Bender, 1938), originally developed by Lauretta Bender for use with adults. Koppitz (1964) has devised a scoring system applicable to children. The basic format of the test is that the child is shown a group of figures and asked to copy them. The eight figures are presented in Figure 2.8. The clinician can look at the child's errors both quantitatively (i.e., number of errors) and qualitatively (i.e., kinds of errors). Some of the different types of errors found are enlargements, compressions, rotations, and distorted angles. While Bender (1970) has praised the Koppitz scoring system, she recommends caution in the use of the Bender-Gestalt with children. She also stresses that when the test is used, the examiner should be sure to consider the total functioning of the child.

Several tests on the market are similar in format to the Bender-Gestalt. The Benton Visual Retention Test (Benton, 1963) and the Developmental Test of Visual-Motor Integration (Beery & Buktenica, 1967), for example, are comparable. These instruments are similar in that the child is to draw figures. The Benton differs slightly in that it can be administered by showing and then removing the figures so that the child draws them from memory.

The Eye-Hand Coordination subtest of the Marianne Frostig Developmental Test of Visual Perception is another device frequently used to test eye-hand coordination.

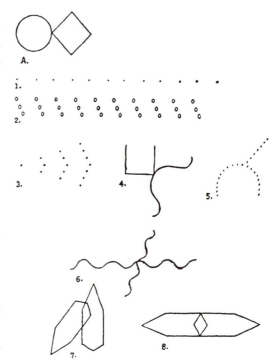

Figure 2.8 Bender-Gestalt test figures.
Source: L. Bender, *A Visual-Motor Gestalt Test and Its Clinical Use*, Research Monograph No. 3, p. 4. Copyright 1938, the American Orthopsychiatric Association, Inc. Reproduced by permission.

On this test, the child is required to draw lines from one point to another on a sheet of paper. The path of the line varies in difficulty from item to item by the number of angles that must be negotiated and the narrowness of the borders within which the line must be drawn.

The Tower Building subtest of the Stanford-Binet is an example of an assessment of eye-hand coordination that does not use pencil-and-paper tasks. The young child is required to copy with his own blocks the tower built by the tester. As with all tests, a child may fail this one for a variety of reasons, but failure to build the tower correctly may indicate eye-hand coordination problems.

Assessment of Tactual and Kinesthetic Abilities

Few tests assess tactual and kinesthetic abilities. Numerous items from visual-motor tests also require the child to use his or her tactual and kinesthetic senses, but not many attempts have been made to construct specific tests of tactual and kinesthetic abilities. Ayres, however, undoubtedly because of her interest in kinesthetic deficits and tactual problems such as tactual defensiveness, has included tests dealing with the tactual and kinesthetic senses in her *Southern California Sensory Integration Tests* (Ayres, 1972). At least five of these tests are designed to measure tactual and kinesthetic abilities: Kinesthesia, Manual Form Perception, Finger Identification, Graphesthesia, Localization of Tactile Stimuli. Here are brief descriptions:

1 Kinesthesia: With his/her eyes shielded, the child is required to move his/her hand to various places on a kinesthesia "chart." For example, the examiner first moves the child's hand and outstretched finger to a certain place on the chart and then guides the hand back to the start. The child is then asked to move the hand back to the place on the chart by himself/herself.

2 Manual Form Perception: Again, the child's eyes are occluded. The examiner places a solid geometric form in one of the child's hands and the child is asked to select from among a number of alternatives the picture of the form identical to the one he is holding.

3 Finger Identification: With his/her vision occluded, the child is to identify which of his/her fingers was touched by the tester.

4 Graphesthesia: With eyes shielded, the child sits with his/her palms down. The examiner "draws" with a pencil eraser a design on the back of one of the child's hands. The child must then reproduce the design.

5 Localization of Tactile Stimuli: The examiner touches the child's visually shielded hand or forearm with a ball-point pen. The child is then required to touch with index finger the place where he/she was touched.

INTERVENTIONS

There are two general approaches to the treatment of the kinds of perceptual problems discussed in this chapter—the *process-training approach* and the *behavioral approach.* We have already described the general nature of these two models in Chapter 1. Our presentation here will be more specific and we will provide concrete descriptions of instructional techniques falling within each of these approaches.

Process-Training Programs

A number of programs have been designed to remediate the kinds of perceptual problems discussed in this chapter. Perceptual training packages were, in fact, the first formalized remedial programs for the learning disabled. While some of these programs stress one or two areas more than the others do (e.g., visual more than visual-motor, tactual, and kinesthetic), most of them include activities aimed at remediating all four—visual, visual-motor, tactual, and kinesthetic—of the disabilities we have been discussing in this chapter.

Getman, Kane, Halgren, and McKee's "The Physiology of Readiness" In 1964, Getman and his colleagues published a manual of practical training activities for children with visual disabilities—*The Physiology of Readiness: An Action Program for the Development of Perception in Children.* This booklet includes activities that Getman had found successful in his many years of clinical work as an optometrist. Getman's program is based to a large extent on the work of A. M. Skeffington, another optometrist (see Getman, 1976). Skeffington contributed almost 40 years of papers through what is known as the Optometric Extension Program.

The program of Getman and his associates is based upon the following assumptions:

1   Academic performance in today's schools depends heavily on form and symbol recognition and interpretation.

2   There are perceptual skills that can be developed and trained.

3   The development of perceptual skills is related to the levels of coordination of the body systems; i.e., the better the coordination of the body parts and body systems, the better the prospects for developing perception of forms and symbols.

4   The child whose perceptual skills have been developed and extended is the child who is free to profit from instruction and to learn independently. The greater the development of the perceptual skills, the greater the capacity for making learning more effective. (Getman et al., 1964, p. iii)

The program of Getman and his co-workers is composed of activities subsumed under six general divisions:

1   General Coordination
2   Balance
3   Eye-Hand Coordination
4   Eye Movements
5   Form Perception
6   Visual Memory (Imagery)

Practice in General Coordination   This aspect of the program is designed to provide children with practice in total body movement. The exercises here deal mostly with move-

ments of the head, arms, and legs. *Some** examples of such activities are:

1   The teacher requires the child to turn his/her head from side to side while the child is lying on the floor. The child is encouraged to turn his/her head until his/her ear touches the floor.

2   While lying on the floor, the child is asked to move his/her arms, with elbows straight, over his/her head until his/her hands touch.

3   While on his/her back, the child moves his/her legs, with knees straight, in scissors fashion.

4   The child is asked to make "angels in the snow" movements. He/she moves his/her arms up over his/her head and spreads his/her legs out and then brings his/her arms back to his sides while moving his/her legs back together. The child repeats this procedure several times.

5   The child is to jump, hop, and skip.

Practice in Balance   These activities involve the use of visual perception for the acquisition of better balance. Most of the activities include the use of a balance beam—a 2-by-4-inch board of about 8 feet in length that is raised a couple of inches off the ground on supports. The child is involved in a number of exercises in which he or she is to walk on the 4-inch width of the balance beam. For example, the child may be asked to

1   walk heel-to-toe along the beam;
2   walk backwards toe-to-heel on the beam.

Practice in Eye-Hand Coordination   For this part of the program the child is engaged in numerous chalkboard exercises. These activities are designed for the purpose of increasing the child's ability to coordinate his/her eyes and hands. Some of the chalkboard activities include having the child use both hands to draw circles, horizontal lines, and vertical lines

* These examples are described so that the reader can get a general idea of the Getman program. For *proper* use of this program and others we describe, the reader should obtain a copy of the program in question.

on the chalkboard. An exercise involving two children has one child place X's on the board while the other one draws lines from one X to the next without taking the chalk off the board.

Practice in Eye Movements Activities in this part of the program attempt to increase the child's ability to move his or her eyes quickly and accurately from one object to another. In one exercise, for example, the child is asked to alternate his/her fixation from his/her thumbs, held in front of him/her, to the teacher, who is standing farther away. This training is for the development of near and far smooth eye movements.

Practice in Form Perception Here two kinds of templates are used—chalkboard and desk templates. The child uses templates of various figures—circle, square, triangle—in order to trace them, first on the chalkboard and then on paper at his/her desk. Once the skill has been mastered, he or she is encouraged to draw the figures without the aid of templates.

Practice in Visual Memory These exercises are for the purpose of developing the child's imagery ability. A tachistoscope is needed so that the teacher can flash slides on the board. The Getman team indicates that if a tachistoscope is not available, one can manually move a piece of cardboard in front of and to the side of the projector lens. The child is shown various figures via the slide projector for very brief exposure periods. After a slide is shown, he/she is asked to respond to one of the figures in a variety of ways: name it, trace it in the air, circle it on a worksheet, trace it on a worksheet, draw a replica of it. Other slides are presented that show more complex figures and require the child to do different activities with them. The teacher can vary the exposure times, decreasing them as the child becomes more proficient.

The Frostig-Horne Visual Perception Training Program Frostig and Horne (1964) have written a commercially available program designed for remediation purposes or for readiness training. Like Getman, Marianne Frostig has been a pioneer in the field of learning disabilities. She is the founder of the Marianne Frostig Center of Educational Therapy in Los Angeles, where many aspects of the Frostig-Horne program are implemented (see Frostig, 1976). The Frostig-Horne program follows closely the areas assessed in the *Marianne Frostig Developmental Test of Visual Perception* (Frostig, Lefever, & Whittlesey, 1964).

Eye-Motor Coordination Exercises The program provides worksheets for the teacher to give to the child. Activities consist of a number of exercises that offer the child an opportunity to coordinate his/her eyes and hands. Boundaries are provided on the worksheets for the child to draw within. The boundaries vary in their direction and shape (curved or straight). The difficulty of the exercises is also controlled by the width of the boundary lines.

Figure-Ground Exercises These worksheets require the child to find and trace figures embedded within other lines and figures. The worksheets are sequenced so that both the figures to be found and the background become more complex.

Perceptual Constancy Exercises The ability trained in this section of the Frostig-Horne program is that of perceptual generalization. The child is trained to recognize that an object remains the same even though it may be presented in a different form, color, size, or context. For example, a child must learn that two objects are both chairs, even though one is smaller and softer than the other.

Position-in-Space Exercises This aspect of the program was included by Frostig and

Horne for helping the child who exhibits reversals. The child is required to place himself/herself in various positions in relation to objects in the classroom. He/she learns to appreciate, for example, the position of being under or over a table. The program provides worksheets that require the child to discriminate figures in various positions.

Spatial Relations Exercises The exercises included here are designed to provide a child with an appreciation of the spatial relationships among objects. Worksheets involve a number of activities in which the child is required to observe spatial relationships.

Kirk and Kirk's Visual Perceptual Training Suggestions Kirk and Kirk (1971) have also made suggestions for training in visual perception. Their remediation techniques are outlined in *Psycholinguistic Learning Disabilities: Diagnosis and Remediation.* They present teaching activities based on how a child scores on their test—the ITPA. While their activities are not as detailed as Getman's or Frostig's, they do list a number of general teaching strategies. Within the sphere of visual reception—the ability to obtain meaning from visually presented stimuli—Kirk and Kirk believe that there may be at least five different reasons for failure. The child may

1 lack prerequisite skills of visual-motor perception;

2 not have the appropriate knowledge and experience;

3 not observe stimuli within his/her visual field;

4 not be able to associate meaning with visual symbols;

5 not be able to use visual imagery.

For each of these five potential visual reception problems, Kirk and Kirk have devised teaching activities. To provide the child with visual-motor perception, for example, the teacher can use many of the same activities recommended by Getman and Frostig. If the child lacks visual experience, he/she is encouraged to explore the environment, and the teacher discusses the things the child sees. For the child who is not observant of objects in his/her visual field, some suggested approaches are to instruct the child to pay attention to the visual environment. One recommended game is to bring the child into a room and then remove the child and ask him/her to name what was in it. The child who has difficulty associating meaning with visual symbols is encouraged to do so by performing such activities as discriminating objects on the basis of color, size, shape, and so forth. Visual imagery is trained, for example, by asking the child to recall and describe pictorially past events.

Newell Kephart's Approach Until his death in the early 1970s, Newell Kephart was in charge of the Newell C. Kephart Glen Haven Achievement Center in Fort Collins, Colorado. It was at this center that he put into practice his training activities devised to help perceptually disabled children achieve the perceptual-motor match. His particular approach was published in the now classic *The Slow Learner in the Classroom* (Kephart, 1960; 2nd. ed., 1971).

Basically, Kephart divided his program into activities involving chalkboard training, sensory-motor training, ocular motor training, and form perception training.

Chalkboard Training Kephart devised a number of elaborate exercises using chalk and chalkboard. He, as well as Getman, noted that a particular advantage of chalkboard over pencil and paper is that spatial directions are more consistent, Up *is* "up" on a chalkboard, whereas up is actually "away from" when a paper is placed on a table before a child. Furthermore, a piece of chalk is easier to hold than a pencil for some children, and the movements required are of a grosser nature than those used with pencil and paper.

Different activities for the chalkboard were recommended by Kephart for a variety of purposes: promoting directionality, crossing the midline, orientation, tracing, copying. To induce directionality, the teacher puts dots on the board at random and the child connects one dot to the next one as the teacher puts them on the board. For the child who has problems in crossing the midline, Kephart suggested that at first the child be asked to draw a line to either the right or left of a center line in front of him or her; gradually, the teacher should require the child to draw lines that cross the midline. Numerous other chalkboard activities were described by Kephart for training eye-hand coordination.

Sensory-Motor Training   The activities contained in this portion of Kephart's program were designed to help the child who has difficulty in coordinating movements of his/her body. A walking board is used for training posture and balance. The child is asked to walk on the balance beam forward, backward, and sideways. Kephart recommended a variety of other procedures for use with the walking board. The balance board, a wooden platform 16 by 16 inches, is also used; the child can be asked, for example, to throw and catch a ball while on the balance board platform. Other training exercises include "angels in the snow" routines as well as the trampoline exercises. Activities on the trampoline are meant to promote dynamic balance: "the development of total bodily coordination throughout the gross muscle systems" (Kephart, 1960, p. 224).

Ocular Motor Training   This program was devised for the purpose of helping the child gain control over the movements of his or her eyes. It includes many activities for the teacher to use in training the child's eye movements.

Bruce Roberts, Photo Researchers, Inc.

Balance beam walking is a common exercise in perceptual-motor training programs.

For example, in order to train ocular pursuit, the teacher draws a "road" on the board with the flat side of a piece of chalk. The child then takes a toy car and follows the road.

Form Perception Training   Training procedures here have been keyed to the developmental level of the child. The exercises include the putting together of puzzles, the construction of designs from matchsticks, and putting pegs in a pegboard. Because Kephart believed in the importance of motor activities for visual development, the activities place a heavy emphasis on motoric skills.

Ray Barsch's Approach   Barsch has articulated a movement approach to education (Barsch, 1976) and advocated what he terms a "Movigenic Curriculum." He has detailed his educational methods in *Achieving Perceptual-Motor Efficiency* (Barsch, 1967). His educational techniques are based on 10 basic constructs:

(1) the organism is designed for movement (2) the objective of movement is survival (3) movement occurs in an energy surround (4) the mechanism for acquiring information is the percepto-cognitive system (5) the terrain of movement is Space (6) developmental momentum thrusts the learner toward maturity (7) movement occurs in a climate of stress (8) feedback is essential to efficiency (9) development occurs in segments of sequential expansion, and (10) communication of efficiency is derived from the visual spatial phenomenon called language. (p. 329)

There are three basic components of Barsch's Movigenic Curriculum: postural-transport orientations, percepto-cognitive modes, and degrees of freedom. The postural-transport orientations include muscular strength, dynamic balance, body awareness, spatial awareness, and temporal awareness. The percepto-cognitive modes (perception and cognition are viewed as practically one and the same thing) include the gustatory, olfactory, tactual, kinesthetic, auditory, and visual. What Barsch calls the Degrees of Freedom are bilaterality, rhythm, flexibility, and motor planning. For each of the above aspects of his program, Barsch (1967) has included a chapter that contains exercises for use with learning-disabled children.

Barsch also sets forth 10 guidelines for teachers who use his curriculum:

1 The teacher should be careful to view the child's movement as "efficient-inefficient" rather than as "successful-failing." Efficiency of movement is the goal.

2 As the child's efficiency increases, the teacher should be aware of the complexity of the child's movements. The teacher should evaluate whether the child is achieving more and more complex skills.

3 "Activities must be planned to give the learner ample opportunities to explore his muscular relationships, varying positions of balance, all parts of his body, all positions of space and varying relationships to time" (p. 331).

4 All six of the perceptual modes—gustatory, olfactory, tactual, kinesthetic, auditory, and visual—must be used by the child.

5 "Activities should be provided to deliberately vary the zones of stimulation presenting opportunities in wide assortments of target sources from near, mid, far and remote space" (p. 331).

6 The teacher should provide the child with experiences that necessitate his/her using a learned task in a variety of ways.

7 The child needs to be encouraged to be the determiner of his/her own activities. The teacher should give the child a number of activities to choose from and encourage the child's initiative.

8 The teacher must bring about a cognitive ability in the child to plan his/her own movements.

9 "A spatial orientation can be applied to all types of performance" (p. 332). All academic areas can be considered within a spatial framework.

10 The teacher need not change his/her own teaching style entirely. The Movigenic Curriculum can be used within the existing framework of the teacher's particular approach.

Bryant Cratty's Approach   Cratty has written several manuals and books dealing with the training of motor skills. He has devised exercises for the purpose of enhancing motor skills as such (e.g., Cratty, 1967) and also for increasing a child's cognitive abilities (e.g., Cratty, 1973). With regard to the remediation of motor development, Cratty divides his activities into those for: (1) perceptions of the body and its position in space; (2) balance; (3) locomotion; (4) agility; (5) strength, endurance, and flexibility; (6) catching and throwing balls; (7) manual abilities; and (8) moving and thinking. The specific exercises under each of these headings are very similar to those used for physical education.

To increase a child's cognitive abilities,

Cratty maintains that the activity must be associated in some way with the higher thought processes that are to be changed. The activity itself will not increase cognitive capabilities. For example, Cratty (1973) includes the following game called "Interference":

To Enhance: Concentration in the presence of distractions, short-term memory, immediate-term memory, ability to mentally rehearse items in a series.

Participants and Equipment: Children ages 5 and older; retarded children ages 8, 9, and older. Variety of playground equipment, ropes, balls, hoops, etc.

Description: Initially a child demonstrates a series of four or five movements, while observers are told that they must remember and later duplicate these movements. Then a second child demonstrates a different series of five movements. Observing children, one by one, are then asked to repeat the first series. Possible interfering effects of second series observed are discussed, with implications for concentration. (p. 35)

Glen Doman and Carl Delacato's Approach Doman, a physical therapist, and Delacato, an educational psychologist, posited a most controversial theory and method for remediating learning disabilities (Delacato, 1959, 1963, 1966). They founded the Institutes for the Achievement of Human Potential in Philadelphia, where they train individuals to carry out their program of "neurological organization."

At least three major elements of their approach have been questioned by numerous authors:

1   The development of the individual—ontogeny—recapitulates the development of the species—phylogeny.
2   The child should be trained to have cerebral dominance, that is, he should be predominantly one-sided with regard to his preferences—right-eyed, right-handed, right-legged.

3   The brain itself is remediated by their procedures.

With respect to the first element, Doman and Delacato advocate the once-popular notion that the individual progresses through stages that parallel the evolutionary development of the human species. For example, they presuppose that the child goes through stages equivalent to the fish, amphibian, reptile, and primate before achieving humanity. Their training activities correspond to these levels (e.g., creeping and crawling exercises). Robbins and Glass (1969) present numerous arguments against this theory.

Regarding the second element, Doman and Delacato believe strongly in the establishment of a consistent laterality, and they even inhibit some children from using their nonpreferred side in order to bring about laterality. They maintain that this cerebral dominance is necessary in order to learn to read. Robbins and Glass (1969) also question Doman and Delacato's theory regarding the need for a consistent lateral preference.

As to the third element, many of the specific activities advocated by Doman and Delacato are the same as those of other perceptual-motor practitioners. The crucial difference in their approach is their focus on remediation. While others, such as Barsch, Frostig, Getman, and Kephart, have from time to time made allusions that imply they believe their remediation activities influence the activity of the brain, Doman and Delacato underline their conviction that their activities remediate the brain. Other perceptual-motor theorists advance their curricula within the framework of the behaviors to be improved.

Indicative of the intense feelings that have been aroused by the Doman-Delacato treatment method was the unprecedented official statement issued in 1968 by a number of professional organizations. The organizations were the American Academy for Cerebral Palsy, American Academy of Physical Medicine and Rehabilitation, American Congress of Rehabilitation Medicine, Canadian Association for Retarded Children, Canadian Rehabilitation Council for the Disabled, and the National Association for Retarded Children. Their lengthy statement makes four major points about the Doman-Delacato procedures:

1 The promotional methods place parents in an uneasy position if they refuse the treatment.

2 The regimens are so demanding that the parents may neglect other family needs and the child may be inhibited from engaging in normal age-appropriate activities.

3 Doman and Delacato's claims of success are exaggerated and undocumented.

4 The theoretical underpinnings of their practices are weak.

The Behavioral Approach

Behaviorists working with children with academic problems differ from followers of the process-training approach in that they *are concerned exclusively with improving skills that are components of academic responses.* In other words, whereas some process-training advocates would assume that patterned crawling or practice in walking on a balance beam will affect a child's ability to read or write or count, behaviorists assume that one must work directly with the specific skills that are involved in performing academic tasks. If, for example, the goal is to teach a child to write, then one must provide instruction in the skills required for forming letters. After specific skills (e.g., writing the letters *a* to *m*) have been taught, however, one may find that a generalization has been learned (e.g., the child may improve overall in his letter-writing ability and be able to learn new letters more quickly).

Because of its focus on teaching specific skills, the behavioral approach requires a "task analysis" of the performances to be developed. A task has been analyzed when it has been broken down into prerequisite and component skills to such an extent that the child's errors in performance can be precisely identified and the subskills that he must learn in order to perform adequately are obvious.

Visual Perceptual Problems From a behavioral standpoint, teaching children to make necessary visual discriminations is an essential element in teaching them beginning reading and arithmetic skills. Children who evidence deficits in form perception or perception of position in space have, from a behavioral perspective, failed to learn appropriate discriminations among visual stimuli. The teacher's task, therefore, is to teach the visual discriminations that will allow the child to make correct academic responses.

An individual has learned a discrimination when he reliably responds to a given stimulus. A child has learned to discriminate *d* from *b* when he reliably responds by saying "dee" when shown the letter *d* and by saying "bee" when shown the letter *b*. If a child reliably calls the correct word when shown the stimulus *dog*, but does not respond "dog" when presented with any other configuration of letters, then he has learned a word discrimination. Discrimination may involve auditory, visual, tactile, or other types of stimuli or complex combinations of stimuli. Behaviorists contend that a crucial factor to be considered in children's visual perceptual difficulties is how to teach them to discriminate the relevant visual stimuli that are a part of academic tasks.

Children's discrimination learning has been studied extensively in the laboratory as well as in the classroom (cf., Bijou & Baer, 1966; Stevenson, 1972). It ordinarily consists of presenting the training stimulus and reinforcing the desired response. In the case of a laboratory experiment, the discrimination training may involve a comparatively simple stimulus, such as a small light mounted on a box, and a relatively simple response, such as pushing a lever protruding from a box. The experimenter may then train children to push the lever when the light is on and not to push it when the light is off. He/she does this by giving the children reinforcers—tokens, trinkets, candies—for pushing the lever when the light is on and withholding the reinforcers for pushing the lever when the light is off. When a child consistently pushes the lever and obtains reinforcement in the "light on" condition but seldom or never pushes the lever in the "light off" condition, he or she has learned a simple visual discrimination. The experimenter may then be interested in studying certain aspects of discrimination by varying the reinforcement procedure, the color or intensity of the light, other stimuli that are paired with the light, and so on. In this way, significant information may be obtained about what discriminations a child can learn and how best to teach certain discriminations.

In the classroom, discrimination training makes use of the same basic principles and procedures employed in the laboratory. If it is desired to teach a child to discriminate his or her name from other words, the teacher must present the child's name, perhaps printed on a card, and provide reinforcement only for the appropriate response—that is, saying the child's name. The teacher must withhold reinforcement for the child's incorrect responses, such as saying his or her name when another child's name is shown, saying his or her name before any card is shown, or saying another child's name when his or her own name card is shown. Whether the teacher is successful in teaching a child to discriminate his/her name, or to make any other discrimination, may de-

pend on precisely how the name and other stimuli are presented, how the teaching trials are timed, how incorrect responses are handled, how reinforcement is given, and so forth.

Acquisition of Initial Visual Discriminations   Much of our knowledge about how children learn beginning reading, writing, and arithmetic skills has been contributed by Arthur W. Staats (Staats, 1973; Staats, Brewer, & Gross, 1970; Staats & Staats, 1963). After more than a decade of careful research, Staats outlined a theory of reading that has as its basic tenet: Learning to read involves the sequential acquisition of a hierarchy of visual discrimination skills. The child must first learn to attend to relevant stimuli, then learn to discriminate simple forms.

> These basic behavioral skills form the basis for learning the alphabet discriminations; these form the basis for learning the elementary reading units (grapheme-phoneme, i.e., letter-sound correspondences); these form the basis for acquiring a large repertoire of word-reading responses; and so on. (Staats, Brewer, & Gross, 1970, p. 76)

Staats's Research on Visual Discrimination   According to Staats, reading, as well as other basic academic skills, proceeds from simpler to more complex tasks in an orderly fashion. Thus, if a child is experiencing learning difficulties or is not performing as expected for his/her age, one must analyze precisely the skills in this hierarchy that the child has acquired and teach those skills that are deficient. If a child is retarded in reading ability, it is essential to determine whether certain component skills have been acquired. If discrimination of the letters of the alphabet has been learned but letter-sound (grapheme-phoneme) correspondences have not been learned, then the child must be instructed on letter-sound tasks. (See Box 2.4 for discussion of Staats's views on reading acquisition.)

Box 2.4
A BEHAVIORAL VIEW OF READING VERSUS ORAL-LANGUAGE LEARNING

The strict behaviorist believes that reading problems can be overcome by adequate reinforcement for reading responses. Arthur W. Staats, a theoretician and researcher from the behaviorist school, has made some interesting comparisons between reading and oral-language problems. Staats maintains that learning oral language and learning to read involve essentially the same principles. Thus *the child who learns oral language can learn to read if appropriate conditions are arranged* (Staats, 1973; Staats & Staats, 1962, 1963). It may be inappropriate and unproductive to attribute a child's reading problems to biological or central nervous system deficits *as long as the child has normal language.* Staats has observed that children are usually given many learning trials during the acquisition of oral language. During the acquisition of reading, on the other hand, children are typically provided with far fewer and more poorly arranged opportunities to learn. In teaching their children to talk, parents speak to their children many thousands of times, giving them many thousands of explicit opportunities to respond and giving them clear, immediate reinforcement or feedback on their performance. But in learning to read, the child typically is faced with a very different situation. He/she may be in a class with 25 other children, be given only a few opportunities to respond each day, and be given delayed reinforcement or ambiguous feedback on his/her performance. Therefore it is helpful to design an instructional procedure that includes a very high frequency of opportunity to respond to explicit tasks and very frequent reinforcement for correct responses.

In order to arrange the optimum conditions for learning the visual discriminations required for reading, Staats devised the apparatus shown in Figure 2.9. The child sits facing the small window in the partition. The teacher sits in the other chair to the side of the partition and places 5-by-8-inch cards with stimuli to be read (e.g., letters or words) in the window. Marbles can be dropped down the chute by the teacher. When a marble drops into the box at the end of the chute, the teacher instructs the child to put the marble in the hole at the upper right corner of the partition (returning it to the container on the teacher's side and receiving a trinket or other reinforcer) or to drop it in one of the tubes on the child's left, where accumulation of marbles can earn the toy displayed above the tube.

In his early research with preschoolers, Staats used marbles as token reinforcers that could be exchanged for trinkets, candies, or toys (Staats, Brewer, & Gross, 1970). At first the children were asked to name pictures. Then, gradually, letters were introduced. The letter *A* was shown and the child was told its name and asked to say it. Letter-naming trials were interspersed with picture-naming trials, and new letters were introduced only when the child had mastered those previously shown. Prompts (i.e., telling the child the letter name

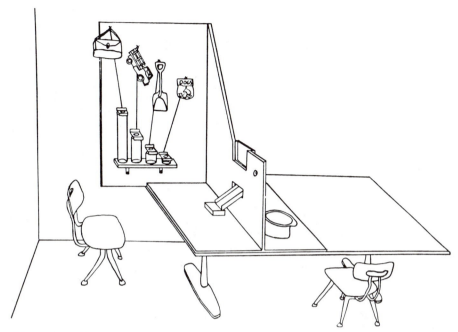

Figure 2.9 The child learning apparatus.
Source: *A. W. Staats, "A General Apparatus for the Investigation of Complex Learning in Children,"* Behaviour Research and Therapy, *1968, 6, 47. Reprinted by permission.*

if he/she did not know it) and picture naming were gradually removed from the trials as the child mastered the tasks. Reinforcement was given very frequently for correct answers, and the teacher was careful to prevent the child from making errors at each stage. Teaching sessions were kept very short (average length 3.2 minutes) and were stopped at the first sign of inattention. Careful records were kept of the stimuli presented, the child's responses, the length of the sessions, and the reinforcers given. Staats and his associates (1970) found that as children learned more letters, they became more efficient learners—fewer trials, less time, and fewer reinforcers were required to learn successive groups of letters (e.g., *Q* to *T* as compared with *A* to *D*).

After the children had learned the letters of the alphabet, they were taught word discrimination tasks. Using essentially the same approach that had been applied in the teaching of letters, teachers taught the children phonetic sets of words (cad, mad, pad, rad, sad, tad, or cat, mat, pat, rat, sat, tat). The children learned phonetic reading skills, and they became more efficient learners as their training progressed. It is important to note that the training in alphabet and word reading was done in about 120 brief sessions and that the children were given thousands of learning trials and earned hundreds of reinforcers.

The work of Staats, Brewer, and Gross showed that very young children (age 3½ to 4½ years) could be taught the visual discrimination and cognitive skills necessary for beginning reading when appropriate motivation (re-

Box 2.5
WORKING WITH VISUAL PERCEPTUAL PROBLEMS: THE USE OF FADING

Fading is an instructional technique frequently used by behaviorists. Fading involves the introduction and gradual elimination of cues or "crutches." For example, if a child cannot discriminate *was* from *saw,* but can discriminate black from red, a color-fading procedure might be employed. *Was* might be written in black ink and *saw* in red ink. The stimuli would then differ along two dimensions—letter configuration or form and color. The child will at first discriminate between the words only on the basis of the color dimension. Over many reading trials the red ink for *saw* can gradually be darkened until, in the final trials, *saw* is black and the words differ only along the dimension of letter configuration. Color, in this example, is the fading dimension, and the child's discrimination is transferred from the color to the configuration dimension.

Many laboratory studies have shown that stimulus fading is an effective technique in teaching visual discriminations to the retarded (cf., Bijou, 1968; Estes, 1970; Stevenson, 1972); even severely retarded children have been taught discriminations that previously seemed impossible for them to learn. Less severely handicapped and normal children also have profited from the use of fading techniques. Corey and Shamow (1972), for example, found that normal nursery-school children acquired and retained oral reading behaviors better when pictures representing the words were superimposed over the words and then gradually faded out. The use of fading techniques in teaching any discrimination is limited primarily by the teacher's ability

Figure 2.10 Possibly techniques of fading in teaching word discrimination.

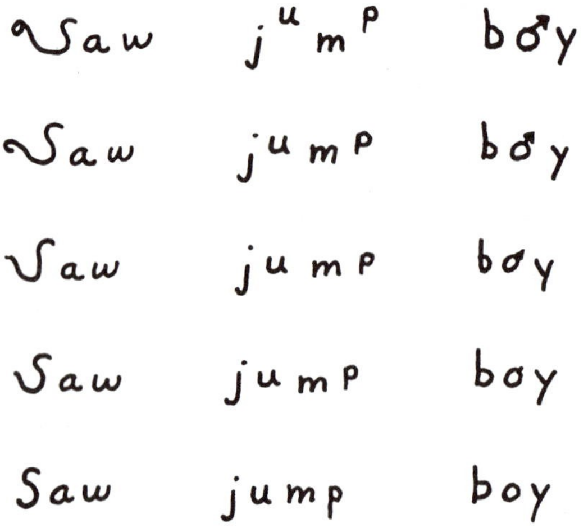

techniques in teaching any discrimination is limited primarily by the teacher's ability to identify and attenuate stimulus dimensions that will help children learn. Many simple fading techniques are known to experienced teachers and can be devised using materials that are readily available. For instance, pictures, dots, underlines, arrows, and other stimuli may be associated with a letter or word and gradually faded in size, as shown in Figure 2.10.

The creative and resourceful teacher will be able to devise simple but effective fading procedures. It must be kept in mind, however, that the child's responses are the best guide to instructional effectiveness. No matter how clever a fading procedure appears to others, it is of no value whatever, if the child can learn the discrimination without it or if it does not result in the child's learning to discriminate.

A feature of fading is that it makes it possible to teach a discrimination with very few errors because training begins with a discrimination the child has already learned and the fading stimulus is eliminated as gradually as possible in order to avoid most errors. This low ratio of errors is a big advantage for teaching the learning disabled because they have experienced failure so often.

inforcement) was provided and tasks were appropriately sequenced. These results suggested to Staats that older children with learning difficulties also could be taught to read if the necessary motivational and instructional techniques were used. Consequently, he devised a token reinforcer system, in which the child was given plastic disks as tokens (which could be exchanged for a wide variety of toys or other items) for correct responses, and a simple, highly structured teaching method. His token reinforcement system was the first use of such procedures in educational behavior modification.

The basic procedure involves reinforcing the child with tokens for the correct reading of new words presented singly. Once learned, these new words are then presented in paragraphs of a story. Similar teaching and reinforcement procedures have been used with a wide variety of children and instructors in a large number of studies (e.g., Ryback & Staats, 1970; Staats & Butterfield, 1965; Staats, Finley, Minke, & Wolf, 1964; Staats, Minke, & Butts, 1970; Staats, Minke, Finley, Wolf, & Brooks, 1964;

Staats, Minke, Goodwin, & Landeen, 1967). In some of these studies, the children were taught by parents, volunteer housewives, high-school seniors, or other nonprofessionals. The results using the Staats techniques have been consistently impressive.

Behavior Modification and Reversal Problems   The remediation of reversal problems has also been the topic of research (see Box 2.6). Deno and Chiang (1979) worked with five severely learning disabled children from 9 to 12 years of age who exhibited reversal problems associated with the letters *b*, *d*, *p*, and *q*. Reinforcement for correct responses and feedback on number correct greatly improved the reversal error rate for four of the five children.

Hasazi and Hasazi (1972) reported an interesting case in which behavior modification was used to reduce incorrect arithmetic responses caused by reversal problems. The subject of their study was an 8-year-old boy who almost invariably reversed the digits in two-digit sums. Otherwise this child was a very capable student. Because his reversal behavior had persisted for nearly a year, he had been referred for several neurological and visual examinations. His teachers had been giving him "extra help" because of his apparent neurological or perceptual deficits. Careful observation of his behavior, however, revealed that his reversals were likely a function of the teacher's attention (i.e., reinforcement) rather than true perceptual problems:

Box 2.6
WORKING WITH REVERSAL PROBLEMS:
THE IMPORTANCE OF INSTRUCTIONAL SEQUENCING

When confronted with children who manifest reversal problems, the inclination of many teachers embracing a behavioral approach is to present the problem letters—b and d, for example—and then reinforce correct labeling ("bee" for b and "dee" for d). Unfortunately behavioral researchers have shown that the most effective method is not quite that simple. They have found that the *sequence* in which potentially reversible letters are presented can be crucial. Both Douglas W. Carnine and Joanna P. Williams advise some time separation between the presentation of letters like b and d. Based on their research (Carnine, 1976, 1980, 1981; Williams & Ackerman, 1971), one can make the following recommendations for teaching the child with reversal problems:

1 Separate in time the learning of b from the learning of d. For example, first teach the child to discriminate b from other nonreversible letters such as a, s, m, f, and r. Have the child practice on these letters for a couple of weeks before attempting to teach him or her the letter d.

2 On the day that you are ready for the introduction of d, do it gradually. Do *not* suddenly present b and d and have the child attempt to learn the difference between the two. Two ways of doing this according to Carnine (1980, 1981) are:

   i Present d along with other letters that are not similar to b, such as a, s, m, f, and r. Ask the child to identify each of them, including d. Once he/she has learned to discriminate d from other dissimilar letters, then present the child with b and d together and require him/her to identify the one as "bee" and the other as "dee."
   ii Using a matching technique, ask the child to make easier matches first before gradually having him/her make more difficult matches. For example, when asking him/her to "find the one on the bottom like the one on the top," present him/her with problems in which 50% of the alternatives are similar, as in Figure 2.11.

Figure 2.11

Then give him/her problems in which 50% of the alternatives are similar, as in Figure 2.12.

Figure 2.12

Finally, give him/her problems in which 100% of the alternatives are similar, as in Figure 2.13.

Figure 2.13

First, Bob was able to discriminate easily between numbers containing the same but reversely ordered digits, such as 12 and 21. Second, he often pointed out reversals on his own paper to the teacher when she failed to notice them. Finally, he was observed on several occasions erasing correctly ordered sums and reversing the order of the digits contained. (Hasazi & Hasazi, 1972, p. 158)

When the teacher withdrew "extra help" (i.e., marked all sums "correct" whether reversed or not) and reinforced correct digit order with attention, Bob's digit reversals decreased to near zero, as shown in the Experimental 1 phase of Figure 2.14. Because Hasazi and Hasazi wanted to make sure that teacher attention was in fact the reinforcer maintaining reversed digits, they instituted a reversal of the contingency: the teacher again attended with "extra help" to Bob's reversals (Baseline 2 in Figure 2.14). After Bob began to write reversed digit sums, just as he had during the first baseline condition, the teacher once more began to ignore reversed digits (Experimental 2). The results shown in Figure 2.14 are convincing evidence that Bob's problem was not primarily neurological or perceptual. The problem was with the teacher's inadvertent reinforcement of digit reversals.

Visual-Motor, Tactual, and Kinesthetic Problems Because the behaviorist stresses working on academic behaviors and because the academic behavior most obviously connected with visual-motor, tactual, and kinesthetic disabilities is that of handwriting, most behavioral research in this area has been on handwriting problems. Although used with other types of problems, *nowhere are the three behavioral techniques of task analysis, shaping,*

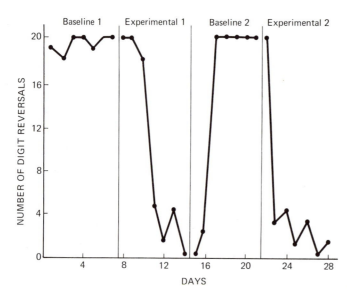

Figure 2.14   Number of digit reversals per day under baseline and experimental conditions. Source: J. E. Hasazi & S. E. Hasazi, "Effects of Teacher Attention on Digit-Reversal Behavior in an Elementary School Child," *Journal of Applied Behavior Analysis,* 1972, 5, p. 160. Reprinted with permission.

and modeling more important than in working with handwriting problems and other problems due to visual-motor, tactual, and kinesthetic disabilities. Task analysis is the breaking down of a complex behavior into its component skills. Shaping is the method of reinforcing successive approximations of a to-be-learned behavior. Modeling is the demonstration by a person to another person of what the first person wishes the second person to do.

Task Analysis   The first concern of the behaviorist working with a child exhibiting poor handwriting is to do a task analysis of handwriting itself. If a child is not writing legibly, the task of writing may be analyzed into the component skills of

1   holding the pencil correctly;

2   making marks with appropriate pressure on the pencil;

3   discriminating legibly formed from illegibly formed letters;

4   forming legible letters when shown a visual model;

5   properly spacing letters and words.

Each of these five component skills is in itself a task that can be analyzed into component or prerequisite subtasks. Holding the pencil correctly, for example, could be broken down into

1   grasping the pencil with the thumb in opposition to the index and middle fingers, the shaft of the pencil forming an angle of approximately 45 degrees with the thumb;

2   placing the thumb and fingers approximately 1 inch from the point of the pencil;

3   curling the fingers naturally toward the palm of the hand;

4   resting the fourth finger and outside edge of the hand on the paper.

The process of task analysis can be extended indefinitely; it must continue until the teacher or other behavior analyst can identify exactly where the child's performance falters and what must be taught if the child is to reach the instructional objective.

Shaping   The process of task analysis outlined above suggests that one can identify a succession of approximations of the final performance desired. It also suggests that in order to teach the final performance, one could reinforce each successive approximation. This method is precisely what is involved in the process of "shaping" behavior. Behavior shaping, the method of reinforcing successive approximations, is to teaching new behavioral repertoires what stimulus fading is to teaching new discriminations. To use a shaping technique, one must begin with reinforcement of a performance that is already in the individual's repertoire. Then, gradually, the criterion for reinforcement is shifted to closer and closer approximations of the terminal goal. Complex visual-motor skills such as writing can be shaped by providing reinforcement, first, for merely holding the pencil and making lines on the paper, and later, for gradually closer approximations of forming legible letters.

The extent to which tasks must be analyzed and the number of approximations shaped in order to teach a skill will depend on the level of the child's functioning. Tasks must be more finely analyzed and steps in the shaping process must be smaller for younger or more severely handicapped children than for older children and those without handicaps. Like stimulus fading, task analysis and behavior shaping are useful only if they help children to learn at a faster rate. It would be ridiculous to analyze a task and attempt to shape a performance in a child who can in one step master the skill being taught; on the other hand, a task analysis or shaping procedure for a child who is having difficulty in learning is adequate only if the child is performing well on each successive approximation.

Modeling In order to reinforce a behavior, one must wait for it to occur; in order to shape a behavior, one must wait specifically for an approximation of the desired performance. That it is possible simply to arrange an environment in which a performance is likely and then wait patiently for approximations that can be reinforced is obvious from the experimental psychology literature. Multitudes of pigeons and rats have been taught, by using behavior shaping, to peck disks or press levers without the experimenter having given them instructions or having shown them how to perform. When a child is being taught a new skill, however, behavioral examples can in some cases completely eliminate the need for shaping. Showing children a model or example of how they are to behave can often make it possible for them to acquire instantaneously, through observational learning, a performance that otherwise might take a considerable amount of time to shape (cf., Bandura, 1969; Cullinan, Kauffman, & LaFleur, 1975).

Reinforcement for appropriate performance is a primary factor in teaching, but task analysis, behavior shaping, and modeling are procedures that greatly enhance the value or effectiveness of reinforcement. *Task analysis* is necessary in order to know precisely what to reinforce. *Shaping* makes it possible for an individual to acquire gradually and systematically a skill that no amount of reinforcement could induce without successive approximations. *Modeling* allows the child to acquire immediately an imitative performance that can be reinforced.

Beginning Writing Skills The work of Staats and his colleagues (Staats, Brewer, & Gross, 1970) has shown that teaching writing skills consists essentially of shaping an imitative set of motor behaviors. In their work, young culturally deprived children approximately 4 years old were taught to write the letters of the alphabet. The teacher began by showing the child how to hold a crayon (and, later in the program, a pencil) and trace a line. Next the child was shown how to trace large letters. After the child learned to trace letters, he/she was taught, through instructions and models, how to copy them, beginning with very large letters that were gradually reduced to primary-size type. Appropriate imitations (i.e., tracing or copying the model letters correctly) were reinforced with tokens in much the same manner as responses were reinforced in Staats's reading program described earlier in this chapter. The tasks gradually increased in difficulty, and gradually a greater accuracy of imitation was required in order to obtain reinforcement. As a result of such instruction, the children learned to write the letters of the entire alphabet after several thousand tries. The slow acquisition of a child's writing performance is shown in Figure 2.15. The response numbered 1 was produced when the child was asked to write the letters in his name prior to instruction. The response numbered 2 shows the first try at tracing the letter *a*. Subsequent tries at copying letter forms show the child's step-by-step acquisition of writing skill. Staats and his associates found that *young children learned new letters in fewer attempts after they had acquired the ability to copy the first few letters.* In other words, the children were able to generalize their learned behaviors to new tasks. This is an important finding since generalization is not easily obtained when working with young and/or handicapped children.

Rayek and Nesselroad (1972) have used even more explicit procedures to teach writing to young handicapped children, and they have obtained good results. Their program includes giving and fading both verbal and visual prompts and reinforcing successive approximations of the terminal goal. Verbal prompts include instructions regarding how to form a letter, and visual prompts include forms to be traced (e.g., lines, which are gradually faded by changing them to dots). The terminal goals include both manuscript and cursive writing. The program combines the use of a number of behavior principles:

First, writing is taught by shaping procedures. It is the gradual shaping of a motor skill to the point where the response approximates a specific model. Second, letters are made up of stroke elements. A task analysis suggests that the elements requiring the least complex motor responses are the horizontal and vertical lines. Slanted lines and curved lines are more complex. For maximum program efficiency, letters containing common elements are grouped into families and taught together. For instance, all letters using straight lines are taught before letters containing slanted lines. According to the task analysis, letters within a given family are ordered according to their difficulty and assigned in that order. Figure 2.16 shows the stroke elements and the letters and numbers which include them. Third, copying a letter from a visual model precedes writing a letter from dictation. This procedure is used to assure that the child is equipped to make the appropriate strokes prior to writing from dictation. Fourth, writing is functional when it is used in practical ways such as writing one's name, words, or stories. Once these meaningful uses of writing are possible for the child, the social interactions which ensue take over to maintain the behavior. (Rayek & Nesselroad, 1972, pp. 171–172)

In most academic programs manuscript writing (printing) is taught before cursive writing. Lovitt (1973) and his colleagues, however, have successfully taught cursive writing from the beginning of the school year without taking into consideration what writing instruction the pupils had previously received. Lovitt's research data appear to support Staats's contention that learning to copy specific letters will improve performance on copying other letters.

Procedures for correcting specific writing problems have not been extensively researched. However, reinforcement, explicit instruction, response cost contingencies for errors, and activities such as labeling, tracing, touching, and copying letters have been used to improve handwriting in learning disabled and normal children (Brigham, Finfrock, Breunig, & Bushell, 1972; Fauke, Burnett, Powers, & Sulzer-Azaroff, 1973; Hopkins, Schutte, & Garton, 1971; Lovitt, 1973).

Lovitt (1973) has taught typing skills to

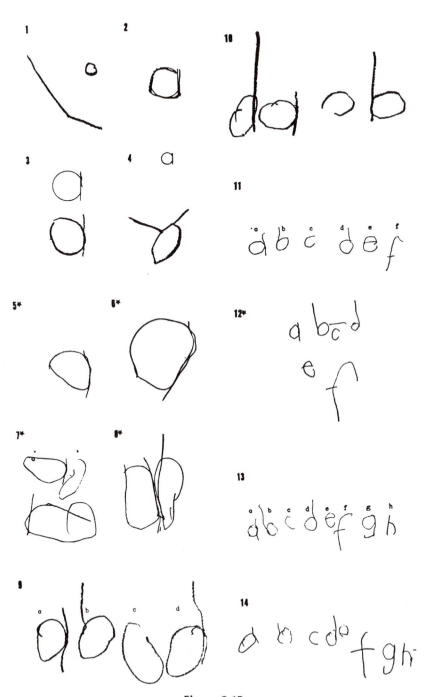

Figure 2.15

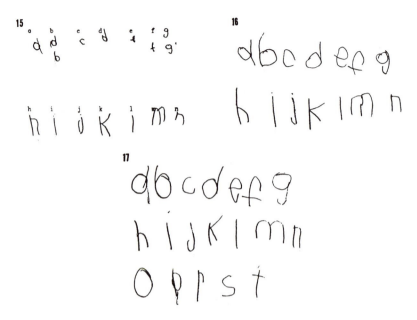

Figure 2.15 (*cont.*) Summary of the writing learning of a 4-year-old child with an IQ of 89.
Source: A. W. Staats, B. A. Brewer, & M. C. Gross, "Learning and Cognitive Development: Representative Samples, Cumulative-Hierarchical Learning, and Experimental-Longitudinal Methods," *Monographs of the Society for Research in Child Development*, 1970, Ser. No. 141, Vol. 35, No. 8, p. 69. Reprinted with permission.

learning disabled children. Typing does have certain advantages over handwriting, especially for individuals who experience difficulty in the visual-motor skills required for writing. Typing is faster (once the basics are learned) and produces a consistent, legible script. Furthermore, it is an intriguing activity for most children; few will have to be coaxed, prodded, or extrinsically reinforced for learning typing skills.

Beginning Arithmetic The most fundamental arithmetic skill is counting. Staats and his colleagues (Staats et al., 1970) have shown that learning to count involves learning three distinct performances:

The child has to learn a sequence of sensorimotor responses that involves attending to the individual objects in the set in order (one at a time, at least at the beginning). He also has to learn a sequence of counting verbal responses. In addition, as a third type of learning, the latter has to be under the control of the former and vice versa. (p. 46)

Specifically, the child must learn (1) the visual-motor skill of touching or moving objects one at a time and in order; (2) the verbal skill of saying the numbers in sequence; and (3) the skill of combining or coordinating the visual-motor and verbal performances.

Staats and his co-workers taught young children to count by systematically developing each of the three skills. In the beginning, the teacher showed the child a card with pictures of one or two objects on it, and prompted the child to say "One dog," "Two fish," and so forth. When the child could discriminate and label numerosity for one and two objects, a

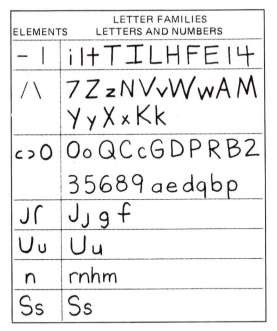

ELEMENTS	LETTER FAMILIES LETTERS AND NUMBERS
− |	i l + T I L H F E I +
/ \	7 Z z N V v W w A M Y y X x K k
c ɔ O	O o Q C c G D P R B 2 3 5 6 8 9 a e d q b p
J ʃ	J ɟ g f
U ᴜ	U ᴜ
n	r n h m
S s	S s

Figure 2.16 Elements and letter families. Source: E. Rayek & E. Nesselroad, "Application of Behavior Principles to the Teaching of Writing, Spelling, and Composition," in G. Semb (Ed.), *Behavior Analysis and Education—1972* (Lawrence, Ks.: University of Kansas, Department of Human Development, 1972). Reprinted with permission.

third object was introduced. When "three" was mastered, the pictures were changed to geometric forms. Next, the child was taught to count dots as the teacher uncovered them with her hand. The correct counting performance was modeled by the teacher, and the child was reinforced (with tokens) for imitating. When the child could count four dots, the teacher arranged objects in a row and modeled the behavior of touching and counting them in order. Later, objects were pulled from a row and counted in order. Still later, objects not arranged in order were moved one at a time from a pile and counted. Finally, rote verbal counting was extended through verbal modeling and imitation.

Parsons (1972) and Grimm, Bijou, and Parsons (1973) have used similar procedures in teaching beginning arithmetic skills to handicapped young children. As with beginning writing, these skills were developed by using a number of basic behavior modification techniques in combination: task analysis, reinforcement, shaping, fading, and modeling.

Visual-motor, motor, tactual, and kinesthetic skills appear to be of value in some children's learning of basic computational skills, as well as in counting. Lovitt and his co-workers (Lovitt, 1973; Smith, Lovitt, & Kidder, 1972) have found that providing objects to manipulate and showing models of problem solutions improved children's computation performance.

CONTROVERSIES SURROUNDING VISUAL, VISUAL-MOTOR, TACTUAL, AND KINESTHETIC DISABILITIES

No aspect of the field of learning disabilities has sparked more controversy than that of training aimed at the remediation of the perceptual processes (see Box 2.7). Heated debates about the value of perceptual training have raged for years. Basically, there are five interrelated issues that can be characterized by the following five questions:

1 How well can visual, visual-motor, tactual, and kinesthetic disabilities be measured?

2 Are visual, visual-motor, tactual, and kinesthetic disabilities present in learning-disabled children?

3 Do visual, visual-motor, tactual, and kinesthetic disabilities cause problems in academic learning, such as reading?

4 How effective is the training of visual, visual-motor, tactual, and kinesthetic processes with regard to academics?

5 Are there any other reasonable causes of problems in academics?

Box 2.7
SOME DO'S AND DON'TS FOR THE TEACHER

Given the turmoil and controversy surrounding the consideration of visual, visual-motor, tactual, and kinesthetic factors in learning disabilities, it is probably wisest for the teacher of learning-disabled children not to have strong biases regarding perception and learning disabilities. There are, however, a number of "dos" and "don'ts" that should guide the teacher in making reasonable decisions about the perceptual abilities of children in his or her class.

DON'T   automatically assume that a child has a visual perceptual problem because he/she has reading problems, even if reading errors appear at first glance to reflect perceptual problems, such as reversal errors.

DO   look for other than perceptually based reasons for failure on academic tasks.

DON'T   rely on a single test score from a perceptual test in assessing a child's perceptual functioning. At least three or four such tests should indicate low perceptual functioning before you conclude that the child has a perceptual problem.

DON'T   place much faith in scores obtained from subtests claiming to assess particular aspects of perceptual functioning, such as figure-background problems or position-in-space problems.

DON'T   attempt to make a placement decision or devise an educational program for a child on the basis of information from perceptual tests without using extreme caution.

DO   use the information gained from the total test scores of several perceptual instruments to form a gross estimate of a child's perceptual functioning. With this estimate in mind, you can perform a task analysis of the academic tasks the child has been failing.

DON'T   rely on perceptual training based on a process-training model to improve a child's academic behavior.

DO   consider the use of behaviorally based interventions for perceptual problems, particularly if the child is having difficulty in the early stages of learning to read.

DON'T   assume that a behaviorally based intervention designed to remediate a specific type of perceptual problem will cure all the child's academic problems, or even all the child's perceptual problems. A disadvantage of the behavioral approach is that a specific set of instructional activities is usually necessary for each type of problem the child has.

DO   be prepared, if using a behaviorally based intervention, to spend a great deal of time devising the instructional program and drilling the child on academic tasks. A disadvantage of the behavioral approach is that it is very time-consuming if carried out appropriately.

How Well Can Visual, Visual-Motor, Tactual, and Kinesthetic Disabilities Be Measured?

One of the major reasons some authorities have questioned the worth of perceptual training is that the tests (e.g., the Bender-Gestalt, Developmental Test of Visual Perception, and Illinois Test of Psycholinguistic Abilities) are notably lacking in reliability and validity (Coles, 1978; Salvia & Ysseldyke, 1981). *Reliability* refers to how likely it is that a particular child will receive the same, or nearly the same, score on a test administered at two different points in time. For example, if on the first testing a child receives a relatively high score on the Position in Space subtest of the Developmental Test of Visual Perception, and 3 months later achieves a low score, it would be difficult to rely on the results of either one of the testings. One cannot place a lot of faith in a test for which there is a great deal of fluctuation in scores from one testing to the next. *Validity* refers to whether a test is measuring what it purports to be measuring. For example, if the developers of a test such as the Developmental Test of Visual Perception claim that they are measuring skills that are important for reading, then how well a child does on each of the subtests should be indicative of how well he/she can read. If, on the other hand, subtest scores do not predict very well how a child will do in reading, then the validity of the subtests can be questioned. These two technical concepts—reliability and validity—are the primary yardsticks by which tests are measured.

As with any issue that is hotly debated, there are two camps, each of which firmly believes in the merits of its own position. The most reasonable conclusions one can draw regarding perceptual testing are:

1 Use of a score on a *single subtest* to attempt to pinpoint a specific type of problem (e.g., posi-

tion-in-space problems or figure-background problems) is highly questionable.

2 If one chooses to use perceptual tests, one should always obtain scores from at least three or four testings in order to corroborate one's findings.

3 Even several testings should be interpreted with caution, especially if these are *subtest* scores.

Are Visual, Visual-Motor, Tactual, and Kinesthetic Disabilities Present in Learning-Disabled Children?

As we have just noted, perceptual tests are highly questionable from a technical point of view. This inadequacy makes it unwise to use the results from perceptual tests as a basis for making placement decisions or for devising educational programs for individual students without exercising a great deal of caution. However, taking total scores rather than subtest scores, and grouping them for research rather than individual instructional purposes, one does find a moderate relationship between scores on perceptual tests and scores in reading achievement (Hallahan & Cruickshank, 1973; Kavale, 1982). In other words, children who score low in visual perception have a better than chance likelihood of scoring low in reading achievement.

Do Visual, Visual-Motor, Tactual, and Kinesthetic Disabilities Cause Problems in Academic Learning, Such as Reading?

Although there is some evidence that perceptual skills are moderately related to reading achievement and that learning-disabled children are more likely than nondisabled children to score more poorly on visual perceptual tests, this does not mean that perceptual problems *cause* reading problems. Simply testing children on two variables such as visual perception and reading and then finding a relationship between the two does not allow one to state that one causes the other. Attempting to answer the next question provides a better way of looking at whether perceptual disabilities cause reading problems.

How Effective Is the Training of Visual, Visual-Motor, Tactual, and Kinesthetic Processes with Regard to Academics?

If it could be demonstrated that training visual perceptual processes increases the reading achievement of learning-disabled children, then one would be in a better position to say that visual perceptual problems cause reading disabilities. Unfortunately the evidence on this matter is mixed, depending on whether one takes a process-training or a behavioral approach to intervention. In general, process-training interventions, such as Frostig's and Kephart's, have not met with much success (Hallahan & Cruickshank, 1973; Myers & Hammill, 1982). The best that can be said is that perceptual training based on a process-training model may have some effect on perceptual skills. However, it does not increase reading achievement. Behavioral interventions, on the other hand, have been successful in improving *early* reading behaviors by focusing on the reinforcement of visual discrimination skills.

Are There Any Other Reasonable Causes of Problems in Academics?

As we pointed out at the very beginning of this chapter, not all learning-disabled children exhibit perceptual problems. This is important to keep in mind, because when the field of learning disabilities was being established, the prevailing notion was that the majority, if not

all, of learning-disabled children have perceptual problems. It is now recognized by most authorities that even if perceptual problems do exist in some learning-disabled children, there are other possible sources for the learning problems. As we will discuss in Chapter 7, there is considerable evidence, for example, that language disabilities may be a cause of reading problems in some learning-disabled children. Frank Vellutino and Isabelle Liberman, in fact, both believe that poor performance on visual perceptual tasks can be attributed to inadequate language rather than visual perceptual disturbances (Liberman & Shankweiler, 1979; Vellutino, 1977). They think, for example, that reversal errors are more likely the result of verbal-response (naming) errors rather than perceptual problems.

Vellutino and Liberman have each conducted a series of studies to back up their claims. The results of a couple of Vellutino's investigations will be mentioned. First, he and his colleagues found that poor readers did much better in the visual recall of words than they did in pronouncing the same words (Vellutino, Steger, & Kandel, 1972; Vellutino, Smith, Steger, & Kaman, 1975). Furthermore, in two clever experiments they found that poor readers were as able as normal readers to remember unfamiliar words (Hebrew) presented visually (Vellutino, Pruzek, Steger, & Meshoulam, 1973; Vellutino, Steger, Kaman, & De-Setto, 1975). Vellutino's implication is that poor readers may not do as well on visual recall of familiar English words because they have not made the verbal-figural associations between the letters and their sounds. However, when Hebrew words are used, both normal and poor readers are equally unfamiliar with the sounds of the letters, and under these conditions of equal verbal-figural familiarity, the poor and normal readers perform similarly. Other researchers have found results similar to those of Vellutino and Liberman (e.g., Allington, Gormley, & Truex, 1976; Gupta, Ceci, & Slater, 1978; Hicks, 1980; Swanson, 1979).

SUMMARY

The term "perception" refers to an individual's ability to organize and interpret sensory information. Disabilities in perception which are closely linked are visual, visual-motor, tactual, and kinesthetic in nature. Of these four perceptual modes, the visual has been the one most often associated with learning-disabled children. Visual perception deficits are not deficits in visual acuity, but in the interpretation of visual information. Using Eleanor Gibson's theory of perceptual development, one can describe a child's visual perceptual deficit as his or her difficulty in discriminating the distinctive features of stimuli, such as the "form" or "position in space" of objects visually present.

Good visual-motor perception requires the coordinating of the visual and motor systems. Advocates of visual-motor training have posited that for many learning-disabled children this "perceptual-motor match" (as Kephart describes it) is particularly hard to achieve. Kephart argues that the coordination of these systems is the foundation of higher conceptual thinking. Kephart's theory also assumed that motor development precedes visual development, and that the sensation from movement serves as feedback for the monitoring of visual-motor activities. But several studies have shown that the opposite sequence, with visual development preceding motor development, is the more valid one. Nevertheless, Kephart's argument that visual and motor development interact to monitor each other has been supported in studies of school children and non-human animals.

Closely related to motor problems are tactual (sensation of touch) and kinesthetic (sensation of movement) problems. Children with such problems may exhibit a tactual "defensiveness," an inability to perform complex motor activities, an inability to form an adequate "body image," or deficits in "laterality."

A variety of commercial tests have been designed to assess perceptual disability; they have proved least valid when used in isolation. But even when deployed in batteries in an effort to isolate the particular perceptual mode responsible for problems in academics, these tests are far from totally accurate.

Once it is assumed that a child has a perceptual disability, one of two general treatment approaches may be employed: the process-training approach or the behavioral approach. The majority of process-training programs are aimed at all four of the perceptual disabilities. For example, Getman and his colleagues have devised a program for visually disabled children which encourages practice in the coordination of perceptual skills, Frostig and her colleagues have developed a similar program specifically for the remediation of the perceptual problems of learning-disabled children, Kirk and Kirk have offered strategies geared to alleviate a child's perceptual difficulties, and Kephart has developed activities that help children to achieve the perceptual-motor match. Also under the rubric of the process-training approach are Barsch's "Movigenic Curriculum" and Cratty's program, both of which have the goal of enhancing a child's motor skills and decreasing his or her cognitive disabilities. Doman and Delacato have proposed a controversial approach to perceptual problems which emphasizes training the child in cerebral dominance, believing that their program remediates deficits in the brain and that the development of an individual is parallel to the development of the species. Research on the efficacy of the Doman-Delacato program has not found it effective.

In contrast to the disciples of the process-training approach, behaviorists want to improve skills that directly affect a child's academic responses; for example, to combat visual perceptual problems, Staats and his colleagues have taught children to make visual discriminations that yield correct responses in reading. Children are reinforced for making correct visual discriminations at increasing levels of difficulty. Likewise, behaviorists have employed stimulus fading to teach visual discriminations and have carefully sequenced instruction and provided reinforcement to prevent letter and digit reversals. In approaching a child's deficits in the visual-motor, tactual, and kinesthetic modes, behaviorists have employed task analysis, reinforcement, shaping, fading, and modeling to improve learning-disabled children's academic performance, such as handwriting and arithmetic computation.

The remediation of the perceptual disabilities of learning-disabled children has traditionally been the most controversial area in this field. Many authorities believe that the tests that claim to identify specific perceptual problems are generally not reliable or valid; even interpretations that are drawn from several subtest scores must be drawn cautiously. Experimenters have found a modest correlation between scores on these perceptual tests and scores in reading achievement, but it is doubtful that perceptual problems cause reading problems in many cases. In fact, recent research indicates that sources other than perceptual deficits may be the cause of many children's learning problems. It is important that teachers be aware of the evidence associated with the controversy over perceptual training programs as they examine the abilities of their students and devise educational interventions.

REFERENCES

ALLINGTON, R.L., GORMLEY, K., & TRUEX, S. (1976). Poor and normal readers' achievement on visual tasks involving high frequency, low discriminability words. *Journal of Learning Disabilities, 9,* 292–296.

AYRES, A. J. (1965). Patterns of perceptual-motor dysfunction in children: A factor analytic study. *Perceptual and Motor Skills, 20,* 335–368.

AYRES, A. J. (1969). Deficits in sensory integration in educationally handicapped children. *Journal of Learning Disabilities, 2,* 160–168.

AYRES, A. J. (1971). Characteristics of types of sensory integrative dysfunction. *American Journal of Occupational Therapy, 25,* 329–334.

AYRES, A. J. (1972). *Southern California Sensory Integration Tests.* Los Angeles: Western Psychological Services.

AYRES, A. J. (1975). Sensorimotor foundations of academic ability. In W. M. Cruickshank & D. P. Hallahan (Eds.), *Perceptual and learning disabilities in children.* Vol. 2: *Research and theory* (pp. 301–358). Syracuse, NY: Syracuse University Press.

BANDURA, A. (1969). *Principles of behavior modification.* New York: Holt, Rinehart, & Winston.

BARSCH, R. H. (1967). *Achieving perceptual-motor efficiency.* Seattle, WA: Special Child Publications.

BARSCH, R. H. (1976). Ray H. Barsch. In J. M. Kauffman & D. P. Hallahan (Eds.), *Teaching children with learning disabilities: Personal perspectives* (pp. 58–93). Columbus, OH: Charles E. Merrill.

BEERY, K. E., & BUKTENICA, N. (1967). *Developmental Test of Visual-Motor Integration.* Chicago: Follett Publishers.

BENDER, L. (1938). *A Visual-Motor Gestalt Test and its clinical use.* Research Monograph No. 3. New York: American Orthopsychiatric Association.

BENDER, L. (1970). Use of the Visual-Motor Gestalt Test in the diagnosis of learning disabilities. *Journal of Special Education, 4,* 29–39.

BENTON, A. L. (1963). *The Revised Benton Visual Retention Test.* New York: Psychological Corp.

BIJOU, S. W. (1968). Studies in the experimental development of left-right concepts in retarded children using fading techniques. In N. R. Ellis (Ed.), *International review of research in mental retardation* (Vol. 3, pp. 65–96). New York: Academic Press.

BIJOU, S. W., & BAER, D. M. (1966). Operant methods in child behavior and development. In W. K. Honig (Ed.), *Operant behavior: Areas of research and application* (pp. 718–789). Englewood Cliffs, NJ: Prentice-Hall.

BORTNER, M., & BIRCH, H. G. (1962). Perceptual and perceptual-motor dissociation in cerebral palsied children. *Journal of Nervous and Mental Diseases, 134,* 103–108.

BRIGHAM, T. A., FINFROCK, S. R., BREUNIG, M. K., & BUSHELL, D. (1972). The use of programmed materials in the analysis of academic contingencies. *Journal of Applied Behavior Analysis, 5,* 177–182.

CARNINE, D. W. (1976). Similar sound separation and cumulative introduction in learning letter sound correspondence. *Journal of Educational Research, 69,* 368–372.

CARNINE, D. W. (1980). Two letter discrimination sequences: High-confusion alternatives first versus low-confusion alternatives first. *Journal of Reading Behavior, 12,* 41–47.

CARNINE, D. W. (1981). Reducing training problems associated with visually and auditorily similar correspondences. *Journal of Learning Disabilities, 14,* 276–279.

CHALL, J. (1967). *Learning to read: The great debate.* New York: McGraw-Hill.

COHEN, S. A. (1969a). Comments from Dr. Cohen. *Journal of Learning Disabilities, 2,* 661.

COHEN, S. A. (1969b). Studies in visual perception and reading in disadvantaged children. *Journal of Learning Disabilities, 2,* 498–507.

COLARUSSO, R. P., & HAMMILL, D. D. (1972). *Motor-Free Visual Perception Test.* San Rafael, CA: Academic Therapy Publications.

COLES, G. (1978). The learning-disabilities test battery—empirical and social issues. *Harvard Educational Review, 48,* 313–340.

COREY, J. R., & SHAMOW, J. (1972). The effects of fading on the acquisition and retention of oral reading. *Journal of Applied Behavior Analysis, 5,* 311–315.

CRATTY, B. J. (1967). *Developmental sequences of perceptual-motor tasks.* Freeport, NY: Educational Activities.

CRATTY, B. J. (1973). *Intelligence in action.* Englewood Cliffs, NJ: Prentice-Hall.

CULLINAN, D., KAUFFMAN, J. M., & LA FLEUR, N. K. (1975). Modeling: Research with implications for special education. *Journal of Special Education, 9,* 209–221.

CUTLER, C. M., CICIRELLI, V. G., & HIRSHOREN, A. (1973). Comparison of discrimination and reproduction tests of children's perception. *Perceptual and Motor Skills, 37,* 163–166.

DELACATO, C. H. (1959). *The treatment and prevention of reading problems: The neurological approach.* Springfield, IL: Charles C. Thomas.

DELACATO, C. H. (1963). *The diagnosis and treatment of speech and reading problems.* Springfield, IL: Charles C. Thomas.

DELACATO, C. H. (1966). *Neurological organization and reading.* Springfield, IL: Charles C. Thomas.

DENO, S. L., & CHIANG, B. (1979). An experimental analysis of the nature of reversal errors in children with severe learning disabilities. *Learning Disability Quarterly, 2(3),* 40–45.

ESTES, W. K. (1970). *Learning theory and mental development.* New York: Academic Press.

FAUKE, J., BURNETT, J., POWERS, M. A., & SULZER-AZAROFF, B. (1973). Improvement of handwriting and letter recognition skills: A behavior modification procedure. *Journal of Learning Disabilities, 6,* 25–29.

FROSTIG, M. (1976). Marianne Frostig. In J. M. Kauffman & D. P. Hallahan (Eds.), *Teaching children with learning disabilities: Personal perspectives* (pp. 164–190). Columbus, OH: Charles E. Merrill.

FROSTIG, M., & HORNE, D. (1964). *The Frostig program for the development of visual perception: Teacher's guide.* Chicago: Follett.

FROSTIG, M., LEFEVER, D. W., & WHITTLESEY, J. R. B. (1964). *The Marianne Frostig Developmental Test of Visual Perception.* Palo Alto, CA: Consulting Psychologist Press.

GETMAN, G. N. (1965). The visuomotor complex in the acquisition of learning skills. In J. Hellmuth (Ed.), *Learning Disorders* (Vol. 1, pp. 49–76). Seattle, WA: Special Child Publications.

GETMAN, G. N. (1976). Gerald N. Getman. In J. M. Kauffman & D. P. Hallahan (Eds.), *Teaching children with learning disabilities: Personal perspectives* (pp. 210–237). Columbus, OH: Charles E. Merrill.

GETMAN, G. N., KANE, E. R., HALGREN, M. R., & MCKEE, G. W. (1964). *The physiology of readiness: An action program for the development of perception in children.* Minneapolis, MN: Publications to Accelerate School Success.

GIBSON, E. J. (1963). Development of perception: Discrimination of depth compared with discrimination of graphic symbols. In J. C. Wright & J. Kagan (Eds.), Basic cognitive processes in children (pp. 5–24). *Monographs of the Society for Research in Child Development*, 28(2, Serial No. 86).

GIBSON, E J. (1969). *Principles of perceptual learning and development.* Englewood Cliffs, NJ: Prentice-Hall.

GIBSON, E. J., GIBSON, J. J., PICK, A. D., & OSSER, H. A. (1962). A developmental study of the discrimination of letter-like forms. *Journal of Comparative and Physiological Psychology*, 55, 897–906.

GRIMM, J. A., BIJOU, S. W., & PARSONS, J. A. (1973). A problem-solving model for teaching remedial arithmetic to handicapped young children. *Journal of Abnormal Child Psychology*, 1, 26–39.

GUPTA, R., CECI, S. J., & SLATER, A. M. (1978). Visual discrimination in good and poor readers. *Journal of Special Education*, 12, 409–416.

HALLAHAN, D. P., & CRUICKSHANK, W. M. (1973). *Psychoeducational foundations of learning disabilities.* Englewoood Cliffs, NJ: Prentice-Hall.

HASAZI, J. E., & HASAZI, S. E. (1972). Effects of teacher attention on digit-reversal behavior in an elementary school child. *Journal of Applied Behavior Analysis*, 5, 157–162.

HELD, R., & HEIN, A. (1963). Movement produced stimulation in the development of visually guided behavior. *Journal of Comparative and Physiological Psychology*, 56, 872–876.

HENDRICKSON, L. N., & MUEHL, S. (1962). The effect of attention and motor response pretraining on learning to discriminate b and d in kindergarten children. *Journal of Educational Psychology*, 53, 236–241.

HICKS, C. (1980). The ITPA Visual Sequential Memory task: An alternative interpretation and the implications for good and poor readers. *British Journal of Educational Psychology*, 50, 16–25.

HOPKINS, B. L., SCHUTTE, R. C., & GARTON, K. L. (1971). The effects of access to a playroom on the rate and quality of printing and writing of first and second grade students. *Journal of Applied Behavior Analysis*, 4, 77–87.

HUTTENLOCHER, J. (1967). Discrimination of figure orientation: Effects of relative position. *Journal of Comparative and Physiological Psychology*, 63, 359–361.

KAVALE, K. (1982). Meta-analysis of the relationship between visual perceptual skills and reading achievement. *Journal of Learning Disabilities*, 15, 42–51.

KEPHART, N. C. (1960). *The slow learner in the classroom.* Columbus, OH: Charles E. Merrill.

KEPHART, N. C. (1971). *The slow learner in the classroom* (2nd Ed.). Columbus, OH: Charles E. Merrill.

KEPHART, N. C. (1975). The perceptual-motor match. In W. M. Cruickshank & D. P. Hallahan (Eds.), *Perceptual and learning disabilities in children.* Vol. 1: *Psychoeducational practices* (pp. 63–69). Syracuse, NY: Syracuse University Press.

KIRK, S. A., & KIRK, W. (1971). *Psycholinguistic learning disabilities: Diagnosis and remediation.* Urbana, IL: University of Illinois Press.

KOPPITZ, E. M. (1964). *The Bender Gestalt test for young children.* New York: Grune & Stratton.

LAVRENT'EVA, T. V., & RUZSKAYA, A. G. (1960). Comparative analysis of touch and vision: Communication v. simultaneous intersensory comparison of form at preschool age. *Dokl. Akad. Pedagog. NAUK RSFSR*, 44, 73–76.

LIBERMAN, I. Y., & SHANKWEILER, D. (1979). Speech, the alphabet, and teaching to read. In L. Resnick & P. Weaver (Eds.), *Theory and practice of early reading* (Vol. 1, pp. 109–132). Hillsdale, NJ: Lawrence Erlbaum Associates.

LOVITT, T. C. (1973). *Applied behavior analysis techniques and curriculum research.* Report submitted to the National Institute of Education.

MYERS, P., & HAMMILL, D. (1982). *Learning disabilities: Basic concepts, assessment practices, and instructional strategies.* Austin, TX: Pro-Ed.

NAYLOR, H. (1980). Reading disability and lateral asymmetry: An information-processing analysis. *Psychological Bulletin*, 87, 531–545.

PARSONS, J. A. (1972). The reciprocal modification of arithmetic behavior and program development. In G. Semb (Ed.), *Behavior analysis and education—1972* (pp. 185–199). Lawrence, KS: Kansas University Department of Human Development.

PICK, H. L., & PICK, A. D. (1970). Sensory and perceptual development. In P. H. Mussen (Ed.), *Carmichael's manual of child psychology* (3rd ed., pp. 773–847). New York: Wiley.

RAYEK, E., & NESSELROAD, E. (1972). Application of behavior principles to the teaching of writing, spelling, and composition. In G. Semb (Ed.), *Behavior analysis and education—1972* (pp. 171–184). Lawrence, KS: University of Kansas Department of Human Development.

REESE, H. W., & LIPSITT, L. P. (1970). *Experimental child psychology.* New York: Academic Press.

ROBBINS, M., & GLASS, G. V. (1969). The Doman-Delacato rationale: A critical analysis. In J. Hellmuth (Ed.), *Educational therapy* (Vol. 2, pp. 321–377). Seattle, WA: Special Child Publications.

RYBACK, D., & STAATS, A. W. (1970). Parents as behavior therapy-technicians in treating reading deficits (dyslexia). *Journal of Behavior Therapy and Experimental Psychiatry, 1,* 109–119.

SALVIA, J., & YSSELDYKE, J. E. (1981). *Assessment in special and remedial education* (2nd ed.). Boston: Houghton Mifflin.

SEKULER, R. W., & ROSENBLITH, J. F. (1964). Discrimination of direction of line and the effect of stimulus alignment. *Psychonomic Science, 1,* 143–144.

SMITH, D. D., LOVITT, T. C., & KIDDER, J. D. (1972). Using reinforcement contingencies and teaching aids to alter the subtraction performance of children with learning disabilities. In G. Semb (Ed.), *Behavior analysis and education—1972* (pp. 342–360). Lawrence, KS: Kansas University Department of Human Development.

STAATS, A. W. (1968a). *Learning, language, and cognition.* New York: Holt, Rinehart, & Winston.

STAATS, A. W. (1968b). A general apparatus for the investigation of complex learning in children. *Behaviour Research and Therapy, 6,* 45–50.

STAATS, A. W. (1973). Behavior analysis and token reinforcement in educational behavior modification and curriculum research. In C. Thoresen (Ed.), *Behavior modification in education,* seventy-second yearbook of the National Society for the Study of Education, Part I (pp. 195–229). Chicago: University of Chicago Press.

STAATS, A. W., BREWER, B. A., GROSS, M. C. (1970). Learning and cognitive development: Representative samples, cumulative-hierarchical learning, and experimental-longitudinal methods. *Monographs of the Society for Research in Child Development, 35*(8, Serial No. 141).

STAATS, A. W., & BUTTERFIELD, W. H. (1965). Treatment of nonreading in a culturally deprived juvenile delinquent: An application of reinforcement principles. *Child Development, 4,* 925–942.

STAATS, A. W., FINLEY, J. R., MINKE, K. A., & WOLF, M. M. (1964). Reinforcement variables in the control of unit reading responses. *Journal of the Experimental Analysis of Behavior, 7,* 139–149.

STAATS, A. W., MINKE, K. A., & BUTTS, P. (1970). A token reinforcement remedial reading program administered by black therapy-technicians to problem black children. *Behavior Therapy, 1,* 331–353.

STAATS, A. W., MINKE, K. A., FINLEY, J. R., WOLF, M. M., & BROOKS, L. O. (1964). A reinforcer system and experimental procedure for the laboratory study of reading acquisition. *Child Development, 35,* 209–231.

STAATS, A. W., MINKE, K. A., GOODWIN, R. A., & LANDEEN, J. (1967). Cognitive behavior modification: 'Motivated learning' reading treatment with sub-professional therapy-technicians. *Behaviour Research and Therapy, 5,* 283–299.

STAATS, A. W., & STAATS, C. K. (1962). A comparison of the development of speech and reading behavior with implications for research. *Child Development, 33,* 831–846.

STAATS, A. W., & STAATS, C. K. (1963). *Complex human behavior.* New York: Holt, Rinehart, & Winston.

Stanford-Binet Intelligence Scale. (1973, rev., 3rd ed.). Boston: Houghton Mifflin.

STEVENSON, H. W. (1972). *Children's learning.* Englewood Cliffs, NJ: Prentice-Hall.

SWANSON, H. L. (1979). Developmental recall lag in learning disabled children: Perceptual deficit or verbal mediation deficiency? *Journal of Abnormal Child Psychology, 7,* 199–210.

TARAKANOV, V. B., & ZINCHENKO, V. P. (1960). Comparative analysis of touch and vision. Communication VI: Voluntary memory of form in preschool children. *Dokl. Akad. Pedagog. NAUK RSFSR, 4,* 49–52.

VELLUTINO, F. R. (1977). Alternative conceptualizations of dyslexia: Evidence in support of a verbal-deficit hypothesis. *Harvard Educational Review, 47,* 334–354.

VELLUTINO, F. R., PRUZEK, R., STEGER, J. A., & MESHOULAM, U. (1973). Immediate visual recall in poor and normal readers as a function of orthographic-linguistic familiarity. *Cortex, 9,* 368–384.

VELLUTINO, F. R., SMITH, H., STEGER, J. A., & KAMAN, M. (1975). Reading disability: Age differences and the perceptual deficit hypothesis. *Child Development, 46,* 487–493.

VELLUTINO, F. R., STEGER, J. A., KAMAN, M., DESETTO, L. (1975). Visual form perception in deficient and normal readers as a function of age and orthographic-linguistic familiarity. *Cortex, 11,* 22–30.

VELLUTINO, F. R., STEGER, J. A., KANDEL, G. (1972). Reading disability: An investigation of the perceptual deficit hypothesis. *Cortex, 8,* 106–118.

WEDELL, K. (1973). *Learning and perceptuo-motor disabilities in children.* New York: Wiley.

WHITE, B. L., CASTLE, P., & HELD, R. (1964). Observations on the development of visually-directed reaching. *Child Development, 35,* 349–364.

WILLIAMS, J. A., & ACKERMAN, M. D. (1971). Simultaneous and successive discrimination of similar letters. *Journal of Educational Psychology, 62,* 132–137.

WOHLWILL, J. S. (1970). Perceptual development. In H. W. Reese & L. P. Lipsitt (Eds.), *Experimental child psychology* (pp. 362–410). New York: Academic Press.

ZAPOROZHETS, A. V. (1965). The development of perception in the preschool child. In P. H. Mussen (Ed.), European research in child development (pp. 82–101). *Monographs of the Society for Research in Child Development, 30*(2, Serial No. 100).

ZINCHENKO, V. P. (1957). Some properties of orienting movements of the hands and eyes and their role in the formation of motor habits. (Authorized summary of candidate's dissertation). Moscow: Institute of Psychology.

ZINCHENKO, V. P. (1960). Comparative analysis of touch and vision. Communication II: Properties of orienting-investigatory eye movements for preschool children. *Dokl. Acad. Pedagog. NAUK RSFSR, 4,* 53–60.

ZINCHENKO, V. P., CHZHI-TSIN, V., & TARAKVANOV, V. V. (1962). Formation of and development of perceptive behavior. *Vop. Psikhol, 8,* 1–14.

ZINCHENKO, V. P., LOMOV, B. F., RUZSKAYA, A. G. (1959). Comparative analysis of touch and vision. Communication I: On so-called simultaneous perception. *Dokl. Akad. Pedagog. NAUK RSFSR, 3,* 71–74.

ZINCHENKO, V. P., & RUZSKAYA, A. G. (1960a). Comparative analysis of touch and vision. Communication III: Visual-haptic transfer in preschool age. *Dokl. Akad. Pedagog. NAUK RSFSR, 4,* 95–98.

ZINCHENKO, V. P., & RUZSKAYA, A. G. (1960b). Comparative analysis of touch and vision. Communication VII: The observable level of perception of form in children of preschool age. *Dokl. Akad. Pedagog. NAUK RSFSR, 4,* 85–88.

Cognitive Disabilities

Cognition is the study of how we go about thinking. It is the study of thought. For many years, the special education profession was not very interested in cognition, largely because of the popularity of behaviorism. Strict behaviorists are interested solely in observable behavior—that is, behavior that can be measured. Thought processes are not observable, so strict behaviorists dismiss cognition as a legitimate area of scientific inquiry. Under the influence of behaviorism, special educators were reluctant to consider that thought processes might be worth studying.

Since the mid-1970s, however, cognitive psychology has been more readily accepted within the psychology community. Many psychologists, including some behaviorists, began to criticize behavioral theory as too simplistic. They seriously questioned whether complex human behavior could be explained solely by stimulus-response connections. As Mahoney (1974) put it:

> There is now an overwhelming body of evidence indicating that a "passive organism" input-output model is sorely inadequate. Not only are there complex causal interactions among environmental and internally-based stimulations, but we know that much of what is "external" is actually mediated. Humans do not passively register the world as it really is; they filter, transform, and construct the experiences which constitute their "reality." (p. 29)

Thus, whereas behaviorists are concerned with the association of stimulus (S) and response (R), cognitive psychologists concentrate on what occurs between the S and the R. They want to know what goes on "inside our heads" before we respond to things in our environment.

ORGANIZATION OF CHAPTER

For the most part, this chapter is organized along historical lines. First we will consider the early work on field dependence and impulsivity—the two areas of cognition that were the first to be studied in learning-disabled children. Then we will discuss the study of memory problems—the area of cognition that has received the most attention in learning-disabled children. Next we will explore the area that has received the most attention of late—the exotic-sounding study of metacognition. Then we will present the major theoretical formulation to come out of the research conducted into these cognitive characteristics—the conceptualization of the learning-disabled child as an *inactive learner*. Finally, we will present the major educational interventions that have been devised for dealing with the cognitive disabilities of learning-disabled children.

THE EARLY RESEARCH—COGNITIVE STYLES

The 1960s witnessed a rapid growth of interest in an area of study that came to be referred to as *cognitive styles*. Until this time, the majority of cognitive psychologists had been interested in the *content* of thinking, i.e., what people were thinking when faced with problem-solving tasks. In the 1960s, however, researchers became interested in the *how* of thinking (Blackman & Goldstein, 1982). They pursued the notion that people have different *styles* of approaching problem-solving tasks and, in fact, could be categorized according to the particular style they used. The researchers considered

these styles to be relatively permanent personality traits, meaning they could be used to explain how the person would behave in a variety of situations. The two cognitive styles that received the most attention, first in normal child development and then in learning disabilities, were the dimensions of *field independence–field dependence* and *reflectivity-impulsivity*.

Field Independence Versus Field Dependence

Field independence–field dependence refers to how much individuals are influenced by their environment when asked to make decisions on perceptual tasks. Persons who are heavily influenced by their environment are termed field dependent. Their perceptions are less accurate because they can be "thrown off" by misleading information in their surroundings. Individuals who are able to focus on the most essential perceptual data without being influenced by inessential details are referred to as field independent. Their perceptions tend to be more accurate than those of individuals who are field dependent.

Three methods have been used to measure field independence. In the most elaborate one, the individual is seated on a chair within a small room. Both the chair and the room can be tilted by the experimenter and the person in the chair. After both the chair and room are tilted so that neither is in a vertical position, the individual is requested to "right" his or her chair to the true vertical. Those who are able to ignore cues from the room and place their chair in close to a true vertical position are categorized as field independent. Those who cannot are classified as field dependent. A second measure, the rod and frame test (RFT), is a more portable and scaled-down version of the first. A picture-frame-like device holds a rod that can be adjusted to various angles within the frame. After placing both the rod and the frame in nonvertical positions, the experimenter asks the individual to adjust the rod to the true vertical. The entire apparatus is in a darkened experimental room so that the person can only be influenced by cues from the rod or the frame or both. Those who are able to disregard cues from the frame and place the rod in an upright position are considered field independent. Those who allow the frame to distort their perceptions are referred to as field dependent. The third method of measurement, the embedded figures test (EFT), is a paper-and-pencil task that requires the individual to locate a geometric figure that is embedded within a context of distracting lines.

Scores on all three of these tests of field independence are highly correlated (Hagen & Kail, 1975), i.e., an individual who scores high on any one of the three is likely to score high on either of the other two. For this reason, the bulk of the research, especially with children, has been conducted using the easy-to-administer EFT.

The earliest research on field independence–dependence was done with nonhandicapped adults and children (Witkin, Dyk, Faterson, Goodenough, & Karp, 1962; Witkin, Goodenough, & Karp, 1967). Developmentally, children generally become more field independent with age.

Two lines of research using field independence–dependence measures are relevant to the area of learning disabilities. First, more than 20 studies have explored the relationship between field independence–dependence and achievement in nonhandicapped children. Second, a number of studies have directly compared the performance of learning-disabled versus non-learning-disabled children on field independence–dependence measures. Both lines of research have generally supported the idea that learning-disabled children are more field dependent than their nonhandicapped peers (Blackman & Goldstein, 1982).

Reflectivity-Impulsivity

A cognitive-style dimension that has received even more attention than field independence–dependence is reflectivity-impulsivity. The notion here is that individuals can be classified according to whether or not they reflect before making decisions when faced with difficult but solvable tasks. Most of these studies have used the matching familiar figures test (MFF) (Kagan, Rosman, Day, Albert, & Phillips, 1964), although some of the more recent ones have used an expanded version of this test (Salkind & Wright, 1977). Figure 3.1 is an example of an item from the MFF. The child is asked to find the figure on the bottom that is exactly like the one on the top. The experimenter records two things: (1) response time, i.e., how long it takes the child to make his or her first choice; and (2) errors, i.e., how many incorrect choices the child makes before he or she gets the correct answer. Impulsive children are those who respond quickly but make many errors, whereas reflective children are those who respond more slowly and make fewer errors. In general, research has shown the reflectivity-impulsivity dimension to be developmentally sensitive, with children becoming more reflective with age.

As in the area of field independence–dependence, the research on reflectivity-impulsivity has taken two general forms that are applicable to the field of learning disabilities. There have been studies of the relationship between achievement and reflectivity-impulsivity in nonhandicapped children, and there have been studies comparing learning-disabled versus nonhandicapped groups on the MFF. In general, the evidence is consistent in supporting

Figure 3.1   Item from Kagan's matching familiar figures test.

the notion that learning-disabled children are impulsive (Blackman & Goldstein, 1982).

Educational Implications

Shortly after the laboratory researchers began to find differences in the cognitive styles of learning-disabled children, some special educators began to advance hypotheses about the educational ramifications of these findings. In particular, they focused on the impulsive responding of learning-disabled children. A major reason for this interest, no doubt, was that the experimental findings were in such

close agreement with clinically based notions about many learning-disabled children. Teachers and school psychologists could easily relate to the idea of the learning-disabled child as one who is too quick to respond. Teachers of the learning disabled, for example, would be the first to tell you that their students don't seem to think before they respond, but instead blurt out the first thing that comes into their heads.

Because of the intuitive appeal of the cognitive-style work to educators, numerous special educators turned their attention to the modification of the dimensions of field dependence and, especially, impulsivity. They hypothesized that impulsivity was a major cause of the behavioral and academic problems of learning-disabled children. Several reviews (e.g., Blackman & Goldstein, 1982; Digate, Epstein, Cullinan, & Switzky, 1978; Epstein, Hallahan, & Kauffman, 1975) of studies attempting to train reflectivity reached similar conclusions:

1   Learning-disabled children can be trained to respond in a more reflective manner.

2   It is not enough to concentrate training efforts on getting the children to slow down. In other words, longer response times do not automatically lead to fewer errors.

3   Those who have provided impulsive children with language-based strategies, e.g., systematically scanning all of the alternatives while saying them aloud, have had the most success in making the cognitive styles of these children more reflective on the MFF.

4   *Most importantly,* however, even though children have been made more reflective on the laboratory-based MFF, this has not made them more reflective in their approach to classroom-based academic tasks nor has it automatically led to improved academic responding.

Given the last conclusion, the work on cognitive styles, at first glance, seems highly disappointing. After all, if training in cognitive styles does not lead to improvement in classroom behavior, then of what use is it? While it is true that the immediate educational payoff for the learning disabled has been minimal, it is important to place this early research on cognitive styles in its proper historical context. It has had a substantial impact on how we now view learning-disabled children and educational programming for them. There have been a number of valuable outcomes of this early work on cognitive styles:

1 It made the learning disabilities field aware that learning-disabled children may have different styles of approaching problem-solving tasks than do their nonhandicapped counterparts.

2 These different styles include impulsivity as well as a lack of task-approach strategies.

3 This impulsivity and nonstrategic approach can be modified by directly teaching learning-disabled children to use task-approach strategies.

4 Language is a useful regulator of impulsive behavior.

5 In order to achieve improvement in academic performance, the focus of the cognitive training needs to be on the academic materials themselves rather than on laboratory-type tasks like the MFF.

Apropos this last point: Since the mid-1970s, learning disabilities professionals have been using some of the same types of training strategies—e.g., self-instruction and strategy training—but have made academic materials the focus of their training activities. Instead of training impulsive children to become more reflective on the MFF and hoping that this would carry over to classroom activities, they have been using self-instruction and the training of strategies as techniques to attack academic tasks directly. We will have more to say about these efforts later in the chapter.

MEMORY STUDIES

The study of memory is another line of cognitive research in learning disabilities that began at about the same time as the work on cognitive styles. Like the latter, the study of memory gained a lot of impetus from the fact that it was seen as logically relevant to the everyday functioning of the learning-disabled child. Teachers were quick to agree that many learning-disabled children display significant difficulties in memory. "In one ear and out the other" is a commonly heard phrase in the teachers' lounge when the topic of conversation is a learning-disabled child.

Consideration of cognition as a legitimate area of study in the learning-disabled child was greatly aided by the research on the memory processes of the learning disabled. A major reason for this is that learning disabilities researchers have been able to borrow from a long tradition of research on memory processes in the areas of experimental and developmental psychology and this research was regarded as rigorous and scholarly.

Memory can be studied in various ways. Some memory tasks require the child to remember auditory material; some require the retention of visual information. Some ask the child to remember things in exactly the same order as they were presented; some do not. Some allow the child only a limited amount of time to study the to-be-remembered material; some do not, and so forth. We will describe here a type of memory task that has been used very often with learning-disabled children—it is referred to as a visual, short-term memory task.

The task we describe is called visual because the to-be-remembered information is visual in nature. This distinguishes it from other memory tasks that assess a different modality, e.g., auditory. It is a short-term memory task because it tests the retention of material over a relatively short period of time—a few seconds or a minute or so at the most. This distinguishes it from long-term memory tasks in which the individual is shown some material and then asked to remember it a number of hours, or even days, later.

In an example of a typical visual, short-term memory task, the experimenter shows the child pictures of familiar things and asks him or her to remember them. The adult, for instance, shows the child a piece of posterboard containing pictures of a cow, horse, banana, dog, apple, orange, and cat. The child is allowed a specified period of time, perhaps 20 seconds, to study the set of pictures. At the end of this study period, the adult covers up the pictures and asks the child to name them. After the student remembers these seven pictures as best he or she can, another seven pictures are presented, with the same instructions. Perhaps 10 of these sets of pictures are shown to the child.

FINDINGS WITH THE LEARNING DISABLED

A number of researchers, using the task just described or one similar to it, have studied the memory processes of the learning disabled. Dozens of studies have delved into the various facets of the memory problems experienced by the learning disabled (e.g., Bauer, 1977; Hallahan, Kauffman, & Ball, 1973; Swanson, 1977, 1979; Tarver, Hallahan, Kauffman, & Ball, 1976; Torgesen & Goldman, 1977; Vellutino, Steger, DeSetto, & Phillips, 1975). The findings of these researchers have been remarkably consistent with regard to three major conclusions:

1 Learning-disabled children exhibit difficulties on these memory tasks relative to their nonhandicapped peers.
2 Their memory problems can be attributed to failure to use certain strategies that nonhandicapped children are accustomed to using.
3 The strategies that nonhandicapped students use spontaneously can be taught to learning-disabled children. When they are taught to use

such strategies, the learning disabled perform on a par with the nonhandicapped.

Memory Strategies and the Learning Disabled

These three conclusions make it obvious that a major underlying factor contributing to learning-disabled children's poor memory performance is their inability to use strategies that would make these tasks easier. There are a variety of different strategies that are often used by the nonhandicapped but not by the learning disabled. Two of the most common are *rehearsal* and *organization*. Rehearsal is the repetition of the names of the to-be-remembered things. For instance, in the above example, it helps considerably if you say the names of the seven stimuli (cow, horse, banana, dog, apple, orange, and cat) over and over again while you are viewing them. If you organize them in some way while you are rehearsing them, this is an even bigger aid to memory. Thus it helps to group the seven stimuli into two smaller categories of animals (cow, horse, dog, cat) and fruits (banana, apple, orange), and then rehearse them within each of these groupings. Learning-disabled children tend not to employ these strategies of rehearsal and organization, although after a few training sessions they are able to pick them up and use them to their benefit.

The major findings of the memory research, therefore, reinforced some of the major conclusions from the work on cognitive styles. Both lines of research pointed to the fact that many learning-disabled children lack strategies for performing on learning tasks. Both also produced evidence that such strategies could be taught to the learning disabled. There was, however, one major difference between the two lines of research. While some of those working in the cognitive-style area had made the mistaken assumption that training cognitive styles in the laboratory setting would automatically carry over into the classroom, few memory researchers made such an assumption. This is not to say, however, that the work of the cognitive-style researchers has not had educational implications. Their conceptualization of the learning-disabled child as deficient in the use of strategies laid the foundation for many of the educational procedures we will discuss later in this chapter.

METACOGNITION

In the 1970s, an outgrowth of the research on memory in developmental psychology came to be known as *metacognition.* John Flavell and his colleagues, who had for many years been studying the memory processes of children, were most responsible for the development of metacognition as an area of study in child development (Flavell, 1970, 1979; Flavell & Wellman, 1977). Flavell noted that even though young children could be trained to use memory strategies like rehearsal, unless they were continually prompted to do so, they reverted to nonrehearsal and subsequent poorer performance. He suggested, therefore, that in order to understand children's memory development more completely, we need to consider what he called "metamemory" factors, or *an individual's understanding of the relevant variables that affect that individual's own memory performance.*

According to Flavell's conceptualization, then, there is a distinction between cognitive strategies and metacognitive strategies. Cognitive strategies—for example, rehearsal—are used to make cognition progress; metacognitive strategies are used to monitor this progress. Thus the young children who reverted to nonrehearsal would be said to have metacognitive deficiencies in that they did not monitor, check, and maintain the use of an efficient cognitive strategy.

The concept of metacognition is not an easy one to understand, though it helps to think of it as an exotic term for the ability to use study skills. It involves two components:

(1) an awareness of what skills, strategies, and resources are needed to perform a task effectively and (2) the ability to use self-regulatory mechanisms to ensure the successful completion of the task, such as planning one's moves, evaluating the effectiveness of one's ongoing activities, checking the outcomes of one's efforts, and remediating whatever difficulties arise (Baker & Brown, 1984; Baker, 1982, pp. 27–28).

Another important thing to keep in mind is that although metacognition grew out of work in memory, there are a variety of different aspects of metacognition besides metamemory. Two others that have particular relevance for learning disabilities are metalistening skills and metacomprehension skills in reading. We now turn to a discussion of metamemory, metalistening, and metacomprehension in the learning disabled.

METACOGNITION IN THE LEARNING DISABLED

Metamemory

One of the first studies of the metacognitive abilities of the learning disabled used a metamemory task that was designed by Flavell and his colleagues (Kreutzer, Leonard, & Flavell, 1975). Learning-disabled children were compared with nondisabled children in their ability to answer questions pertaining to how they would go about trying to remember information (Torgesen, 1979). Children were asked to respond to items such as the following:

If you wanted to phone a friend and someone told you the phone number, would it make any difference if you called right away after you heard the number or if you got a drink of water first?

Why? What would you do if you wanted to try to remember a phone number?

The learning disabled had more difficulty than their nondisabled peers answering these meta-memory questions. In reply to "What would you do if you wanted to try to remember a phone number?" most students in both groups said they would write it down. However, when asked, "What would you do if you did not have a pencil and paper to write it down?" 86% of the nondisabled students but only 46% of the learning-disabled children replied that they would use verbal rehearsal as a technique. In addition, the results generally showed that the learning-disabled children could only generate a very narrow range of solutions to memory problems.

Metalistening

Anecdotal reports paint a picture of the learning-disabled child as a very poor listener. Learning disabilities teachers often describe these children as "looking as though they understand what you are telling them, although their subsequent behavior often belies the fact that they have understood a word that you have been saying to them." This kind of informal observation was supported by a study comparing the listening comprehension skills of learning-disabled and nonhandicapped elementary-school students (Kotsonis & Patterson, 1980). The adult told the children that they were going to play a game that involved several rules. She then presented one rule at a time, asking the children after each rule presentation if they thought they now had enough information to know how to play the game. The learning-disabled children were much more likely than their nondisabled peers to voice a readiness to play even though by objective standards they had not yet heard enough information to play the game appropriately. They were less aware of the insufficiency of their information.

Box 3.1
IS IT EASIER TO REMEMBER THAT A TALL BOY PLAYED BASKETBALL OR THAT THE HUNGRY BOY PLAYED BASKETBALL?

Good readers know when and where to concentrate their efforts. As efficient readers, we know it takes less effort to read *People* magazine than to read a textbook. Unfortunately, poor readers are not as adept at making this kind of distinction. They do not adjust their reading style to fit the level of the reading material. An interesting study by Owings, Peterson, Bransford, Morris, and Stein (1980) demonstrates this strategy deficiency nicely. What they did was to compare the most and the least successful fifth-grade readers' reading behavior on an easy versus a difficult reading passage. The difficult passage is reprinted below:

Talking at Recess

All the boys got together during recess and talked about what they had done the day before. The sleepy boy had eaten a hamburger. The hungry boy had played basketball. The thirsty boy had taken a nap. The sick boy had played a trick on his brother. The tall boy had done his homework. The strong boy had drunk some Kool-Aid. The smart boy had helped his father cut wood. The funny boy had gone to the doctor. When the bell rang, all the boys ran to the door and lined up to go indoors. (p. 252)

The easier passages contained identical words, but the subject-predicate pairings were logical: "The tall boy played basketball"; "The hungry boy ate a hamburger." After reading one of the passages, children were asked questions, such as "What did the hungry boy do?"

As you would expect, the less successful readers were less able to answer the comprehension questions. In addition, the results clearly point out that the poor readers were less able to adjust their reading style to match the level of the passage. The poor readers spent an equal amount of time studying both paragraphs, whereas the good readers spent more time on the difficult passage. The poor readers were unable to explain why the difficult passages were in fact harder to learn. Furthermore, Owings et al., believe that the less successful did not even notice the difference in difficulty between the two passages until they were asked to tell which paragraph made sense and which one was mixed up.

Source: R. D. Kneedler, with D. P. Hallahan, & J. M. Kauffman. *Special Education for Today* (Englewood Cliffs, N.J. Prentice-Hall, 1984). p. 87.

Metacomprehension in Reading

The academic area to which the concept of metacognition is most applicable is reading. Many learning-disabled children have difficulties in the area of reading comprehension (see Box 3.1), and the study of metacomprehension has helped special educators understand and remediate these problems. A number of research studies have been generated on reading comprehension (Anderson, 1980; Baker & Anderson, 1982; Baker & Brown, 1980; Bos & Filip, 1982; Brown, 1980; Forrest & Waller, 1981; Paris & Myers, 1981; Wong, 1982). This research has pointed to the following metacomprehension strategies as being deficient in many learning-disabled children:

1 *Clarifying the purposes of reading.* Before efficient readers even begin to read, they have a mind-set about the general purpose of their reading. Their approach to reading to obtain the gist of a news article is different from their approach to reading to gain information from a textbook on which they will be tested. Learning-disabled children are not as adept at adjusting their reading style to fit the difficulty level of the material.

They tend to approach all reading passages with the same degree of concentration and effort, whereas nonhandicapped readers take more time and effort when faced with more difficult material.

2 *Focusing attention on important parts of passages.* Closely related to the first point, researchers have found that the learning disabled have difficulty in picking out the main idea of a paragraph. Good readers spend more time and effort focusing on the major ideas contained in paragraphs they read.

3 *Monitoring one's level of comprehension.* Efficient readers also know when they are not comprehending what they are reading. Even the best readers occasionally find that they do not fully understand something they have been reading. Knowing when you are and are not understanding something is an important metacomprehension skill.

4 *Rereading and scanning ahead.* When good readers do note that they are having problems comprehending material, they often use a couple of basic metacomprehension strategies that the learning disabled do not use as readily. They stop and reread portions of the passage and/or scan ahead for information that will help them understand what they are reading.

5 *Consulting external sources.* When good readers encounter a word they do not know, they

Rhoda Sidney

The efficient reader alters his reading style to match the purpose and content of the reading material. Reading a comic versus reading schoolwork often involves different reading styles.

are more likely than learning-disabled children to rely upon external sources for help. For example, they realize that consulting a dictionary, asking others for help, and using contextual cues are good methods of helping them figure out specific words that are giving them difficulty.

In addition to this list of suggestions for increasing the metacomprehension abilities of the learning disabled, a variety of other metacognitive training ideas have been developed. We will discuss some of them in the section of this chapter on "Educational Methods for Cognitive Disabilities."

THE CONCEPT OF THE PASSIVE LEARNER WITH STRATEGY DEFICITS

The bulk of the research on the cognitive disabilities of the learning disabled has led some authorities to conclude that many learning-disabled children are passive individuals who lack strategies for attacking academic problems (Hallahan, Kneedler, & Lloyd, 1983; Torgesen, 1977). In addition to the research on cognitive styles, memory, and metacognition indicating that learning-disabled children have problems in spontaneously applying strategies, there is ample evidence that many of them exhibit "learned helplessness"—the belief that their efforts will not result in desired outcomes (Seligman, 1975). They have learned to expect failure no matter how hard they try, and this expectation leads them to "give up," or lose motivation. For example, when learning-disabled children fail on a task, they are less likely than nonhandicapped children to blame their failure on a lack of effort (Pearl, Bryan, & Donahue, 1980). In other words, learning-disabled individuals tend to minimize the value of effort. They tend to believe that no amount of

Box 3.2
CAN THE IQ-ACHIEVEMENT DISCREPANCY OF THE LEARNING DISABLED BE EXPLAINED BY THE CONCEPT OF PASSIVITY?

The concept of the passive learner has undoubtedly had a substantial impact on how the learning-disabled child is approached educationally. The notion of the learning-disabled child as passive has also led to theoretical speculation about the major defining characteristic of learning disabilities—the discrepancy between the child's actual level of achievement and the expected level based on the child's IQ. Torgesen (1977) has speculated:[1]

One possible explanation for the IQ-achievement discrepancy in learning disabled children, at least for the early primary grades, is provided by an examination of the different requirements for attaining an average IQ versus attaining average achievement in school. An intelligence measure at first grade is essentially a measure of the skills and knowledge the child has attained in his preschool years. Learning in young children which takes place outside of school may be viewed as being primarily incidental learning (Flavell, 1971). In other words, the young child does not set out to learn things with the express purpose of being able to recall them later. His learning arises as a natural and un-self-conscious product of his normal interaction with the environment. What he learns is mostly about relationships among things (Gibson, 1969), and these relationships are given concretely and naturally in the world of his experience. Thus, at first grade, the IQ test score may be interpreted as a measure of incidentally learned knowledge and skill.

Once the child enters school, however, he is faced with a much different kind of challenge to his learning abilities. For the first time, he is exposed to a requirement to learn material so that it may be efficiently recalled later. This learning is self-conscious, and it often requires that the child associate things which are outside of his natural experience. The relationships are not naturally given; he must generate them.... No longer is it sufficient to merely let things happen; the child must make them happen in very special, strategic ways. He must develop efficient study habits, and he must actively create organization and structure. In essence, he must develop and use new techniques of intelligence....

Many children who have learned sufficiently in their early years to attain an average IQ score may be relatively immature with regard to the kind of cognitive and personal awareness required to use efficient strategies in self-conscious learning. At the end of first grade, when IQ scores based on incidental learning are compared with achievement scores based on intentional learning, some children are going to have an IQ-achievement discrepancy as a result of their failure to adapt to new learning challenges. The discrepancy will not be the result of any specific cognitive defect, but will be due to more general cognitive and personality factors as they influence the ability to use efficient learning strategies. (p. 30)

[1] From J. K. Torgesen, "The role of nonspecific factors in the task performance of learning disabled children: A theoretical assessment." *Journal of Learning Disabilities.* p. 30, 1977. Reprinted by special permission of The Professional Press, Inc.

Paul S. Conklin, Monkmeyer

Some authorities believe that many of the characteristics of learning disabled children fit the pattern of a passive child who is lacking strategies for attacking academic problems.

effort will help them achieve. They are prone to view themselves as helpless when faced with academic tasks.

Given the cognitive and metacognitive disabilities as well as the motivational problems of the learning disabled, there is little wonder that some authorities have referred to the learning disabled as passive. As Hallahan & Kauffman (1982) summarize:

> Many of the psychological and behavioral characteristics we have mentioned can be summed up by saying that the learning-disabled child is a passive individual lacking in strategies for attacking academic problems. Specifically, research points to the learning-disabled child as one who tends to not believe in his or her own abilities (learned helplessness), have an inadequate grasp of what strategies are available for problem solving (poor metacognitive skills), and be unable to produce appropriate learning strategies spontaneously. *The picture we get is of a child who does not actively involve himself or herself in the learning situation.*

These observations have led Torgesen . . . to refer to the learning-disabled child as an inactive learner. Hallahan has also concluded that a major difficulty many learning-disabled children have, which affects how they go about attempting to learn in a variety of situations, is their inability to use task-approach skills spontaneously (Hallahan & Bryan, 1981; Hallahan & Reeve, 1980). But there is a bright side to the generalization that many learning-disabled children are inactive, passive learners: This inactivity can be overcome. Given appropriate experiences, learning-disabled children can be taught to use appropriate task-approach strategies. (p. 116)

In the next section, we discuss some of the educational methods that have been devised for combating the passive learning style of some learning-disabled children.

EDUCATIONAL METHODS FOR COGNITIVE DISABILITIES

In the 1970s, the field of special education witnessed the "birth" of a new set of educational procedures designed to deal with the recently developed interest in the cognitive disabilities of the learning disabled. This new educational approach was *cognitive-behavior modification* (CBM). Actually, CBM had been used for many years with adults for treating a variety of clinical problems. It was not until a great deal of evidence had accumulated that some learning-disabled children are passive learners with strategy deficits, however, that some within the learning disabilities field began to embrace the CBM approach.

In attempting to define CBM, it helps to contrast it with the more traditional behavior modification. *Whereas in behavior modification one attempts to modify observable behaviors, in CBM one tries to modify unobservable thought processes.* Two additional features of CBM differentiate it from behavior modification, and they have made it attractive to those who hold to the conceptualization of the learning-disabled child as one with a passive learning style and strategy deficits. First, most CBM techniques emphasize providing the individual with strategies for learning. Second, CBM stresses teaching the person self-initiative. The emphasis is on the child's full awareness and independent participation in the instructional

Table 3.1   Teacher Techniques and Student Outcome

Procedures That Appear to Foster Student Dependency and Failure	*Procedures That Appear to Foster Student Motivation and Self-Control*
Norm-referenced evaluation and grading based on peer comparisons.	Criterion-referenced evaluation and grading.
Teacher use of labels such as *distractible, poor memory, impulsive,* to rationalize child's learning problem.	Realistic teacher expectation of child performance considering child's prerequisite skills and level and amount of information to be learned.
Teacher attitude that child's lack of learning is due to deficits within the child.	Child's lack of learning attributed to use of inappropriate instructional strategies.
Low teacher expectation for child performance.	Teaching of self-instructional strategies of inner speech, memory rehearsal, mnemonics, drill, etc., to enable child to direct own learning.
Achievement testing conducted at end of year to evaluate child's learning.	Direct measurement of skills conducted frequently to measure effectiveness of teaching method and child's learning.
Large-group instruction geared to middle-ability group.	Small group instruction based on child's level and needs.
Instructional content presented in large units of knowledge.	Instructional content presented by the task analysis method with information broken down to manageable steps of learning.
Evaluative feedback very general. Lack of information given in feedback on how to improve performance.	Evaluative feedback specific with demonstration of how to complete problem correctly.
Teacher as sole director of learning experiences.	Child as collaborator in choosing learning experiences, setting goals, charting skills that have been mastered.
Teacher always places the child in the "being helped" role, thus emphasizing his dependent position.	Role reversal where the child as a peer tutor helps another child with the same problem.

Source: L. Grimes, "Learned Helplessness and Attribution Theory: Redefining Children's Learning Problems," *Learning Disability Quarterly*, 1981, 4, 91–100.

process. Table 3.1 highlights the differences between teaching approaches, such as CBM, that attempt to foster independence and self-control and those that encourage dependency.

Many different types of educational procedures fall under the label of CBM. There are, of course, debates within the field over whether particular techniques should truly be considered CBM. For the purposes of this chapter, we will discuss three kinds of CBM treatments for cognitive disabilities: *self-instruction, academic strategy training,* and *metacomprehension training.*

Self-Instruction

Self-instruction was the first type of CBM procedure to be used with learning-disabled children. Donald Meichenbaum of the University of Waterloo in Canada pioneered the use of this treatment with the learning disabled. In developing his procedures, Meichenbaum relied a great deal on the earlier work of the well-known Soviet language development researchers Luria and Vygotsky. Vygotsky (1962) and Luria (1961) viewed language as playing a critical role in the child's overall cognitive development. Luria, for example, posited that the normal child goes through three stages in which his or her behavior is controlled by (1) the external speech of adults, (2) the overt speech of the child himself or herself, and (3) the covert speech of the child himself or herself. The last stage, inner language, is what enables the child to perform higher-level cognitive operations.

The following training sequence, based on that developed by Meichenbaum and Goodman (1971), has served as the prototype for many subsequent self-instruction efforts:

1 The adult performs the task while verbalizing aloud:
   a   questions about the task;
   b   self-guiding instructions on how to solve the task;
   c   self-evaluation of performance.

2 The child performs the task while the adult instructs aloud.
3 The child performs the task while verbalizing aloud.
4 The child performs the task while verbalizing in a whisper.
5 The child performs the task while verbalizing covertly.

The following is an example of the kinds of self-instruction that have been used by Meichenbaum. These are a set of instructions for use on a task requiring the copying of line patterns:

Okay, what is it I have to do? You want me to copy the picture with the different lines. I have to go slow and be careful. Okay, draw the line down, down, good; then to the right, that's it; now down some more and to the left. Good, I'm doing fine so far. Remember to go slow. Now back up again. No, I was supposed to go down. That's okay. Just erase the line carefully. . . . Good. Even if I make an error I can go slowly and carefully. Okay, I have to go down now. Finished. I did it. (Meichenbaum & Goodman, 1971, p. 117)

After a decade of research by himself and others, Meichenbaum (1981) set forth 10 guidelines for the development of self-instructional programs:

1 Make a careful analysis of the target behaviors that you want to change.
2 Listen for the strategies that the child is presently using, paying special attention to whether they are inappropriate.
3 Use training tasks that are as close as possible to those target behaviors that you want to change.
4 Collaborate with the child in devising the self-instruction routine rather than imposing the regimen on him or her.
5 Be sure that the child has all the skills that are necessary to use the self-instructions.
6 Give the child feedback about the utility of the self-instructions for performance.
7 Explicitly point out other tasks and settings in which the self-instructions can be used.

David Strickler, Monkmeyer

It is often recommended that the development of self-instruction training regimen be a collaborative effort between child and teacher.

8 Use a variety of trainers, settings, and tasks to increase the chances that the child will learn to use the self-instructions successfully outside the training setting.
9 Anticipate failures and include failure management in the training activities.
10 Train until a reasonable criterion of performance has been reached, then follow up with "booster" sessions in order to provide a better chance that the trained skills will be maintained.

Two Criteria for the Successful Use of Self-Instructions

Research reviews on the use of self-instructions with the learning disabled have revealed two features that appear especially critical for the success of self-instructional training in correcting the academic problems of the learning disabled (Hallahan, Kneedler, & Lloyd, 1983; Hallahan, Lloyd, Kauffman, & Loper, 1983):

1 The training should be done on the academic materials themselves. Training on laboratory-type tasks in the hope that the child will carry over the self-instructions to classroom activities is relatively fruitless.
2 The more specific the set of self-instructions, the greater the chance they will succeed. Some, for example, have taught children to verbalize very broad statements as they approach a problem, such as, "What is my problem? What is it I have to do? What is my plan?" While at first glance such general self-statements are appealing because they seem to apply to multiple situations, research has not borne this out. The evidence is more in favor of teaching children to use specific sets of strategies that apply to specific kinds of problems.

An Example of the Successful Use of Self-Instruction

The following procedures were used successfully to improve the handwriting performance of a learning-disabled boy (Kosiewicz, Hallahan, Lloyd, & Graves, 1982). Note how the self-instructions are focused on the academic material and are very specific in nature. The student was given single words as well as paragraphs to copy. He was trained to use the following strategies:

1   He said the word to be copied.
2   He said the first syllable of the word.
3   He said the name of each letter in the syllable three times.
4   He named each letter in the syllable as he wrote it.
5   He repeated each of the above steps for each syllable of the remaining syllables in the word.

A Final Word on Self-Instruction: How Important Is the Verbalization?

Every self-instruction routine, of course, contains many components. Two of the major ones are *the use of verbalization and the use of one or more strategies.* The feature that has been most identified with self-instruction techniques is self-verbalization. It is thus ironic that the research that has been done on the subject suggests that the actual verbalization (especially the overt verbalization aspect) may not be a necessary component of the training regimen (Hallahan, Kneedler, & Lloyd, 1983). What appears to be more important to the success of self-instruction training is the fact that it can teach children specific strategies for working on academic problems. This focus on academic strategies is also the major focus of the next approach to cognitive disabilities that we will consider—academic strategy training.

Academic Strategy Training

Academic strategy training teaches children to use step-by-step systems for solving academic problems. Actually, the principles behind strategy training have been around for some time. For example, there have long been advocates of training students to use word-attack strategies in learning how to read (Chall, 1967). In such phonics-based approaches, children are taught to (1) scan from left to right, (2) say sounds for letters as they are encountered during the scanning, (3) blend these sounds together as they say them during scanning, and (4) say the product of steps 1–3 at a normal rate of speaking. What gives the more recent academic strategy training approaches a different slant is the far greater emphasis they place on the systematic use of strategies for a wide variety of academic tasks.

Major Aspects of Academic Strategy Training

In order to use academic strategy training, the teacher needs to plan ahead with regard to the following three things: (1) task classes, (2) strategies, and (3) preskills. Table 3.2 presents a plan for strategy training for simple multiplication problems. The first step, the specification of a task class, requires the teacher to determine on what type of academic problem the child will be working. Answering all comprehension questions requiring answers about sequences of events in the reading material, finding entries in reference books, and solving equations for unknowns are all examples of task classes. The second step, specification of the strategy, is a plan of action for achieving an objective or set of objectives. The third step, specification of preskills, is frequently referred to as task analysis. It involves "walking through" the strategy in order to determine what preskills the child will need to be taught in order to use the strategy.

Effectiveness of Academic Strategy Training

In general, research on the use of academic strategy training has demonstrated its effectiveness. One group of researchers (Hallahan et al.,

Table 3.2 Aspects of Instructional Design for Attack Strategy Training

Task Class for Multiplication Facts

Description: Multiplication of any number (0–10) by any number (0–10).
Examples: $0 \times 6 =$ __; $3 \times 9 =$ __; $7 \times 4 =$ __; $8 \times 8 =$ __; $10 \times 1 =$ __
Objective: Given a page of unordered multiplication problems written in horizontal form with factors from 0 to 10, the student will write the correct products for the problems at a rate of 25 problems correct per minute with no more than 2 errors per minute.

Attack Strategy for Multiplication Facts

Attack Strategy: Count by one number the number of times indicated by the other number.

Steps in Attack Strategy:	Examples:
1 Read the problem.	$2 \times 5 =$ __
2 Point to a number that you know how to count by.	student points to 2
3 Make the number of marks indicated by the other number.	$2 \times 5 =$ __
4 Begin counting by the number you know how to count by and count up once for each mark, touching each mark.	///// "2, 4, ..."
5 Stop counting when you've touched the last mark.	"... 6, 8, 10"
6 Write the last number you said in the answer space.	$2 \times 5 = \underline{10}$ /////

Task Analysis Showing Preskills for Multiplication Attack Strategy

1 Say the numbers 0 to 100.
2 Write the numbers 0 to 100.
3 Name $\times$ and $=$ signs.
4 Make the number of marks indicated by numerals 0 to 10.
5 Count by numbers 1 to 10.
6 End counting-by sequences in various positions.
7 Coordinate counting-by and touching-marks actions.

Source: D. Cullinan, J. Lloyd, & M. H. Epstein, "Strategy Training: A Structured Approach to Arithmetic Instruction," *Exceptional Education Quarterly*, 1981, 2(1), 41–49.

1983), for example, reached the following conclusions:

Our major conclusions are relatively straightforward. We have learned that elementary-aged LD students can learn to use strategies for attacking academic tasks. Strategies can be taught for a variety of academic areas. These strategies can be taught in very short periods of time (as quickly as a few minutes when the component skills have been taught previously), and the effects of training are often quite dramatic. Transfer of use of the strategy to other items for which it is applicable will occur when students have been taught the component skills required for applying the strategy to the generalization items. Also, students will continue to apply them correctly without further training. Apparently, teaching strategies that require identical component skills may facilitate learning of later strategies. We have learned that it is possible for students to learn closely related strategies without confusing them, but we are not sure whether this is always the case or to what extent it is affected by pupil age, choice of strategies, or other instructional procedures. And we have learned that it may not be necessary for students to verbalize the steps in strategies.

Considered in conjunction with the research of others using similar procedures (e.g., Carnine, 1980; Kameenui, Carnine, & Maggs, 1980; Smith & Lovitt, 1975), we think that strategy training offers a viable approach to remediation of academic achievement deficits. Further studies must define the limits of strategy training and identify the conditions under which it is of optimal use to teachers.[2]

Metacomprehension Training

Out of the burgeoning interest in the metacognitive problems of the learning disabled has come a flurry of activity in devising instructional programs to increase the metacognitive abilities of these children. For example, much effort has gone into applying metacognitive principles to learning-disabled children's reading problems. While a metacognitive approach may not be as applicable to decoding problems (Baker, 1982), many authorities have noted that the training of certain metacognitive skills may hold great promise for correcting the reading comprehension problems of the learning disabled. Thus most of the activity in this area has focused on metacomprehension training rather than on some other aspect of metacognition, such as metamemory.

At the Elementary Level

One of the most active researchers in this area has been Bernice Wong of Simon Fraser

[2] From D. P. Hallahan, R. J. Hall, S. O. Ianna, R. D. Kneedler, J. W. Lloyd, A. B. Loper, and R. E. Reeve (1983). "Summary of Research Findings at the University of Virginia Learning Disabilities Research Institute," *Exceptional Education Quarterly, 4*(1), pp. 107–108. Reprinted with permission of the publisher, PRO-ED, 5341 Industrial Oaks Blvd, Austin TX 78735.

University in Canada. She has been quite successful in using metacomprehension training to improve the reading comprehension of learning-disabled students. For example, in one study she assessed the value of having learning-disabled children focus their attention on the main ideas of paragraphs they were reading (Wong, 1979). She compared the reading comprehension of two groups of learning-disabled children, one of which received special training and one of which did not. The specially trained group received the following metacognitive treatment. Before each paragraph of a story, the adult read aloud questions pertaining to the main ideas of the paragraph. The same questions were printed in the children's copies of the stories. On a subsequent test that assessed their recall, the children who had received the questions did much better than the group that had not. In particular, they improved their comprehension of the most thematically important ideas in the story.

Wong and Jones's (1982) method of teaching learning-disabled students to use self-questioning strategies while reading is another good example of the successful application of metacomprehension instruction. Learning-disabled students taught to use the following set of metacomprehension strategies while reading greatly improved their reading comprehension:

1 Ask yourself, What am I studying the passage for?
2 Find the main ideas and underline them.
3 Think of a question about each main idea and write it down.
4 Look back at your questions and answers to see how they provide you with more information.

At the Secondary Level

Because the focus of metacomprehension training is on comprehension problems rather than decoding problems, and because learning-disabled students at the secondary level are more likely than their younger counterparts to have comprehension but not decoding difficulties, some authorities have suggested that metacomprehension training may be even more useful at the secondary-school level. The best known educational program for the learning disabled at the secondary level with a metacomprehension focus is Multipass. Multipass was developed by researchers at the University of Kansas. Based on the SQ3R method developed years ago (Robinson, 1946), Multipass involves having the child make many "passes" (hence the name Multipass) through the reading material. The three major passes are the Survey, Size-Up, and Sort-Out. These three passes are embedded in a context of highly individualized programming and a heavy reliance on ensuring that the child achieves certain performance goals before moving on to the next stage. The following passage describes the three passes in Multipass:

> The purpose of the Survey Pass was to familiarize the student with the main ideas and the organization of the chapter. Thus, this previewing pass required the student to: (a) read the chapter title, (b) read the introductory paragraph, (c) review the chapter's relationship to other adjacent chapters by perusing the table of contents, (d) read the major subtitles of the chapter and notice how the chapter is organized, (e) look at illustrations and read their captions, (f) read the summary paragraph, and (g) paraphrase all the information gained in the process.
>
> The Size-Up Pass was designed to help students gain specific information and facts from a chapter without reading it from beginning to end. This pass required the student to first read each of the questions at the end of the chapter to determine what facts appeared to be the most important to learn. If the student was already able to answer a given question as a result of the Survey Pass, a checkmark . . . was placed next to the question. The student now progressed through the entire chapter following these steps: (a) look for a textual cue (e.g., bold-face print, subtitle, colored print, italics); (b) make the cue into a question (e.g., if the cue was the italicized vocabulary word *conqueror*, the student asked, "What

does the conqueror mean?"; if the cue was the subtitle "The Election of 1848," the student might ask, "Who won the election of 1848?" or "Why was the election of 1848 important?"); (c) skim through the surrounding text to find the answer to the question; and (d) paraphrase the answer to yourself without looking in the book. When the student reached the end of the chapter using these four steps for each textual cue, he/she was required to paraphrase all the facts and ideas he/she could remember about the chapter.

> The Sort-Out Pass was included to get students to test themselves over the material presented in the chapter. In this final pass, the student read and answered each question at the end of the chapter. If the student could answer a question immediately, he/she placed a checkmark next to it. If the student was unable to answer the question, however, the answer was sought by (a) thinking in which section of the chapter the answer would most likely be located, (b) skimming through that section for the answer, (c) if the answer was not located, thinking of another relevant section, and (d) skimming that section, and so on until the student could answer the question. A checkmark was then placed next to the question, and the student moved on to answer the next question. (Schumaker, Deshler, Alley, Warner, & Denton, 1982, pp. 298–299)

The Use of Metacognitive Training in Perspective

Although the formal use of metacognitive training has a relatively brief history, it has already enjoyed a great deal of success. Most authorities in this area are quite optimistic about its future. More and more teachers are beginning to use metacognitive principles in their everyday classroom routines, and many experienced teachers have noted how often they were using metacognitive-based ideas in their instruction without realizing it. Even the most ardent proponents of metacognitive training, however, have noted that it is hardly a panacea for all the academic difficulties of learning-disabled children. For example, as Baker (1982) has noted, the metacognitive approach to reading does not lend itself well to decoding problems. It appears that the more a child's academic problem is due to lack of lower-level skills, such as grapheme-phoneme correspondence or basic multiplication facts, the less effective a metacognitive approach will be. For these more basic kinds of problems, many agree that cognitive training, such as self-instruction or academic strategy training, is more appropriate.

SUMMARY

Cognition is the study of thinking. Recently, special educators have begun to be interested in the cognitive processes of exceptional children. Many researchers have examined the cognitive disabilities of learning-disabled children and have developed educational techniques accordingly.

In the 1960s cognitive investigators of the learning disabled examined the child's "cognitive style" of approaching a problem or a task. The cognitive styles that have been studied most intensively are "field independence-field dependence" and "reflectivity-impulsivity." Researchers labeled "field independent" those students who attend to the essential details of a task while ignoring the inessential details. Children who attend equally to essential and inessential details or who attend more to inessential than to essential details are called "field dependent." Studies have demonstrated that learning-disabled children are significantly more "field dependent" than their nonhandicapped peers.

Students are classified within the cognitive style of reflectivity-impulsivity according to whether or not they pause to reflect before making decisions while trying to solve a difficult task. The majority of studies of this cognitive style have employed a version of the Matching Familiar Figures Test (MFF). The results of this research generally indicate that learning-disabled children tend to be more impulsive than their nonhandicapped peers.

Many laboratory researchers have sought to modify field dependence and impulsivity in learning-disabled children. Some investigators, for example, have tried to train learning-disabled children to be more reflective. The results of their studies have indicated that learning-disabled children can learn to respond in a more reflective manner by practicing aloud a review of solutions to a problem. But while this research has improved the reflectivity of children as measured by the MFF, the researchers noted a distinct lack of generalization from the laboratory to the classroom. Trained children were not significantly more reflective in approaching classroom academic tasks.

The study of the memory processes of learning-disabled children began at about the same time as research on cognitive styles. Representative memory studies have revealed that learning-disabled children, when compared with their nonhandicapped peers, exhibit difficulties with short-term memory tasks. These difficulties may be attributed to a failure to use memory strategies which nonhandicapped children use spontaneously. Subsequent memory research, however, indicates that learning-disabled children can be taught these common strategies (such as rehearsal and organization). Thus, though investigated independently, the issues of cognitive style and memory have led researchers to the same conclusion—that many learning-disabled children lack performance strategies which can, however, be taught successfully in the laboratory, although the "carry-over" of this learning to the classroom has been inadequate so far.

As an outgrowth of this search for a basis of learning disability in memory, researchers have studied "metacognition" and, more specifically, "metamemory." Flavell and his colleagues found that good learning performance depends not only on the child's use of cognitive memory strategies (e.g., rehearsal), but also on his or her monitoring of such strategies while engaged in learning tasks. "Metacognitive strategies," then, are just as necessary for good learning as are cognitive strategies. Metalistening and metacomprehension in reading have also been studied in learning-disabled children. Studies of metamemory, metalistening, and metacomprehension have indicated that many learning-disabled children are deficient on metacognitive tasks.

The study of the cognitive disabilities of the learning disabled has led some authorities to characterize these children as "passive" learners who lack strategies for attacking academic problems. Fortunately, recent research has indicated that such passivity can be combatted. There is evidence that educators can teach these children task approach skills by means of cognitive behavior modification (CBM) programs, in which researchers attempt to modify unobservable thought processes while teaching both strategies for learning and personal initiative.

One example of CBM is self-instruction, a procedure in which children learn to verbalize silently the questions, directions, and judgments that affect their performance. Research has indicated that self-instruction training, in order to be most effective, should be implemented with academic materials from the classroom and should be specific to a particular task. Likewise, children have learned systems for solving problems with academic strategy training. Elementary-aged learning-disabled students can be taught strategies for a variety of academic areas in a short period of time. It has also been found that students will continue to apply the strategies correctly without further training. Also, Wong and her colleagues have achieved improvement in learning-disabled children's comprehension skills by teaching them metacomprehension strategies. In addition, secondary-level students have learned systematically to read and examine academic material via the program Multipass.

Metacognitive training has been successful in surmounting the academic problems of some learning-disabled children. The results of research suggest that metacognitive training is most appropriate for students who have acquired the basic academic skills whereas academic strategy training or self-instruction may be more appropriate for students who lack basic academic skills.

REFERENCES

ANDERSON, T. H. (1980). Study strategies and adjunct aids. In P. J. Spiro, B. C. Bruce, & W. F. Brewer (Eds.), *Theoretical issues in reading comprehension* (pp. 483–502). Hillsdale, NJ: Erlbaum.

BAKER, L. (1982). An evaluation of the role of metacognitive deficits in learning disabilities. *Topics in Learning and Learning Disabilities, 2*(1), 27–35.

BAKER, L., & ANDERSON, R. I. (1982). Effects of inconsistent information on text processing: Evidence for comprehension monitoring. *Reading Research Quarterly, 17,* 281–294.

BAKER, L., & BROWN, A. L. (1980). *Metacognitive skills and reading* (Tech. Rep. No. 188). Champaign, IL: University of Illinois, Center for the Study of Reading.

BAKER, L., & BROWN, A. L. (1984). Cognitive monitoring in reading. In J. Flood (Ed.), *Understanding reading comprehension*. Newark, DE: International Reading Association.

BAUER, R. H. (1977). Memory processes in children with learning disabilities: Evidence for deficient rehearsal. *Journal of Experimental Child Psychology, 24,* 415–430.

BLACKMAN, S., & GOLDSTEIN, K. M. (1982). Cognitive styles and learning disabilities. *Journal of Learning Disabilities, 15,* 106–115.

BOS, C. S., & FILIP, D. (1982). Comprehension monitoring skills in learning disabled and average students. *Topics in Learning and Learning Disabilities, 2*(1), 79–85.

BROWN, A. L. (1980). Metacognitive development and reading. In R. J. Spiro, B. C. Bruce, & W. F. Brewer (Eds.), *Theoretical issues in reading comprehension* (pp. 453–481). Hillsdale, NJ: Erlbaum.

CARNINE, D. W. (1980). Preteaching versus concurrent teaching of the component skills of a multiplication problem-solving strategy. *Journal of Research in Mathematics Education, 11,* 375–379.

CHALL, J. (1967). *Learning to read: The great debate.* New York: McGraw-Hill.

CULLINAN, D., LLOYD, J. W., & EPSTEIN, M. H. (1981). Strategy training: A structured approach to arithmetic instruction. *Exceptional Education Quarterly, 2*(1), 41–49.

DIGATE, G., EPSTEIN, M. H., CULLINAN, D., & SWITZKY, N. H. (1978). Modification of impulsivity: Implications for improved efficiency in learning for exceptional children. *Journal of Special Education, 12,* 459–468.

EPSTEIN, M. H., HALLAHAN, D. P., & KAUFFMAN, J. M. (1975). Implications of the reflectivity-impulsivity dimension for special education. *Journal of Special Education, 9,* 11–25.

FLAVELL, J. H. (1970). Developmental studies of mediated memory. In H. W. Reese & L. P. Lipsitt (Eds.), *Advances in child development and behavior,* Vol. 5 (pp. 182–211). New York: Academic Press.

FLAVELL, J. H. (1971). What is memory development the development of? *Human Development, 14,* 272–278.

FLAVELL, J. H. (1979). Metacognition and cognitive monitoring: A new area of cognitive-developmental inquiry. *American Psychologist, 34,* 906–911.

FLAVELL, J. H., & WELLMAN, H. M. (1977). Metamemory. In R. V. Kail & J. W. Hagen (Eds.), *Perspectives on the development of memory and cognition* (pp. 3–33). Hillsdale, NJ: Erlbaum.

FORREST, D. L., & WALLER, T. G. (April, 1981). *Reading ability and knowledge of important information.* Paper presented at the meeting of the Society for Research in Child Development, Boston, MA.

GIBSON, E. J. (1969). *Principles of perceptual learning and development.* New York: Appleton-Century-Crofts.

GRIMES, L. (1981). Learned helplessness and attribution theory: Redefining children's learning problems. *Learning Disability Quarterly, 4,* 91–100.

HAGEN, J. W., & KAIL, R. V. (1975). The role of attention in perceptual and cognitive development. In W. M. Cruickshank & D. P. Hallahan (Eds.), *Perceptual and learning disabilities in children.* Vol. 2: *Research and theory* (pp. 165–192). Syracuse, NY: Syracuse University Press.

HALLAHAN, D. P., & BRYAN, T. H. (1981). Learning disabilities. In J. M. Kauffman & D. P. Hallahan (Eds.), *Handbook of special education* (pp. 141–164). Englewood Cliffs, NJ: Prentice-Hall.

HALLAHAN, D. P., HALL, R. J., IANNA, S. O., KNEEDLER, R. D., LLOYD, J. W., LOPER, A. B., & REEVE, R. E. (1983). Summary of research findings at the University of Virginia Learning Disabilities Research Institute. *Exceptional Education Quarterly, 4*(1), 94–113.

HALLAHAN, D. P., & KAUFFMAN, J. M. (1982). *Exceptional children.* Englewood Cliffs, NJ: Prentice-Hall.

HALLAHAN, D. P., KAUFFMAN, J. M., & BALL, D. W. (1973). Selective attention and cognitive tempo of low achieving and high achieving sixth grade males. *Perceptual and Motor Skills, 36,* 579–583.

HALLAHAN, D. P., KNEEDLER, R. D., & LLOYD, J. W. (1983). Cognitive behavior modification techniques for learning disabled children: Self-instruction and self-monitoring. In J. D. McKinney & L. Feagans (Eds.), *Current topics in learning disabilities,* Vol. 1. New York: Ablex Publishing.

HALLAHAN, D. P., LLOYD, J. W., KAUFFMAN, J. M., & LOPER, A. B. (1983). Academic problems. In R. J. Morris & T. R. Kratochwill (Eds.), *Practice of child therapy: A textbook of methods* (pp. 113–141). New York: Pergammon Press.

HALLAHAN, D. P., & REEVE, R. E. (1980). Selective attention and distractibility. In B. K. Keogh (Ed.), *Advances in special education,* Vol. 1 (pp. 141–181). Greenwich, CT: J.A.I. Press.

KAGAN, J., ROSMAN, B. L., DAY, D., ALBERT, J., & PHILLIPS, W. (1964). Information processing in the child: Significance of analytic and reflective attitudes. *Psychological Monographs, 78* (1, Whole No. 578).

KAMEENUI, E., CARNINE, D. W., & MAGGS, A. (1980). Instructional procedures for teaching reversible passive voice and clause constructions to three mildly handicapped students. *The Exceptional Child, 27*(1), 29–40.

KNEEDLER, R. D., with HALLAHAN, D. P., & KAUFFMAN, J. M. (1984). *Special education for today.* Englewood Cliffs, NJ: Prentice-Hall.

KOSIEWICZ, M. M., HALLAHAN, D. P., LLOYD, J. W., & GRAVES, A. W. (1982). Effects of self-instruction and self-correction procedures on handwriting performance. *Learning Disability Quarterly, 5,* 71–78.

KOTSONIS, M. E., & PATTERSON, C. J. (1980). Comprehension-monitoring skills in learning disabled children. *Developmental Psychology, 16,* 541–542.

KREUTZER, M. A., LEONARD, C., & FLAVELL, J. H. (1975). An interview study of children's knowledge about memory. *Monographs of the Society for Research in Child Development, 40* (1, Serial No. 159).

LURIA, A. (1961). *The role of speech in the regulation of normal and abnormal behaviors.* New York: Liveright.

MAHONEY, M. J. (1974). *Cognition and behavior modification.* Cambridge, MA: Ballinger.

MEICHENBAUM, D. (April, 1981). *Teaching thinking: A cognitive behavioral approach.* Paper presented at the meeting of the Society for Learning Disabilities and Remedial Education, New York.

MEICHENBAUM, D., & GOODMAN, J. (1971). Training impulsive children to talk to themselves: A means of developing self-control. *Journal of Abnormal Psychology, 77,* 115–126.

OWINGS, R. A., PETERSON, G. A., BRANSFORD, J. D., MORRIS, C. D., & STEIN, B. S. (1980). Spontaneous monitoring and regulation of learning: A comparison of successful and less successful fifth graders. *Journal of Educational Psychology, 72,* 250–256.

PARIS, S. G., & MYERS, M. (1981). Comprehension monitoring, memory, and study strategies of good and poor readers. *Journal of Reading Behavior, 13,* 5–22.

PEARL, R., BRYAN, T., & DONAHUE, M. (1980). Learning disabled children's attributions for success and failure. *Learning Disability Quarterly, 3*(1), 3–9.

ROBINSON, F. P. (1946). *Effective study.* New York: Harper & Brothers.

SALKIND, N. J., & WRIGHT, J. C. (1977). The development of reflection-impulsivity and cognitive efficiency: An integrated model. *Human Development, 20,* 377–387.

SCHUMAKER, J. B., DESHLER, D. D., ALLEY, G. R.,

WARNER, M. M., & DENTON, P. H. (1982). Multipass: A learning strategy for improving reading comprehension. *Learning Disability Quarterly, 5,* 295–304.

SELIGMAN, M. E. P. (1975). *Helplessness: On depression, development and death.* San Francisco: Freeman.

SMITH, D. D., & LOVITT, T. C. (1975). The use of modeling techniques to influence the acquisition of computational arithmetic skills in learning disabled children. In E. Ramp & G. Semb (Eds.), *Behavior analysis: Areas of research and application* (pp. 283–308). Englewood Cliffs, NJ: Prentice-Hall.

SWANSON, H. L. (1977). Response strategies and stimulus salience with learning disabled and mentally retarded children on a short-term memory task. *Journal of Learning Disabilities, 10,* 635–642.

SWANSON, H. L. (1979). Developmental recall lag in learning disabled children: Perceptual deficit or verbal mediation deficiency? *Journal of Abnormal Child Psychology, 7,* 199–210.

TARVER, S. C., HALLAHAN, D. P., KAUFFMAN, J. M., & BALL, D. W. (1976). Verbal rehearsal and selective attention in children with learning disabilities: A developmental lag. *Journal of Experimental Child Psychology, 22,* 375–385.

TORGESEN, J. K. (1977). The role of nonspecific factors in the task performance of learning disabled children: A theoretical assessment. *Journal of Learning Disabilities, 10,* 27–34.

TORGESEN, J. K. (1979). Factors related to poor performance in reading disabled children. *Learning Disability Quarterly, 2*(3), 17–23.

TORGESEN, J. K., & GOLDMAN, T. (1977). Verbal rehearsal and short-term memory in reading disabled children. *Child Development, 48,* 56–60.

VELLUTINO, F. R., STEGER, J. A., DESETTO, L., & PHILLIPS, F. (1975). Immediate and delayed recognition of visual stimuli in poor and normal readers. *Journal of Experimental Child Psychology, 19,* 223–232.

VYGOTSKY, L. (1962). *Thought and language.* New York: Wiley.

WITKIN, H. A., DYK, R. B., FATERSON, H. F., GOODENOUGH, D. R., & KARP, S. A. (1962). *Psychological differentiation.* New York: Wiley.

WITKIN, H. A., GOODENOUGH, D. R., & KARP, S. A. (1967). Stability of cognitive style from childhood to young adulthood. *Journal of Personality and Social Psychology, 7,* 291–300.

WONG, B. Y. L. (1979). Increasing retention of main

ideas through questioning strategies. *Learning Disability Quarterly, 2*(2), 42–47.

WONG, B. Y. L. (1982). Understanding the learning disabled student's reading problems: Contributions from cognitive psychology. *Topics in Learning and Learning Disabilities, 1*(4), 43–50.

WONG, B. Y. L., & JONES, W. (1982). Increasing metacomprehension in learning disabled and normally achieving students through self-questioning training. *Learning Disability Quarterly, 5,* 228–240.

Attention Disabilities and Hyperactivity

Learning-disabled children are frequently described by their teachers and parents as inattentive and hyperactive. It is not unusual for the parents to relate numerous incidents from the child's early years that depict him or her as an exceedingly rambunctious pest, always into places where a child should not be. This very same child, when confronted with the demands of the school situation, can quickly become a nightmare for even the best of teachers. It often only takes one of these children in a classroom to create chaos.

THE EARLY WORK: STRAUSS SYNDROME

Much of the early interest in attention problems and hyperactivity in the learning disabled was triggered by work in the 1930s and 1940s with the mentally retarded. Through a series of studies (Strauss & Werner, 1942; Werner & Strauss, 1939, 1940, 1941) with purportedly brain-injured, mentally retarded children, Heinz Werner and Alfred Strauss identified what later came to be known as the "Strauss Syndrome." They believed that children who are mentally retarded as a result of brain injury display a particular set, or syndrome, of behavioral characteristics—distractibility, hyperactivity, and perceptual-motor problems.

Much of Werner and Strauss's theorizing was based on clinical impressions rather than controlled research. They did, however, conduct a series of laboratory investigations concerning the behavioral characteristics of distractibility. They studied the ability of retarded children to discriminate figure from background. They looked at figure-background ability in a number of modalities, but their most intensive investigations were in the visual realm. They presented slides of familiar objects (e.g., sailboat, hat, iron, cup) embedded in backgrounds (e.g., wavy lines) to each child at very fast exposure times, such as half a second. After each slide had been exposed, the experimenter asked the child, "What did you see?" Werner and Strauss found that some of the children were more likely to respond to the background by saying, for example, that they saw the wavy lines than were another group, who were more likely to respond to the figure by saying, for example, that they saw the sailboat. The group responding to the background consisted of children whom Werner and Strauss had diagnosed as brain injured, whereas the group correctly responding to the figure were considered non-brain-injured. Werner and Strauss hypothesized that brain injury in the mentally retarded leads to distractibility—an inability to focus on the task at hand. They believed that this distractibility or, as they considered it, forced responsiveness to stimuli was closely related to the motor restlessness or hyperactivity that they were observing in mentally retarded children diagnosed as brain damaged.

CRITICISMS OF WERNER AND STRAUSS

This work of Werner and Strauss did not go uncriticized. Specifically, the procedures used to form their brain-injured and non-brain-injured groups were attacked as being inappropriate (Sarason, 1949). One way in which an individual could be classified as brain injured was on the basis of behavior alone. Even if no direct evidence of a lesion was obtained through neurological tests and there was no indication of brain damage in the medical history of the individual (e.g., abnormal birth), a child was classified as brain injured if he or she displayed behavior clinically observed to occur in brain-damaged individuals. Although Werner and Strauss could be faulted on the grounds of having formed their brain-damaged group on other than stringent neurological evidence, the case against them would not have been so damaging had they used, for classification pur-

poses, behaviors other than those on which they eventually were to compare the brain-injured and non-brain-injured subjects (e.g., forced responsiveness to stimuli). Circular logic is evident in their comparing in experimental tests the two groups—brain injured and non–brain injured—on behaviors used to place the children differentially into one or the other group in the first place.

While the numerous criticisms from others certainly weaken the inference drawn by Werner and Strauss that brain damage is a *cause* of distractibility and hyperactivity, these faults do not negate the fact that these two researchers did find evidence of a sizable subgroup of retarded children who did exhibit a forced responsiveness to stimuli. It is important to point out here that up until this time mental retardation was perceived as a relatively homogeneous state. All retarded were considered to be alike, and consequently no differential or individual educational or psychological programming was initiated on their behalf. By dispelling the long-standing notion that there were no individual differences among the retarded, the work of Werner and Strauss had revolutionary impact.

STRAUSS SYNDROME APPLIED TO CHILDREN OF NORMAL INTELLIGENCE

Werner and Strauss both worked at the Wayne County Training School in Michigan. It so happened that a number of other individuals who would eventually figure in the development of the field of learning disabilities were also on staff there. One such individual important for our discussion of attention and hyperactivity was William Cruickshank. In 1957, he published the results of a major study in which he replicated the work of Werner and Strauss with cerebral-palsied children of near-normal, normal, and above-normal intelligence (Cruickshank, Bice, & Wallen, 1957). Cruickshank found that cerebral-palsied children of normal intelligence exhibited poor figure-ground relationships, presumably owing to their distractibility. This study served as a conceptual bridge between lowered and normal intelligence. In other words, it showed that an individual did not need to be retarded in order to display the behavioral characteristics of inattention and hyperactivity.

Bolstered by the results of his study of the cerebral palsied, Cruickshank extended his work to children who would by today's standards be considered learning disabled. He pointed out that many children of normal intelligence who did not have any obvious signs of brain damage, such as cerebral palsy, also exhibited attention difficulties and hyperactivity. In the late 1950s, he established an educational program for these children (we will describe it in detail later in the chapter).

The term *Strauss Syndrome* is out of fashion today because of its origin in the notion that attention problems and hyperactivity are caused by brain damage. As you will read later in the chapter, special educators are now inclined to think there is a multiplicity of possible causes of inattention and hyperactivity. Although one does not hear or see much reference to the Strauss Syndrome today, professionals in the learning disabilities field are still very much concerned with how to deal with inattention and hyperactivity. The terminology may have changed, but the problems of inattention and hyperactivity remain.

THE RELATIONSHIP BETWEEN INATTENTION AND HYPERACTIVITY

The relationship between hyperactivity and inattention is a strong one. It is rare for a teacher or parent to refer to a child as having one of these problems without also having the other.

In fact, it is interesting to note, that what people mean by a "hyperactive child" is usually a child who exhibits attentional problems as much or more than excessive motor activity (see Box 4.1). Most authorities believe that the major problems of children labeled hyperactive lie more in the domain of attention than in that of overactivity.

DSM-III: ATTENTION DEFICIT DISORDER

Indicative of the prevailing view that attention difficulties are more basic than hyperactivity problems is the way the issue is dealt with in the third edition of the American Psychiatric Association's *Diagnostic and Statistical Manual of Mental Disorders* (DSM-III) (1980). In 1968, the second edition of the DSM included a category of "Hyperkinetic Reaction of Childhood." In 1980, however, DSM-III renamed the disorder "Attention Deficit Disorder with Hyperactivity" and "Attention Deficit Disorder without Hyperactivity." Table 4.1 on p. 113 outlines the diagnostic criteria that are listed in DSM-III for attention deficit disorder with hyperactivity. The criteria for attention deficit disorder without hyperactivity are exactly the same except for the absence of hyperactivity.

Evaluation of DSM-III Criteria

Most professionals who work closely with hyperactive children agree that the definition of attention deficit disorder with hyperactivity is a vast improvement over the previous conceptualization of the problem as primarily one of overactivity. Whalen (1983) notes, however, it is still too early to tell how well accepted the definition will be by professionals. At this point, the major objection to the DSM-III treatment of the problem is that it does not go far enough in specifying how to operationalize

Box 4.1
HYPERACTIVE CHILDREN ARE NOT JUST CHILDREN WHO MOVE A LOT

"Hyperactive children are not just children who move a lot. High activity level is in itself no disease. There are other reasons for moving about than hyperactivity; for instance, nervousness. And, paradoxical though it may sound, many hyperactive children and most hyperactive adults do not move more than is customary. The label "hyperactivity" is deceptive. It was applied early in history of knowledge about the disorder before it was realized that motor restlessness is a secondary, inconstant, and transient characteristic of these children's behavior. In the listing of characteristic symptoms that follows, we will consider it first but not give it primary importance. In fact, we prefer to call these children 'underfocusers.' This indicates that they fail to maintain concentration and are apt to make premature decisions that are often wrong or ill-advised and get them into trouble. This is their basic problem and it is with regards to this that they need help.

The children are restless. They continually and unpredictably shift position and change what they are doing. Overall, they may be very active or not very active; more importantly, they move when others think it wise to be still.

We must differentiate this restlessness from the repetitive movement patterns of people who are anxious and drum their fingers, smooth their hair, straighten their tie, or twitch.

They are inattentive. They flit from one thing to another. They are not just distractible, they welcome distractions.

This inattentiveness must be distinguished from that of the child who is merely bored, or preoccupied with other matters.

They are hasty. They lack impulse control and crave immediate gratification. They come to conclusions and expect consequences without having done the necessary physical or mental work.

Again, we must distinguish this from the behavior of children who are merely uninterested or otherwise preoccupied.

They resist limit setting. The child opposes discipline with whining manipulations or temper tantrums of spiraling intensity. Both threats and bribes are ineffective and punishment does not deter.

We must distinguish this behavior from that of the ill-bred or spoiled child, and that of the individual who is angry or even psychotic.

They are emotionally unstable. Lacking self-control, they express each change in mood and bewilder with mood changes.

This must be distinguished from the child who has a so-called 'affective disorder,' such as primary mania or depression.

They are inconsequential. They seem to have trouble in connecting cause with effect. Disapproval of their anti-social behavior perpetually catches them by surprise.

We must distinguish this from the actions of children who really do not understand, either because they are ill-raised or retarded.

They are accident-prone. Their carelessness and uninhibited curiosity bring them physical injury as well as social mishaps.

We must distinguish this from the adversities that befall those who are inexperienced, untaught, or so preoccupied that they are oblivious to hazards.

They are socially inept. They are friendly but so insensitive and lacking in empathy that their friends soon drift away.

This is quite different from the situation of 'loners,' who prefer their own company.

They are emotionally superficial. Their style is bland, defensive and denying. They keep relationships at a shallow level.

Distinguish this from anxiety, self-centered obliviousness, or the inappropriate interactions of people who are psychotic and have disordered thoughts.

No single one of these attributes is in itself diagnostic of hyperactivity. On the other hand, no child is likely to show all of them. Among the younger, pre-school children, restless, accident-prone and recalcitrant behavior would be most noticeable. Among grade-schoolers, those children would be conspicuous who are inattentive, hasty and disruptive. In high school, social ineptitude takes its toll, and the inconsequentiality may lead to antisocial and delinquent behavior. The motor restlessness now has gone. Among adults, failure to consolidate relationships and hold down jobs may be the most apparent characteristics."

Source: M. Kinsbourne & J. M. Swanson, "Hyperactivity," *Learning Disabilities: Information Please,* 1978, Quebec Association for Children with Learning Disabilities (pp 1–2).

the criteria set forth. Barkley (1982), for example, would like to see the adoption of specific cutoff points on well-standardized rating scales of hyperactivity.

Barkley also believes there is one characteristic of most hyperactive children that is overlooked by the DSM-III criteria—a deficit in rule-governed behavior (compliance, self-control, and problem solving). Barkley cites the classic distinction made by Skinner (1954) between contingency-shaped and rule-governed behavior:

A contingency-shaped behavior is developed and maintained by the naturally occurring consequences for that behavior. For instance, the response of avoiding a hot stove may develop because of the child's previous experience of being burned by one; such avoidance is contingency

shaped. In contrast, rule-governed behavior occurs when the person's behavior is elicited by a command, rule, or other linguistic stimulus. The community, usually the parents, often arranges consequences for compliance or noncompliance with the rule; these may be far different from those natural consequences that would occur in the absence of the rule. Many children learn to avoid hot stoves not because they have previously been burned by them, but because parents have provided rules (commands) to the child to avoid hot objects and have consequated the child's behavior to this or other commands depending on whether compliance or noncompliance occurred. (Barkley, 1982, p. 158)

In Barkley's example, then, the hyperactive child is one who would be more apt to learn not to touch the hot stove only after he or she went ahead and touched it. The nonhyperac-

Table 4.1   Diagnostic Criteria for Attention Deficit Disorder with Hyperactivity

The child displays, for his or her mental and chronological age, signs of developmentally inappropriate inattention, impulsivity, and hyperactivity. The signs must be reported by adults in the child's environment, such as parents and teachers. Because the symptoms are typically variable, they may not be observed directly by the clinician. When the reports of teachers and parents conflict, primary consideration should be given to the teacher reports because of greater familiarity with age-appropriate norms. Symptoms typically worsen in situations that require self-application, as in the classroom. Signs of the disorder may be absent when the child is in a new or a one-to-one situation.

The number of symptoms specified is for children between the ages of 8 and 10, the peak age range for referral. In younger children, more severe forms of the symptoms and a greater number of symptoms are usually present. The opposite is true of older children.

A Inattention. At least three of the following:

1   often fails to finish things he or she starts;
2   often doesn't seem to listen;
3   easily distracted;
4   has difficulty concentrating on schoolwork or other tasks requiring sustained attention;
5   has difficulty sticking to a play activity.

B Impulsivity. At least three of the following:

1   often acts before thinking;
2   shifts excessively from one activity to another;
3   has difficulty organizing work (not because of cognitive impairment);
4   needs a lot of supervision;
5   frequently calls out in class;
6   has difficulty awaiting turn in games or group situations.

C Hyperactivity. At least two of the following:

1   runs about or climbs on things excessively;
2   has difficulty sitting still or fidgets excessively;
3   has difficulty staying seated;
4   moves about excessively during sleep;
5   is always "on the go" or acts as if "driven by a motor."

D Onset before the age of 7.

E Duration of at least 6 months.

F Not due to schizophrenia, affective disorder, or severe or profound mental retardation.

Source: American Psychiatric Association, *Diagnostic and Statistical Manual of Mental Disorders* (DSM-III), Washington, D.C.: American Psychiatric Association, 1980 (p. 43).

tive child, on the other hand, could be inhibited from touching the stove by a mother's warnings not to go near it.

INATTENTION VERSUS HYPERACTIVITY: SOME GENERAL CONCLUSIONS

Given the present state of knowledge it is best to assume that essentially what most individuals mean when they say a child is hyperactive is that the child has attentional problems (Barkley, 1982; Douglas, 1972; Whalen, 1983). In other words, the attentional problems the child has usually surpass the problems created by any

excess degree of movement. The following two guidelines also apply:

1   Virtually all hyperactive children also have attentional problems. (These children would fit the attention deficit disorder with hyperactivity category of DSM-III.)

2   A very few children have attentional problems without also being considered hyperactive. (These children would fit the attention deficit disorder without hyperactivity category of DSM-III.) In fact, some (e.g., Barkley, 1982) have recommended doing away with the categoric distinction between hyperactivity and nonhyperactivity and just retaining one category: attention deficit disorder with hyperactivity.

Sybil Shelton/Paul Arnold

Most authorities agree that a child who has excess motor activity or hyperactivity will very likely also have additional problems.

DEFINING ATTENTION PROBLEMS IN THE LEARNING DISABLED

During the first half of this century, child development specialists did not pursue attention as a topic for study. This was because behaviorism was so popular during this period and behaviorists are, by definition, interested only in observable behaviors. Attention, being something that is not easily definable in terms of observable behavior, was thus viewed by behaviorists as not worthy of study. In the 1950s, however, interest in attention surged. One of the reasons for this was that research psychologists were curious to solve some of the practical problems that had arisen during combat in World War II (Krupski, 1981). For example, military personnel wanted to know how best to train radar specialists to use their attention to detect enemy aircraft. Once attention in adults became a legitimate area for study, the door was open for child psychologists to look at the development of attention in children. And as child development specialists began to investigate attention, they developed a variety of research strategies that professionals in the learning disabilities field adopted.

Research on the attentional problems of the learning disabled can be divided into laboratory-based investigations and those that have taken place in the classroom. It is evident from the variety of ways that attention has been studied, particularly in the laboratory, that there is no one way of defining attention.

Laboratory Studies of Attention

Keogh and Margolis (1976) believe attention is not a unitary function but is multifaceted in nature. They conceptualize the attention difficulties of learning-disabled children as falling into three different categories: *com-*

ing to attention, decision making, and maintaining attention.

Coming to Attention Keogh and Margolis (1976) note that many learning-disabled children have difficulty "getting . . . into the task, of focusing . . . attention to ensure clear understanding of the task and its requirements" (p. 279). Closely related to the notion of coming to attention is the concept of selective attention. Selective attention is the ability to focus on the relevant features of a task without being distracted by its irrelevant aspects. A number of researchers, using a variety of experimental tasks, have concluded that learning-disabled children have selective attention problems with both auditory and visual material (see Hallahan & Reeve, 1980, for a review of these studies, and Pelham, 1981, for a critical appraisal of the selective-attention literature).

In addition to the research evidence showing that learning-disabled children often have difficulty picking out the important cues of various learning tasks, teachers have also noted the trouble such children have in focusing. These are the children who have not completed the assigned seatwork but are able to tell the teacher how many stray pencil marks there are on the page. When faced with a new task, such children have difficulty determining what are the relevant cues to which they should be attending. Both Keogh and Margolis (1976) and Hallahan (1975) have noted that some of this seemingly inattentive behavior may in fact be learning-disabled children's way of seeking to gain information. Instead of concentrating on the task before them, they may be looking for cues on how to perform the task from extraneous sources in their environment. In other words, some learning-disabled children may have difficulty in choosing between appropriate and inappropriate sources of information to help in solving problems.

Decision Making In the last chapter, we discussed impulsivity versus reflectivity. A wealth of research indicates that learning-disabled children are more impulsive decision makers. When faced with problem-solving situations, they tend to choose one of the first alternatives that comes into their heads rather than weighing many alternatives before deciding.

Maintaining Attention Learning-disabled children also have difficulty in sticking to a task once they begin it. The ability to maintain attention has been studied in the laboratory through the use of vigilance tasks. A typical vigilance task is the Continuous Performance Test (CPT) (Rosvold, Mirsky, Sarason, Bransome, & Beck, 1956). On the CPT, the child sits before an apparatus containing a revolving drum. As the child sits there, letters continually come into view on the drum at the approximate rate of one letter every second. The child is instructed to press a response key every time a particular letter—an X, for example—appears on the drum. In a 5-minute period, the child is exposed to about 300 letters, with the correct X appearing 80 times. On a more difficult version of the task, the child is told to press the response key only when he or she sees an X that has been immediately preceded by an A. On the more difficult A-X version, there are 60 possible correct responses in a 5-minute period.

In general, investigators have found that learning-disabled children perform more poorly than their nonhandicapped peers on vigilance tasks (Pelham, 1981). They make fewer correct detections of the target stimulus and press the key more often when they should not (more false alarms). Furthermore, their performance deteriorates more quickly over time. As Pelham (1981) notes, there is a considerable difference of opinion on just how these differences should be interpreted. Some, for example, believe such differences indicate physiologically based arousal problems in the learning disabled.

Others argue that they are due to the learning-disabled children's long history of failure—that these children lack the motivation to engage themselves in such boring tasks as the CPT (Douglas & Peters, 1979). If the latter is the case, then the learning-disabled child's poor vigilance performance would be considered a consequence rather than a cause of learning problems. There is also the possibility that both positions are correct—i.e., learning-disabled children have problems maintaining attention that lead to learning problems that lead to further attentional problems.

Classroom Studies of Attention

Virtually all teachers who have had learning-disabled children in their classrooms will attest to the fact that they have attentional problems. It is thus not surprising that investigators who have studied the attentional behavior of learning-disabled children in classroom settings have concluded that these children are more inattentive than their nonhandicapped peers (Hallahan, 1975).

Researchers in this area typically observe children while they are engaged in classroom work. They record such things as the frequency with which the children engage in non-task-oriented behaviors like looking at or talking to other children or getting out of their seat. Bryan (1974), for instance, found a group of third-grade learning-disabled children to be task oriented 68% of the time in comparison to their nonhandicapped peers, who were on-task 88% of the time.

An Interactional Approach to Defining Attention Problems

Krupski (1981) posits that attention difficulties need to be considered in the context of interaction among three variables—*child, task demands, and setting demands.* It is her position that a particular child's attention will vary according to the kind of task on which he or she is working and within what type of situation the work is occurring.

Child   The child variable refers to whether or not the child has been identified as handicapped. Krupski notes that exceptional children, in general, are often candidates for attentional problems. The learning disabled and mentally retarded are especially vulnerable to such problems. According to Krupski, however, these children are not inattentive in all situations. Whether or not they will have attentional difficulties depends on the other two variables of task and setting demands.

Task Demands   Krupski breaks down tasks with regard to whether they require voluntary or involuntary attention. Tasks requiring an active effort to pay attention on the part of the child fall into the category of voluntary attention. A vigilance task, such as the CPT, is a perfect example of an activity requiring voluntary attention. In addition, most academic tasks children are faced with in school fall into the category of voluntary attention. Colorful and exciting television programs, on the other hand, fit into the category of involuntary attention. Such activities do not require much active effort on the part of the child to attend. Instead, the child's attention is captured by the salience of the task itself. In many free-play situations in school, the child needs only involuntary attention.

The more the task requires voluntary rather than involuntary attention, the more the learning-disabled child is at a disadvantage. Krupski (1981) has reported the results of a study that highlights the importance of the voluntary-involuntary attention distinction. She observed learning-disabled and nonhandicapped children engaging in a variety of tasks in their classroom. Before she began the observations, she categorized the various classroom activities according to how much they required voluntary attention. Type 1 tasks required a high degree of voluntary attention (e.g., reading and mathe-

Everett C. Johnson, Leo de Wys, Inc.

Some activities do not require much active effort on the part of the child to pay attention. Such activities, referred to as requiring involuntary attention, are less of a problem for learning disabled children than are tasks requiring voluntary attention.

matics); Type 2 tasks needed an intermediate degree of voluntary attention (e.g., copying letters and penmanship); Type 3 tasks needed the lowest amount of voluntary attention (e.g., artwork). Whereas the nonhandicapped students were on-task about 80% of the time regardless of the task, the learning-disabled group's attention was influenced substantially by the degree of voluntary attention needed to perform the activity. For Type 1 tasks, they were on-task 69% of the time; for Type 2 tasks, they were on-task 78% of the time; and for Type 3 tasks, they were on-task 92% of the time.

Setting Demands Not only can the task impose certain demands on the child, but so can the environmental setting. In certain situations, a greater degree of attention is expected than in other settings. In particular, the amount of structure imposed on the child has a great deal of influence on how he or she will attend. The work of Routh with hyperactive children indicates that in free-play situations the attentional behavior of hyperactive and nonhandicapped children is quite similar. Under structured conditions, however, where the children are expected by adults to display on-task behavior, the hyperactive children are much less attentive than their nonhandicapped peers (Routh & Schroeder, 1976; Routh, Schroeder, & O'Tuama, 1974).

PREVALENCE

In considering the prevalence of attention problems and hyperactivity, a number of interrelated questions can be asked:

1   How prevalent is the attention deficit disorder with hyperactivity in the general school-age population?
2   How prevalent is the attention deficit disorder with hyperactivity in the learning-disabled school-age population?
3   How prevalent is the attention deficit disorder with hyperactivity in the general adult-age population?
4   How prevalent is the attention deficit disorder without hyperactivity?

Most authorities agree that approximately 3% to 5% of the general school-age population exhibit an attention deficit disorder with hyperactivity, making it one of the most common reasons for referral to child guidance clinics (Barkley, 1982). They also agree that there is considerable overlap between this group of children and the learning disabled. Safer and Allen (1976), for example, estimate that 39% of learning-disabled children are also hyperactive.

Considerable controversy surrounds the question of whether hyperactive children outgrow their problem behavior. At one time, many authorities believed that hyperactivity diminished over time, that by adolescence, and certainly by adulthood, it vanished. Today, however, the evidence is not so clear-cut. There is still not a great deal of data on this topic, but what data there are indicate that many hyperactive children continue to have problems associated with their hyperactive behavior well into adolescence and adulthood (e.g., Ackerman, Dykman, & Peters, 1977; Hechtman, Weiss, Perlman, Hopkins, Wener, 1981). However, as Henker and Whalen (1980) indicate:

> The problems do tend to change in form or at least in mode of expression. Problems may also decrease in intensity as these individuals leave highly structured academic environments and enter more flexible school or work settings, which offer greater options for achieving a match between personal styles and situational demands.

> In general, however, social and attentional problems often persist. (p. 322)

At the present time, there are no available data on how many children fall into the classification of attention deficit disorder without hyperactivity. It is apparent, however, that very few children are being classified in this way by professionals compared with the sister classification of attention deficit disorder with hyperactivity. There are two possible reasons for this. It could be that (1) indeed, there are few children who fall into this classification; or (2) these types of children, because they do not display obvious and highly disruptive hyperactive behaviors, are going unrecognized.

CAUSES

On one thing authorities are in unanimous agreement—there is no one cause of attention and hyperactivity problems (see Box 4.2). As Whalen (1983) states:

> Similar behaviors may have quite different origins, just as the source of a headache may be hypertension, a brain tumor, dietary insufficiency, and so forth. And ... the behaviors of hyperactive youngsters are not all that similar; behavioral diversity is the rule rather than the exception. Thus there is no reason to expect that a unitary etiological process will be uncovered. (p. 170)

Not only are the possible causes multiple, but trying to pick out the one cause, or group of causes, for individual cases is usually fruitless. One can rarely identify with any assurance the exact cause(s) of a particular child's attention problems and hyperactivity.

The many causes that have been advanced by different theorists have been categorized by Whalen (1983) into three somewhat interdependent groups—*early biological, physical environmental,* and *psychosocial influences.* The

---

Box 4.2
HYPERACTIVITY = HETEROGENEITY

At one time, it was common to hear professionals (e.g., psychologists, physicians, special education teachers) refer to a child as having the *hyperactive* or *hyperkinetic syndrome*. Use of this terminology is on the decline, however, because it is quite misleading. The term *syndrome* implies homogeneity with regard to causal factors, behavioral characteristics, and treatment procedures. Children identified as hyperactive, however, are anything but homogeneous with regard to causes, symptoms, or intervention methods. An apt synonym for hyperactivity is heterogeneity.

The notion that it is questionable to refer to hyperactive children as exhibiting a syndrome did not gain favor until a great many futile efforts to discover such a syndrome had been made. As Henker and Whalen (1980) state:

So far, however, data-based attempts to demonstrate the existence of this "classical hyperactive" have fallen short of meeting scientific criteria. One of the most perplexing findings is that characteristics that correlate conceptually and theoretically often fail to correlate (or show only modest relationships) when empirical studies are conducted (Klein & Gittelman-Klein, 1975; Langhorne, Loney, Paternite, & Bechtoldt, 1976; Routh & Roberts, 1972; Sandberg, Rutter, & Taylor, 1978; Werry, 1968). For example, in a . . . study of multiple measures of attention and activity level, Ullman, Barkley, and Brown (1978) found no consistent relationships between these two response domains; in other words, predictions of attentiveness from measures of motoric activity (or vice versa) could not be made at better than chance levels. (p. 343)

---

discussion of causes that follows closely conforms to Whalen's groupings.

EARLY BIOLOGICAL INFLUENCES

Familial-Genetic

Whalen points out that evidence of a genetic basis for hyperactivity is only suggestive. Some studies have shown that parents of hyperactive children are more likely to have been hyperactive themselves than are the parents of nonhyperactive children. In addition, studies of twins have tended to show that the activity levels of identical twins are more similar than are the activity levels of fraternal twins. Both of these lines of research are merely suggestive, however, because an environmental explana-

tion cannot be ruled out in either of them. For example, a parent who was, or is, hyperactive could, by serving as an inattentive, hyperactive model, influence his or her child to be inattentive and hyperactive. In the case of the twin studies, parents of identical twins might be more likely to treat the two children similarly than might the parents of fraternal twins.

Central Nervous System (CNS) Problems

Beginning with the theorizing of Werner and Strauss in the 1930s and 1940s about the "Strauss Syndrome," the notion that some kind of CNS dysfunction is at the root of attention and hyperactivity problems has enjoyed a good deal of popularity. Again, however, the research in this area is controversial. Using a modification of Barkley's conceptualization of this area, the evidence for CNS dysfunction falls into three groups—*neurological soft signs, CNS arousal disturbances,* and *prenatal and perinatal stress.*

Neurological Soft Signs Neurological soft signs are behavioral indices of CNS dysfunction. They include such things as clumsiness, balance problems, and poor fine-motor coordination. They are referred to as "soft" signs because they are not always indicative of CNS dysfunction. They are not terribly accurate predictors of neurological problems. Although soft signs tend to appear more often in children with verifiable CNS dysfunction, they are also sometimes exhibited by perfectly normal individuals. The major drawback to soft signs as an index of CNS dysfunction is that, being behavioral in nature, they are a step removed from their supposed cause—a malfunctioning of the brain. In other words, an inference must be made that a problem in the brain (which is not observed directly) is causing a deviation in behavior (which can be observed directly).

CNS Arousal Disturbances As Whalen notes, there is a long history of speculation concerning the arousal mechanisms of the brain as causal factors in attention and hyperactivity disturbances. Unfortunately the hypotheses advanced have not been overwhelmingly convincing, with some investigators claiming that overarousal is the key factor and others arguing that underarousal is at the heart of the problem (e.g., Browning, 1967). In recent years, however, the evidence has been more on the side of underarousal (Hastings & Barkley, 1978). One of the hypotheses is that such children, being underaroused, seek an excess amount of stimulation from their environment. This stimulus seeking manifests itself in off-task behavior and hyperactivity.

Prenatal and Perinatal Stress Complications during pregnancy and during the birth process can result in CNS disorders. Prematurity, for example, can cause injury to the brain, resulting in a variety of disorders such as cerebral palsy. The degree to which such factors result in hyperactivity, however, is open to debate (Whalen, 1983).

Minor Physical Anomalies

Waldrop and Halverson (1971) have reported a series of studies that link the presence of minor physical anomalies with hyperactivity in children ranging in age from preschool to early elementary years. These studies show that there is a tendency for hyperactive children to possess more minor physical anomalies (e.g., fine "electric" hair, low-seated ears, abnormal head circumference, webbing of the two middle toes) than nonhyperactive children. Since such anomalies are often associated with congenital defects, such as Down's syndrome, Waldrop and Halverson suggest that some hyperactive children may have a subtle chromosomal irregularity or may have had an impediment to proper embryological development.

It is difficult to digest all the many studies and theories relating to the possibility of early biological causes of hyperactivity and attentional problems. Whalen (1983) sums it up well when she states that the area

is laced with methodological problems, contradictory findings, and unsuccessful attempts at replication. Even when reliable measurements can be obtained, their meaning is ambiguous and, in most cases, it is not yet possible to separate cause from concomitant from consequence. Understanding is further clouded by the fact that the biological deviations found in subgroups of hyperactive children are also found among normal populations and in youngsters with diverse disorders that have no apparent similarity to hyperactivity. . . . Perhaps the best characterization at the present time is that these research enterprises are generating tantalizing and potentially consequential clues about brain-behavior relationships. The specificity, validity, and impact of such information should increase dramatically with progressive refinements in biomedical theory and technology. However, this work is still far from providing either definitive answers about the etiologies of hyperactivity, or information that has direct clinical utility for the diagnosis and treatment of hyperactive children. (pp. 175–176)

PHYSICAL ENVIRONMENTAL INFLUENCES

Today a great deal of attention is being paid, even in the popular media, to environmental hazards that are potentially harmful to young children or unborn children. More and more doctors, for instance, are recommending that pregnant women limit their intake of subtle "poisons" such as tobacco, caffeine, food additives, and alcohol. There has been speculation that these substances are responsible for a variety of birth defects and behavioral disturbances (such as hyperactivity), and indeed it is now well established that mothers who drink heavy amounts of alcohol during pregnancy are placing their unborn children at risk for a variety of physical and behavioral problems (Delaney & Hayden, 1977). This area of research into physical environmental influences, however, has been a hotbed of wild and exaggerated claims. Whalen believes, however, that two areas are worthy of exploration regarding a link to hyperactivity—lead poisoning and diet.

Lead Poisoning

Lead was first recognized as a potential source of brain damage when it was used in paint. Although lead-based paint is now outlawed, environmentalists point to high levels of lead in automobile exhaust as a potential hazard. The hypothesis forwarded is that even rela-

tively low levels of lead in the air over a long period of time can accumulate to the point at which damage to the brain can occur. The evidence for a relationship between such subtle lead poisoning and hyperactivity, although not overwhelming, is enough to consider it worthy of further research (Whalen, 1983).

Diet

Gaining widespread media attention has been the notion that food allergies are at the root of attention problems and hyperactivity. Feingold (1975) has been the best known proponent of the food allergy theory. He believes that approximately 50% of hyperactive children can be helped by the Feingold Diet—a diet that eliminates artificial food colorings and foods such as apples, oranges, tomatoes, and

With the Fiengold diet, children are restricted not only from eating foods with artificial food coloring but also from ingesting foods with salicylates (e.g., apples, oranges, tomatoes, strawberries).

Mimi Forsyth, Monkmeyer

strawberries that naturally contain a substance called salicylate.

Most careful reviews of research on the importance of food allergies in causing hyperactivity indicate that such claims have been exaggerated (Henker & Whalen, 1980; Spring & Sandoval, 1976). At best, it appears that a small subgroup of hyperactive children may respond favorably to the Feingold Diet (Conners, 1980).

PSYCHOSOCIAL INFLUENCES

As Whalen points out, even though many people believe that poor parenting or teaching can lead to hyperactive behavior, there is no solid research evidence to back this up. A point of view gaining favor is that there is a reciprocal relationship between child behavior and that of adults. This notion is gaining acceptance with regard to other child behavior problems as well as in the area of hyperactivity and attentional problems. As Kneedler (1984) states:

> Psychologists and educators, traditionally, have been preoccupied with the idea that the infant and young child are shaped by their parents and other aspects of their environment. The hypothesis that infants or children themselves could exert the same influence on their parents was for many years largely ignored. In the 1970s, however, Bell introduced us to the notion that the direction of influence is a two-way street (Bell, 1971; Bell and Harper, 1977). Sometimes, the parent changes the behavior of the infant or child; sometimes, the reverse is true. Observe a young infant and his or her parents objectively and you'll wonder why it took so long for psychologists to discover that the behavior of a parent is often shaped by the behavior of the child. Note how the parent responds to the cries of the child. Note too how quickly a smile from the baby can bring loving caresses from the parent. (pp. 313–314)

The classic study of Thomas, Chess, and Birch (1968) was the forerunner of the present conceptualization of child-adult relationships as reciprocal in nature. These researchers pointed out that infants are born with certain types of temperaments, some being more difficult than others to handle. How adults interact with their difficult infant, then, can determine to a great extent what type of behavior the young child grows up exhibiting.

Whalen notes that the same kind of reciprocal relationship may also hold between teachers and children:

> Some teachers seem to have unusually high "detection thresholds," that is, they are relatively unlikely to perceive a child as deviant and in need of special help. At the other extreme are teachers with low thresholds who view a wide range of behaviors as changeworthy and refer many students for evaluation and remediation. These individual differences not only have an impact on day-to-day interactions in the classroom, but they may also influence the likelihood that a child is diagnosed, and even the type of treatment given. The same variations can be observed among pediatricians and other practitioners. (Whalen, 1983, p. 181)

ASSESSMENT

Reliable and valid measurement of attention and hyperactivity is not easily accomplished (see Box 4.3). With regard to attention problems, in fact, there is no one instrument that is widely used for clinical purposes. Most measures of attention have been designed exclusively for use in experimental laboratory settings. Some psychologists, however, have used scores on three subtests of the Wechsler Intelligence Scale for Children—Revised (WISC-R) as an indicator of potential attention problems. This practice is based on the fact that learning-disabled children identified as having attentional problems have been found to score poorly on the subtests of Digit Span, Coding, and Arithmetic. These three subtests have sometimes been referred to as a freedom-from-distractibility factor and, more recently, as a sequencing ability factor (Bannatyne, 1974; Kaufman, 1979).

Hyperactivity, too, has been measured in experimental settings by mechanical devices. It was hoped when they were first developed that the instruments used in experimental situations would eventually be applicable to school and home settings. Unfortunately, this has not been the case. Mechanical devices are expensive, are susceptible to failure, and may result in the child's acting differently. One device, for instance, requires the child to wear an experimental wristwatch on his arm or leg—or both. How much the child moves is recorded by the hands on the wristwatch. It has been reported that some children take a great deal of pleasure in shaking their arms or legs in order to see the watch hand move around (and thus record excessive movement).

There are, however, a number of hyperactivity rating scales that have had considerable use by psychologists and teachers (Poggio & Salkind, 1979). The most common are the Werry-Weiss-Peters Activity Scale (Werry, 1968), which is designed for parents to fill out, and the Conners (1969, 1973) checklists. The Werry-Weiss-Peters consists of 31 items that are rated on a 3-point scale of "No," "Some," and "Much." Some example items are: "When watching television, does the child get up and down during the program?" "During meals, does the child wriggle?" "When doing homework, does the child talk too much?" Conners has devised a scale for parents and one for teachers. His most popular one, however, is a 10-item rating scale that has been used by both teachers and parents. Raters are asked to rate such behaviors as "Restless (overactive)," "Excitable, impulsive," and "Inattentive, distractible," using the four categories of "Not at all," "Just a little," "Pretty much," and "Very much."

Box 4.3
HYPERACTIVITY AND THE "DOCTOR'S OFFICE EFFECT"

When parents believe that their child is hyperactive, one of the first professionals they turn to for advice is their physician. Unfortunately, parents of a hyperactive child sometimes find it difficult to get a physician to agree with them that their child is indeed hyperactive. There are numerous anecdotal reports of the frustration of parents (and teachers, too) who have seen their usually hyperactive child behave relatively normally when in the presence of a doctor. This disparity in behavior has come to be referred to as the "doctor's office effect." The following account by Cantwell (1979) of his encounter with a preschool patient is apt:

When I interviewed his parents, the history they gave was a disaster. They described a small tyrant who ruled the house: he was up all night running around, had learned to unhook the screen door, and had been found walking down Ventura Boulevard in his Pampers, had put himself in the clothes dryer and turned it on, and so on. My next move was to examine the child himself. He appeared abnormal in some minor respects: an articulation problem that made his speech hard to follow, low frustration tolerance, and a mannerism of twirling a tuft of hair and at times pulling it out. Yet he played reasonably quietly with the blocks and with the Fisher-Price dollhouse for some 45 minutes. To his parents and teacher he was a disaster—yet to me he looked pretty good, so I began to wonder what was going on.

The boy then walked outside my office, where there is a group of secretarial desks. One woman was away from her desk, and he climbed up on her chair and started pounding the typewriter. When she returned and asked him to get down, he jumped down, kicked her in the shins, and yelled—because of his articulation problem— "Duck you, bitch!" He then lay down and began kicking and screaming; it took his mother another 45 minutes to calm him sufficiently to take him home.

The main point of this story is . . . the relative normality shown in the one-to-one situation with me. This is almost standard in such cases, possibly because the child is somewhat frightened and his adrenal output is up. If he is seen repeatedly, the honeymoon with the doctor will eventually wear off, but a single visit can be misleading.[1]

Though such anecdotal reports are eye-openers, they hardly meet the standards of scientific rigor that would convince one that such a thing as a "doctor's office effect" really exists. Realizing that research was needed on this important topic, Sleator and Ullmann (1981) conducted a study that has convincingly supported the idea that physicians are at a distinct disadvantage when it comes to observing a true indication of a child's hyperactivity. One of their major findings, for example, was that of 95 children who had been rated hyperactive by teachers (scoring a mean of 22 points on Conners's 10-item rating scale compared with a mean of 4 points for a normal control group), only 20 (21%) were rated hyperactive by physicians on the first office visit. Furthermore, a 3-year follow-up revealed that there were no differences between these two groups—those rated hyperactive by both teachers and physicians and those rated hyperactive by teachers but not physicians—on such things as teachers' ratings of hyperactivity, grade in school, grade-point average, the number on stimulant medication, the amount of medication prescribed, and duration of drug treatment. In other words, for all practical purposes, the two groups were viewed as essentially the same and were being treated virtually identically, even though 3 years earlier the physicians had identified only the first group as hyperactive on the basis of an initial office visit. Such occurrences are the things that parental frustrations are made of.

[1] From D. P. Cantwell (1979). "The Hyperactive Child." *Hospital Practice*, Vol. 14, p. 68. Reprinted with permission.

EDUCATIONAL METHODS

Treatment interventions for learning-disabled children with hyperactivity and attention difficulties can be categorized under four general headings: *stimulus reduction, drugs, behavior modification,* and *cognitive-behavior modification.* These approaches should not be viewed as necessarily competing; teachers frequently use aspects of more than one of these methods.

Stimulus Reduction

As noted earlier in the chapter, Cruickshank, expanding on the earlier work of Werner and Strauss, made educational recommendations for hyperactive and inattentive children. Believing that the major problem of these children was their distraction by extraneous stimulation, Cruickshank developed a program that emphasized the reduction of inessential stimuli and enhancement of stimuli essential for learning. At the same time, his program was highly structured, that is, highly teacher directed (Cruickshank, Bentzen, Ratzeburg, & Tannhauser, 1961).

Reduced Environmental Stimulation and Enhancement of Teaching Materials Cruickshank recommended that the distractible child be placed in a classroom that is as devoid as possible of extraneous environmental stimuli. Cruickshank implemented many of the suggestions of Werner and Strauss as well as adding some innovations of his own. Some of the major modifications he recommended for the classroom were:

1 The walls and ceiling should be sound-treated.
2 The floor should be carpeted.
3 The windows should be opaque so that they will admit light but the child cannot see objects outside.
4 Book shelves and cupboards should have doors so that objects inside them will be hidden from view.
5 Bulletin boards should be covered or undecorated except for specific, brief periods of the day.
6 Cubicles—three-sided work areas—should be used for the most distractible children when they are involved in tasks requiring concentration.

The entire classroom, however, should not be bland. To contrast with the blandness of those aspects of the environment not involved in the teaching activity itself, the material directly necessary for instruction should be designed to draw the child's attention to it. The use of vivid colors to highlight the instructional materials was thus suggested. In learning to read, for example, the distractible child would be presented with a few words, or maybe only one word, per page, and these words would be in bold colors. This modification of the reading task was introduced purposely to contrast with the usual reading text wherein a page of print might contain many words plus miscellaneous pictures.

A Structured Program Cruickshank reasoned that because the distractible child is so much at the mercy of his impulses, his program should be heavily structured. Unable to provide his own structure, the distractible child can become quite disoriented in a classroom environment that promotes the idea of having children make a number of decisions for themselves. Many kinds of classrooms that are appropriate for the average child—an open, non-directive classroom, for example—may be most harmful for the impulse-ridden, distractible child. Cruickshank provides an example of what is involved in a structured program:

> Specifically, what is meant by a structured program? For example, upon coming into the classroom the child will hang his hat and coat on a given hook—not on any hook of his choice, but on the same hook every day. He will place his lunch box, if he brings one, on a specific shelf each day. He will then . . . follow the teacher's instructions concerning learning tasks, use of toilet, luncheon activities, and all other experiences until the close of the school day. The day's program will be so completely simplified and so devoid of choice (or conflict) situations that the possibility of failure experience will be almost completely minimized. The learning tasks will be within the learning capacity and within the limits of frustration and attention span of the child. This will mean that a careful study of the child's attention span will have to be made. If it is determined that he has an attention span of four minutes, then all teaching tasks should be restricted to four minutes. (Cruickshank, Bentzen, Ratzeburg, & Tannhauser, 1961, p. 18)

Effectiveness of Stimulus Reduction Cruickshank undertook a demonstration-pilot study of the procedures just outlined (Cruickshank, Bentzen, Ratzeburg, & Tannhauser, 1961). A comparison was made of children in the modified classrooms and those in nonmodified classrooms. The results after 1 year of the program were not overwhelmingly positive. The experimental group made gains in perceptual-motor abilities, as assessed by the Bender-Gestalt, and on the degree of distractibility, as measured by the figure-background test used by Werner and Strauss. But no gains were made in intelligence or academic achievement. After 1 year, the children left the experimental program and the gains were erased.

Other researchers have also attempted to evaluate the efficacy of aspects of the Cruickshank program. Hallahan and Kauffman (1975) have reviewed these efforts (Gorton, 1972; Jenkins, Gorrafa, & Griffiths, 1972; Rost & Charles, 1967; Shores & Haubrich, 1969; Slater, 1968; Sommervill, Warnberg, & Bost, 1973) and found numerous methodological problems:

1   None of the purported efficacy studies was an exact replication of the *total* program devised by Cruickshank. The major component that the researchers concentrated on was stimulus reduction.
2   The stimulus reduction employed varied widely in kind and probably in quantity and quality. The specific methods used ranged from total seclusion of individual children to attempts to seclude an entire classroom.
3   There are serious questions with respect to how distractible the children studied really were.
4   The duration of the studies was usually short.

Because of the above limitations, the following two conclusions from the review of these studies of reduced environmental stimuli *must be treated as tentative:*

1   They generally supported the notion that attending skills were increased.
2   In terms of academic achievement and other higher-level measures, no advantage was found.

Drugs

Stimulant drugs are the most common form of drug treatment given to hyperactive and in-

attentive children. The most frequently used drug for such purposes is methylphenidate (Ritalin is the brand name). It would be difficult to find a more controversial topic in all of special education than the issue of drug treatment of hyperactive children. The popular media, in fact, have given widespread coverage to the use and misuse of such treatment. Unfortunately, the reporting on this issue in both professional journals and the popular media has not always been accurate, and thus a number of misconceptions have arisen. It has frequently been reported, for instance, that large numbers of America's youth are being drugged inappropriately (Schrag & Divoky, 1975). Most estimates, however, place the prevalence of drug treatment of children at about 1% to 2% (Sandoval, Lambert, & Sassone, 1980).

Another myth surrounding the use of stimulants is that they exert a paradoxical effect in that while they calm down hyperactive children, they "hype up" nonhyperactive children. Some clinicians, in fact, have mistakenly assumed that they could use this information to diagnose hyperactivity: If the child responds to the medication by becoming more calm, this, they believe, proves that he or she is hyperactive. Research now points to the conclusion that stimulants actually increase both hyperactive and nonhyperactive children's ability to focus on the task at hand (Henker & Whalen, 1980).

The one thing most authorities now agree on is that the use of medication to control hyperactivity and inattention is a very complex method of treatment. The doctor, parents, teachers, and child need to work together as a team or the medication might not only be ineffective but might even have disastrous effects. Just a few of the reasons why this high degree of communication among all parties is necessary are outlined below.

Importance of Dosage Level   It has become apparent that dosage levels are of critical importance in the use of stimulants for hyperactive children. Complicating the situation is the growing evidence that different dosages affect different types of behavior (Sprague & Sleator, 1977). There is a relatively direct relationship between dosage level and behavioral change as perceived by teacher ratings. The higher the dosage, the more likely the teacher is to rate the child's behavior as improved, or less hyperactive. The relationship between dosage level and performance on cognitive tasks, however, is not one-to-one. Too high a dose actually results in detrimental performance. The fact that dosage levels have differing effects on social and cognitive behavior can unwittingly lead to too high a dosage level for some children. As Pelham (1983) states:

> One of the problems with previous studies of drug effects on learning is the dosages of psychostimulants that have been administered in the great majority of studies (and in *all* long-term studies) have been considerably higher than the doses shown to maximize cognitive improvement. . . . Teacher ratings show greatest improvement with high doses of medication, with the result that the great majority of children in these studies have received mean doses of stimulants that improve *social behavior* but are 50% to 400% higher than the dose that Sprague and colleagues have recommended as the maximum to improve *cognitive abilities*. (pp. 15–16)

Potential Adverse Responders Evidence has accumulated that not all hyperactive children respond favorably to stimulant medication. In fact, one of the major proponents of drug treatment for hyperactivity, Kinsbourne (Kinsbourne & Swanson, 1978), estimates that at least 40% of hyperactive children should not be medicated because they have an adverse response to the drugs.

Brief Time Course for Effects of Drugs Another factor that makes the administration of stimulants so complicated is the time course of these drugs. Methylphenidate, for example, has a very brief time period during which it is effective (Kinsbourne & Swanson, 1978; Pelham, 1983). It takes about 2 to 3 hours for the drug to reach its maximum effectiveness, and then the effects subside until about 6 hours after ingestion they are totally gone. This means that the teacher should plan to take advantage of that time period during which the drug is most effective, but such planning is not easily done.

Acquisition Versus Productivity Pelham (1983) points out that some of the past researchers who did not find stimulant effects on learning may have been too quick to claim that such drugs were not at all useful for improving academic performance. The important distinction that needs to be made is between academic tasks that require the child to learn new responses and those in which the child needs to practice responses that have already been learned to some degree. Drugs do not appear to benefit the acquisition of new skills, but they do help the child to produce more academic work with which he or she is already somewhat familiar. Thus, although there are many situations for which drugs would not be beneficial, there do appear to be some tasks for which they are helpful. Specifically, typical seatwork tasks during which the teacher has assigned the child some work on which he or she needs practice would seem the most likely to benefit from the effects of stimulant medication.

Possible Side Effects A number of potential side effects, both physiological and psychological, are associated with stimulant medication. Possible physiological side effects are a decrease in appetite and an increase in sleeplessness. With regard to psychological side effects, some authorities have expressed fears that giving children drugs might lead to undesirable motivational changes in the child and the adults who deal with that child. The concern here is that both the child and the adults may become psychologically dependent on the medication. For example, misbehavior might automatically be blamed on the child's forgetting to take his or her medicine.

Drugs Are Not Enough   Most authorities agree that drugs are rarely, if ever, enough for the treatment of learning-disabled children with hyperactivity and attentional problems. At best, medication is only one aspect of a treatment regimen for such children. Special teaching techniques are required if these children are to learn in the academic setting. The next two sections discuss two general treatment approaches that can be used by teachers.

Behavior Modification

A behavior modification approach to problems of attention and hyperactivity assumes that attention and motoric behavior can be measured through direct observation. In the case of motoric behavior, there is little doubt that it can be easily observed—such things as

out-of-seat behavior are readily measured. Attention is a bit more difficult to observe, but it, too, can be measured. As Hallahan and Kauffman (1975) state:

> Behaviors such as looking at the teacher, following directions, engaging in a single activity, writing answers, or in some other manner giving correct responses or exhibiting task-oriented activity have been recorded as measures of attention in the classroom. A behavior modification analysis of attention implies that such attending responses are a function of specific consequences which can be varied systematically to increase or decrease attending behavior (Martin & Powers, 1967). A number of studies have shown that task attention, study behavior, or orientation to teacher can be increased by reinforcing those behaviors with teacher attention or other social or material consequences. These studies have demonstrated the effectiveness of a variety of reinforcement procedures in different settings and with children varying in age, behavioral description, and diagnostic label. (p. 239)

Figure 4.1   Record of study behavior for Levi, an often disruptive first-grader.
Source: R. V. Hall, D. Lund, & D. Jackson, "Effects of Teacher Attention on Study Behavior," *Journal of Applied Behavior Analysis*, 1968, 1, p. 9. Reprinted by permission.

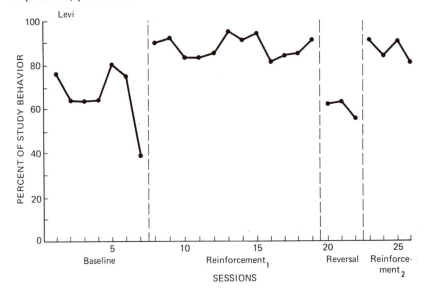

Among the many studies of reinforcement of task attention or study behavior is a now classic report by Hall, Lund, and Jackson (1968). One of the six subjects of their study was Levi, a first-grader selected because he was often disruptive. Each day during the experiment, an observer recorded Levi's attention to the teacher and his academic tasks. Every 10 seconds, the observer recorded whether or not Levi was attending, and the percent of study behavior (i.e., percent of 10-second intervals Levi was studying) was plotted for each day. Figure 4.1 shows the results of differential teacher attention for study and nonstudy behavior. During baseline sessions, the teacher gave Levi almost no attention when he was studying but frequently attended to him when he was disruptive (i.e., not studying, making noise, or disturbing others). When the teacher ignored Levi's disruptive and inattentive actions and attended to him frequently while he was engaged in study behaviors, his study behavior increased dramatically (as shown in Reinforcement₁). A reversal of the relationship between teacher attention and study behavior

(i.e., providing teacher attention for nonstudy behavior and ignoring studying) produced a reversal in Levi's percent of study behavior—it dropped from about 90% to about 60%. Reinstatement of teacher attention for study behavior (Reinforcement₂) resulted in Levi's once more becoming studious. Hall and his co-workers obtained essentially the same results with the other five children included in their report.

Reinforcing the idea, noted earlier in the chapter, of a strong relationship between inattention and hyperactivity were the findings for Levi's disruptive behavior. When Levi's teacher shifted her attention to attentive study behaviors, not only did Levi's attention increase, but his disruptive behavior declined as well, as can be seen from Figure 4.2.

Time after time it has been shown that differential social attention from the teacher, parent, or other person caring for the child has had a salutary effect on disruptive or disturbing behavior (cf. Becker, 1971; and Krumboltz & Krumboltz, 1972). The essential elements of good classroom control appear to be: (1) mak-

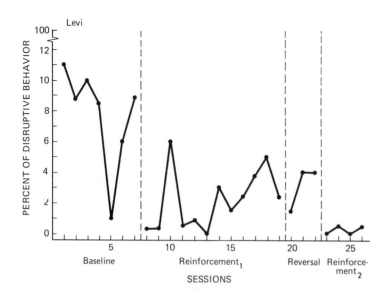

Figure 4.2 Record of disruptive behavior for Levi, a first-grader. *Source:* R. V. Hall, D. Lund, & D. Jackson, "Effects of Teacher Attention on Study Behavior," *Journal of Applied Behavior Analysis,* 1968, 1, p. 10. Reprinted by permission.

ing clear rules regarding behavior; (2) giving frequent praise to the children who follow the rules; (3) ignoring disruptive or inappropriate behavior unless it is dangerous or intolerable; and (4) when misbehavior cannot be allowed to continue, giving soft, private reprimands to the rule violator (Madsen, Becker, & Thomas, 1968; Madsen, Madsen, Saudargas, Hammond, Smith, & Edgar, 1970).

Although these elements of classroom control may be useful to improve the behavior of most children, they are clearly insufficient tools for controlling the behavior of some hyperactive youngsters. More incisive methods of behavior modification are often successful with such children. These methods may involve using stronger reinforcers than social attention. Token reinforcers, games, and other material rewards or activities, given contingent on appropriate or nonhyperactive behavior, are often sufficient to change behavior in a desirable direction. The control of persistently occurring behaviors that are inimical to classroom order and learning sometimes requires punishment, either in the form of response cost or application of punishing stimuli. In some cases, it has been found that enlisting the child's parents or peers as agents of reinforcement is of value. Finally, because children learn a great deal by observing and imitating others, peers and adults have effectively served as exemplars for hyperactive children.

Cognitive Behavior Modification

As was discussed in the last chapter, cognitive behavior modification (CBM) involves the modification of thought processes. Whereas in behavior modification, one would attempt to modify such observable behavior as children's getting out of their seats, in CBM one might try to decrease children's getting out of their seats by getting them to think through what it is they must do to stay seated and concentrate on their work.

Hallahan and his colleagues have noted that CBM procedures might be particularly appropriate for attention problems and hyperactivity because they stress teaching children self-initiative (Hallahan, Kneedler, & Lloyd, 1983; Hallahan, Lloyd, Kauffman, & Loper, 1983; Kneedler & Hallahan, 1984). They point out that all the other major approaches to dealing with children with attention and hyperactivity problems—stimulus reduction, drugs, behavior modification—emphasize external controls. They all involve doing something to the children: shielding them from distractors, giving them pills, administering reinforcers to them. Some authorities are concerned that individuals using these types of techniques might unwittingly be reinforcing the very passivity in learning-disabled children that has proved to be so detrimental to their performance. CBM thus appeals to some because its emphasis is on the child's full awareness and independent participation in the intervention.

CBM for attentional problems and hyperactivity can take many forms. One method that has been particularly successful is self-monitoring (Hallahan & Sapona, 1983). In self-monitoring, the individual evaluates his or her own behavior and then keeps a record of that evaluation. Hallahan and his colleagues have designed a procedure in which children ask themselves the question, "Was I paying attention?" every time they hear a tone on an audiocassette tape recorder. The tones have been prerecorded by the teacher so that they occur at random intervals, with the average interval being about 45 seconds. If the child can answer "yes," then he or she makes a check in the Yes column on a sheet of paper; if the answer is "no," then he or she makes a check in the No column. Gradually, the children are weaned from reliance on the tones and recording sheets. The following is a sample set of instructions for the self-monitoring procedure. (See Box 4.4 for an example of the approach in action.)

Box 4.4
SELF-MONITORING OF ATTENTION: A PLAY WITH ONE ACTOR

The following scene shows how the self-monitoring procedure might be implemented.

Scene: A classroom of students engaged in various activities. One teacher is walking about the room, preparing for her next activity. Some students are sitting in a semicircle facing another teacher and answering questions. Other students are sitting at their desks and writing on papers or in workbooks. Edwin is working at his own desk. The teacher picks up some pages that have green strips of paper attached at the top.

Teacher: (*Walking up to Edwin's desk*): Edwin, here are your seatwork pages for today. I'm going to start the tape and I want you to self-record as you have been doing. What are you going to ask yourself when you hear the beep?

Edwin: (*Taking papers*): Was I paying attention?

Teacher: Okay, that's it. (*Turning away.*) Bobby, Jackie, and Anne, it's time for spelling group. (*Starts a tape recorder and walks toward front of room where three students are gathering.*)

Edwin: (*Begins working on his assignments; is continuing to work when a tone comes from the tape recorder. Edwin's lips barely move as he almost inaudibly whispers*): Was I paying attention? Yes. (*He marks on the green strip of paper and returns to work. Later, another tone comes from the tape recorder. Edwin whispers.*) Was I paying attention? Yes. (*He marks on the green strip of paper and returns to work. Later, as the students in one group laugh, Edwin looks up and watches them. While he is looking up, a tone occurs.*) Was I paying attention? No. (*He marks the strip of paper and begins working again. He continues working, questioning himself when the tone occurs, and recording his answers.*)

Source: D. P. Hallahan, J. W. Lloyd, and L. Stoller, *Improving Attention with Self-Monitoring: A Manual for Teachers.* (Charlottesville: University of Virginia Learning Disabilities Research Institute, 1982, p. 8).

"Johnny, you know how paying attention to your work has been a problem for you. You've heard teachers tell you, 'Pay attention,' 'Get to work,' 'What are you supposed to be doing?' and things like that. Well, today we're going to start something that will help you help yourself pay attention better. First we need to make sure that you know what paying attention means. This is what I mean by paying attention." (Teacher models immediate and sustained attention to task.) "And this is what I mean by not paying attention." (Teacher models attentive and inattentive behaviors and requires the student to categorize them.) "Okay, now let me show you what we're going to do. While you're working, this tape recorder will be turned on. Every once in a while, you'll hear a little sound like this:" (Teacher plays tone on tape). "And when you hear that sound, quietly ask yourself, 'Was I paying attention?' If you answer 'yes,' put a check in this box. If you answer 'no,' put a check in this box. Then go right back to work. When you hear the sound again, ask the question, answer it, mark your answer, and go back to work. Now, let me show you how it works." (Teacher models entire procedure.) "Now, Johnny, I bet you can do this. Tell me what you're going to do every time you hear a tone. Let's try it. I'll start the tape and you work on these papers." (Teacher observes student's implementation of the entire procedure, praises its correct use, and gradually withdraws.) (Hallahan, Lloyd, and Stoller, 1982, p. 12)

SUMMARY

The study of the hyperactivity and attention problems of the learning disabled derives largely from the work of Werner and Strauss (in the 1930s and 1940s) with brain-injured, mentally retarded children. Although their work has been subsequently criticized, their interest in attentional processes greatly influenced the field of learning disabilities' concern for attentional problems and hyperactivity.

Today, researchers relate inattention and hyperactivity, searching for evidence that what people call "hyperactivity" has its deeper basis in inattention, not in overactivity. Accordingly, the American Psychiatric Association's *Diagnostic and Statistical Manual of Mental Disorders* (DSM-III) in 1980 renamed and divided the disorder into: Attention Deficit Disorder with Hyperactivity or Attention Deficit Disorder without Hyperactivity. Most professionals accept this definition, even though Barkley has argued persuasively that this distinction is unnecessary because the Attention Deficit Disorder without Hyperactivity occurs but rarely.

Laboratory studies have isolated three types of attentional problems of learning-disabled children: *coming to attention, decision-making*, and *maintaining attention*. The first refers to the difficulty they have discerning the relevant features of a task from the irrelevant ones; these children also make poor decisions because they tend to decide impulsively; finally, these children perform deficiently (in comparison with nonhandicapped peers) on "vigilance tasks," a finding which has led researchers to search for a cause in the child's physiological arousal system or in his or her history of failure at academic tasks.

Classroom studies have also found that many learning-disabled children have problems in attention. Krupski has suggested that such inattentiveness is a seemingly simple effect of a complex cause—the debilitating interaction of *child, task demands*, and *setting demands*. If a *child* is labelled "handicapped," then he or she is more likely to show those attention problems that occur when the *task demands* a child's voluntary attention (i.e., his or her active effort). *Setting demands* tend to decrease the child's attentiveness when the setting is a structured one.

Although most authorities agree that about 3 percent to 5 percent of the general, school-age population exhibit an attention deficit disorder with hyperactivity, there is considerable controversy surrounding more particular questions about the prevalence of this disorder.

Authorities agree, though, that there is no one cause of attention and hyperactivity problems. Whalen has categorized possible causes in three somewhat interdependent groups: *early biological, physical environmental*, and *psycho-social* influences. Should it exist, the *early biological* influence may be familial-genetic, in which case attention problems and hyperactivity would be inherited. However, research in support of this is merely suggestive, and it fails to rule out environmental explanations. Whether inherited or not, these problems may originate in a dysfunctional central nervous system, in which case neurological "soft signs," arousal disturbances, or prenatal and perinatal stress may cause later dysfunctional behavior. However, research has failed to specify the effect of these central nervous system problems on attentive and hyperactive behavior. In addition, minor physical anomalies have been correlated with hyperactivity in children although no biological link has been determined. In general, biological influences have proven hard to study, and biological deviations found in hyperactive children have also been found in normal individuals and in children with diverse disorders.

Physical environmental influences that may be causing attentional problems and hyperactivity include lead poisoning (e.g., from automobile exhaust) and diet.

The *psycho-social* influences possibly leading to hyperactivity include a reciprocal relationship between adults and children in that each can influence the other. Research indicates that some children are born with distinct types of temperaments, and that adults' responses to a more difficult temperament may shape the child's behavior for the worse.

The general tentativeness of these claims about causal factors indicates that attention and hyperactivity are difficult constructs to measure. The Wechsler Intelligence Scale for Children-Revised (WISC-R) contains subtests that attempt to identify attention problems, and hyperactivity has been measured by experimental devices and rating scales (e.g., the Werry-Weiss-Peters Activity Scale and the Conner's checklists).

The difficulty of assessing and explaining the origin of attention problems and hyperactivity has not led to a scarcity of treatments, however. Treatments include stimulus reduction, drugs, behavior modification, and cognitive behavior modification.

Cruickshank developed a program that reduces inessential stimuli and enhances stimuli that are essential for learning; this program has led to an increase in the attentive behavior of children, but has not demonstrated significant improvement in their academic performance.

The use of stimulant drugs with children remains highly controversial and surrounded by misconceptions. Research shows that dosage levels that improve the child's social behavior are detrimental to his or her cognitive performance, and not all hyperactive children will respond favorably to medication. Stimulants are only effective for a short time. In addition, drugs do not appear to aid the child in acquiring new academic skills, but may increase his or her productivity with familiar academic work. Potential side effects of taking stimulants include: insomnia, decreased appetite, and psychological dependence on the drugs. Most authorities agree that drug treatment is rarely, if ever, sufficient to improve the performance of hyperactive children. Other specific teaching techniques, such as behavior modification and cognitivie behavior modification, must also be employed.

Using behavior modification, for example, social reinforcement from teachers, parents, and peers, token reinforcement, and modelling are successful means to redirect the inattentive and hyperactive child's attention to academic tasks. Likewise, cognitive behavior modification (CBM) directs the child's attention to the task, but forces him or her to take initiative for improving his or her performance. For example, the CBM technique of self-monitoring requires that the individual evaluate and record his or her attending behavior during periods of independent work.

REFERENCES

ACKERMAN, P. T., DYKMAN, R. A., & PETERS, J. E. (1977). Teenage status of hyperactive and non-hyperactive learning disabled boys. *American Journal of Orthopsychiatry, 47,* 577–596.

American Psychiatric Association. (1980). *Diagnostic and statistical manual of mental disorders* (3rd ed., DSM-III). Washington, D.C.

BANNATYNE, A. (1974). Programs, materials, and

techniques. *Journal of Learning Disabilities, 7,* 265–283.

BARKLEY, R. A. (1982). Guidelines for defining hyperactivity in children: Attention deficit disorder with hyperactivity. In B. B. Lahey & A. E. Kazdin (Eds.), *Advances in clinical child psychology.* Vol. 5 (pp. 137–180). New York: Plenum Press.

BECKER, W. C. (Ed.) (1971). *An empirical basis for change in education: Selections on behavioral psychology for teachers.* Chicago: Science Research Associates.

BELL, R. Q. (1971). Stimulus control of parent or caretaker behavior by offspring. *Developmental Psychology, 4,* 63–72.

BELL, R. Q., & HARPER, L. V. (1977). *Child effects on adults.* Hillsdale, NJ: Erlbaum.

BROWNING, R. M. (1967). Hypo-responsiveness as a behavioral correlate of brain damage in children. *Psychological Reports, 20,* 251–259.

BRYAN, T. S. (1974). An observational analysis of classroom behaviors of children with learning disabilities. *Journal of Learning Disabilities, 7,* 26–34.

CANTWELL, D. P. (1979). The "hyperactive" child. *Hospital Practice, 14,* 65–73.

CONNERS, C. K. (1969). A teacher rating scale for use in drug studies with children. *American Journal of Psychiatry, 126,* 884–888.

CONNERS, C. K. (1973). Rating scales for use in drug studies with children. *Psychopharmacology Bulletin* (Special Issue—Pharmacotherapy with Children), 24–84.

CONNERS, C. K. (1980). *Food additives and hyperactive children.* New York: Plenum Press.

CRUICKSHANK, W. M., BENTZEN, F. A., RATZEBURG, F. H., & TANNHAUSER, M. T. (1961). *A teaching method for brain-injured and hyperactive children.* Syracuse, NY: Syracuse University Press.

CRUICKSHANK, W. M., BICE, H. V., & WALLEN, N. E. (1957). *Perception and cerebral palsy.* Syracuse, NY: Syracuse University Press.

DELANEY, S., & HAYDEN, A. (1977). Fetal alcohol syndrome: A review. *American Association for the Education of the Severely and Profoundly Handicapped, 2,* 164–168.

DOUGLAS, V. I. (1972). Stop, look, and listen: The problems of sustained attention and impulse control in hyperactive and normal children. *Canadian Journal of Behaviour Science, 4,* 259–282.

DOUGLAS, V. I., & PETERS, K. G. (1979). Toward a clearer definition of the attention deficit of hyperactive children. In G. A. Hale & M. Lewis (Eds.), *Attention and cognitive development* (pp. 173–247). New York: Plenum Press.

FEINGOLD, B. F. (1975). *Why your child is hyperactive.* New York: Random House.

GORTON, C. E. (1972). The effects of various classroom environments on performance of a mental task by mentally retarded and normal children. *Education and Training of the Mentally Retarded, 7,* 32–38.

HALL, R. V., LUND, D., & JACKSON, D. (1968). Effects of teacher attention on study behavior. *Journal of Applied Behavior Analysis, 1,* 1–12.

HALLAHAN, D. P. (1975). Distractibility in the learning disabled child. In W. M. Cruickshank & D. P. Hallahan (Eds.), *Perceptual and learning disabilities in children.* Vol. 2: *Research and theory* (pp. 195–218). Syracuse, NY: Syracuse University Press.

HALLAHAN, D. P., & KAUFFMAN, J. M. (1975). Research on the education of distractible and hyperactive children. In W. M. Cruickshank & D. P. Hallahan (Eds.), *Perceptual and learning disabilities in children.* Vol. 2: *Research and theory* (pp. 221–256). Syracuse, NY: Syracuse University Press.

HALLAHAN, D. P., KNEEDLER, R. D., & LLOYD, J. W. (1983). Cognitive behavior modification techniques for learning disabled children: Self-instruction and self-monitoring. In J. D. McKinney & L. Feagans (Eds.), *Current topics in learning disabilities.* Vol. 1. (pp. 207–244). New York: Ablex Publishing.

HALLAHAN, D. P., LLOYD, J. W., KAUFFMAN, J. M., & LOPER, A. B. (1983). Academic problems. In R. J. Morris & T. R. Kratochwill (Eds.), *Practice of child therapy: A textbook of methods* (pp. 113–141). New York: Pergamon Press.

HALLAHAN, D. P., LLOYD, J. W., & STOLLER, L. (1982). *Improving attention with self-monitoring: A manual for teachers.* Charlottesville, VA: University of Virginia Learning Disabilities Research Institute.

HALLAHAN, D. P., & REEVE, R. E. (1980). Selective attention and distractibility. In B. K. Keogh (Ed.), *Advances in special education.* Vol. 1: *Basic constructs and theoretical orientations* (pp. 141–181). Greenwich, CT: J.A.I. Press.

HALLAHAN, D. P., & SAPONA, R. H. (1983). Self-monitoring of attention with learning-disabled children: Past research and current issues. *Journal of Learning Disabilities, 16,* 616–620.

HASTINGS, J., & BARKLEY, R. (1978). A review of psychophysiological research with hyperkinetic children. *Journal of Abnormal Child Psychology, 6*, 413–447.

HECHTMAN, L., WEISS, G., PERLMAN, T., HOPKINS, J., & WENER, A. (1981). Hyperactives as young adults: Prospective ten-year follow-up. In K. G. Gadow & J. Loney (Eds.), *Psychosocial aspects of drug treatment for hyperactivity* (pp. 417–442). Boulder, CO: Westview Press.

HENKER, B., & WHALEN, C. K. (1980). The changing faces of hyperactivity: Retrospect and prospect. In C. K. Whalen & B. Henker (Eds.), *Hyperactive children: The social ecology of identification and treatment* (pp. 321–363). New York: Academic Press.

JENKINS, J. R., GORRAFA, Q., & GRIFFITHS, S. (1972). Another look at isolation effects. *American Journal of Mental Deficiency, 76*, 591–593.

KAUFMAN, A. S. (1979). *Intelligent testing with the WISC-R.* New York: Wiley.

KEOGH, B. K., & MARGOLIS, J. (1976). Learn to labor and wait: Attentional problems of children with learning disorders. *Journal of Learning Disabilities, 9*, 276–286.

KINSBOURNE, M., & SWANSON, J. M. (1978). Hyperactivity. *Learning Disabilities: Information Please.* Montreal: Quebec Association for Children with Learning Disabilities.

KLEIN, D. F., & GITTELMAN-KLEIN, R. (1975). Problems in diagnosis of minimal brain dysfunction and the hyperkinetic syndrome. *International Journal of Mental Health, 4*, 75.

KNEEDLER, R. D., & HALLAHAN, D. P. (1984). Self-monitoring as an attentional strategy for academic tasks with learning disabled children. In B. Gholson & T. Rosenthal (Eds.), *Applications of cognitive development theory.* New York: Academic Press.

KNEEDLER, R. D., with HALLAHAN, D. P., & KAUFFMAN, J. M. (1984). *Special education for today.* Englewood Cliffs, NJ: Prentice-Hall.

KRUMBOLTZ, J. D., & KRUMBOLTZ, H. B. (1972). *Changing children's behavior.* Englewood Cliffs, NJ: Prentice-Hall.

KRUPSKI, A. (1981). An interactional approach to the study of attention problems in children with handicaps. *Exceptional Education Quarterly, 2* (3), 1–10.

LANGHORNE, J. E., LONEY, J., PATERNITE, C. E., & BECHTOLDT, H. P. (1976). Childhood hyperkinesis: A return to the source. *Journal of Abnormal Psychology, 85*, 201–209.

MADSEN, C. H., BECKER, W. C., & THOMAS, D. R. (1968). Rules, praise, and ignoring: Elements of elementary classroom control. *Journal of Applied Behavior Analysis, 1*, 139–150.

MADSEN, C. H., MADSEN, C. K., SAUDARGAS, R. A., HAMMOND, W. R., SMITH, J. B., & EDGAR, D. E. (1970). Classroom RAID (Rules, Approval, Ignore, Disapproval): A cooperative approach for professionals and volunteers. *Journal of School Psychology, 8*, 180–185.

MARTIN, G. L., & POWERS, R. B. (1967). Attention span: An operant conditioning analysis. *Exceptional Children, 33*, 565–570.

PELHAM, W. E. (1981). Attention deficits in hyperactive and learning-disabled children. *Exceptional Education Quarterly, 2* (3), 13–23.

PELHAM, W. E. (1983). The effects of psychostimulants on academic achievement in hyperactive and learning-disabled children. *Thalamus, 3* (1), 2–48. Newsletter of the International Academy for Research in Learning Disabilities.

POGGIO, J. P., & SALKIND, N. J. (1979). A review and appraisal of instruments assessing hyperactivity in children. *Learning Disabilities Quarterly, 2*, 9–22.

ROST, K. J., & CHARLES, D. C. (1967). Academic achievement of brain injured and hyperactive children in isolation. *Exceptional Children, 34*, 125–126.

ROSVOLD, H. E., MIRSKY, A. F., SARASON, I., BRANSOME, E. D., & BECK, L. H. (1956). A continuous performance test of brain damage. *Journal of Consulting Psychology, 20*, 343–352.

ROUTH, D. K., & ROBERTS, R. D. (1972). Minimal brain dysfunction in children: Failure to find evidence of a behavioral syndrome. *Psychological Reports, 31*, 307–314.

ROUTH, D. K., & SCHROEDER, C. S. (1976). Standardized playroom measures as indices of hyperactivity. *Journal of Abnormal Child Psychology, 4*, 199–207.

ROUTH, D. K., SCHROEDER, C. S., & O'TUAMA, L. A. (1974). Development of activity level in children. *Developmental Psychology, 10*, 163–168.

SAFER, D. J., & ALLEN, R. P. (1976). *Hyperactive children: Diagnosis and management.* Baltimore, MD: University Park Press.

SANDBERG, S. T., RUTTER, M. O., & TAYLOR, E. (1978). Hyperkinetic disorder in psychiatric clinic attenders. *Developmental Medicine and Child Neurology, 20*, 279–299.

SANDOVAL, J., LAMBERT, N., & SASSONE, D. (1980). The identification and labeling of hyperactivity in children: An interactive model. In C. K. Whalen & B. Henker (Eds.), *Hyperactive children: The social ecology of identification and treatment* (pp. 145–171). New York: Academic Press.

SARASON, S. B. (1949). *Psychological problems in mental deficiency.* New York: Harper.

SCHRAG, P., & DIVOKY, D. (1975). *The myth of the hyperactive child.* New York: Pantheon Books.

SHORES, R. E., & HAUBRICH, P. A. (1969). Effects of cubicles in educating emotionally disturbed children. *Exceptional Children, 36,* 21–26.

SKINNER, B. F. (1954). *Science and human behavior.* New York: Macmillan.

SLATER, B. R. (1968). Effects of noise on pupil performance. *Journal of Educational Psychology, 59,* 239–243.

SLEATOR, E. K., & ULLMANN, R. K. (1981). Can the physician diagnose hyperactivity in the office? *Pediatrics, 67,* 13–17.

SOMMERVILL, J. W., WARNBERG, L. S., & BOST, D. E. (1973). Effects of cubicles versus increased stimulation on task performance by first-grade males perceived as distractible and nondistractible. *The Journal of Special Education, 7,* 169–185.

SPRAGUE, R., & SLEATOR, E. (1977). Methylphenidate in hyperkinetic children: Differences in dose effects on learning and social behaviors. *Science, 198,* 1274–1276.

SPRING, C., & SANDOVAL, J. (1976). Food additives and hyperkinesis: A critical evaluation of the evidence. *Journal of Learning Disabilities, 9,* 560–569.

STRAUSS, A. A., & WERNER, H. (1942). Disorders of conceptual thinking in the brain-injured child. *Journal of Nervous and Mental Diseases, 96,* 153–172.

THOMAS, A., CHESS, S., & BIRCH, H. G. (1968). *Temperament and behavior disorders in children.* New York: New York University Press.

ULLMAN, D. G., BARKLEY, R. A., & BROWN, H. W. (1978). The behavioral symptoms of hyperkinetic children who successfully responded to stimulant drug treatment. *American Journal of Orthopsychiatry, 48,* 425–437.

WALDROP, M. F., & HALVERSON, C. F. (1971). Minor physical anomalies and hyperactive behavior in young children. In J. Hellmuth (Ed.), *Exceptional infant.* Vol. 2: *Studies in abnormalities* (pp. 343–380). New York: Brunner/Mazel.

WERNER, H., & STRAUSS, A. A. (1939). Problems and methods of functional analysis in mentally deficient children. *Journal of Abnormal and Social Psychology, 34,* 37–62.

WERNER, H., & STRAUSS, A. A. (1940). Causal factors in low performance. *American Journal of Mental Deficiency, 45,* 213–218.

WERNER, H., & STRAUSS, A. A. (1941). Pathology of figure background relation in the child. *Journal of Abnormal and Social Psychology, 36,* 236–248.

WERRY, J. S. (1968). Studies of the hyperactive child. IV: An empirical analysis of minimal brain dysfunction syndrome. *Archives of General Psychiatry, 19,* 9–16.

WHALEN, C. K. (1983). Hyperactivity, learning problems, and the attention deficit disorders. In T. H. Ollendick & M. Hersen (Eds.), *Handbook of child psychopathology* (pp. 131–199). New York: Plenum Press.

Social and Emotional Disabilities

In Chapter 4, we discussed inattention and hyperactivity. Certainly these are behavioral characteristics of learning-disabled children that may reflect social or emotional problems. They are characteristics that upset parents and teachers and hamper the child's social acceptance and emotional adjustment. But learning-disabled children may exhibit behavior problems besides those we discussed in Chapter 4. In fact, they may show a wide variety of indications that they are emotionally troubled and socially maladjusted.

WHEN IS PROBLEM BEHAVIOR A DISABILITY?

Normal children exhibit problem behavior. This statement may at first seem surprising, since we tend to think of normal children as those who are not troublesome to their parents, teachers, or other adults. But research shows very clearly that most children sometimes exhibit behavior that their parents and/or their teachers consider to be a problem. And most normal children realize that they are at times a "problem" to adults. Obviously, then, a reasonable person cannot conclude that any child who is seen as a problem is emotionally disturbed, learning disabled, or has a social or emotional disability (Wood, 1982).

More than a generation ago, demographic studies of children's behavior indicated that normal children are far from problem free. The California Growth Study (MacFarlane, Allen, & Honzik, 1954) and research by Lapouse and Monk (1958) showed that ordinary children exhibit, at some time during their development, behaviors their parents consider to be undesirable. These behaviors might include temper tantrums, overactivity, finickiness about food, specific fears, excessive shyness or withdrawal, or lying. Moreover, Griffiths (1952) found that normal children themselves are aware that their behavior is sometimes a problem.

More recently, Rubin and Balow (1978)

found that during a 3-year period most children were considered to be a behavior problem in school by at least one of their teachers. Achenbach and Edelbrock (1981) reported that problem behavior of some type was noted by most parents at some time during their children's upbringing.

When is problem behavior a disability in the context of school? Only when children exhibit problem behavior that is comparatively extreme and long lasting are they considered to have a disability. Bower (1981) made extensive studies of the problems of schoolchildren in California. On the basis of his observations, he concluded that a child may be considered emotionally handicapped in school if he or she exhibits one or more of the following five types of behavior to a marked extent and over a long period of time:

1 An inability to learn that cannot be explained by intellectual, sensory, or health factors.

2 An inability to build or maintain satisfactory interpersonal relationships with peers and teachers.

3 Inappropriate types of behavior or feelings under normal conditions.

4 A general, pervasive mood of unhappiness or depression.

5 A tendency to develop physical symptoms, pains, or fears associated with personal or school problems.

Bower's definition is particularly noteworthy because it provided the basis for the federal definition of emotional disturbance in the rules and regulations accompanying PL 94-142. It is also relevant to the social-emotional problems of LD students.

You may have noted that Bower's first characteristic (inability to learn) seems quite similar to the primary characteristic of learning disability. Yet Bower is describing the characteristics of emotionally disturbed (ED), not learning-disabled, children. As we discussed in Chapter 1, the characteristics of ED and LD children

overlap. One cannot make a sharp distinction between these groups of children on the basis of their learning and behavioral characteristics, in spite of the assertions of federal regulations and some authors that LD children are *not* emotionally disturbed.

Beyond the ED-LD distinction, you should consider in more detail what Bower means by a social-emotional handicap. In short phrases, Bower suggests that emotionally handicapped children

don't learn,

can't relate,

act strange,

are sad,

get sick.

Academic learning is extremely important for school-age children, and research has shown that most children with serious emotional problems have academic deficits (Kauffman, 1985). But Bower notes that in addition to their failure to learn academic skills, emotionally handicapped children don't seem to learn from experience (i.e., they make repeated and seemingly mindless errors in social-interpersonal situations as well as on academic tasks). Emotionally handicapped students don't merely fail to get along with teachers and classmates, they seem not to have the ability to develop friendships, show understanding of others, and enjoy playing and working with other people. The actions of these children are strange because they seem unable to read social cues and make their behavior fit the circumstances—their reactions are not what one would expect for a child of given age, sex, and intelligence. Emotionally handicapped children don't seem to get much joy out of life. Their lives seem filled with sadness that squelches pleasure in nearly every situation. And such children frequently get physically ill, especially when they are confronted by a stressful situation at home or in school. In fact, just going to school may be an extremely stressful event that precipitates physical symptoms. These characteristics are often seen in LD students.

Remember that not every emotionally-handicapped or LD child will show all these types of behavior, and many normal children will exhibit one or more of these characteristics occasionally. A child may be considered socially or emotionally handicapped if he or she demonstrates one or more of these characteristics to an unusual degree and for a considerable period of time.

Another point to keep in mind is that a child's problem behavior or apparent disability may actually be a reasonable response to an unreasonably stressful or nondemanding environment. If a child's behavior changes very quickly for the better when he or she is placed in appropriate circumstances, then the "disability" is not so much a problem of the child as it is a fault of the environment.

The notion that a child's behavior is responsive to and interactive with the way other people act toward him or her is a basic concept in *ecological* psychology. The ecological view of social and emotional disabilities includes the assumption that one can never adequately assess a child's behavior without also assessing the way others (especially parents, teachers, and peers) treat him or her. Certainly one must always consider carefully the context in which behavior occurs before making judgments about its significance.

Normal social behavior is defined by social and cultural standards. These standards vary among cultures and social groups and change with such factors as time, socioeconomic conditions, and political realities (see Box 5.1). Therefore, one cannot arbitrarily classify a given social behavior as desirable or undesirable but must take into account the context in which the behavior occurs. When and where a behavior occurs will influence how it is evalu-

ated. Normality or abnormality of social and emotional behavior, then, must be defined with specific situational variables in mind. Moreover, the developmental characteristics of children must be considered when judging whether or not a given problem is significant (Campbell, 1983).

Bower's five types of behavior constitute a good general description of the characteristics of emotionally handicapped LD children, but they are not a framework for classifying behavior problems. Other researchers have suggested useful ways of grouping or clustering behaviors so that one can accurately and reliably describe the type of disability the child has.

Dimensions of Social-Emotional Disability

Psychiatric classifications of children's behavioral disabilities have not been highly reliable, nor have they been of much help to educators (see Achenbach, 1982; Achenbach & Edelbrock, 1978, 1983; Hobbs, 1975; Quay, 1979). Behavioral researchers have attempted to identify types or clusters of deviant behaviors that can be described more reliably and that have more meaning for teachers. These researchers have turned to quantitative methods of determining interrelationships among behavior problems. Their methods are "multivariate," meaning that a large number of variables are intercorrelated using complex statistical procedures such as factor analysis. The results of these statistical procedures reveal which behavior problems tend to cluster or occur together (i.e., form a syndrome).

In one of the earliest statistical studies, Peterson (1961) began by examining the problems listed in the case folders of over 400 referrals to a child guidance clinic. On the basis of the frequency with which these problems occurred, he selected 58 items describing behavioral difficulties and compiled them in a check-

Box 5.1
BEHAVIORAL STANDARDS CHANGE WITH TIME

In North Carolina in 1848, behaviors that today we often accept or overlook were punished severely. Gnagey (1969) reported the following examples of mid-19th century misbehaviors and recommended punishments:

Playing cards at school (10 lashes)

Swearing at school (8 lashes)

Drinking liquor at school (8 lashes)

Telling lies (7 lashes)

Boys and girls playing together (4 lashes)

Quarreling (4 lashes)

Wearing long fingernails (2 lashes)

Blotting one's copybook (2 lashes)

Neglecting to bow when going home (2 lashes)

It is interesting to note that some of the behaviors considered unacceptable in schools a century and a half ago are still considered highly inappropriate (e.g., drinking liquor at school), while others that were severely punished are now commonplace in schools (e.g., playing cards) or even encouraged (boys and girls playing together). Corporal punishment is still used in many schools in the United States, though it is increasingly being defined as ill-advised or illegal. Moreover, Rose (1983) has found that corporal punishment is widely used with mildly handicapped children in today's schools.

Teachers must always be aware of the cultural and personal biases they have about child behavior and its management. But this does not mean that every behavioral standard or prohibition the teacher may impose is questionable or that every kind of child behavior can be justified. What behavioral standards imposed by most schools on children do you think are silly or will be seen as silly a couple of decades from now? What behavioral standards do you think will and should persist? What kinds of classroom management and discipline procedures do you think can be justified? Should nonhandicapped and handicapped children be subjected to the same methods of discipline?

list. The format of the checklist required ratings of 0 (no problem), 1 (mild problem), or 2 (severe problem) for each of the 58 items. Teachers of kindergarten through sixth grade completed the checklist for a total of more than 800 children, and the scores were then subjected to factor analysis. Peterson's interpretation of the factor analysis suggested the existence of two major dimensions: "conduct problem," which implied a tendency to express impulses against society; and "personality problem" or neuroticism, which comprised a variety of elements suggesting low self-esteem, social withdrawal, and dysphoria (sad mood).

Since Peterson's original study, a great deal of research has been done using the behavior problem checklist. Four factors or dimensions of behavioral deviance are typically found in any large sample of schoolchildren. Von Isser, Quay, and Love (1980) summarized the four dimensions as follows:

1 *Conduct disorder* involves such characteristics as overt aggression, both verbal and physical; disruptiveness; negativism; irresponsibility; and defiance of authority—all of which are at variance with the behavioral expectations of the school and other social institutions.

2 *Anxiety-withdrawal* stands in considerable contrast to conduct disorders, involving, as it does, overanxiety, social withdrawal, seclusiveness, shyness, sensitivity, and other behaviors implying a retreat from the environment rather than a hostile response to it.

3 *Immaturity* characteristically involves preoccupation, short attention span, passivity, daydreaming, sluggishness, and other behavior not in accord with developmental expectations.

4 *Socialized aggression* typically involves gang activities, cooperative stealing, truancy, and other manifestations of participation in a delinquent subculture (pp. 272–273).

For more detailed listing of the characteristics associated with each of the four dimensions, see Table 5.1. (*Note:* Not every study has revealed all four dimensions, and different labels have sometimes been given to dimensions. *Anxiety-withdrawal,* for example, has sometimes been called *personality problem; immaturity* has sometimes been called *immaturity-inadequacy;* and *conduct disorder* has sometimes been referred to as *unsocialized aggression.*)

During the past two decades, research has accumulated to establish the pervasiveness, reliability, and validity of these behavioral dimensions (Quay, 1979). Note that these are di-

Table 5.1 Characteristics Defining Four Behavioral Dimensions

Frequently Found Characteristics Defining Conduct Disorder

Characteristics

Fighting, hitting, assaultive
Temper tantrums
Disobedient, defiant
Destructiveness of own or other's property
Impertinent, "smart," impudent
Uncooperative, resistive, inconsiderate
Disruptive, interrupts, disturbs
Negative, refuses direction
Restless
Boisterous, noisy
Irritability, "blows up" easily
Attention-seeking, "show-off"
Dominates others, bullies, threatens
Hyperactivity
Untrustworthy, dishonest, lies
Profanity, abusive language
Jealousy
Quarrelsome, argues
Irresponsible, undependable
Inattentive
Steals
Distractibility
Teases
Denies mistakes, blames others
Pouts and sulks
Selfish

Frequently Found Characteristics Defining Anxiety-Withdrawal

Characteristics

Anxious, fearful, tense
Shy, timid, bashful
Withdrawn, seclusive, friendless
Depressed, sad, disturbed
Hypersensitive, easily hurt
Self-conscious, easily embarrassed
Feels inferior, worthless
Lacks self-confidence

Easily flustered
Aloof
Cries frequently
Reticent, secretive

Frequently Found Characteristics Defining Immaturity

Characteristics

Short attention span, poor concentration
Daydreaming
Clumsy, poor coordination
Preoccupied, stares into space, absentminded
Passive, lacks initiative, easily led
Sluggish
Inattentive
Drowsy
Lack of interest, bored
Lacks perseverance, fails to finish things
Messy, sloppy

Frequently Found Characteristics Defining Socialized Aggression

---

Characteristics

Has "bad companions"
Steals in company with others
Loyal to delinquent friends
Belongs to a gang
Stays out late at night
Truant from school
Truant from home

Source: H. C. Quay, "Classification," in H. C. Quay & J. S. Werry (Eds.), *Psychopathological Disorders of Childhood* (2nd ed.) (New York: Wiley, 1979), pp. 17–21.

mensions of disordered behavior, not types of children—that is, the research on which these dimensions are based involves sorting behaviors into clusters, not sorting children into categories. A given child may indeed exhibit behavior problems that fall under just one dimension, but nothing prevents a child from exhibiting problems associated with more than one dimension (e.g., conduct disorder and immaturity).

Since the late 1960s, researchers have examined the Quay-Peterson checklist ratings of LD children (McCarthy & Paraskevopoulos, 1969; Paraskevopoulos & McCarthy, 1969). In most ways, the ratings of LD children have been found to parallel those of emotionally disturbed children, although LD children tend to receive less extreme scores than disturbed children. The type of behavior problem most frequently observed by teachers of LD, as well as ED and normal students, is conduct disorder. However, recent studies have shown that LD students may tend to exhibit problems constituting a definite "attention deficit" or hyperactivity dimension that non-LD students do not. These studies also reveal that the dimensions of problem behavior may differ somewhat depending on students' age and sex (Epstein, Bursuck, & Cullinan, in press; Epstein, Cullinan, & Lloyd, 1984; Epstein, Cullinan, & Rosemeir, 1983; Epstein, Kauffman, & Cullinan, 1984).

The behavioral dimensions described by Quay (see Quay, 1977, 1979) do not represent a *diagnostic* system of classification. They are helpful to educators, however, in that they convey objective information about how children behave. That is, if a teacher knows that a child is rated high on the conduct disorder dimension, then it can be predicted that the child will exhibit behaviors of a certain type. Such information is likely to be more useful than a psychiatric label in teaching and managing the child in a classroom.

Social-Emotional Disabilities Among the Learning Disabled

Most authorities agree that learning-disabled children often exhibit social-emotional behavior that is a serious problem. In fact, nearly every textbook on learning disabilities has a chapter or section on problems that could be described as social-emotional disabilities. Yet the official government definition and criteria for determining the existence of a learning disability make no mention of social-emotional problems, except to exclude emotional disturbance as a cause of the learning disability (recall our discussion of definition in Chapter 1).

The evidence of social-emotional disabilities in learning-disabled children comes not only from anecdotal descriptions and reports by teachers and parents but from research as well. Most descriptions of children who are learning disabled include references to behavior that is irritating to adults, to problems in relating to other children, and to negative self-perceptions. Observational studies and research involving behavior ratings and other estimates of social relations confirm the social difficulties of learning-disabled children (Bryan, Pearl, Donahue, Bryan, & Pflaum, 1983; Deshler & Schumaker, 1983; Hallahan & Bryan, 1981; Pearl, Bryan, & Donahue, 1983; Serafica & Harway, 1979). On the basis of research evidence, we can say that many LD children (1) are rated by adults as having behavior problems, (2) are not well liked by their peers and do not relate well to them, (3) appear to behave differently in interactions with regular and special teachers, and (4) show evidence of faulty social cognitions.

Ratings by Adults Ratings of learning-disabled children on the Behavior Problem Checklist have indicated that they show the same types of problems as emotionally disturbed children, though to a lesser degree (Quay, 1977). For example, McCarthy and Paraskevopoulos (1969) found that LD children were rated higher on the conduct disorder, immaturity, and anxiety-withdrawal dimensions than were non-LD children, though emotionally disturbed children were rated higher on all three dimensions than were the learning disabled. Cullinan, Epstein, and Lloyd (1981) reported that LD children, especially boys, were rated as showing more behavior problems than non-LD children. In that study, the LD children showed the highest ratings on characteristics related to the anxiety-withdrawal (personality problem) dimension. Gajar (1977), however, found that LD children scored highest on the immaturity dimension.

Other studies involving parents and teachers also indicate that learning-disabled children are perceived negatively by adults. Owen, Adams, Forrest, Stolz, and Fisher (1971) studied what parents of LD children said about their children during interviews. These parents reported that, compared to non-LD siblings, their LD children had poor verbal ability, did not like to listen, were difficult to talk to, had difficulty expressing themselves, and found it hard to control their impulses. Bryan and McGrady (1972) found that teachers rated learning-disabled children as less cooperative, less attentive, less able to organize themselves, less able to cope with new situations, less socially acceptable to others, less willing to accept responsibility, less able to complete assignments, and less tactful than their classmates. McKinney, McClure, and Feagans (1982) found that both teacher ratings and behavioral observation differentiated LD from non-LD children. LD children were less task oriented, more distractible, and more introverted than their non-LD classmates. Perlmutter, Crocker, Cordray, and Garstecki (1983) reported that the high-school students teachers most often singled out as presenting behavior problems tended to be LD students. Perhaps understandably, teachers tend to prefer non-LD to LD children (Garrett & Crump, 1980).

It is possible that adults rate LD children negatively simply because they know these children have been identified as LD, and the label leads them to have negative expectations and to be too quick to see problems in the children's behavior. At least one study, however, suggests that this is *not* always the case, that unbiased adults may simply notice that LD children exhibit socially obtuse or unappealing behavior. Bryan and Perlmutter (1978) made videotapes of learning-disabled children teaching and playing games with other children and then showed the tapes to female undergraduate students who did not know the children or even the purpose of the experiment. After they watched the tapes, the undergraduates were given questionnaires on which they rated the children's physical and emotional status, sociability, and dominance. Learning-disabled children were more likely to be rated as having poorer physical and emotional status and as less sociable and less dominant than non-LD children. These findings were significant, however, only for LD girls. Apparently, LD girls tend to have greater social deficits than LD boys, or female raters are more sensitive to the social behavior of girls, or both.

Taken together, the studies of adult perceptions of learning-disabled children strongly indicate that LD children are viewed negatively. That is, adults are likely to report that an LD child exhibits undesirable, maladaptive behavior.

Peer Relations   Several studies indicate that learning-disabled children, especially if they are white females, tend to be unpopular with their classmates. Bryan (1974, 1976) asked third-, fourth-, and fifth-graders in regular elementary classes in which LD children were placed to name three classmates who were their friends and three whom they did not want to sit next to in class. Compared to their non-LD classmates, LD children received fewer positive choices and more negative choices. White LD girls were rejected more often than were LD boys or non-LD children of either sex. Non-LD white girls were most often chosen as

friends. Studies by Siperstein, Bopp, and Bak (1978), Scranton and Ryckman (1976), and Garrett and Crump (1980) yielded similar results, i.e., LD children are not as popular as non-LD children with their classmates. Bruinincks (1978) found that not only were LD children less popular than their nonhandicapped peers but they overestimated their social status with their peers, which suggests that these children seriously misperceive interpersonal interactions.

Most studies of the low peer acceptance of LD children have been done with children of elementary-school age. Two studies of high-school students suggest, to the contrary, that learning disability is not necessarily associated with low peer acceptance. Sabornie (1983) found that LD high-school students in regular classes were no less socially accepted than were nonhandicapped students. Sabornie's findings may be different from those of other studies not only because he studied the social status of older students but also because the LD students he studied were as well known to their classmates as were nonhandicapped students. Perlmutter et al. (1983) discovered that (1) although LD adolescents were *generally* less well liked by their peers than were non-LD students, *some* LD adolescents were quite popular with their regular classmates; and (2) most LD high-school students were rated in the neutral range rather than in the disliked range on a sociometric scale.

To sum up, as Asher and Taylor (1981) point out, appraisal of the social status of LD children typically indicates that they do not enjoy popularity and close friendships with their nonhandicapped peers. But more research using a variety of methods to assess LD and other handicapped children's peer relations is needed. Not entirely clear at this point is the extent to which most LD children are able to establish close friendships with, are merely accepted or tolerated by, and are actively rejected by their nonhandicapped and handicapped peers. Moreover, many LD adolescents appear to have a different type of social relationship with their peers than do LD children in elementary school.

The research on learning-disabled children's interactions with their peers has suggested why some LD children may be unpopular or rejected. In their communication with other children their own age, they are prone to be more competitive, rejecting, bossy, and less competent at explaining things or giving accurate information (Bryan & Bryan, 1978; Bryan & Pflaum, 1978; Bryan, Wheeler, Felcan, & Henek, 1976). They are less adept than their non-LD peers at influencing others in problem-solving situations (Bryan, Donahue, & Pearl, 1981) and less able to take the perspective of another person (Wong & Wong, 1980). In the light of this evidence of their characteristic ways of responding to their peers, it is not difficult to see why LD children are often friendless or even actively rejected by classmates.

Interactions with Teachers   Hallahan and Bryan (1981) reviewed what little research has been done on the classroom interactions of teachers and LD students. In general, teachers appear to interact more with younger than with older children, and more with children who are having difficulty than with children who are not having academic problems. However, this general finding may not hold for a child who has been labeled LD or after the teacher has experienced failure in helping a child. Then different patterns of teacher-child interaction may be found, depending on the teacher's experience, the setting (e.g., regular or special class), and the child's age, sex, race, and behavioral style.

Children with certain behavioral characteristics associated with learning disabilities apparently induce teachers to respond to them in particular ways. Ianna, Hallahan, and Bell (1982), for example, trained a teenage confederate to play the parts of a distractible and a nondistractible child during sessions in which he was taught various tasks by a prospective special education teacher. As a group, teachers in this situation made significantly more demands on the confederate's attention, gave more instruction, and asked him more often about his performance when he played the part of a distractible child. While, however, some teachers increased their demands, instructions, and questions related to the tasks to be taught, others allowed the confederate to lead them into activities that were irrelevant to the task. Thus there was considerable variability in the way teachers responded to distractible behavior.

Learning-disabled children may tend to have different interactions with special teachers than they do with teachers in regular classes. Bryan (1974) observed that LD children received more praise and less criticism when interacting with teachers in resource rooms than when interacting with teachers in regular classes. Perlmutter et al. (1983) found that teachers of special classes tended to view LD adolescents as less socially competent than did regular class teachers.

Though relatively little is actually known about teacher interactions with LD children, the available research suggests, first, that teacher interactions with LD and normal children do differ and second, that more positive teacher–LD child interactions occur in special education than in regular education settings.

Social Cognitions   Social cognition refers to one's ability to interpret social cues accurately, to interpret affective messages accurately, to express factual and affective information in an understandable way, to develop empathy, to take the perspective of another, to make accurate self-appraisals, and so on. Children deficient in these abilities are virtually certain to have difficulties in social relationships. As we noted earlier in the discussion of peer relationships, LD children tend to have problems in social cognitions. Their poor relationships with peers and adults often seem to be at least partly the result of their misperceptions of both their own behavior and the social situations in which they find themselves (Bryan et al., 1983; Hallahan & Bryan, 1981).

Relationship to Other Disabilities

Research supports the notion that academic problems and disordered school behavior are related (see Kauffman, 1985). Although a child who has one or more of the other disabilities discussed in this book will not necessarily show social and emotional disabilities as well, the chances that he or she will do so are quite high.

Perhaps the suggestion that a child who has marked difficulty with academic work will probably exhibit emotional difficulties is merely common sense. School is, after all, one of the central features of a child's life, and it is hard to imagine how a child's emotional and social functioning could not be adversely affected by academic failure. Yet some children are remarkably resilient and seem unaffected emotionally by events and circumstances that are highly destructive for others (see Rutter, 1979).

Another commonsensical idea is that social-emotional disabilities have a negative influence on children's academic performance. Most children who are considered emotionally disturbed have academic deficits. But not all disturbed children have academic disabilities; some, in fact, excel in school despite their social or emotional troubles (see Kauffman, 1985).

Although a correlation between academic and social-emotional disabilities clearly exists, the causal relationship between them is not clear. That is to say, neither the extent to which academic failure causes social-emotional problems nor the degree to which social-emotional disabilities cause a child to fail at school has been demonstrated. Most likely, academic and social-emotional disabilities exert a reciprocal influence—each contributes to the other (Glidewell, 1969; Glidewell, Kantor, Smith, & Stringer, 1966; Sanders, 1983).

Pertinent work by Center, Deitz, and Kaufman (1982) suggests one way in which LD children's academic experience might contribute to their inappropriate behavior. Center and his colleagues found that when the academic tasks given to behavior-disordered children were too difficult for their abilities, so that they experienced failure on most items, the children's inappropriate behavior increased. Given that the tasks LD children are expected to perform typically are too difficult for them, it is a reasonable guess that the phenomenon recorded by Center and his colleagues will occur. Some of the problem behavior exhibited by LD children may be at least partly a function of their consistently being expected to perform tasks for which they simply haven't the requisite skills. Then, once they begin to misbehave in the classroom, their behavioral characteristics (e.g., inattention, failure to follow instructions, bothering other children) may result in negative teacher perceptions and interference with learning.

Significance of Social-Emotional Disabilities

According to the federal definition and some respected authorities in the field (e.g., Ross, 1977), emotional disturbance is the result, not the cause, of learning disability. Even if this is accepted as fact, LD children's social-emotional problems often interfere with their learning and, in and of themselves, constitute a serious disability that calls for remediation.

While remediation of LD children's academic disabilities often results in improvement in their social-emotional behavior, academic remediation alone will not eliminate all such children's behavior problems.

As stated by Gable, Strain, and Hendrickson (1979), "a youngster's ability to acquire and apply a full repertoire of social skills represents a major step in successfully negotiating our public school system. For children classified as learning disabled . . . , many of whom have been excluded from the mainstream of public education, untold problems result from their inadequate and inappropriate social behavior" (p. 33). Although social skills and emotional stability may not be prerequisites for attaining academic competence, they obviously facilitate school learning. Moreover, they are themselves areas of learning and development that are critical for successful adaptation to the school and to the larger society.

CAUSAL FACTORS

The causes of children's social-emotional disabilities are not known in the vast majority of cases. Professionals frequently make guesses, but can very seldom demonstrate that a suspected cause actually did produce a disability. Usually guesses about causes are not very helpful because the suspected cause is not something that can be changed, and knowledge of the cause often does not lead to an effective intervention. Nevertheless, knowledge of possible causes may lead to more intelligent guesses and to the possibility of prevention.

Known and suspected causes of behavioral disabilities can be clustered into three major groups: *biological, family,* and *school-related.* Other causes related to sociocultural factors, such as the influence of television, are beyond the scope of this chapter. Our discussion here is limited also to those social-emotional disabilities most likely to be observed in children who carry the label learning disabled (i.e., we will not consider causes related to the severe behavioral disabilities associated with autism or schizophrenia).

Biological Factors

Biological contributions to disordered behavior include genetics, nutrition, brain injury, temperament, and physical illness (see Willis, Swanson, & Walker, 1983). These factors (especially genetics, nutrition, and brain injury) are frequently suggested as possible causes of hyperactivity, distractibility, and impulsivity. But, as we saw in Chapters 3 and 4, only scant evidence exists that these are the actual or only causes of such behavioral problems in most cases. The same conclusion holds for other types of behavioral problems associated with learning disabilities—we know that one of these biological factors might account for the problem in a given case, but we cannot often prove that it does (Kauffman, 1985; Ross & Ross, 1982).

In short, although we know there are possible biological causes of LD children's behavioral difficulties, pinpointing a biological cause for a particular problem is usually impossible. And even if there is good reason to suspect that a biological factor has contributed to the child's problem, that knowledge has few if any implications for intervention. For example, knowledge that a child's misbehavior is a result of a genetic factor has no implications for teaching the child. Behavioral disorders do not require genetic counseling or medical intervention except in extremely rare circumstances. Aside from correcting faulty nutrition or providing medical treatment, knowledge that a behavioral problem is caused by a nutritional factor has no implications for educational programming. Brain injury that results in a learning or behavior problem can seldom be corrected by surgery, and knowing that a child's brain has been injured is not useful in designing an educational intervention. Finally, biological interventions that are successful in changing maladaptive behavior do not necessarily point to a biological cause for the disorder (Ross, 1980). For example, some LD children's behavior problems are ameliorated by stimulant drugs, but a child's behavioral improvement with drug treatment does not necessarily mean that the problem was caused by brain injury or any other biological defect (Whalen & Henker, 1980).

Family Factors

Because learning disabilities often appear to "run in the family," some people have speculated that if a learning disability is not genetically transmitted, then it must be caused by family interaction. Children undoubtedly learn many of their attitudes and values from their parents and siblings. A child's family might unwittingly teach him or her undesirable attitudes toward school and academic learning, for example. A home environment that lacks educational stimulation is likely to produce children who have learning problems (Gesten, Scher, & Cowen, 1978). Moreover, research indicates that parental discipline and other aspects of child rearing can contribute to children's behavior problems (Martin, 1975). Discipline that is too lax or too restrictive, especially if the parent is generally hostile toward the child, and inconsistent management of the child at home are likely to foster social-emotional problems.

While family factors may play a major role in children's behavior problems, one cannot often pinpoint the family interactions that are at fault. This is partly because the child's behavior can be a cause of parental behavior as well as a result of it (Patterson, 1980). Consider the fact that a child who exhibits disordered behavior is not typically pleasant to live with—regardless of the origin of the problem, the youngster will cause consternation in most adults. Box 5.2 provides an extreme example of the type of exasperating child behavior that could easily cause parents to interact in a negative, hostile way with the child or simply give up attempts to provide reasonable discipline.

Discovering ways in which families can handle the inappropriate behavior of an LD child is more realistic than trying to find the apparent cause of the child's disordered behavior. Although little is known about how families cause children's behavior problems, quite a lot is known about how families can learn to manage the problems effectively (Patterson, 1971; Patterson, Reid, Jones, & Conger, 1975). Consequently, the teacher must be ready to work with the child's parents and/or to refer the parents to professionals trained to offer guidance about behavior management in the home.

Box 5.2
HOME WRECKER: TYKE LEAVES TRAIL OF TERROR

GRAND RAPIDS, Mich. (UPI)—It's not difficult to follow the trail of toddler Robin Hawkins—it's strewn with disasters.

In the last two months the 2-year-old has chalked up $2,296.37 in damages, including a wrecked car, television, dishwasher and refrigerator.

Robin's trail of terror began with the toilet. Alice the cat got dunked, drowned and flushed.

Her father, Rowlf, neatly tallied the expenses in a yellow tablet: $62.75 for the plumber, $2.50 for Alice.

That was only the beginning.

Robin decided to give teddy bear a bath—atop the heating element in the dishwasher. That cost her father $375 for repairs, $25 for smoke damage and, of course, $8 for the teddy bear.

Then there was the refrigerator. Robin stuck some magnetic letters in the vents just before the family left home for the weekend, causing the motor to burn out. The cost: $310 for the refrigerator, $120 in spoiled food and $3.75 for the magnetic letters.

"That evening, we sat down to watch TV," said Hawkins, an East Grand Rapids police officer. "Robin had twisted the fine tune so far that it broke inside."

Cost: $115.

The next day Mrs. Hawkins went to pick up her husband from his second job as a part-time security officer. Robin was left asleep in her safety seat, the keys were in her mother's purse inside the car.

"We heard the car start up and we ran outside, just in time to watch the car start down the street," Hawkins said.

Robin ran into a tree. Cost: $1,029.52 in repairs.

A few days later, Robin tried to play some tapes in the family stereo. Cost: $36 for tapes and $35 for tape deck repairs.

Shortly afterwards, the couple parked their car halfway in the garage after a shopping trip because they were planning to unload groceries. Robin was strapped in her safety seat.

"My wife had the keys, so we figured everything was OK," Hawkins said.

Everything was OK, until they heard a loud noise and went outside to find the automatic garage door bouncing off the hood of the car with you know who locked inside, pushing the remote control. Cost: $120.

Robin also lifted $620 out of the cash register at a supermarket, drilled 50 holes in the walls of a rental property owned by her parents, painted walls with nail polish and slipped the garden tractor out of gear so it rolled down the driveway, narrowly missing a neighbor out on a walk.

The grand total including miscellaneous damage of $53.85 comes to $2,296.37.

"Some day when she comes and asks me why she isn't getting any allowance, I'll show her this," Hawkins said, waving the yellow pad containing his daughter's damages.

Source: Home Wrecker: Tyke Leaves Trail of Terror. *The Daily Progress,* July 29, 1982, pp. A1, A8. Reprinted with permission.

School-Related Factors

Certain characteristics of schooling appear in some cases to be causal factors in troublesome behavior, and these are the ones teachers should be most concerned about. That is, the teacher ought first to make certain that the child's school experience is not contributing to social-emotional problems. The following questions, based on Kauffman's (1985) discus-

Teachers must evaluate the ways in which their own teaching and behavior management methods might contribute to children's social and emotional problems.

sion of how schools can cause behavior disorders, will help a teacher evaluate the extent to which his or her class might be a contributing factor.

Am I Sufficiently Sensitive to the Child as an Individual?   A school environment that is conducive to appropriate behavior must allow children sufficient freedom to demonstrate their individuality. Teachers who demand strict uniformity and regimentation and who are unable to tolerate and encourage appropriate differences among children are likely to increase the tendency of some children to exhibit problem behavior.

Are My Expectations for the Child Appropriate for His or Her Abilities?   Expectations that are too high for the child's ability lead to constant feelings of failure; expectations that are too low lead to boredom and lack of

progress. A good teacher adjusts expectations to fit the child's level of ability, so that improvement is always both possible and challenging.

Am I Consistent in Managing the Child and the Classroom?   One of the most significant features of a good school experience for any child, but especially one who exhibits behavior problems, is a high degree of structure. By structure we mean that instructions to the child are clear, expectations that instructions will be followed are firm, and consequences for behavior are consistent (see Haring & Phillips, 1962). When the child is being managed consistently, the classroom routine and the consequences for behavior are highly predictable. Inconsistent management is one factor that is almost certain to increase the tendency of any child to misbehave.

Am I Offering Instruction in Skills That Are of Value to the Child?   Often children do not see the relevance for their lives of the skills they are being taught in school. If they see what they are being asked to do as a waste of their time, they are likely to behave inappropriately in protest or out of boredom or frustration. One of the teacher's tasks is to teach skills that are important to the child and to find ways of making "uninteresting" skills worth the child's time to learn, perhaps by offering meaningful rewards for learning.

Am I Giving Reinforcement for the Right Kind of Behavior?   In many classes, children with behavior problems are ignored when they are behaving well and given a lot of attention (usually in the form of criticisms and reminders or threats) when they misbehave. This arrangement is certain to perpetuate the children's behavioral difficulties.

Are Desirable Models of Behavior Being Demonstrated?   Children are great imitators. If the teacher's behavior is a desirable model for children to imitate, then appropriate conduct will be encouraged. Children also imitate their peers. The teacher should call attention to the appropriate behavior of students that provides a good example for others.

Clearly, academic failure and extreme learning problems can set the stage for social and emotional problems (Meyer, 1983; Sanders, 1983). Likewise, a child who exhibits social-emotional problems is more likely than a well adjusted child to fail at school. Frequently it is impossible to unravel the first cause of a child's problems because academic and social-emotional difficulties affect each other reciprocally.

ASSESSMENT

Adequate assessment of a child's behavior should serve several purposes: diagnosis, design of an intervention program, and evaluation of the outcome of intervention. Diagnosis refers not merely to assignment of the child to a category but also to clear description of the nature of the problem the child's behavior presents. The assessment information used in diagnosis should lead logically to an initial plan for correcting the behavior problem; it should also provide the basis for evaluating the effectiveness of attempts to deal with the problem.

We mentioned previously that traditional psychiatric classifications of children's behavior disorders are of little value to educators. Indeed, traditional approaches to the assessment of childhood behavior disorders offer relatively little beyond assignment of a child to a category. Ysseldyke and Shinn (1981) noted that the typical psychoeducational evaluation is seldom helpful to teachers. A competently conducted behavioral assessment, however, contributes much to clear description, effective intervention, and reliable evaluation.

Behavioral assessment does not focus exclusively on the child's problem behavior. Rather, it includes consideration of the child's thoughts and feelings, the social and physical circumstances surrounding the child, and the child's physical well-being as well as the child's behavior. It is a problem-centered approach that relies on the most accessible, reliable sources of information to obtain a complete and realistic view of the child and the context in which his or her behavior is causing difficulty (Mash & Terdal, 1981).

Screening

The initial step in the assessment process is screening. Learning-disabled children or, for that matter, all children in a given school or district may be screened for social-emotional problems. Only infrequently, however, are entire student bodies screened for behavior problems in a systematic way. Typically, teachers are merely told that they may refer for evaluation any child they believe has a serious emotional or behavioral problem. Sometimes a child referred by a teacher because of an apparent social-emotional problem is labeled LD because the child also exhibits deficits in academic learning that are thought to contribute to the unacceptable behavior. Sometimes a child already identified as LD is referred for further evaluation because the teacher notices persistent undesirable social-emotional responses. In any case, screening involves procedures that determine whether or not a child should be studied further. Screening is a method of identifying *suspected* problems.

Although the most common means of screening for social-emotional problems is unstructured teacher observation, ranking or rating devices are sometimes used. The teacher may be asked to rank each child in the class in terms of how well given behavioral descriptions match the child's behavior. Or the teacher might be asked to rate children on a set of behavioral characteristics, indicating the degree to which each behavior is exhibited by or is a problem for each child. Some screening instruments also include self-ratings, and some include ratings by peers or parents. The major purpose of all screening instruments is to sift out those students who are very different from the norm in their behavior, or at least to identify those who are different in the perceptions of others. These students are then considered candidates for more extensive assessment.

Numerous screening instruments are available. They vary widely in format and proven value. Some are global checklists that cover many facets of behavior and can be used by many different raters in a variety of settings. Others are specific to a particular type of behavior problem, setting, or observer (see Mash & Terdal, 1981; O'Leary & Johnson, 1979). An example of a screening instrument designed to be used in the classroom by teachers is *A Process for In-School Screening of Children with Emotional Handicaps* (Bower & Lambert,

1962; Lambert, Hartsough, & Bower, 1979). This scale includes teacher, self-, and peer assessment for children from kindergarten through high school. The *Behavior Rating Profile* (Brown & Hammill, 1983) is a set of several instruments designed to assess the "ecology" of children's behavior. Students rate themselves, are included in a sociogram, and are rated by parents, teachers, and peers. Other rating scales may be used to identify specific types of behavioral problems, such as a deficit in social interaction with peers (see Hops & Greenwood, 1981).

Multisituational Assessment

If a screening procedure or preliminary observation indicates a need for in-depth analysis of a child's behavior, it is necessary to obtain information from a variety of sources in order to describe the problem usefully and plan an intervention. The assessment should lead to a clear picture of the various facets of the child's behavior in a variety of situations. Assessment thus typically involves testing the child's abilities, interviewing concerned individuals, and observing the child's behavior.

Testing Children referred for social-emotional problems must be tested to determine both their general abilities and specific abilities in academic subjects. Assessment of intelligence and academic abilities is important because of the roles that expectations and failure can play in children's misbehavior. Intelligence and achievement tests are used to help psychologists and teachers determine what can reasonably be expected of a child and whether or not his or her current educational placement is appropriate. We will not elaborate on the assessment of intelligence and academic achievement here; other chapters contain detailed discussions of cognitive disabilities and specific academic disabilities. The important point to remember is that an adequate assessment of the child whose classroom *behavior* is a problem always includes thorough testing of the abilities required for academic performance.

Personality tests or other types of tests designed to reveal important things about the child's emotional health are sometimes administered. Tests in which children are asked to complete sentences, draw human figures (themselves or their families, for example), tell stories about pictures, or describe inkblots supposedly reveal much about the child's self-perception and view of the world. In the hands of a highly skilled examiner, such tests are undoubtedly useful devices for establishing rapport with the child and drawing out the child's feelings about significant aspects of his or her life. Nevertheless, the reliability and validity of most such tests are not very high, and one must be cautious in interpreting the results (Mash & Terdal, 1981; O'Leary & Johnson, 1979). Interviews and observations typically are more useful methods of assessing the child for the purpose of understanding the problem and planning an intervention program.

Interviewing   When a child's behavior is a serious cause for concern, assessment must include asking interested parties about their views of the problem. The child's parents and teachers should be interviewed whenever possible, and frequently it is helpful to talk with the child (if he or she has the necessary verbal skills) and siblings and peers as well. The intent of such interviews should be to get as accurate a picture as possible of the perceptions the child and those most important in the child's life have of the problem.

Interviewing is not simple. One must have considerable skill in establishing rapport with people and drawing out of them the information most relevant to the case. Moreover, the interviewer must have a keen sense of what is most important to find out. Although some interviews are structured by a predetermined series of questions, others are freewheeling con-

versations guided only by the interviewer's general plan and sensitivity to human problems.

A general plan for an interview might follow the outline suggested by Kanfer and Grimm (1977). They suggest that an interviewer inquire about the child's behavior and the circumstances in which it occurs with the following types of questions in mind:

1   What *behavioral deficits* does the child exhibit? What skills does the child lack that, if acquired, would allow satisfactory adjustment? What appropriate behaviors does the child need to learn?

2   What *behavioral excesses* does the child exhibit? What specific things does the child do too often or too intensely?

3   What does the child do that indicates *inappropriate environmental control?* What does the child do that is considered deviant in its context or that demonstrates inefficient organization?

4   What does the child do that reflects *inappropriate responses to self?* How does the child's behavior reflect misperceptions of his or her abilities, unrealistic evaluations of self, or inaccurate descriptions of internal states?

5   To what extent does the child's behavior seem to be a function of *inappropriate contingencies?* Under what circumstances and for what specific behaviors is the child punished or rewarded?

Interviews are extremely valuable in finding out what people think about a problem. The information gained from them is often crucial in determining an intervention plan, because what people think about a problem influences how they respond to suggestions and changes in their environment. But interviews alone are not adequate for assessment of behavior problems. Direct observation is required to complete the assessment process.

Observing   Observing the child's behavior and the behavior of those who interact with him or her is the single most important key to adequate assessment. Direct observation not only provides information about the accuracy of perceptions and the appropriateness of feelings about behavior but typically provides the beginning point for intervention as well. Kauffman (1985) suggests that adequate behavioral observation allows one to answer at least the following questions:

In what settings (home, school, math class, or playground) is the problem behavior or behavioral deficit exhibited?

With what frequency, duration, and amplitude does the behavior appear in various settings?

What happens immediately before the behavior occurs that seems to set the occasion for it, and what happens immediately afterward that may serve to strengthen or weaken the response?

What other inappropriate responses are observed?

What appropriate behaviors could be taught or strengthened to lessen the problem?

The mechanics of direct observation are beyond the scope of this chapter (see Alberto & Troutman, 1982; Kerr & Nelson, 1983; Mash & Terdal, 1981, for discussion and illustration of observation and recording techniques). Suffice to say that adequate assessment requires not only that behavior be observed directly but that it be recorded accurately as well. Direct observation and recording allow one to pinpoint the problem, analyze the environmental factors that contribute to it, and plan an intervention designed to produce specific behavioral improvement.

APPROACHES TO TREATMENT

Traditional Approaches to Therapy

Traditional approaches to treatment of behavior problems of the kind most often seen in LD children are play therapy, psychoanalytic therapy, relationship therapy, client-centered psychotherapy, and similar interventions (see Sanders, 1983; Silver, 1983; Tuma & Sobotka, 1983). These traditional approaches, though often described as distinctly different, share many common elements and are in practice more similar than dissimilar (Tuma & Sobotka, 1983). The essence of these approaches consists of helping the child gain insight into his or her behavior by expression of feelings (through oral language or play) in the presence of an empathic, accepting therapist. Although some research supports the effectiveness of traditional therapies with children, the evidence is not strong (Hobbs & Lahey, 1983; Tuma & Sobotka, 1983). Indeed, some seasoned clinicians have suggested that the insight traditional psychotherapies aim to help children acquire is not particularly important in behavioral change (Hobbs, 1974).

Psychoeducational Approach

In the education of emotionally disturbed children, the psychoeducational approach has a long and distinguished history (see Rezmierski, Knoblock, & Bloom, 1982). This approach emerged from treatment programs for disturbed children in the 1940s and 1950s. It is an attempt to deal therapeutically with the reality demands of the school using principles of psychoanalytically oriented psychology. In the psychoeducational approach, emphasis is placed on the ego, the rational aspect of personality. Therapeutic techniques are aimed at the management of "surface" behavior—the child's observable behavior, which is assumed to be primarily a symptom of deeper problems (Long & Newman, 1965; Morse, 1965).

Among the techniques developed by proponents of the psychoeducational approach is the Life-Space Interview, or LSI (see Morse, 1974; Morse & Wineman, 1965). The LSI is a way of talking to children about their misbehavior at or near the time it occurs in an attempt to help them (1) recognize their feelings, (2) understand how and why they became involved in conflict or misbehavior, and (3) discover what they can do to avoid future problems. Although the LSI and other psychoeducational techniques have been widely acclaimed over the years and their effectiveness is supported by anecdotal evidence, very little empirical research can be found to confirm their efficacy. Moreover, the approach itself remains somewhat vague and nonspecific as a theoretical model (Rezmierski et al., 1982).

Structured Classroom Approach

In the 1940s, Alfred Strauss and Heinz Werner and their colleagues began developing a new approach to management of the behavior of children with learning problems (Strauss & Lehtinen, 1947). During the 1950s and 1960s, their methods were further developed by Cruickshank, Bentzen, Ratzeburg, and Tannhauser (1961) with brain-injured and hyperactive children, and by Haring and Phillips (1962) with emotionally disturbed children. Although Strauss and his colleagues and Cruickshank et al. based their teaching methods on the assumption that a neurological deficit was an important cause of children's behavior problems and recommended perceptual training as part of their total program, their methods of behavior management, as well as those of Haring and Phillips, were straightforward. Therefore one need not assume neurological or perceptual deficits before using a structured approach.

The structured approach to managing behavior problems in the classroom, as described by Haring and Phillips (1962), consisted of three main elements: clear directions, firm expectations, and consistent follow-through. Haring and Phillips believed that many children who exhibit inappropriate behavior in school and at home do so because they have not been given clear, simple instructions about how they

are to behave. Often, too, adults' expectations that misbehaving children will do as they are told are not firmly held, so the children learn that they can ignore those instructions. Moreover, Haring and Phillips noted, children with behavior problems typically do not experience consistent consequences for their behavior. Adults, such children learn, make worthless promises and hollow threats; therefore the consequences of their behavior are unpredictable.

Structuring the environment of the child means making it highly predictable. The child is never left in doubt about what is expected of him or her. The consequences of choosing to behave in a given way are stated very clearly, and positive consequences consistently follow desirable behavior, while predictable negative consequences are always applied for undesirable behavior. A routine is established for the school day so that the child can anticipate the demands that will be made for performance and the sequence of work and play that will be scheduled.

The structured approach seems commonsensical, and its emphasis on consistent consequences is similar to the behavior modification techniques that have been widely used for the past decade. Formal evaluations of the structured approach have generally supported its effectiveness (e.g., Haring & Phillips, 1962).

Current Behavioral Approach

Since the late 1960s, the behavioral approach to intervention in children's disorders has gained wide acceptance, been applied to every type of social-emotional disability, become increasingly sophisticated, and grown to include a variety of techniques (see Morris & Kratochwill, 1983). Behavior problems such as hyperactivity and distractibility have been dealt with very successfully in many cases by arranging appropriate contingencies of reinforcement (see, e.g., the case of Levi discussed in Chapter 4 and Figures 4.1 and 4.2). The management of troublesome social-emotional behavior by behavioral techniques is the topic of many books (e.g., Kerr & Nelson, 1983; Morris & Kratochwill, 1983) and cannot be discussed here in detail. We will describe briefly only four major behavioral strategies for dealing with social-emotional disabilities: (1) reinforcement of appropriate behavior, (2) time-out from positive reinforcement, (3) response cost contingencies, and (4) cognitive-behavior modification.

Reinforcement of Appropriate Behavior

The key element in any behavioral strategy for dealing with undesirable behavior is reinforcement for desirable responses. The "trick" that behavioral psychologists and teachers perform when they are successful is to arrange *differential* reinforcement for appropriate behavior—i.e., they make certain that rewards follow desirable behavior and that negative consequences follow undesirable behavior. This strategy requires that the teacher or other intervention agent supply consequences that the

child desires (e.g., teacher attention, preferred activities, tangible items) following good behavior and negative consequences (e.g., the child's being ignored, loss of rewards, social isolation) following negative behavior. The case of Levi (see Chapter 4) is instructive here. The strategy of reinforcing appropriate behavior to reduce inappropriate activity is discussed in detail by Polsgrove and Reith (1983) and Deitz and Repp (1983).

Time-Out from Positive Reinforcement

A wide variety of behavioral strategies involving aversive procedures have been used in special education (see Polsgrove, 1983). One of the most common is time-out, a punishment procedure. Although reinforcement for appropriate behavior will resolve many behavior problems, it is clearly insufficient in some cases. Some situations require direct suppression of maladaptive behavior in addition to reinforcement of desirable behavior.

Time-out is a punishing consequence because for a period of time the child cannot ob-

Learning disabled children often must be taught the self-control and social skills that allow them to be popular and happy with their peers.

A. Chwatsky, Leo de Wys, Inc.

tain reinforcement, i.e., cannot earn rewarding consequences. It does not necessarily entail isolating the child from human contact. It may mean that the child is consistently (1) ignored when inappropriate behavior is observed, (2) required to discontinue participation in an ongoing rewarding activity for a short period of time contingent on misbehavior, (3) excluded for a brief period from the setting in which the misbehavior occurred, or (4) secluded briefly from peers and/or adults contingent on misbehavior. Although time-out can be misused, it is a humane and effective strategy when properly employed (Nelson & Rutherford, 1983). Proper use of time-out always involves reinforcement for appropriate behavior and use of the least restrictive or aversive form of punishment that is effective.

An example of how reinforcement and a time-out contingency that did not require isolating the child were combined has been provided by Kubany, Weiss, and Sloggett (1971). They were faced with the problem behavior of Henry, a bright (IQ 120) 6-year-old whom they described as hyperactive, loud, demanding, oppositional, and disruptive. He would not sit at his desk, which he separated from the other children and piled with debris. Ordinarily, he refused any schoolwork, except reading aloud to the class. Much of his time was spent drawing pictures of sea life on the chalkboard and narrating stories about them. Then too,

> Henry's incessant talking and loud outbursts made it almost impossible for the teacher to carry out her routine. His misbehavior was all the more salient as the class was in general well behaved. Some of Henry's deviant behaviors were smearing and spraying paint on desks and floors, unraveling rolls of tape, destroying a pegboard with a hammer, chipping away at the sidewalk outside the classroom with a screwdriver and hammer, throwing temper tantrums during which he turned over desks and chairs, not returning to the classroom after recess, sometimes from morning recess not until lunch-time. This caused considerable consternation among school personnel since they are responsible for students' well-being throughout the school day. When asked what Henry liked to do, the teacher included "swearing" and "tipping over his chair." When we came upon the scene, Henry's mother was about to take him to a child psychiatrist, and school administrators were considering a plan to place him on a half-day schedule or possibly even to remove him from the public school and place him in a special class for emotionally handicapped children. (p. 174)

Henry's teacher had tried scolding and reprimanding him, only to find that his behavior became even worse. During the time that baseline data were recorded, she usually ignored his misbehavior, but Henry received much attention from his peers. Kubany and his associates designed an intervention procedure with several considerations in mind: the necessity for a time-out contingency for Henry's misbehavior, the peer attention he was receiving for misbehavior, and the impossibility of isolating Henry during time-out because of the nature of the school setting. They obtained a large (9-by-9-inch) 15-minute electric timer and fitted it with a false face with numbers 1 through 6 at 2-minute intervals and a red star at the end of the series. "Henry's Clock" was printed across the center of the timer. On the first day of the intervention procedure the teacher explained the contingencies to the entire class. The procedure was in effect only from the end of the afternoon recess until the end of the school day, the most troublesome time. As long as Henry was in his seat and quiet, the clock was running and a treat (a trinket or candy) was dropped in a "Sharing Jar" for each 2 minutes of running time (a treat was given for each 15 minutes of running time after the first day). Henry was allowed to distribute the treats to the rest of the class at the end of the day. Each time the clock reached the end of a cycle Henry also earned a red star, which was placed on a "Good Behavior Chart" posted at the front of the room. The earned treats and stars constituted reinforcement for behavior incompatible with disruption. Time-out was provided for disruptive behavior by the teacher's turning off the clock until Henry had behaved appropriately for 15 seconds—that is, as long as Henry was misbehaving, the clock was off, time did not accumulate, and treats and stars were not earned and thus he was "in time-out." The rather dramatic effects of this intervention are shown in Figure 5.1. A "reversal" (i.e., return to baseline conditions) and reinstatement of the reinforcement/time-out contingency demonstrated the causal relationship between the intervention procedure and behavioral improvement. Henry's overall behavior improved so markedly that the Kubany team judged special class placement to be obviated.

Response Cost Contingencies Another form of punishment for misbehavior is response cost—withdrawing earned or awarded reinforcers contingent on an undesirable response. This strategy is discussed in detail by

Walker (1983), who has used it in a variety of settings including playgrounds and classrooms. To be properly employed, a response cost contingency must be fully explained to and understood by the child, be used in the context of an ongoing system of reinforcement for appropriate behavior, and include feedback to the child that keeps him or her informed of when reinforcers are lost and for what reason. The amount of reinforcers lost must be proportional to the seriousness of the misbehavior, the loss should follow misbehavior immediately, and the child should never accumulate negative points (i.e., reinforcers not yet awarded or earned should not be withheld).

An example of a response cost contingency for reducing inappropriate behavior in a special class for learning-disabled children is provided by the work of Lloyd, Kauffman, and Weygant (1982). They worked with two 7-year-old girls, Meg and Joan, who frequently sucked their thumbs at school. A response cost contingency, by which tokens that could be used to "purchase" special reinforcing activities were lost

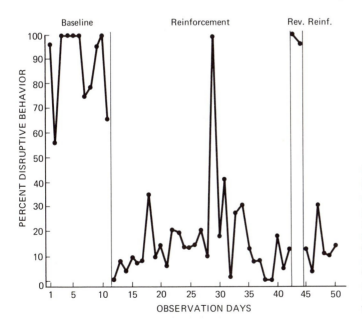

Figure 5.1 Henry's disruptive behavior during baseline, reinforcement, reversal, and reinforcement phases.
Source: E. S. Kubany, L. E. Weiss, & B. B. Sloggett, "The Good Behavior Clock: A Reinforcement/Time-Out Procedure for Reducing Disruptive Classroom Behavior," *Journal of Behavior Therapy and Experimental Psychiatry,* 1971, 2, p. 175. Reprinted with permission.

when thumbsucking was observed, effectively reduced the girls' thumbsucking. The contingency is described as follows:

> The response cost procedure was implemented by having a teacher or aide remove a chit (slip of coloured paper) from a stack of chits held by the child whenever she was observed to have her thumb in her mouth. A new stack of chits was given to the child at the beginning of each day and the contingency was explained. On days when the child had sufficient chits remaining at the end of the school day she was allowed to select a special activity as a reinforcer, such as reading a story to a group of kindergarten children, extra recess, and so on from a menu of activities known to be reinforcing for her. The number of chits given each day and the number required to earn selection of a special reinforcing activity were determined for each child individually by the teacher and observers and were based on thumbsucking frequency during baseline. Initially, the criterion was set to ensure reward and was made gradually more stringent on subsequent days. (p. 170)

Cognitive-Behavior Modification Cognitive-behavioral interventions are, as we discussed in previous chapters, relatively recent additions to the behavioral approach. They are attempts to modify what children think and say to themselves about their problems rather than simply to change unacceptable behavior without regard to the child's cognitions. Cognitive-behavior modification is different from traditional insight-oriented approaches in that it does not rely on the assumption that insight into the unconscious motivations for one's behavior will produce behavioral change. Rather, it deals directly with problem behavior, what the individual thinks and feels in the circumstances in which the behavior is exhibited, and the way one can control thoughts and feelings as well as overt responses. In the case of social-emotional disorders, the child may be taught specific problem-solving skills involving interpersonal behavior.

Kazdin and Frame (1983) provide an example of how a cognitive-behavioral strategy might be applied to the problems of an aggressive child (see Box 5.3). Note that Kazdin and Frame mention at the end of their case description the fact that such strategies have not been evaluated over a long period of time and that experimental evidence of their effectiveness in producing behavioral change is lacking. Future research may indicate the power of cognitive-behavioral therapy with aggressive children, but at present one cannot assume that it is a proven method.

Box 5.3
A SELF-INSTRUCTION STRATEGY FOR AN AGGRESSIVE BOY

Dave was an 11-year-old Caucasian boy who was referred by a local mental health center to an in-patient psychiatric facility for evaluation and treatment. He was hospitalized because his parents felt they could no longer manage him at home given the severity and frequency of his aggressive behavior. Dave had a 6-year history of aggressive behavior, theft, and truancy. His aggressive acts were often severe. For example, on one occasion, his fighting led to the loss of vision in one eye of one of his classmates at school. At the time of admission, his current teacher feared her own welfare and refused to have him in class because of the physical abuse he inflicted on her. Hospitalization was precipitated in part by Dave's serious stabbing of his younger sister.

Apart from aggressive acts, Dave had a history of theft from stores, including small appliances and games and money from cash registers. Other problems were sporadic over his childhood including encopresis and enuresis, but they were associated with clear episodes of family stress (e.g., separation of the mother and father, death of a grandparent who had lived in the home). Although these problems had continued until his hospitalization, they were viewed as relatively minor in significance given the magnitude and consistency of his aggressive acts and rule breaking.

Upon admission to the hospital, the parents indicated that they would only agree to keep Dave in the home if treatment would have direct impact on his aggressive acts. A twofold treatment approach was recommended in which Dave would receive cognitive therapy and the parents would receive parent management training. The father's frequent altercations with the law and brief incarcerations made him an unlikely candidate to attend treatment. Also, the mother felt that she had already tried everything and could not begin to work in treatment for him.

While in the hospital, Dave received cognitive therapy approximately three times per week for a total of 20 sessions. During treatment, Dave learned and rehearsed problem-solving steps that could be applied in everyday situations (see Spivack, Platt, & Shure, 1976). The steps consisted of training the child to ask the following questions or to make the following statements:

1 What am I supposed to do?
2 I need to look at all of my possibilities.
3 I have to focus in (concentrate).
4 I have to make a choice.
5 How well did I do?

In the early sessions, Dave practiced the steps while working on academic or pre-academic tasks, such as deciding what comes next in a series of pictures or what answer might be correct to basic arithmetic problems. In these sessions, learning the steps and responding to each one before proceeding are critical. The specific tasks are not crucial except insofar as they develop use of the problem-solving approach. Training continued with games such as playing checkers or Cat-and-Mouse (a board game utilizing checkers and board).

After the steps were well learned, they were applied to interpersonal situations that were enacted through role-play with the therapist. In each situation, the therapist modeled how the approach was used (as the child) while Dave served as the other person in the situation (e.g., parent or teacher). Dave then enacted the situation while using the steps and receiving prompts, as necessary, to execute the approach correctly.

The situations primarily involved provocative interactions with others in a variety of social situations. The situations included being blamed (justly or unjustly) by teachers for something he had done in class, arguing with siblings or peers, being confronted by the police, and interacting in a variety of situations with others. By the end of treatment, the situations were those that Dave viewed as especially problematic. Also, near the end of treatment, Dave visited his home and spent the weekends with his parents, so he could begin to apply steps to everyday situations outside of the hospital.

The practice weekends impressed the parents, who agreed to take Dave home to give him another chance. The mother was explicit with the hospital staff in noting that if he did not control his aggression, he would have to be institutionalized, and they would not want him home again. The parents were fully apprised of the nature of the treatment and the progress that had been made. Also, they were encouraged to prompt or praise his use of the steps in situations at home.

In the hospital over the course of treatment, Dave made noticeable progress. He frequently avoided arguments and physical fights. He invoked the steps, by his own report and by that of the ward staff, in a variety of situations where he previously would have engaged in fighting. In one instance he was teased by two boys for his attire. He previously would have beaten both of them, especially since they were smaller than he. Dave mentioned instances such as these with enthusiasm in the treatment sessions and stated (as part of his self-evaluation) that he had done well.

Follow-up contact was continued with the family after Dave was discharged. Up to 8 months after treatment Dave remained in the home and, by his parents' anecdotal reports and on objective measures, was doing well. Teacher ratings also indicated that his classroom behavior was no longer a problem. By no means was Dave's behavior representative of a model student. His academic performance was average in most subjects, but this was regarded as much better than expected given his checkered history. Also, his problem behaviors were reported as within the range of classroom disruption of other children. Serious aggressive acts were no longer evident, and truancy, not specifically focused on in treatment, had ceased.

Obviously, the success of treatment of this one case would need to be evaluated over a longer term, especially since the prognosis for such children is poor. Moreover, the extent to which treatment accounted for change was not evaluated. Nevertheless, the case illustrates the approach and its application to seriously aggressive children.

Source: A. E. Kazdin & C. Frame, "Aggressive Behavior and Conduct Disorders," in R. J. Morris & T. R. Kratochwill (Eds.), *The Practice of Child Therapy* (New York: Pergamon, 1983), pp. 179–180.

Programs Designed to Teach Social Skills

The usual school curriculum, especially reading and social studies, provides opportunities for discussion of social behavior, feelings, motivations, and so on. Furthermore, classroom incidents, such as teasing, bullying, sharing, and cooperating, provide the perceptive and competent teacher with frequent opportunities to discuss social learning or teach social skills. The usual curriculum and classroom incidents, however, relegate social learning to the realm of the adventitious or incidental. Clearly it would be desirable, at least for those children with social-emotional problems, to have a planned program for teaching specific social skills.

In the early 1960s, Ojemann and his colleagues devised a curriculum intended to replace children's "nonthinking" (surface) analysis of social problems with a "thinking" (causal) one (Hawkins & Ojemann, 1960; Kremenak & Ojemann, 1965; Ojemann, 1961). Stories, cartoons, hypothetical incidents, problems, and activities provide the beginning point for discussion that seeks to bring out the dynamic reasons for behavior. The assumption underlying this curriculum is that through gaining insight into the dynamics of behavior (i.e., causal factors, such as feelings of inferiority or rejection), children will learn how to behave more adaptively. Little research is available to support this assumption.

More recently, a variety of programs have been developed for teaching what Spivack and Shure (1982) call "interpersonal cognitive problem-solving skills" (ICPS). These programs have ranged from instruction appropriate for preschoolers to activities developed specifically for children in the middle elementary grades to guidelines for working with adolescents. Although the specific techniques employed in such programs have varied (e.g., videotapes, group discussion, role playing, peer competition, dialogue with an adult), Spivack and Shure (1982) point out the commonalities:

> They have all accepted the rationale that there are ICPS skills that mediate interpersonal adjustment, and that training programs should focus on enhancing relevant cognitions while not directly controlling terminal overt adjustment behaviors. All presume that it is necessary to focus somewhat on prerequisite language and/or conceptual skills, on the exploration of feelings, and on the fact that people feel in different ways. (p. 361)

Although it has been demonstrated that well-adjusted children have a higher level of ICPS than children who are not well adjusted, there is little evidence that training in ICPS improves children's overt social behavior.

Goldstein (1974) prepared a social learning curriculum aimed primarily at remediating the social learning deficits of mildly retarded children and youths. The goals of his curriculum are to teach critical thinking and independent action so that students will become socially and occupationally competent. The students are taught skills ranging from recognizing and reacting appropriately to emotions to communicating and getting along with others to managing their own personal affairs (e.g., finances, leisure time, travel, and health).

An outgrowth of the psychoeducational approach in recent years is a curriculum designed to teach children self-control (Fagen, 1979; Fagen & Long, 1979; Fagen, Long, & Stevens, 1975). This curriculum includes step-by-step lessons in which children are led through activities intended to help them acquire a generalized ability to control their own behavior. The capacity for self-control is seen as a composite of eight different skill areas that can be taught in units, as shown in Table 5.2. The rationale for the curriculum is explained by Fagen et al. (1975) as follows:

> Taken together, the eight skills represent an integration of cognitive and affective factors which mediate possibilities for regulating action. The presence of these skills enables a learner to make personally and socially acceptable choices regarding task requirements—choices which preclude the feelings of inadequacy which so often accompany task performance or nonperformance. Through mastery of these self-control skills, the learner incorporates the necessary self-pride and respect for open-minded reflection on available alternatives.

> The self-control curriculum focuses on the internal or mediating processes for skill achievement. Thus, tasks are predominantly process-oriented, with few activities requiring correct answers or narrow outputs. We affirm that inner experiences (affects or thoughts) can be treated operationally so that significant improvement can occur in process skills which mediate response outcomes. (p. 44)

Some evidence suggests that the curriculum is effective in improving certain aspects of self-control (Fagen & Long, 1979).

Table 5.2 Self-Control Curriculum: Overview of Curriculum Areas and Units

Curriculum Area	*Curriculum Unit*
Selection	1 Focusing and concentration 2 Mastering figure-ground discrimination 3 Mastering distractions and interference 4 Processing complex patterns
Storage	1 Developing visual memory 2 Developing auditory memory
Sequencing and ordering	1 Developing time orientation 2 Developing auditory-visual sequencing 3 Developing sequential planning
Anticipating consequences	1 Developing alternatives 2 Evaluating consequences
Appreciating feelings	1 Identifying feelings 2 Developing positive feelings 3 Managing feelings 4 Reinterpreting feeling events
Managing frustration	1 Accepting feelings of frustration 2 Building coping resources 3 Tolerating frustration
Inhibition and delay	1 Controlling action 2 Developing part-goals
Relaxation	1 Developing body relaxation 2 Developing thought relaxation 3 Developing movement relaxation

Source: S. A. Fagen, N. J. Long, & D. J. Stevens, *Teaching Children Self-Control: Preventing Emotional and Learning Problems in the Elementary School* (Columbus, Ohio: Charles E. Merrill, 1975), p. 77. Reprinted by permission.

At the Center at Oregon for Research in the Behavioral Education of the Handicapped, four comprehensive behavior management packages have been developed, tested, and validated. These programs, known by the acronyms CLASS, PASS, PEERS, and RECESS, were designed specifically for the following types of social-emotional disabilities: acting-out behavior, low academic survival skills, social withdrawal, and socially negative-aggressive behavior (Walker, Hops, & Greenwood, 1981). The Oregon programs are based on such behavior modification strategies as reinforcement of appropriate behavior, response cost, and time-out. Teachers of LD children will find in these behavior management packages many field-tested techniques for dealing with social-emotional disabilities.

During the past few years, researchers have shown increased interest in the social skills deficits of the learning disabled, particularly LD adolescents (Deshler & Schumaker, 1983; Gresham, 1981; Schumaker, Deshler, Alley, & Warner, 1983; Zigmond & Brownlee, 1980). The University of Kansas Institute for Research in Learning Disabilities focused much of its effort on defining the social skills in which LD adolescents are deficient and devising a curriculum for teaching those skills (Schumaker et al., 1983). The Kansas researchers' curriculum includes individual and group instruction and programmed written materials designed to teach general social skills (e.g., initiating positive interactions, giving and receiving appropriate criticism and compliments, responding to requests) that can be applied in a variety of situations. Although the initial results are encouraging, extensive field testing of the programs will be necessary to validate them.

We note here that while social skills training programs seem to hold great potential for improving the behavior and social acceptability of handicapped children, relatively little research is available as yet to indicate their effectiveness. Not much is known about which social skills are most important to teach, in which settings they should be taught, or the type of child to whom they can be taught effectively (Gresham, 1981; Hops, 1983; Strain, Odom, & McConnell, 1984). Strain and his colleagues suggest that if social skills are to be improved, then the behavior of the handicapped child's peers must be modified also, not just the behavior of the target child. That is, an effective program of social skills training must include procedures to teach normal peers how to react to the target child because social skills require reciprocal exchanges—changing only the handicapped child's behavior typically results in one-sided social initiations and is therefore likely to fail. The reciprocal nature of social interactions must be taken into account in any social skills training program, whether for preschoolers or adolescents.

SUMMARY

Bower describes the emotionally handicapped child as one who cannot learn at school, behaves strangely, does not relate well to his or her peers and teachers, generally appears to be unhappy, and tends to develop the physical symptoms, pains, or fears associated with personal or school problems. Such a definition applies only to those children who demonstrate one or more of these characteristics to an unusual degree and for a considerable time. Research indicates that many learning-disabled children possess these characteristics, which inhibit their academic performance and their success in social relationships.

Researchers have tried to classify problem behaviors of the emotionally handicapped; in trying to identify behavioral "syndromes," they have correlated problem behaviors by means of quantitative, statistical procedures (such as factor analysis) that reveal which behaviors tend to cluster or occur together. In a sample of schoolchildren, four syndromes are typically found by such means: conduct disorder, anxiety-withdrawal, immaturity, and socialized aggression. Recently, research has accumulated to establish the pervasiveness, reliability, and validity of these behavioral dimensions.

Teachers and researchers agree that learning-disabled children exhibit behavior that is characteristic of these syndromes. Adults tend to perceive and rate LD children negatively, and learning-disabled children in elementary school tend to be less popular than their peers. Although learning-disabled high school students may be generally less likable than their nondisabled peers, some seem quite popular and most are probably socially neutral in the eyes of their peers. Researchers have identified behavioral characteristics of LD children which may influence their popularity: they are poor communicators in social situations, less adept at influencing peers in problem situations, and have difficulty adopting the perspectives of others. Researchers have also suggested that learning-disabled and "normal" children interact differently with their teachers. It appears that more positive interactions occur between LD children and their special education teachers than between LD children and their regular class teachers. In general, it is clear that learning-disabled children tend to misperceive or misinterpret behavioral cues in social interactions. This deficiency in social cognition contributes to their poor relationships with peers and adults.

Research shows that a correlation exists between disturbed behavior in school and deficient academic performance. Disturbances in behavior may be the result or the cause of a learning disability. Once learned, inappropriate behavior contributes to academic problems. Consequently, remediation of both social-emotional and academic deficiencies is required.

Seldom is it possible to isolate the causes of social-emotional behavior problems. Researchers suspect that the causes are biological, familial, or school-related. Experimenters typically can identify possible biological contributions to problem behavior (i.e., genetics, nutrition, brain injury, temperament, illness), but seldom can determine a single cause. Research also indicates that a parent's overly harsh, lax, or inconsistent discipline may contribute to the child's problems. Finally, school-related factors that may adversely affect a child's behavior include a teacher's inflexible approach, inappropriate expectations for the child's performance, inconsistent management, instruction in irrelevant skills, reinforcement of misbehavior, and undesirable models.

Regardless of the cause of problem behavior, traditional means of assessment have been inadequate; they have failed to consider the design and evaluation of a treatment plan in addition to the diagnosis. In contrast, behavioral assessment includes screening to find children who require further evaluation, testing of academic abilities, interviewing significant individuals in the child's environment, and observing the child's behavior in a variety of settings.

Once the child's problem behavior has been identified, a variety of treatment plans may be introduced, including traditional psychotherapy, a psychoeducational approach, a structured classroom approach, or a behavioral approach. The current behavioral approach includes these strategies: reinforcement of appropriate behavior, time-out from positive reinforcement, response cost contingencies, and cognitive behavior modification. Educators have successfully used this approach to improve the social-emotional behavior of learning-disabled children.

The school curriculum has expanded to teach children social skills and problem-solving strategies. While little research is available to indicate the most effective components of a social skills program, teachers and researchers agree that these programs someday may indeed be shown to improve the social behavior of emotionally handicapped children.

REFERENCES

ACHENBACH, T. M. (1982). Assessment and taxonomy of children's behavior disorders. In B. B. Lahey & A. E. Kazdin (Eds.), *Advances in clinical child psychology*, Vol. 5 (pp. 2–38). New York: Plenum.

ACHENBACH, T. M., & EDELBROCK, C. S. (1978). The classification of child psychopathology: A review of empirical efforts. *Psychological Bulletin*, 85, 1275–1301.

ACHENBACH, T. M., & EDELBROCK, C. S. (1981). Behavior problems and competencies reported by parents of normal and disturbed children aged four through sixteen. *Monographs of the Society for Research in Child Development*, 46, whole No. 1 (serial no. 188).

ACHENBACH, T. M., & EDELBROCK, C. S. (1983). Taxonomic issues in child psychopathology. In T. H. Ollendick & M. Hersen (Eds.), *Handbook of child psychopathology* (pp. 65–93). New York: Plenum.

ALBERTO, P., & TROUTMAN, A. (1982). *Applied behavior analysis for teachers.* Columbus, OH: Charles E. Merrill.

ASHER, S. R., & TAYLOR, A. R. (1981). Social outcomes of mainstreaming: Sociometric assessment and beyond. *Exceptional Education Quarterly,* 1(4), 13–30.

BOWER, E. M. (1981). *Early identification of emotionally handicapped children in school* (3rd ed.). Springfield, IL: Charles C Thomas.

BOWER, E. M., & LAMBERT, N. M. (1962). *A process for in-school screening of children with emotional handicaps.* Princeton, NJ: Educational Testing Service.

BROWN, L. L., & HAMMILL, D. D. (1983). *Behavior rating profile: Manual.* Austin, TX: Pro-Ed.

BRUININCKS, V. (1978). Actual and perceived peer status of learning disabled students in mainstream programs. *Journal of Special Education,* 12, 51–58.

BRYAN, J., & PERLMUTTER, B. (1978). Female adults' judgments of learning disabled children. Unpublished manuscript, University of Illinois-Chicago Circle.

BRYAN, T. H. (1974). Peer popularity of learning disabled children. *Journal of Learning Disabilities,* 7, 621–625.

BRYAN, T. H. (1976). Peer popularity of learning disabled children: A replication. *Journal of Learning Disabilities,* 9, 307–311.

BRYAN, T. H., & BRYAN, J. (1978). *Understanding learning disabilities* (2nd ed.). Sherman Oaks, CA: Alfred.

BRYAN, T. H., DONAHUE, M., & PEARL, R. (1981). Learning disabled children's peer interactions during a small-group problem-solving task. *Learning Disability Quarterly,* 4, 13–22.

BRYAN, T. H., & MCGRADY, H. (1972). Use of a teacher rating scale. *Journal of Learning Disabilities,* 5, 199–206.

BRYAN, T. H., PEARL, R., DONAHUE, M., BRYAN, J., & PFLAUM, S. (1983). The Chicago Institute for the Study of Learning Disabilities. *Exceptional Education Quarterly,* 4(1), 1–22.

BRYAN, T. H., & PFLAUM, S. (1978). Social interactions of learning disabled children: A linguistic, social and cognitive analysis. *Learning Disability Quarterly,* 1, 70–79.

BRYAN, T. H., WHEELER, R., FELCAN, J., & HENEK, T. (1976). Come on, Dummy: An observational study of children's communications. *Journal of Learning Disabilities,* 9, 661–669.

CAMPBELL, S. B. (1983). Developmental perspectives in child psychopathology. In T. H. Ollendick & M. Hersen (Eds.), *Handbook of child psychopathology* (pp. 13–40). New York: Plenum.

CENTER, D. B., DEITZ, S. M., & KAUFMAN, M. E. (1982). Student ability, task difficulty, and inappropriate classroom behavior. *Behavior Modification,* 6, 355–374.

CRUICKSHANK, W. M., BENTZEN, F., RATZEBURG, F., & TANNHAUSER, M. A. (1961). *A teaching method for brain-injured and hyperactive children.* Syracuse, NY: Syracuse University Press.

CULLINAN, D., EPSTEIN, M. H., & LLOYD, J. W. (1981). School behavior problems of learning disabled and normal girls and boys. *Learning Disability Quarterly,* 4, 163–169.

DEITZ, D. E. D., & REPP, A. C. (1983). Reducing behavior through reinforcement. *Exceptional Education Quarterly,* 3(4), 34–47.

DESHLER, D. D., & SCHUMAKER, J. B. (1983). Social skills of learning disabled adolescents: Characteristics and interventions. *Topics in Learning and Learning Disabilities,* 3(2), 15–23.

EPSTEIN, M. H., BURSUCK, W., & CULLINAN, D. (in press). Patterns of behavior problems among the learning disabled: II. Boys aged 12–18, girls aged 6–11, girls aged 12–18. *Learning Disability Quarterly.*

EPSTEIN, M. H., CULLINAN, D., & LLOYD, J. W. (1984). Patterns of behavior problems among the learning disabled: III. Replication across ages and sexes. Unpublished manuscript, Northern Illinois University.

EPSTEIN, M. H., CULLINAN, D., & ROSEMEIR, R. (1983). Patterns of behavior problems among the learning disabled: Boys aged 6–11. *Learning Disability Quarterly,* 6, 305–312.

EPSTEIN, M. H., KAUFFMAN, J. M., & CULLINAN, D. (1984). Behavior problem factors of behaviorally disordered students. Unpublished manuscript, Northern Illinois University.

FAGEN, S. A. (1979). Psychoeducational management and self-control. In D. Cullinan & M. H. Epstein (Eds.), *Special education for adolescents: Issues and perspectives* (pp. 235–271). Columbus, OH: Charles E. Merrill.

FAGEN, S. A., & LONG, N. J. (1979). A psychoeducational curriculum approach to teaching self-control. *Behavioral Disorders, 4,* 68–82.

FAGEN, S. A., LONG, N. J., & STEVENS, D. J. (1975). *Teaching children self-control: Preventing emotional and learning problems in the elementary school.* Columbus, OH: Charles E. Merrill.

GABLE, R. A., STRAIN, P. S., & HENDRICKSON, J. M. (1979). Strategies for improving the status and social behavior of learning disabled children. *Learning Disability Quarterly, 2,* 33–39.

GAJAR, A. H. (1977). Characteristics and classification of educable mentally retarded, learning disabled, and emotionally disturbed students. Unpublished doctoral dissertation, University of Virginia.

GARRETT, M. K., & CRUMP, W. D. (1980). Peer acceptance, teacher preference, and self-appraisal of social status among learning disabled students. *Learning Disability Quarterly, 3,* 42–48.

GESTEN, E. L., SCHER, K., & COWEN, E. L. (1978). Judged school problems and competencies of referred children with varying family background characteristics. *Journal of Abnormal Child Psychology, 6,* 247–255.

GLIDEWELL, J. C. (1969). The child at school. In J. G. Howells (Ed.), *Modern perspectives in international child psychiatry* (pp. 733–759). New York: Brunner/Mazel.

GLIDEWELL, J. C., KANTOR, M. B., SMITH, L. M., & STRINGER, L. A. (1966). Socialization and social structure in the classroom. In L. W. Hoffman & M. L. Hoffman (Eds.), *Review of child development research,* Vol. 2 (pp. 221–256). New York: Russell Sage Foundation.

GNAGEY, W. J. (1969). *The psychology of discipline in the classroom.* New York: Macmillan.

GOLDSTEIN, H (1974). *The social learning curriculum.* Columbus, OH: Charles E. Merrill.

GRESHAM, F. M. (1981). Social skills training with handicapped children: A review. *Review of Educational Research, 51,* 139–176.

GRIFFITHS, W. (1952). *Behavior difficulties of children as perceived and judged by parents, teachers, and children themselves.* Minneapolis, MN: University of Minnesota Press.

HALLAHAN, D. P., & BRYAN, T. H. (1981). Learning disabilities. In J. M. Kauffman & D. P. Hallahan (Eds.), *Handbook of special education* (pp. 41–164). Englewood Cliffs, NJ: Prentice-Hall.

HARING, N. G., & PHILLIPS, E. L. (1962). *Educating emotionally disturbed children.* New York: McGraw-Hill.

HAWKINS, A. S., & OJEMANN, R. H. (1960). *A teach-ing program in human behavior and mental health, Book 5: Handbook for fifth grade teachers.* Iowa City: State University of Iowa.

HOBBS, N. (1974). Nicholas Hobbs. In J. M. Kauffman & C. D. Lewis (Eds.), *Teaching children with behavior disorders: Personal perspectives* (pp. 142–167). Columbus, OH: Charles E. Merrill.

HOBBS, N. (1975). *The futures of children.* San Francisco: Jossey-Bass.

HOBBS, S. A., & LAHEY, B. B. (1983). Behavioral treatment. In T. H. Ollendick & M. Hersen (Eds.), *Handbook of child psychopathology* (pp. 427–460). New York: Plenum.

HOPS, H. (1983). Children's social competence and skill: Current research practices and future directions. *Behavior Therapy, 14,* 3–18.

HOPS, H., & GREENWOOD, C. R. (1981). Social skills deficits. In E. J. Mash & L. G. Terdal (Eds.), *Behavioral assessment of childhood disorders* (pp. 347–396). New York: Guilford.

IANNA, S. O., HALLAHAN, D. P., & BELL, R. Q. (1982). The effects of distractible child behavior on adults in a problem-solving setting. *Learning Disability Quarterly, 5,* 126–132.

KANFER, F. H., & GRIMM, L. G. (1977). Behavioral analysis: selecting target behaviors in the interview. *Behavior Modification, 1,* 7–28.

KAUFFMAN, J. M. (1985). *Characteristics of children's behavior disorders* (3rd ed.). Columbus, OH: Charles E. Merrill.

KAZDIN, A. E., & FRAME, C. (1983). Aggressive behavior and conduct disorder. In R. J. Morris & T. R. Kratochwill (Eds.), *The practice of child therapy* (pp. 167–192). New York: Pergamon.

KERR, M. M., & NELSON, C. M. (1983). *Strategies for managing behavior problems in the classroom.* Columbus, OH: Charles E. Merrill.

KREMENAK, S., & OJEMANN, R. H. (1965). *Learning: The on-your-own series. Programs A, B, & C.* Iowa City: University of Iowa.

KUBANY, E. S., WEISS, L. E., & SLOGGETT, B. B. (1971). The good behavior clock: A reinforcement/time-out procedure for reducing disruptive classroom behavior. *Journal of Behavior Therapy and Experimental Psychiatry, 2,* 173–179.

LAMBERT, N. M., HARTSOUGH, C. S., & BOWER, E. M. (1979). *A process for the assessment of effective student functioning: Administration and use manual.* Monterey, CA: Publishers Test Service.

LAPOUSE, R., & MONK, M. (1958). An epidemiological study of behavior characteristics in children. *American Journal of Public Health*, 48, 1134–1144.

LLOYD, J. W., KAUFFMAN, J. M., & WEYGANT, A. D. (1982). Effects of response cost contingencies on thumbsucking and related behaviours in the classroom. *Educational Psychology*, 2, 167–173.

LONG, N. J., & NEWMAN, R. G. (1965). Managing surface behavior of children in school. In N. J. Long, W. C. Morse, & R. G. Newman (Eds.), *Conflict in the classroom* (pp. 352–362). Belmont, CA: Wadsworth.

MACFARLANE, J., ALLEN, L., & HONZIK, M. (1954). *A developmental study of the behavior problems of normal children between twenty-one months and fourteen years.* Berkeley and Los Angeles: University of California Press.

MARTIN, B. (1975). Parent-child relations. In F. D. Horowitz (Ed.), *Review of child development research*, Vol. 4 (pp. 463–540). Chicago: University of Chicago Press.

MASH, E. J., & TERDAL, L. G. (1981). Behavioral assessment of childhood disturbance. In E. J. Mash & L. G. Terdal (Eds.), *Behavioral assessment of childhood disorders* (pp. 3–76). New York: Guilford.

MCCARTHY, J. M., & PARASKEVOPOULOS, J. (1969). Behavior patterns of learning disabled, emotionally disturbed, and average children. *Exceptional Children*, 36, 69–74.

MCKINNEY, J. D., MCCLURE, S., & FEAGANS, L. (1982). Classroom behavior of learning disabled children. *Learning Disability Quarterly*, 5, 42–52.

MEYER, A. (1983). Origins and prevention of emotional disturbances among learning disabled children. *Topics in Learning and Learning Disabilities*, 3(2), 59–70.

MORRIS, R. J., & KRATOCHWILL, T. R. (Eds.) (1983). *The practice of child therapy.* New York: Pergamon.

MORSE, W. C. (1965). Intervention techniques for the classroom teacher. In P. Knoblock (Ed.), *Educational programming for emotionally disturbed children: The decade ahead* (pp. 29–41). Syracuse, NY: Syracuse University Press.

MORSE, W. C. (1974). William C. Morse. In J. M. Kauffman & C. D. Lewis (Eds.), *Teaching children with behavior disorders: Personal perspectives* (pp. 198–216). Columbus, OH: Charles E. Merrill.

MORSE, W. C., & WINEMAN, D. (1965). Group interviewing in a camp for disturbed boys. In N. J.

Long, W. C. Morse, & R. G. Newman (Eds.), *Conflict in the classroom* (pp. 374–380). Belmont, CA: Wadsworth.

NELSON, C. M., & RUTHERFORD, R. B. (1983). Time-out revisited: Guidelines for its use in special education. *Exceptional Education Quarterly*, 3(4), 56–67.

OJEMANN, R. H. (1961). Investigations on the effects of teaching an understanding and appreciation of behavior dynamics. In G. Caplan (Ed.), *Prevention of mental disorders of children* (pp. 378–397). New York: Basic Books.

O'LEARY, K. D., & JOHNSON, S. B. (1979). Psychological assessment. In H. C. Quay & J. S. Werry (Eds.), *Psychopathological disorders of childhood* (2nd ed.) (pp. 210–246). New York: Wiley.

OWEN, F. W., ADAMS, P. A., FORREST, T., STOLZ, L. M., & FISHER, S. (1971). Learning disorders in children: Sibling studies. *Monographs of the Society for Research in Child Development*, 36, serial no. 144.

PARASKEVOPOULOS, J., & MCCARTHY, J. M. (1969). Behavior patterns of children with special learning disabilities. *Psychology in the Schools*, 7, 42–46.

PATTERSON, G. R. (1971). *Families.* Champaign, IL: Research Press.

PATTERSON, G. R. (1980). Mothers: The unacknowledged victims. *Monographs of the Society for Research in Child Development*, 45, serial no. 186, whole no. 5.

PATTERSON, G. R., REID, J. B., JONES, R. R., & CONGER, R. E. (1975). *A social learning approach to family intervention.* Vol. 1: *Families with aggressive children.* Eugene, OR: Castalia.

PEARL, R., BRYAN, T., & DONAHUE, M. (1983). Social behaviors of learning disabled children: A review. *Topics in Learning and Learning Disabilities*, 3(2), 1–14.

PERLMUTTER, B. F., CROCKER, J., CORDRAY, D., & GARSTECKI, D. (1983). Sociometric status and related personality characteristics of mainstreamed learning disabled adolescents. *Learning Disability Quarterly*, 6, 20–30.

PETERSON, D. R. (1961). Behavior problems of middle childhood. *Journal of Consulting Psychology*, 25, 205–209.

POLSGROVE, L. (Ed.) (1983). Aversive control in the classroom. *Exceptional Education Quarterly*, 3, whole No. 4.

POLSGROVE, L., & REITH, H. J. (1983). Procedures for reducing children's inappropriate behavior in special education settings. *Exceptional Education Quarterly, 3*(4), 20–33.

QUAY, H. C. (1977). Measuring dimensions of deviant behavior: The Behavior Problem Checklist. *Journal of Abnormal Child Psychology, 5,* 277–289.

QUAY, H. C. (1979). Classification. In H. C. Quay & J. S. Werry (Eds.), *Psychopathological disorders of childhood* (2nd ed.) (pp. 1–42). New York: Wiley.

REZMIERSKI, V. E., KNOBLOCK, P., & BLOOM, R. B. (1982). The psychoeducational model: Theory and historical perspective. In R. L. McDowell, G. W. Adamson, & F. H. Wood (Eds.), *Teaching emotionally disturbed children* (pp. 47–69). Boston: Little, Brown.

ROSE, T. L. (1983). A survey of corporal punishment of mildly handicapped students. *Exceptional Education Quarterly, 3*(4), 9–19.

ROSS, A. O. (1977). *Learning disability: The unrealized potential.* New York: McGraw-Hill.

ROSS, A. O. (1980). *Psychological disorders of children* (2nd ed.). New York: McGraw-Hill.

ROSS, D. M., & ROSS, S. A. (1982). *Hyperactivity: Current issues, research, and theory* (2nd ed.). New York: Wiley.

RUBIN, R., & BALOW, B. (1978). Prevalence of teacher identified behavior problems: A longitudinal study. *Exceptional Children, 45,* 102–111.

RUTTER, M. (1979). Maternal deprivation, 1972–1978. New findings, new concepts, new approaches. *Child Development, 50,* 283–305.

SABORNIE, E. J. (1983). A comparison of the regular classroom sociometric status of EMR, LD, ED, and nonhandicapped high school students. Unpublished doctoral dissertation, University of Virginia.

SANDERS, M. (1983). Assessing the interaction of learning disabilities and social-emotional development. *Topics in Learning and Learning Disabilities, 3*(2), 37–47.

SCHUMAKER, J. B., DESHLER, D. D., ALLEY, G. R., & WARNER, M. M. (1983). Toward the development of an intervention model for learning disabled adolescents: The University of Kansas Institute. *Exceptional Education Quarterly, 4*(1), 45–74.

SCRANTON, T. R., & RYCKMAN, D. (1976). Sociometric status of learning disabled children in an integrative program. *Journal of Learning Disabilities, 9,* 402–407.

SERAFICA, F. C., & HARWAY, N. I. (1979). Social relations and self-esteem of children with learning disabilities. *Journal of Clinical Child Psychology, 8,* 227–233.

SILVER, L. B. (1983). Therapeutic interventions with learning disabled students and their families. *Topics in Learning and Learning Disabilities, 3*(2), 48–58.

SIPERSTEIN, G. R., BOPP, M., & BAK, J. (1978). Peers rate LD children on who is the smartest, best looking, and most athletic. *Journal of Learning Disabilities, 10,* 98–102.

SPIVACK, G., PLATT, J. J., & SHURE, M. B. (1976). *Problem solving approach to adjustment.* San Francisco: Jossey-Bass.

SPIVACK, G., & SHURE, M. B. (1982). The cognition of social adjustment. In B. B. Lahey & A. E. Kazdin (Eds.), *Advances in clinical child psychology,* Vol. 5 (pp. 323–372). New York: Plenum.

STRAIN, P. S., ODOM, S. L., & MCCONNELL, S. (1984). Promoting social reciprocity of exceptional children: Identification, target behavior selection, and intervention. *Remedial and Special Education, 5*(1), 21–28.

STRAUSS, A. A., & LEHTINEN, L. E. (1947). *Psychopathology and education of the brain-injured child.* New York: Grune & Stratton.

TUMA, J. M., & SOBOTKA, K. R. (1983). Traditional therapies with children. In T. H. Ollendick & M. Hersen (Eds.), *Handbook of child psychopathology* (pp. 391–426). New York: Plenum.

VON ISSER, A., QUAY, H. C., & LOVE, C. T. (1980). Interrelationships among three measures of deviant behavior. *Exceptional Children, 46,* 272–276.

WALKER, H. M. (1983). Applications of response cost in school settings: Outcomes, issues, and recommendations. *Exceptional Education Quarterly, 3*(4), 47–55.

WALKER, H. M., HOPS, H., & GREENWOOD, C. R. (1981). RECESS: Research and development of a behavior management package for remediating social aggression in the school. In P. S. Strain (Ed.), *The utilization of classroom peers as behavior change agents* (pp. 261–303). New York: Plenum.

WHALEN, C. K., & HENKER, B. (1980). The social ecology of psychostimulant treatment: A model for conceptual and empirical analysis. In C. K. Whalen & B. Henker (Eds.), *Hyperactive children: The social ecology of identification and treatment* (pp. 3–51). New York: Academic Press.

WILLIS, D. J., SWANSON, B. M., & WALKER, C. E.

(1983). Etiological factors. In T. H. Ollendick & M. Hersen (Eds.), *Handbook of child psychopathology* (pp. 41–64). New York: Plenum.

WONG, B. Y. L., & WONG, R. (1980). Role-taking skills in normal achieving and learning disabled children. *Learning Disability Quarterly, 3,* 11–18.

WOOD, F. H. (1982). Living with the emotionally disturbed—burden or opportunity? *B. C. Journal of Special Education, 6,* 1–10.

YSSELDYKE, J. E., & SHINN, M. R. (1981). Psychoeducational assessment. In J. M. Kauffman & D. P. Hallahan (Eds.), *Handbook of special education* (pp. 418–440). Englewood Cliffs, NJ: Prentice-Hall.

ZIGMOND, N., & BROWNLEE, J. (1980). Social skills training for adolescents with learning disabilities. *Exceptional Education Quarterly, 1*(2), 77–83.

Spoken-Language Disabilities

Spoken language is the primary means by which most people communicate. We listen to what other people have to say, and we tell other people what we have to say by using spoken language. Without language skills, we could not enjoy a stand-up comedian's routine or understand a well-prepared lecture. We could not tell someone else about a good movie we had seen or whisper a kind word to a close friend.

It was pointed out in Chapter 2 that students with visual, motor, or visual-motor handicaps have captured most of the attention of those in the field of learning disabilities. Historically, disabilities in spoken language were relatively neglected. In an analysis of the learning disabilities literature from 1966 to 1970, Hallahan and Cruickshank (1973) found that there were more than three times as many journal articles dealing with perceptual-motor behavior

as there were with language. Since that time, emphasis on language performance has increased.

The neglect of language skills in the early development of learning disabilities was unfortunate for many reasons. First, because of the basic importance of language in everyday life, the language difficulties students experience should be a foremost target for remediation. Second, the need for language skills in virtually all areas of academic achievement means that these skills are crucial to success in school. Third, estimates of the prevalence of disorders of spoken language among students with learning disabilities reveal that they are among the most common problems LD students experience.

The spoken-language disabilities of students with learning disabilities are the topic of this chapter. The characteristics of these problems, means for assessing them, and methods for helping students overcome them are presented in the following sections.

CHARACTERISTICS

Difficulties in learning language skills have been seen as quite common in learning disabilities for many years. Influential figures such as Orton (1937), Kirk (1976), Strauss and Kephart (1955), and Johnson and Myklebust (1967) emphasized the importance of language in their work.

Terminology

Competence-Performance Language theorists emphasize a distinction between *competence* and *performance*. Competence refers to the hidden knowledge of language that nearly all people are presumed to have. Performance refers to language behavior, both listening and speaking. Often confused with the competence-performance issue is the comprehension-production dichotomy. Comprehension refers to a person's ability to understand what is spoken, and production refers to his or her ability to use language expressively. The competence-performance issue is the more general of the two in that it applies to both comprehension and production. The comprehension-production distinction is concerned with the more concrete differentiation between listening and speaking.

The practical importance of the comprehension-production dichotomy is that comprehension usually develops prior to production. Eisenson (1972) provided an example of this:

> Almost all children can detect fine shades of differences before they can themselves produce them. A child may persist in his "kicky" for *kitty,* but reject this pronunciation from an adult; he

may still produce "wawipop" at age five but resent such an offering from an older person. What the child is demonstrating by this apparently inconsistent language behavior is that at age four or five he has better phonemic discrimination, and so better expectations in regard to listening, than he has motor control over his own production. (p. 17)

Linguistic Terms Linguistics—the study of language—has emphasized several aspects of language. These include *phonology, syntax, morphology, semantics,* and, somewhat recently, *pragmatics*. Each of these features of language is described in Table 6.1 on p. 178.

Teachers of LD students often work with speech pathologists on diagnostic and remedial procedures for those students who have disabilities in spoken language. The field of speech pathology has produced a great deal of work on language problems. One area of study of speech pathology that is related to learning disabilities but is considered to be more in the realm of speech pathology is *aphasia*. Aphasia refers to difficulty in acquiring a system of language (Eisenson, 1972).

Normal Language Development

The major milestones in the normal development of language have been documented (e.g., Menyuk, 1972). At birth, the infant cries. Starting with the birth cry, believed to be a reflex response to the pain of breathing on his or her own, the infant for several weeks engages in crying as a response to discomfort. Crying of this sort has been termed "undifferentiated crying" because it does not seem to change on the basis of various states of discomfort (Eisenson, 1972).

At about 2 months of age, the infant begins to use two new responses. Cooing sounds emerge and the infant's crying seems to differ according to the situations in which it occurs. These differences in crying can be thought of

Table 6.1 Terms Used in Linguistics

Term	Meaning	Examples
Phonology	The sound system of language	A letter may have different sounds under different conditions: s = "sss" in *hiss* but "zzz" in *his*.
Syntax	The grammatic structure of language	These sentences have different structures but equivalent meanings: "His hair is red" and "He has red hair."
Morphology	The units of meaning of language and how they are expressed	The word *women* has two meaningful parts: woman & plural.
Semantics	The meaning of language	The sentence "Nothing is too good for him" has two possible meanings.
Pragmatics	The use of different language depending on circumstances	To an authority figure one might say, "I disagree" but to a friend one might say, "Aw, come off it."

as based on whether the child is physically uncomfortable or socially isolated.

From about 3 to 6 months of age, the infant engages in babbling. This stage is often considered a crucial one for the later development of speech because it causes changes in the infant's environment (Eisenson, 1972) and it is important for the child to learn that he or she can operate on the environment by making noises. Infants learn this when adults, particularly parents, attend to and reinforce babbling.

At about 8 or 9 months of age, according to Eisenson, the child enters a stage of echolalia. At this point, the infant begins to imitate speech sounds. If an adult says something, the child will attempt to say the same thing.

At about 1 year of age the child utters his or her first words. Primitive sentences are formed at about 18 months. From this point on, language acquisition occurs exceedingly rapidly in terms of the complexities of language that are to be mastered. By 3 or 4 years, the child is able to use most of the basic types of sentences of the language, although subtle and complex ones must still be learned during later years (C. Chomsky, 1969).

Atypical Development and Problems

Pupils with language disabilities may have difficulties in any of several areas of language. Although some studies (Semel & Wiig, 1975) have reported that learning-disabled students differ from normally achieving pupils on both expressive and receptive language skills, it seems they have greater difficulty using spoken language to express themselves than they do understanding the spoken language of others (Hessler & Kitchen, 1980; Noel, 1980; Wong & Roadhouse, 1978). Some of the specific areas of language that may cause difficulties are *phonology, statement repetition, syntax, morphology, semantics,* and *pragmatics.* Each area is discussed in the following sections.

Phonology

Development As already noted, the first sounds produced by infants are crying, cooing, and babbling. How speakers arrive at understanding and producing the sounds used in language is the province of phonemic development and use, or phonology. Shortly after birth, infants are capable of discriminating be-

Language skills develop very rapidly. During infancy, young children learn many things about language from everyday interactions with those around them.

tween sounds on the bases of frequency, intensity, and duration; a few months later, they can discriminate between speech and nonspeech sounds and friendly and unfriendly voices (Menyuk, 1972).

Children learn to discriminate sounds on the basis of their distinctive features (Jacobson, 1941/1968), much as they use distinctive features to discriminate visual patterns (see discussion of Eleanor Gibson's work in Chapter 2). Some of the aspects that children use to hear differences are the consonantal, nasal, strident, and voiced features of speech sounds. These and other distinctive features of speech can be used to predict which sounds will be more or less difficult to discriminate. The first actual speech sounds that children use are those that are highly discriminable on the basis of distinctive features. That children's first words often are "mama" and "papa" is predicted by a distinctive features analysis because these words are composed of easily discriminable speech sounds (Menyuk, 1972) and are most likely to

be reinforced and shaped by attention and other forms of reinforcement from parents.

Problems Problems with phonological production or speech are usually referred to as articulation problems. Mastery of articulation requires the development of control over the muscles used in speaking but does not necessarily imply difficulties with understanding spoken language. Students with articulatory problems *may* or *may not* have difficulties with understanding speech.

Problems with *auditory discrimination* have often been discussed in the field of learning disabilities. Auditory discrimination refers to an individual's skill in telling the difference between sounds. One test of auditory discrimination would be to show a child pictures of a rake and a lake and then tell him or her to touch the picture of a "lake"; in this way, one could tell whether the sounds were heard correctly. In a review of many studies of the relationship between phonological skills and reading, Kavale

(1981b) found that auditory discrimination correlated with reading achievement. However, the correlation is not particularly great (Gersten & Carnine, 1984) and it is unclear to what extent this relationship indicates a need for training (Hammill & Larsen, 1974b; Rozin & Gleitman, 1977; Sabatino, 1973).

Problems with phonemic *segmentation* are said to exist when children cannot separate words into their parts (sounds). Rhyming, for example, requires that the last sounds of a word be held constant while the first sounds are changed. Skill in segmenting words into their constituent sounds appears to be closely related to early reading achievement (Rozin & Gleitman, 1977), and this relationship led Tarver and Ellsworth (1981) to argue that difficulties with phonemic segmentation may be fundamental to learning-disabled students' difficulties with reading.

Problems with *sound blending* may also reflect children's difficulties with phonology. Sound blending—essentially the opposite of phonemic segmentation—is used to collapse separated phonemes into a whole. For example, the sounds *mmm, iii, sss,* and *t* can be blended into the word *mist.* Sound blending correlates with reading achievement and discriminates good from poor readers, with poor readers having weaker sound-blending skills (Kass, 1966; Kavale, 1981b; Richardson, DiBenedetto, & Bradley, 1977; Richardson, DiBenedetto, Christ, & Press, 1980). However, the relationship between sound blending and reading is thought to be less obvious when scores are controlled for IQ (Hammill & Larsen, 1974b; Harber, 1980a; Larsen, Rogers, & Sowell, 1976), although some evidence contradicts this (e.g., Richardson et al., 1980).

Statement Repetition   Many skills are required for understanding and using spoken language. Some of these skills are quite rudimentary and others are quite complicated. For example, the ability to rephrase a sentence so that it is changed from passive to active voice is fairly complicated; one must alter many words in the sentence. In contrast, the ability to repeat a statement is relatively simple; one must say only what one heard.

However, statement repetition is fundamental, for without this skill, students cannot hold a statement in memory long enough to think about it, change it, or do much of anything else with it. It has been repeatedly reported that learning-disabled students do poorly on statement repetition tasks (Hessler & Kitchen, 1980; Hresko, 1979; McNutt & Li, 1980; Vogel, 1974; Wiig & Roach, 1975; Wong & Roadhouse, 1978). Performance on statement repetition tasks may be affected by many of the spoken-language skills described elsewhere. For example, pupils with weaker phonemic skills may have to work so hard at pronouncing words they have heard that when they try to say a complicated word, they forget the remainder of a sentence they are repeating. But statement repetition is clearly one of the skills required for successful learning, and one in which many learning-disabled students are deficient.

Syntax   Syntax refers to the patterns people use to put words together into sentences and is roughly equivalent to "grammar." Studies of syntax have been greatly influenced by N. Chomsky's (1965) view of language as an innate ability of humankind. According to this view, people have an underlying understanding of language (see earlier discussion of competence) that gives them the ability to use different sentence structures to say the same things and very similar structures to say things with different meanings.

Development   Before the age of 3 or 4, at which time they will have mastered most of the basic grammatical structures, children pass through two major stages in their development of syntax. For some time, they use one-word utterances to stand for entire sentences (McNeill,

1970). Later they begin to string words to-gether in rudimentary sentences that omit non-essential words such as articles. For example, a child may say "Allgone shoe" in place of the sentence "The shoe is not here." Usually these beginning forms of syntax give way to more so-phisticated forms long before children enter preschool and as they grow toward adulthood, children and adolescents learn to use sentences that are longer, include more clauses, and so forth.

Problems Learning-disabled students, how-ever, experience problems with syntax. For ex-ample, Hresko (1979) reported that learning-disabled students' repetitions of sentences re-vealed difficulties with declarative forms of sentences and various kinds of clauses. Also, comparisons of learning-disabled and normally achieving students have revealed that LD pupils have greater difficulty selecting a picture to which a sentence refers and choosing a sen-tence that describes a picture (Semel & Wiig, 1975). Furthermore, when the syntax of a sen-tence makes it ambiguous (e.g., "He laughed at the church"), learning-disabled pupils are less likely to realize that it can be interpreted in more than one way (Wiig, Semel, & Abele, 1981).

Some problems with syntax remain even after many years of schooling. For example, Fayne (1981) found that learning-disabled ado-lescents do not understand to what a pronoun refers as well as their normally achieving peers, and Wiig and Semel (1975) found that LD ad-olescents are more likely than their normal peers to produce grammatically incorrect sen-tences. In addition, although their sentences do become longer and more complex as they grow older (Andolina, 1980), learning-disabled chil-dren and adolescents still seem to use sentences that are simpler than those used by their peers (Simms & Crump, 1983).

Morphology Children learn not only the phonology and syntax of their language but also how to change parts of words in ways that change meaning. For example, they learn that by adding an ending to most nouns they can indicate more than one of that thing (e.g., girl + s = more than one girl). These rules of grammar (called morphological rules) have been found to be particularly important for learning disabilities. Berko (1958) developed a widely used method of studying morphology that is illustrated in Figure 6.1. Children are shown pictures of objects and told about them; then they are asked to complete sentences re-quiring the use of particular inflections (changes) in the words for the objects.

Development Children develop morpho-logical rules at a young age. One rule refers to the addition of a letter to the end of a word to indicate that it is plural, as illustrated above. Of course, some words do not follow the usual rules of inflection; for example, the word *fish* may be both the singular and the plural form; the plural of the word *man* does not require the addition of a phoneme, but the change of one (the *aaa* becomes an *eee* to make *men*).

Problems Students with reading disabil-ities do not use morphological rules as well as their peers (Kass, 1966; Vogel; 1974, Wiig, Semel, & Crouse, 1973), regardless of whether they are being tested on real or nonsense words (Vogel, 1974). Their difficulties are particu-larly striking when the plural of a word requires adding a complex ending, such as *box, boxes* (Vogel, 1977); when they must give the third person singular possessive; and when they are asked to create an adjective form of a word (Wiig et al., 1973).

Semantics Semantics is the feature of lan-guage having to do with meaning. Although semantics involves the study of the meanings of words in groups, particularly sentences, most of the information we have about the semantics of learning-disabled pupils has to do with their knowledge of word meanings.

This dog has spots. He is spotty. But this dog has even more spots. He is _____ .

This boy can shake things. Here he is shaking. He does it every day. Every day he _____ .

These are lags. They have hats. Whose hats are they? They are the _____ .

Figure 6.1 Examples of morphological tasks with which learning-disabled children have trouble.
From S. A. Kirk, J. J. McCarthy, and W. D. Kirk (1968). *Examiner Manual: Illinois test of psycholinguistic abilities*, Rev. Ed. Champagne, University of Illinois Press, p. 8. Reprinted with permission.

Studies about the semantic problems of pupils with learning disabilities have produced many conflicting findings. For example, learning-disabled pupils have been shown to have relatively impoverished vocabularies in two studies (Ackerman, Peters, & Dykman, 1971; Myklebust, Bannochie, & Killen, 1971) but not in a third (Wiig & Semel, 1975). Similarly, learning-disabled students have been reported to have more difficulty than their normally achieving peers in using words to label pictures in one study (Wiig & Semel, 1975) but not in another (German, 1979). These disagreements among studies may be attributed to differences in how the researchers defined *learning disabled* when selecting their samples (see discussions of definition in Chapters 1 and 10), how the students' performance was measured, and other factors (e.g., age of pupils tested).

It does appear, however, that pupils with language disabilities have at least some problems with semantics. They have difficulty completing an orally presented sentence that has a common word missing, and they find it hard to name an object that has been described by its features (parts and function). Their problems are more apparent when the words that are missing and the words for the objects described are "low-frequency" words (do not occur often in children's reading materials) (German, 1979). Furthermore, LD pupils have difficulties in understanding sentences in which an ambiguous word is used; for example, they may not realize that the sentence, "He was drawing a gun," can have two different meanings (Wiig et al., 1981). Also, LD adolescents take longer and make more errors than their normally achieving peers when asked to name antonyms (e.g., told "brother," they were to say "sister") and make more errors when trying to define common words such as *robin, bridge,* and *opinion* (Wiig & Semel, 1975).

The study of pragmatic aspects of language reveals that people use language differently depending on social situations. These students would use different language if they were talking to their parents or teachers.

Ken Karp

Pragmatics Pragmatics refers to the way in which language is used in social situations. People alter how they speak depending on whom they are speaking to, why they are speaking, and other factors. For example, most children use shorter and simpler sentences when talking to someone clearly younger than themselves than when talking to someone nearly the same age or older (Shatz & Gelman, 1973). However, boys (but not girls) classified as learning disabled use more complicated and longer communication patterns when explaining to younger children how to play a game than when explaining to their age-mates how to play the same game (Bryan & Pflaum, 1978). Also, pupils with learning disabilities are less effective in providing descriptive information about objects than their normally achieving peers (Noel, 1980). That is, when they are required to describe something so that another person can select it from an array of choices, they will not do as well as normally learning students. Normally learning students used labels more frequently and LD students used terms referring to the shape of objects more frequently.

Mistakes in how they use language may lead to social problems for learning-disabled pupils, as discussed in the previous chapter. For example, Bryan, Wheeler, Felcan, and Henek (1976) reported that learning-disabled students used more competitive statements in their conversations with peers, but normally achieving students made more comments showing consideration. Speaking competitively may cause hard feelings and even lead to arguments and fights. Thus, poor spoken language skills may be related to the social problems of LD pupils.

ASSESSMENT

Traditionally, it was assumed that children's general language ability was best assessed by measuring their IQ. Because intelligence tests rely heavily on language abilities, IQ was considered a good indicator of verbal ability. This was thought to be particularly true with such IQ tests as the Wechsler Intelligence Scale for Children—Revised or WISC-R (Wechsler, 1974) that have subtests designed to assess language performance (e.g., vocabulary).

However, one of the major influences on learning disabilities during the 1960s and 1970s was the development and use of tests specifically intended to measure language abilities. Occasionally, these instruments were used as *screening* devices—i.e., they were administered to determine whether individual students were so different from their peers that they needed further testing. More often, however, they were used as *diagnostic* devices—i.e., they were administered to determine what deficits should be remediated or at what point in an instructional program a student should begin work. Although there are other legitimate purposes for assessment (see Ysseldyke & Shinn, 1981), these two are particularly important for those working with the language problems of learning-disabled students. In the following sections, assessment programs for screening and diagnosing the spoken-language skills of students with learning disabilities are described.

Screening of spoken language skills usually follows a referral. The referral is likely to come from a regular class teacher who has noticed that a student seems different from his or her peers. Referrals may also be based on observed scores on instruments measuring performance in another area. For example, some reading tests provide information about students' vocabulary development; a low score on one of these instruments may encourage educators to refer students for screening.

As mentioned previously, most of the instruments used for diagnosis are also used for screening; these will be considered together in this section. Some of the instruments, however, were designed to focus on one or a few spoken-language skills, while others were created to assess many skills. These types will be considered separately in the following subsections.

Tests of Specific Areas

Spoken-language competence may be divided into many subareas. Some of these subareas that have been of particular concern to people who work with LD students are *auditory discrimination, vocabulary, sentence comprehension*, and *expression*.

Auditory Discrimination   Two important tests of auditory discrimination are the *Auditory Discrimination Test* (Wepman, 1958, 1973), and the *Goldman-Fristoe-Woodcock Test of Auditory Discrimination* (Goldman, Fristoe, & Woodcock, 1970). Wepman's test has been one of those most frequently used in learning disabilities to assess auditory perceptual ability. In it, a young child is presented with two words and asked whether they are alike or different. The words are either the same or different with regard to their beginning, middle, or ending sounds (e.g., *mop-pop, bed-bad, rap-rat*). Children who mistakenly identify words as the same when they are actually different, or different when they are actually the same, are thought to have difficulties in discriminating the sounds of speech.

The Goldman-Fristoe-Woodcock test also is designed to assess auditory discrimination abilities, but it does so slightly differently from the Wepman. In the Goldman-Fristoe-Woodcock, a tape recorder plays individual words to the child and he or she is required to select the one picture from among four choices that corresponds to the word. The four pictures show words in which only the initial or final consonant sounds differ. Mistakes on the choices of pictures are thought to indicate difficulties in

discriminating specific sounds of the spoken language.

Vocabulary   The *Peabody Picture Vocabulary Test—Revised* (Dunn & Dunn, 1981), along with its prior edition, is probably the most widely used test of vocabulary after the vocabulary subtest of the WISC-R. The Peabody is designed for use with individuals ranging in age from 2½ to 40. It requires the subject to select from among four drawings the one that corresponds to a word said by the examiner. The Peabody is frequently administered to give a quick estimate of IQ based solely on vocabulary.

Sentence Comprehension and Expression   The *Northwestern Syntax Screening Test* (Lee, 1971) and the *Carrow Elicited Language Inventory* or CELI (Carrow, 1974) assess students' comprehension and use of sentences. The Northwestern test is a two-part screening instrument that provides information about students' understanding of syntax. On one part of the test, designed to assess comprehension of sentences, the subject selects from among four drawings. The examiner reads two sentences, repeats one of them, and then asks the subject which picture illustrates the sentence that was said twice. Then the subject is told to indicate which picture corresponds to the other sentence. In the second part, the examiner shows pictures and says pairs of sentences, then points to a picture and requests that the subject repeat the sentence corresponding to it. The examiner points to another picture and asks the subject to repeat the sentence of the given pair that corresponds to it.

The CELI is a diagnostic instrument for evaluating young students' verbal expression. The examiner says a sentence and then the student repeats it. Each sentence is scored on the basis of whether the student's imitation included various grammatical parts (e.g., pronouns, prepositions, conjunctions, and so forth). Thus the examiner can learn which parts of the grammar of spoken language the student uses correctly in statement repetition tasks.

Comprehensive Tests

In contrast to tests of specific aspects of spoken language, several comprehensive tests have been designed to assess many facets of spoken language. Usually, these tests include several subtests for assessing components of language competence that may resemble tests of specific aspects of spoken language. For example, one subtest of a comprehensive test may be designed to evaluate verbal expression skills.

The language test that has received the most mention within the field of learning disabilities is the *Illinois Test of Psycholinguistic Abilities* or ITPA (Kirk, McCarthy, & Kirk, 1968). The ITPA has done much to further the development of the field of learning disabilities (see also Kirk, 1976). In particular, it has stressed the idea of intraindividual assessment and of testing for educational purposes. Because of its integral association with the field of learning disabilities, the ITPA is discussed in some detail here (see also Box 6.1).

The ITPA was designed to allow clinicians to assess specific processes presumed to be associated with school success. The history of the instrument (see Kirk, 1969, for a recounting) reveals that the purpose of the test was to make it possible to identify a student's deficit areas and then adjust instruction to meet that student's individual needs. The presumption underlying this approach is that individuals have unique strengths and weaknesses that can be identified by examining performance on tasks that tap very specific skills.

Clearly the idea of intraindividual differences is central to the field of learning disabil-

ities. Since its publication, however, the ITPA—as well as, to some extent, the idea of intraindividual differences—has received substantial criticism. The test has been criticized on these grounds: The idea of underlying processes governing behavior has not been substantiated; the subtests do not actually measure different abilities or processes; the standardization of the test was inadequate; and the test's reliability was too low to make it trustworthy for deciding such important matters as how or what students should be taught. These criticisms, and others, are discussed in detail in Engelmann (1967), Hallahan and Cruickshank (1973), Mann (1971), Sedlak and Weiner (1973), Waugh (1975), and Ysseldyke and Salvia (1974).

More recently, the *Test of Language Development* or TOLD (Newcomer & Hammill, 1977) was developed. The focus of the TOLD is on assessment of the major aspects of spoken language, including phonology, syntax, and semantics. Five subtests and two supplementary tests are included. The five subtests are (1) Picture Vocabulary, (2) Oral Vocabulary, (3) Grammatical Understanding, (4) Sentence Imitation, and (5) Grammatical Completion. The two supplementary tests are Word Discrimination and Word Pronunciation. The TOLD may be used as both a diagnostic and a screening device.

The *Utah Test of Language Development* (Mecham, Jex, & Jones, 1967) and the *Slingerland Screening Tests for Identifying Children with Specific Language Disability* (Slingerland, 1970) are other more general tests sometimes used by learning disabilities specialists. The Utah test is a comprehensive spoken-language assessment device designed for use with atypical students. Several language behaviors are measured, including repetition of digits, naming of colors, naming of pictures, and following directions. Also included are items re-

Box 6.1
ITPA

The ITPA was designed to correspond to Osgood's (1957a, 1957b) communications model, which is composed of (1) *channels* of communication, (2) psycholinguistic *processes* of communication, and (3) *levels* of organization. Channels refer to the various sensory modalities through which information can pass (e.g., visual-motor or auditory-verbal). Processes refer to the actions happening to the information in the channels; the processes are reception (input of information), association (manipulations of concepts or linguistic information), and expression (output of information). Levels refer to how much "thinking" is required; the levels of organization are representational (information is manipulated symbolically) and automatic (information is manipulated without conscious effort and is more rote or habitual).

The 12 subtests of the ITPA are shown schematically in Figure 6.2. Six subtests can

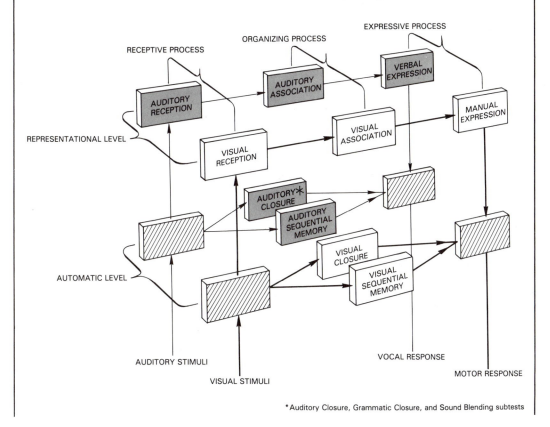

*Auditory Closure, Grammatic Closure, and Sound Blending subtests

Figure 6.2 Subtests of the ITPA.
From S. A. Kirk, D. J. McCarthy, and W. D. Kirk (1968). Examiner's manual: Illinois test of psycholinguistic abilities, Rev. Ed. Champaign IL: University of Illinois Press, p. 8. Reprinted with permission.

be given at the representational level. Two involve the receptive process (Visual Reception and Auditory Reception), two involve the organizing process (Visual-Motor Association and Auditory-Vocal Association), and two involve the expressive process (Motor Expression and Verbal Expression). Six other subtests can be given at the automatic level: Visual Sequential Memory, Auditory Sequential Memory, Visual Closure, Auditory Closure, Grammatic Closure, and Sound Blending.

Each of the subtests was designed so that responding to the items on it required that the subject use only one ability and so that the items increase in difficulty the further through a subtest the subject goes. These are descriptions of the subtests:

> Visual Reception: Child is shown picture of an object and then shown pictures of four other objects; she or he must select the one which is from the same category.
>
> Auditory Reception: Child is asked to answer "Yes" or "No" to questions like "Do dogs eat?" "Do dogs fly?" "Do mute musicians vocalize?"
>
> Visual-Motor Association: Child chooses a picture of an object that goes with a stimulus (e.g., shown a bone, child chooses dog rather than pipe, rattle, or pencil).
>
> Auditory-Vocal Association: Child completes verbal analogies (e.g., "Bread is to eat; milk is to _____").
>
> Motor Expression: Child demonstrates what to do with a pictured object (e.g., strums and fingers the frets of a guitar).
>
> Verbal Expression: Child describes common objects (e.g., nail), earning a higher score by giving more complex and thorough descriptions.
>
> Visual Sequential Memory: Child is shown a card depicting a series of shapes and then must arrange tile with those shapes on them into the same order from memory.
>
> Auditory Sequential Memory: Child repeats sequences of numbers said by examiner.
>
> Visual Closure: Child is shown a line drawing and directed to find objects in it; many of which may be only shown in part.
>
> Auditory Closure: Child is asked to say what examiner said although examiner omits some sounds when saying item (e.g., given "re/ig//ator," child should say "refrigerator").
>
> Grammatic Closure: Child gives correct grammatical form to complete statements shown in pictures (e.g., given "This man is painting. He is a _____," the child should say "painter").
>
> Sound Blending: Child is given words separated into sounds and asked to say them (e.g., given "z-ee-f," child should say "zeef").

quiring non-spoken-language skills such as copying of designs and reading.

The Slingerland was intended to be used as a screening device for young children. Some of its subtests measure spoken-language skills in the areas of auditory discrimination, auditory perception, auditory memory, word and sentence imitation, and story retelling. Others were designed to assess such areas as visual copying, visual memory, and visual discrimination.

INTERVENTIONS

Intervention in the language disorders of students with learning disabilities is influenced by several factors. Among these influences are the theoretical conceptions of language that teachers adopt and the programs and materials available for teaching. In the following sections, these topics are discussed.

Behavioral Versus Nativistic Approaches

Although there are many theoretical explanations of how language is acquired—and therefore how it ought to be taught—most positions fall into two broad camps: behavioral and nativistic. The behavioral position explains language behavior in terms of *learning*; the nativistic position considers language to be a *native* ability. Simple descriptions of the theoretical aspects of these approaches and resulting interventions are presented in the following paragraphs.

Behavioral Many people think that learning principles can be used to explain language acquisition. Skinner (1957) popularized the position that operant conditioning is the primary means of learning language. Since then, others (e.g., Jenkins & Palmero, 1964; Staats, 1968, 1974) have expanded on these ideas.

According to behavioral explanations, the speaking behavior of individuals is learned. Children's language skills are "taught" by the environment. Processes such as modeling (children hear others saying words and observe the effects that speaking has) and reinforcement (the use of language has effects on the child's environment) influence performance. Production of words is *shaped*: Environmental contingencies may reward a toddler for saying "cah-cah" but will only reward an older child for saying "car." Word meanings are learned by *differential reinforcement*: People around a

child will react one way if he or she says "blue" when pointing to a blue object and another way if he or she says "blue" when pointing to a red object. Syntactic skills are developed by learning *response classes*: Children can say, "I see," and then nearly anything else (e.g., "you," "a dog," "a girl who is running," "the point you are trying to make"), depending on the circumstances.

Interventions based on a behavioral approach are direct and systematic. Specific language skills are identified and activities are designed to get students to use those skills. As the students use them, their teachers provide reinforcement of accurate usage and correction of mistakes. For example, if a student does not know the usual plural form of *man* (e.g., the student says "mens" rather than "men"), the

Teachers use expansion to help students learn better language skills.

Paul Conklin, Monkmeyer

teacher might model the correct form ("Listen to me say it: men"), provide the student with an opportunity to repeat it correctly ("How do you say it?"), and praise common usage ("That's it! *Men.* You said it correctly!"). The teacher might then provide other opportunities for practice under different conditions to help the student remember the pronunciation. For example, while showing a picture of adult males, the teacher might say, "Tell me about these people. Are they boys? That's correct; they're not boys. What are they? Yes! They are *men.*" Related morphological forms (e.g., *wo-men*) might be assessed and taught, if necessary.

Nativistic   In contrast to the behavioral position, which stresses the importance of the environment and its influence on the behavior of the speaker, the nativistic position emphasizes the importance of innate abilities and the interpretations of the listener. The nativistic orientation was originally based largely on N. Chomsky's (1957) work on syntax, then received a big boost from his review of Skinner's (1957) work (N. Chomsky, 1959). One of the leading advocates of the nativistic position is McNeill (1966, 1970). McNeill and others emphasize the idea that language abilities are genetically transmitted, that there is an understanding of language "wired" into the brain at birth.

One of the main reasons nativists advocate this idea is that language performance is incredibly diverse. Any page of a newly written book, for example, is very unlikely to have on it lines of print that have appeared in the exact same form anywhere else (except quotations, of course). Similarly, children speak sentences they have never previously heard. According to nativists, such diversity negates any possible behavioral explanation of language.

Furthermore, according to the nativistic position, the fact that different strings of words can represent very similar ideas suggests that there is an underlying structure to language.

For example, the idea in the sentence "Jane played the song" can also be stated in another form without changing the idea: "The song was played by Jane." According to nativists, not only do these two sentences have the same "deep structure"—the same abstract basis—but children possess the innate ability to understand that these two sentences have the same deep structure.

Interventions based on a nativistic position deemphasize the importance of direct teaching and stress the value of discovery learning. Although nativists consider environment important, their approach is based less on having teachers initiate instruction and more on having them respond to children's use of language. According to McNeill (1970):

> A language is thus acquired through [a child's] discovering the relations that exist between the surface structure of its sentences and the universal aspects of the deep structure, the latter being a manifestation of children's own capacities. The interaction between children's innate capacities and their linguistic experience occurs at this point, in the acquisition of transformations—and it is here that parental speech must make its contributions. (p. 1088)

One of the primary means nativists use to encourage acquisition of language is *expansion.* Expansion refers to an adult responding in an interpretive way to children's utterances: the adult *expands* on what a child says. For example, if the child says "Doggie gone," the adult might say "Yes, the doggie is gone." In this way, it is hoped that the child will learn the more grammatically complete form for the idea that he or she expressed when saying "Doggie gone."

Programs and Techniques

Most of the actual interventions that have been used with learning-disabled children and adolescents have not been exclusively aligned with one or the other of the basic approaches to language. In fact, the interventions have been based more on clinical and classroom experience than on any theory.

Psycholinguistic Psycholinguistic interventions were particularly popular during the 1960s and 1970s. Among the interventions in this group were many that were based on the ITPA (Kirk et al., 1968) and others that, although not expressly related to the test, were based on many of the same assumptions. It was assumed that specific language abilities or processes could be isolated and that each skill could be trained using educational techniques. For example, inability to remember sequences as measured by the Auditory Sequential Memory subtest of the ITPA might be remediated by providing extensive practice in following multistep directions (e.g., "Go to the door, open it, close it, walk backward to the bookshelf, touch a big red book, come back to your seat, and sit down") and other activities.

There have been many programs and recommendations about psycholinguistic training. For example, Kirk and Kirk (1971) provided specific remedial recommendations, and a book by Bush and Giles (1977) has chapters that correspond exactly with the subtests of the ITPA. Similarly, there are kits that include many activities for work on various processes. For example, the *MWM Program for Developing Language Abilities* (Minskoff, Wiseman, & Minskoff, 1972) and the *GOAL Program* (Karnes, 1972) both contain teaching manuals that describe activities and materials for carrying out the activities (e.g., picture cards) that are designed to teach the processes measured by the ITPA.

Probably the most widely known program related to psycholinguistic training is the *Peabody Language Development Program* (Dunn, Smith, Dunn, Horton, & Smith, 1981). This program, the revised version of an immensely popular earlier one, is composed of four kits and is designed to be used with children of preschool, primary-, and elementary-school age.

Unlike many other programs with ties to psycholinguistics, the Peabody program does not recommend activities for specific processes; instead, it is aimed at general language development. The kits include teachers' manuals and other materials (e.g., picture cards, puppets) for use in daily lessons. The Peabody program also emphasizes the use of behavior modification techniques.

Many studies of remedial training based on the ITPA have reported that these activities are ineffective. For example, Hammill and Larsen (1974a) reviewed the results of 39 studies and found that fewer than half of the comparisons made in the studies favored pupils given psycholinguistic training. However, advocates of psycholinguistic training (e.g., Lund, Foster, & McCall-Perez, 1978) disagreed with these analyses. More recently, Kavale (1981a) examined research on psycholinguistic training and reported that there was some evidence of effectiveness.

Cognitive-Psycholinguistic Cognitive-psycholinguistic interventions are most closely associated with nativistic theory. In the early development of the field of learning disabilities, the term *psycholinguistic* was almost invariably associated with the ITPA. More recently, however, it has been used to refer to approaches that are influenced by the study of the mixture of psychology and linguistics—an area dominated by advocates of nativistic (and antibehavioristic) theory. Cognitive-psycholinguistic authorities generally do not align themselves with the ITPA and related training programs.

Lee, Koenigsknecht, and Mulhern (1975) described methods of intervention that are consistent with the cognitive-psycholinguistic approach. The techniques they advocate are rooted in conversation with children and are very similar to the process of expansion, discussed previously. In this approach, the teacher presents stories (arranged according to level of linguistic difficulty) and then asks questions in order to get students to use various forms of sentences. Using the sentence that a student utters as a base, the teacher employs one of several different techniques to encourage a more grammatically acceptable sentence. For example, when a student uses the wrong inflection of a verb in a sentence (e.g., "He eated bananas"), the teacher might (1) ask the pupil to repeat the sentence ("What did you say?") in the hope that it will then be said correctly by the pupil; (2) repeat the mistaken statement ("He eated bananas?") to encourage the pupil to make the correction; or (3) ask the pupil whether the statement was correct ("Is 'He eated bananas' correct?") to encourage self-correction. Lee and colleagues report that their experience with these techniques leads them to believe they are effective and that some experimental data confirm their belief.

Semel has developed two programs that are consistent with cognitive-psycholinguistic ideas. One is the *Sound-Order-Sense* program (SOS; Semel, 1970) and the other is the *Semel Auditory Processing Program* (SAPP; Semel, 1976). The SOS program is designed to help children develop listening skills that they can use in comprehending spoken language. As its name implies, the activities in the SOS program stress *sound* (perception of sounds), *order* (remembering the order of things that have been said), and *sense* (semantics). There are special features of the program, such as books printed in a way that allows pupils to know immediately whether they have answered correctly. SOS includes 2 years of daily lessons designed to be used with children of primary-school age.

The SAPP is designed to help children develop skills in processing and interpreting language. Activities were selected to provide work

In many language intervention programs, teachers work with several children in a group. A common activity is having children describe an object.

on auditory memory, morphology, syntax, semantics, and other types of language skills. The activities (e.g., morphemic segmentation, sentence completion) used to encourage learning of language skills are deliberately varied to induce more general learning. The entire program is composed of three levels and can be used with students ranging from 3 years old to the teen years. In a study undertaken to evaluate the results of the SAPP, Semel and Wiig (1981) reported LD students of elementary-school age made substantial gains on several measures of language development during the time their teachers were following the program.

Task Analytic Task-analytic interventions are most closely associated with a behavioral perspective on language. In task-analytic programs, activities are designed to teach specific subskills of language and to help students integrate these subskills into more general language competence. DISTAR Language (Engelmann & Osborn, 1977), the comprehension strand of the *Corrective Reading* program (Engelmann, Becker, Hanner, & Johnson, 1978), and the Monterey language program (Gray & Ryan, 1973) are examples of task-analytic programs.

The DISTAR Language program (Engelmann & Osborn, 1977) includes three levels and is designed to be used with children in the primary grades. Unlike the psycholinguistic and cognitive-psycholinguistic programs, which are concerned with global language ability, DISTAR's purpose is to teach the language used in the classroom. Of course, in doing so, it attempts to foster general language development. Daily lessons with scripts for the teacher to follow include activities for work on basic skills (e.g., descriptions, pronouns, asking questions) and lead up to work on traditional language activities (e.g., identification of subjects and predicates). Teaching techniques include group instruction, modeling, frequent responding, correction, and reinforcement. DISTAR Language programs were a part of the Direct

Instruction Model tested in the Follow-Through program. According to evaluations of the Follow-Through program, the Direct Instruction Model was the most effective of nine major approaches (Abt Associates, 1976, 1977) and was the only model that had positive effects on children's language performance (House, Glass, McLean, & Walker, 1978). Other studies have revealed similar evidence of effectiveness (Gersten & Maggs, 1982; Maggs & Morath, 1976; Weller, 1979).

The comprehension strand of the *Corrective Reading* program (Engelmann et al., 1978) is very similar to DISTAR Language. It includes two levels, Thinking Basics and Comprehension Skills, with scripted daily lessons for the teacher to follow. Unlike DISTAR Language, which is designed for young children, these comprehension programs are written for older students who need remedial work. According to Engelmann and colleagues (1978), these students

> do not have well-developed recitation skills. They cannot repeat sentences they hear, so they have trouble retaining and answering questions about information that is presented. These students are often prevented from comprehending what they read because they don't even understand the material when it is presented orally. (p. 8)

The program teaches language and thinking skills such as description, classification, definition, analogies, deductions, and vocabulary. After the skills have been taught, they are systematically integrated into the students' reading and writing tasks. Some preliminary evidence indicates that the program has effects on oral vocabulary and reading comprehension (Lloyd, Cullinan, Heins, & Epstein, 1980).

The Monterey program, described by Gray and Ryan (1973), is composed of a highly structured series of tasks, presentation techniques, and evaluation guidelines. Because the program is designed to be used with children who have severe language deficits, it begins with very rudimentary skills, such as naming pictured nouns, and progresses to more sophisticated skills, such as describing events. The teacher uses models, prompts, and reinforcers to increase the students' language production. Interestingly, aspects of the Monterey program are based on a nativistic perspective (e.g., the sequence of syntax tasks was drawn from nativistic work), even though the program has a strong behavioral orientation. Evaluations of the program have shown that it is effective (Gray & Ryan, 1973; Matheny & Panagos, 1978).

SUMMARY

Mastery of oral language skills is necessary not only in everyday life, but also in virtually all areas of academic learning. It is important to understand spoken-language disabilities, because they very often accompany learning disabilities.

Those who study language skills concern themselves with people's *competence* (the hidden knowledge of language) and *performance* (language behavior). Authorities believe that the ability to comprehend spoken language develops before the ability to produce it. Linguists describe listening and speaking skills according to several characteristics: *phonology, syntax, morphology, semantics,* and *pragmatics.*

Learning-disabled pupils may have difficulties in any of the various aspects of language performance. Some research in learning disabilities has suggested that certain phonological skills (particularly, segmenting words into sounds and blending sounds into words) present difficulties for learning-disabled students. Other research reveals that these pupils have difficulty imitating statements. Still other research shows that learning-disabled students perform less well than their normally achieving peers in the areas of syntax and semantics. Furthermore, they lag behind their peers in mastering automatic rules of language such as those that are used when changing a word into another of its forms (refer back to Figure 6.1). Finally, learning-disabled children and youth do not modify their use of language to fit the demands of the social situations in which they find themselves.

Assessment of language performance has been accomplished by the use of many different tests. Among these are tests of specific skills such as those designed to measure auditory discrimination and tests of a more general nature. Often, the latter tests are composed of several subtests devoted to performance in specific areas of language development, and the scores from these subtests may be combined to estimate a level of general language development.

Instructional approaches to language learning have differed about the relative importance of people's inherent language competence and the effects of environmental factors. Nativistic approaches place greater emphasis on responding to pupils' spontaneous language, but behavioral approaches place greater emphasis on structuring environments that support higher language achievement. Successful developmental and remedial language programs, although they may seem inclined in one or the other direction, incorporate features consistent with both nativistic and behavioral approaches.

REFERENCES

Abt Associates. (1976). *Education as experimentation: A planned variation model* (Vol. III-A). Cambridge, MA: Author.

Abt Associates. (1977). *Education as experimentation: A planned variation model* (Vol. IV). Cambridge, MA: Author.

ACKERMAN, P. T., PETERS, J. E., & DYKMAN, R. A. (1971). Children with specific learning disabilities: WISC profiles. *Journal of Learning Disabilities, 4,* 150–166.

ANDOLINA, C. (1980). Syntactic maturity and vocabulary richness of learning disabled children at four age levels. *Journal of Learning Disabilities, 13*, 372–377.

BERKO, J. (1958). The child's learning of English morphology. *Word, 14*, 150–177.

BRYAN, T. H., & PFLAUM, S. (1978). Social interactions of learning disabled children: A linguistic, social and cognitive analysis. *Learning Disability Quarterly, 1*(3), 70–79.

BRYAN, T. H., WHEELER, R., FELCAN, J., & HENEK, T. (1976). "Come on, Dummy:" An observational analysis of children's communications. *Journal of Learning Disabilities, 9*, 661–669.

BUSH, W. J., & GILES, M. T. (1977). *Aids to psycholinguistic teaching* (2nd ed.). Columbus, OH: Charles Merrill.

CARROW, E. (1974). *Carrow Elicited Language Inventory.* Austin, TX: Learning Concepts.

CHOMSKY, C. (1969). *The acquisition of syntax in children from 5 to 10.* Cambridge, MA: MIT Press.

CHOMSKY, N. A. (1957). *Syntactic structures.* The Hague: Mouton.

CHOMSKY, N. A. (1959). Review of *Verbal Behavior* by B. F. Skinner. *Language, 35*, 26–58.

CHOMSKY, N. A. (1965). *Aspects of the theory of syntax.* Cambridge, MA: MIT Press.

DUNN, L. M., & DUNN, L. (1981). *Peabody Picture Vocabulary Test—Revised.* Circle Pines, MN: American Guidance Service.

DUNN, L. M., SMITH, J. O., DUNN, L. M., HORTON, K. B., & SMITH, D. D. (1981). *Peabody language development kits—Revised.* Circle Pines, MN: American Guidance Service.

EISENSON, J. (1972). *Aphasia in children.* New York: Harper & Row.

ENGELMANN, S. (1967). The relationship between psychological theories and the act of teaching. *Journal of School Psychology, 5*, 92–100.

ENGELMANN, S., BECKER, W. C., HANNER, S., & JOHNSON, G. (1978). *Corrective reading* (series guide). Chicago: Science Research Associates.

ENGELMANN, S., & OSBORN, J. (1977). *DISTAR Language.* Chicago: Science Research Associates.

FAYNE, H. R. (1981). A comparison of learning disabled adolescents with normal learners on an anaphoric pronominal reference task. *Journal of Learning Disabilities, 14*, 597–599.

GERMAN, D. J. N. (1979). Word-finding skills in children with learning disabilities. *Journal of Learning Disabilities, 12*, 176–181.

GERSTEN, R., & CARNINE, D. (1984). On the relationship between auditory-perceptual skills and reading: A response to Kavale's meta-analysis. *Remedial and Special Education, 5*(1), 16–19.

GERSTEN, R. M., & MAGGS, A. (1982). Teaching the general case to moderately retarded children: Evaluation of a five year project. *Analysis and Intervention in Developmental Disabilities, 2*, 329–343.

GOLDMAN, R., FRISTOE, M., & WOODCOCK, R. W. (1970). *Goldman-Fristoe-Woodcock Test of Auditory Discrimination.* Circle Pines, MN: American Guidance Service.

GRAY, B., & RYAN, B. (1973). *A language program for the nonlanguage child.* Champaign, IL: Research Press.

HALLAHAN, D. P., & CRUICKSHANK, W. M. (1973). *Psychoeducational foundations of learning disabilities.* Englewood Cliffs, NJ: Prentice-Hall.

HAMMILL, D. D., & LARSEN, S. C. (1974a). The effectiveness of psycholinguistic training. *Exceptional Children, 41*, 5–14.

HAMMILL, D. D., & LARSEN, S. C. (1974b). The relationship of selected auditory perceptual skills and reading ability. *Journal of Learning Disabilities, 7*, 429–435.

HARBER, J. R. (1980). Auditory perception and reading: Another look. *Learning Disability Quarterly, 3*(3), 19–29.

HESSLER, G., & KITCHEN, D. (1980). Language characteristics of a purposive sample of early elementary learning disabled students. *Learning Disability Quarterly, 3*(3), 36–41.

HOUSE, E. R., GLASS, G. V., MCLEAN, L. D., & WALKER, D. F. (1978). No simple answer: Critique of the Follow-Through evaluation. *Harvard Educational Review, 48*, 128–160.

HRESKO, W. (1979). Elicited imitation ability of children from learning disabled and regular classes. *Journal of Learning Disabilities, 12*, 456–461.

JACOBSON, R. (1968). *Child language, aphasia, and general sound laws* (A. Keiler, Trans.). The Hague: Mouton. (Original work published in 1941.)

JENKINS, J. J., & PALMERO, D. S. (1964). Mediation processes and the acquisition of linguistic structure. In U. Bellugi & R. Brown (Eds.), The acquisition of language. *Monographs of the Society for Research in Child Development, 29*(1, Whole No. 92).

JOHNSON, D. J., & MYKLEBUST, H. R. (1967). *Learning disabilities: Educational principles and practices.* New York: Grune & Stratton.

KARNES, M. (1972). *The GOAL program: Language development.* Springfield, MA: Milton Bradley.

KASS, C. E. (1966). Psycholinguistic disabilities of

children with reading problems. *Exceptional Children, 32,* 533–539.

KAVALE, K. (1981a). Functions of the Illinois Test of Psycholinguistic Abilities (ITPA): Are they trainable? *Exceptional Children, 47,* 496–510.

KAVALE, K. (1981b). The relationship between auditory perceptual skills and reading ability: A meta-analysis. *Journal of Learning Disabilities, 14,* 539–546.

KIRK, S. A. (1969). Illinois Test of Psycholinguistic Abilities: Its origin and implications. In J. Hellmuth (Ed.), *Learning disorders* (Vol. 3; pp. 395–427). Seattle: Special Child.

KIRK, S. A. (1976). S. A. Kirk. In D. P. Hallahan & J. M. Kauffman (Eds.), *Teaching children with learning disabilities: Personal perspectives* (pp. 238–269). Columbus, OH: Charles Merrill.

KIRK, S. A., & KIRK, W. E. (1971). *Psycholinguistic learning disabilities: Diagnosis and remediation.* Urbana, IL: University of Illinois Press.

KIRK, S. A., MCCARTHY, J., & KIRK, W. E. (1968). *Illinois Test of Psycholinguistic Abilities.* Urbana, IL: University of Illinois Press.

KNAPCYZK, D. R., & LIVINGSTON, G. (1974). The effects of prompting question asking upon on-task behavior and reading comprehension. *Journal of Applied Behavior Analysis, 7,* 115–122.

LARSEN, S., ROGERS, D., & SOWELL, V. (1976). The use of selected perceptual tests in differentiating between normal and learning disabled children. *Journal of Learning Disabilities, 9,* 85–90.

LEE, L. (1971). *Northwestern Syntax Screening Test.* Evanston, IL: Northwestern University Press.

LEE, L., KOENIGSKNECHT, R. A., & MULHERN, S. T. (1975). *Interactive language development teaching.* Evanston, IL: Northwestern University Press.

LLOYD, J., CULLINAN, D., HEINS, E. D., & EPSTEIN, M. H. (1980). Direct instruction: Effects on oral and written language comprehension. *Learning Disability Quarterly, 3*(4), 70–76.

LUND, K., FOSTER, G. E., & MCCALL-PEREZ, F. C. (1978). The effectiveness of psycholinguistic training: A reevaluation. *Exceptional Children, 44,* 310–319.

MAGGS, A., & MORATH, P. (1976). Effects of direct verbal instruction on intellectual development of institutionalized moderately retarded children: A 2-year study. *Journal of Special Education, 10,* 357–364.

MANN, L. (1971). Psychometric phrenology and the new faculty psychology. *Journal of Special Education, 5,* 3–14.

MATHENY, N., & PANAGOS, J. M. (1978). Comparing the effects of articulation and syntax programs on syntax and articulation improvement. *Language, Speech, and Hearing Services in Schools, 9,* 57–61.

MCNEILL, D. (1966). Developmental psycholinguistics. In F. Smith & G. A. Miller (Eds.), *The genesis of language: A psycholinguistic approach* (pp. 15–84). Cambridge: MIT Press.

MCNEILL, D. (1970). The development of language. In P. H. Mussen (Ed.), *Carmichael's manual of child psychology* (Vol. 1, 3rd ed., pp. 1061–1161). New York: Wiley.

MCNUTT, J. C., & LI, J. C-Y. (1980). Repetition of time-altered sentences by normal and learning disabled children. *Journal of Learning Disabilities, 13,* 25–29.

MECHAM, M., JEX, J. L., & JONES, J. D. (1967). *Utah Test of Language Development.* Salt Lake City, UT: Communication Research Associates.

MENYUK, P. (1972). *The development of speech.* New York: Bobbs-Merrill.

MINSKOFF, E. H., WISEMAN, D. E., & MINSKOFF, J. G. (1972). *The MWM program for developing language abilities.* Ridgefield, NJ: Educational Performance Association.

MYKLEBUST, H. R., BANNOCHIE, M. N., & KILLEN, J. R. (1971). Learning disabilities and cognitive processes. In H. R. Myklebust (Ed.), *Progress in learning disabilities,* (Vol. 2; pp. 213–251). New York: Grune & Stratton.

NEWCOMER, P. L., & HAMMILL, D. D. (1977). *Test of Language Development.* Austin, TX: Pro-Ed.

NOEL, M. M. (1980). Referential communication abilities of learning disabled children. *Learning Disability Quarterly, 3*(3), 70–87.

ORTON, S. T. (1937). *Reading, writing and speech problems in children.* New York: Norton.

OSGOOD, C. E. (1957a). A behavioristic analysis. In J. Bruner (Ed.), *Contemporary approaches to cognition* (pp. 75–117). Cambridge, MA: Harvard University Press.

OSGOOD, C. E. (1957b). Motivational dynamics of language behavior. In M. R. Jones (Ed.), *Nebraska symposium on motivation* (Vol. 5; pp. 348–424). Lincoln, NE: University of Nebraska Press.

RICHARDSON, E., DIBENEDETTO, B., & BRADLEY, C. M. (1977). The relationship of sound blending to reading achievement. *Review of Educational Research, 47,* 319–334.

RICHARDSON, E., DIBENEDETTO, B., CHRIST, A., & PRESS, M. (1980). Relationship of auditory and visual skills to reading retardation. *Journal of Learning Disabilities, 13,* 77–82.

ROZIN, P., & GLEITMAN, L. R. (1977). The structure

and acquisition of reading II: The reading process and the acquisition of the alphabetic principle. In A. S. Reber & D. L. Scarborough (Eds.), *Toward a psychology of reading: The proceedings of the CUNY Conference* (pp. 55–141). Hillsdale, NJ: Erlbaum.

SABATINO, D. A. (1973). Auditory perception: Development, assessment, and intervention. In L. Mann & D. A. Sabatino (Eds.), *First review of special education*, (Vol. 1; pp. 49–82). Philadelphia: JSE Press.

SEDLAK, R., & WEENER, P. (1973). Review of research on the Illinois Test of Psycholinguistic Abilities. In L. Mann & D. A. Sabatino (Eds.), *First review of special education* (Vol. 1; pp. 113–163). Philadelphia: Buttonwood Farms.

SEMEL, E. (1970). *Sound-order-sense* (Levels 1–2). Chicago: Follett.

SEMEL, E. (1976). *Semel auditory processing program.* Chicago: Follett.

SEMEL, E. M., & WIIG, E. H. (1975). Comprehension of syntactic structures and critical verbal elements by children with learning disabilities. *Journal of Learning Disabilities, 8,* 46–51.

SEMEL, E. M., & WIIG, E. H. (1981). Semel auditory processing program: Training effects among children with language-learning disabilities. *Journal of Learning Disabilities, 14,* 192–197.

SHATZ, M., & GELMAN, R. (1973). The development of communication skills: Modifications in the speech of young children as a function of the listener. *Monographs of the Society for Research in Child Development, 38*(5, Serial No. 152).

SIMMS, R. B., & CRUMP, W. D. (1983). Syntactic development in the oral language of learning disabled and normal students at the intermediate and secondary level. *Learning Disability Quarterly, 6,* 155–165.

SKINNER, B. F. (1957). *Verbal behavior.* Englewood Cliffs, NJ: Prentice-Hall.

SLINGERLAND, B. H. (1970). *Slingerland screening test for identifying children with specific language disability* (2nd ed.). Cambridge MA: Educators Publishing Service.

STAATS, A. W. (1968). *Learning, language, and cognition.* New York: Holt, Rinehart & Winston.

STAATS, A. W. (1974). Behaviorism and cognitive theory in the study of language: A neopsycholinguistics. In R. L. Schiefelbusch & L. L. Lloyd (Eds.), *Language perspectives: Acquisition, retardation, and intervention* (pp. 615–646). Baltimore, MD: University Park Press.

STRAUSS, S. A., & KEPHART, N. C. (1955). *Psychopathology and education of the brain-damaged child.* New York: Grune & Stratton.

TARVER, S. G., & ELLSWORTH, P. S. (1981). Written and oral language for verbal children. In J. M. Kauffman & D. P. Hallahan (Eds.), *Handbook of special education* (pp. 491–511). Englewood Cliffs, NJ: Prentice-Hall.

VOGEL, S. A. (1974). Syntactic abilities in normal and dyslexic children. *Journal of Learning Disabilities, 7,* 103–109.

VOGEL, S. A. (1977). Morphological ability in normal and dyslexic children. *Journal of Learning Disabilities, 10,* 41–49.

WAUGH, R. (1975). The ITPA: Ballast or bonanza for the school psychologist. *Journal of School Psychology, 13,* 201–208.

WECHSLER, D. (1974). *Manual for the Wechsler Intelligence Scale for Children—Revised.* New York: Psychological Corporation.

WELLER, C. (1979). The effects of two language training approaches on syntactical skills of language-deviant children. *Journal of Learning Disabilities, 12,* 470–479.

WEPMAN, J. M. (1958). *Auditory Discrimination Test.* Chicago: Language Research Associates.

WEPMAN, J. M. (1973). *Auditory Discrimination Test* (rev. ed.). Chicago: Language Research Associates.

WIIG, E. H., & ROACH, M. A. (1975). Immediate recall of semantically varied "sentences" by learning disabled adolescents. *Perceptual and Motor Skills, 40,* 119–125.

WIIG, E. H., & SEMEL, E. M. (1975). Productive language abilities in learning disabled adolescents. *Journal of Learning Disabilities, 8,* 578–586.

WIIG, E. H., SEMEL, E. M., & ABELE, E. (1981). Perception of ambiguous sentences by learning disabled twelve-year-olds. *Learning Disability Quarterly, 4,* 3–12.

WIIG, E. H., SEMEL, E. M., & CROUSE, M. A. (1973). The use of English morphology by high-risk and learning disabled children. *Journal of Learning Disabilities, 6,* 457–465.

WONG, B. Y. L., & ROADHOUSE, A. (1978). The Test of Language Development (TOLD): A validation study. *Learning Disability Quarterly, 1*(3), 48–61.

YSSELDYKE, J. E., & SALVIA, J. A. (1974). Diagnostic-prescriptive teaching: Two models. *Exceptional Children, 41,* 181–186.

YSSELDYKE, J. E., & SHINN, M. R. (1981). Psychoeducational evaluation. In J. M. Kauffman & D. P. Hallahan (Eds.), *Handbook of special education* (pp. 418–440). Englewood Cliffs, NJ: Prentice-Hall.

Reading Disabilities

Without doubt, reading disabilities are debilitating to children and adolescents. Students with reading disabilities fall behind very rapidly in nearly all school subjects. They are likely to develop negative concepts of themselves and lose any motivation to succeed that they may have had. They have very limited access to the rich worlds found in books by Laura Ingalls Wilder, C. S. Lewis, Judy Blume, S. E. Hinton, or any of the other authors that many students enjoy. Furthermore, reading has become nearly essential for adult employment and is almost a necessity for obtaining a driver's license and other adult "privileges."

Reading disabilities are nearly synonymous with learning disabilities. In the general school population, between 10% and 15% of the students have reading disabilities (Harris & Sipay, 1980), but reading problems are the most common academic deficit among students labeled learning disabled (Norman & Zigmond, 1980). It has been estimated that over 85% of all LD students have reading disabilities (Kaluger & Kolson, 1978). Furthermore, teachers in learning disabilities programs report that they place more emphasis on reading instruction than on any other area (Kirk & Elkins, 1975). Thus there is a large overlap between the fields of reading and learning disabilities that has resulted in strong debate among professionals working in these areas (see Lerner, 1975).

CHARACTERISTICS

Around the turn of the century, Morgan (1896) and Hinshelwood (1917) reported the first extensive descriptions of reading disabilities. Later, important observations about students with reading disabilities were made by Monroe (1932), who developed an assessment system for analyzing students' mistakes during oral reading and described remedial procedures, and Orton (1937), who suggested that reading problems were the result of teaching methods that were inappropriate for some students' level of neurological development. Since the work of these pioneers, much more about

Christopher G. Knight, Photo Researchers, Inc.

Problems in reading usually make it very difficult for LD students to learn and make progress in other academic areas.

the characteristics of reading disabilities has been learned and controversies have developed about many aspects of the field.

Definition and Terminology

There is no widely accepted definition of reading disabilities. Experts disagree about what kinds of reading problems represent reading disabilities and about how severe a deficit must be before it qualifies as a reading disability. Some people maintain that most mistakes in reading words do not indicate a reading problem and that only those students who have significant difficulty with understanding what they have read should be judged to have reading disabilities. Others argue that students who read at less than a certain standard of accuracy (perhaps less than 90% of the words correct) have reading disabilities.

Definitions of reading disabilities (and other similar terms) usually refer to retardation in reading that is serious enough to hamper a student's progress in school and that has persisted for some time. Reading retardation is considered serious if a student is behind at least one grade level in the primary and elementary years or two grade levels in the secondary years. Many definitions (e.g., Critchley, 1970) indicate that students with reading disabilities must also have normal intelligence and conventional educational opportunities before they can be said to have reading disabilities. Some definitions (e.g., Spache, 1976) even include phrases specifying that students from lower socioeconomic groups should not be considered reading disabled unless they have serious problems in comparison to their peers from the same socioeconomic group. As a result, a student in one part of a city might be judged to have a reading disability, while a student with identical intelligence levels and reading skills *but from a poorer neighborhood* of the same city would not be considered reading disabled.

Additionally, there is no consensus about what terms among the many that have been used are the most appropriate labels for reading disability. Some of the terms used in the past are no longer heard. Hinshelwood (1917), for example, titled his book about reading problems *Congenital Word Blindness*, and Orton (1937) used the descriptive label *strephosymbolia* (twisted symbols), but today these terms are usually found only in historical discussions. However, several other terms used earlier to refer to certain types of reading disabilities have persisted.

Dyslexia   The term *dyslexia* comes from Greek and means "difficulty with reading." A dyslexic is a person who has dyslexia. It has medical connotations and is more often used by physicians and by those who believe that reading problems are the result of biological (particularly neurological) problems. Dyslexia also suggests a severe reading disability, perhaps because students with quite serious deficits are more likely to be taken to medical clinics than are other students.

Corrective Reader   The term *corrective reader* is more educational in origin than dyslexic and is usually used to refer to students whose reading difficulties are not so severe that intensive remedial efforts are warranted. The difficulties experienced by a student labeled a corrective reader might be less persistent and might involve problems only in reading accuracy, fluency, rate, or comprehension.

Remedial Reader   The term *remedial reader* is also more educational than dyslexic. It is used to indicate students who need extensive and intense remedial education in the area of reading. Students considered remedial readers are likely to have serious difficulties both with accuracy, fluency, and rate of reading and with understanding what they have read. The reading problems of students with learning disabilities are more similar to the reading problems of remedial readers than to those of corrective readers.

Problems Related to Reading Disabilities

Researchers have tried to identify problems that are related to reading disabilities so that pupils with reading deficits can be understood better and so that possible causes and correlates can be treated. The evidence they have discovered reveals that the reading problems of learning-disabled students separate them from their normally achieving peers in many ways. Furthermore, these reading problems are related to many other difficulties.

Reading Performance Problems   When pupils with learning disabilities read, they often do not accurately say what is on the page in front of them. They make many different kinds of mistakes. For example, they may mispronounce or skip words, add extra words, or substitute one word for another. The material in Box 7.1 illustrates what it is like to listen to a learning-disabled pupil read.

Reading performance requires use of phonological, syntactic, and semantics skills (see discussion of these skills in Chapter 6). *Phonological* skills are used when readers convert written words into their oral-language equivalents; these skills are most obvious when students read aloud. *Syntactic* skills involve using the grammatical structure of written material to aid reading. *Semantic* skills refer to those aspects of language knowledge that help readers to use meaning and to understand what is being read. Capable readers use all of these skills in a smoothly functioning way, drawing

---

Box 7.1
HOW IT SOUNDS TO HEAR A LEARNING-DISABLED STUDENT READ

The following example shows what the reading of a learning-disabled student sounds like. This passage was drawn from an elementary level social studies textbook. Next to the passage were pictures of factory workers and automobiles with prominent white tires.

Here is what the student said:

Then Ford had uh other i . . . a better idea. Take the worrrk to the men. He deee . . . A long rope was hooked onto the car . . . wheels . . . There's no rope on there. The rope pulled the car . . . auto . . . the white wheels along . . . pulled the car all along the way. Men stood still. Putting on car parts. Everybody man . . . put on, on, a few parts. Down the assembly line went the car. The assembly line saved . . . time. Cars costed still less to buh . . . bull . . . d . . . build. Ford cuts their prices on the Model T again.

Here is the actual passage the student was to read:

Then Ford had another idea. Take the work to the men, he decided. A long rope was hooked onto a car axle and wheels. The rope pulled the axle and wheels along. All along the way, men stood still putting on car parts. Down the assembly line went the car. The assembly line saved more time. Cars cost still less to build. Ford cut the price of the Model T again.

Source: W. R. Fiedler & G. Feeney. (1972). *Inquiring about cities: Studies in geography and economics.* New York: Holt, Rinehart & Winston (p. 211).

---

on each of them to a greater or lesser degree at various times as the need arises. Learning-disabled readers may have difficulty with any or all of these skills.

Phonology Young children's play with spoken words often reflects phonological skills. Saying words that rhyme or that start with the same sound (*bah, bay, boo, bo*) requires phonological skills. More sophisticated language games indicate mastery of phonological skills; for example, speaking in "pig latin" requires moving some of the sounds of words.

Children who have difficulty with beginning reading usually do not have strong phonological skills and seem unaware of how the sound system of our language works. For example, although we immediately realize that the word *mow* is said more quickly than the word *motorcycle* and therefore would be a shorter written word, many young children do not (Rozin, Bressman, & Taft, 1974). Poor readers also have difficulty segmenting the sounds that make up words. Segmenting refers to the ability to separate words into parts; having students say the word *blackboard* without saying "black" requires segmenting skills. Children who have weak segmentation skills when they start kindergarten are likely to have difficulty with beginning reading and probably will be in the lowest group at the end of the year (see Liberman, Shankweiler, Liberman, Fowler, & Fischer, 1977).

Sound blending, another phonological skill, is used when letter sounds or other word parts are collapsed into a word said at a normal rate of speech. Sound blending has been found to be highly and positively correlated with performance on later reading tests in many studies (e.g., Chall, Roswell, & Blumenthal, 1963). In other studies (e.g., Kass, 1966), it has been reported that LD students' low achievement in reading is related to inadequate auditory closure and sound blending skills (for further information, see sections on these skills in Chapter 6). However, the correlations between these abilities and reading achievement may be misleading. Auditory closure and sound blending are not closely related to reading achievement when the contributions of age and IQ to reading achievement are controlled (e.g., Harber, 1980; Larsen, Rogers, & Sowell, 1976). These findings may indicate that general ability (IQ) is the cause of the relationship, or that more specific abilities such as sound blending are important only during the early stages of reading. The latter explanation is probably more accurate because training in sound blending has been an important part of effective procedures for teaching beginning reading skills (e.g., Carnine, 1977; Jeffrey & Samuels, 1967).

One aspect of reading that clearly requires phonological skill is associating letters with sounds. The association between letters and sounds is sometimes called the alphabetic principle, sound-symbol relationship, or phoneme-grapheme relationship. Children who do not know the common sounds for letters will have difficulty "sounding out" unfamiliar words. Pflaum (1980) reported that learning-disabled students who depended on letter-sound cues in oral reading comprehended what they read better than learning-disabled students whose oral reading did not indicate reliance on phonology. Theories about visual perceptual problems causing difficulty with the sound-symbol relationship (e.g., saying /b/ for d) dominated in the field of learning disabilities during the 1960s and much of the 1970s. However, these problems apparently stem from deficits in verbal skills (e.g., Vellutino, 1977). As summarized by Tarver and Ellsworth (1981):

> Orientation or rotation confusions (e.g., *b/d*, *saw/was*) may be explained as difficulties in establishing visual-*verbal* relationships rather than difficulties in stabilizing visual-*spatial* relationships. The evidence suggests that these confusions are not due to *misperceptions*, but to *mislabeling* of the visual stimuli because of a more basic deficit in the ability to remember the names of letters and/or words. (p. 494)

Ability to use phonological skills is crucial to success in early reading, when what a child says while looking at a book must come under the control of the print on the page. Phonological skills are used extensively in translating the written material into more familiar oral language, but other skills are used in reading, and learning-disabled students may have difficulty with them, too.

Syntax   Syntactic skills are called on when readers use the grammatical structure of written materials. Syntax does not help with reading a list of unrelated words, but it is helpful in reading phrases and sentences. For example, given the phrase *beside the* _____, syntactic skills (and some semantics skills; see the following discussion) allow us to make a reasonable guess that the next word will be a noun, probably naming some kind of object. Even more importantly, syntactic skills allow readers to work on clusters of related words in a sentence—phrases—rather than on each word separately. For example, in the sentence, *The small boy holding a cap ran very fast to home-plate*, there are four phrases. Efficiency is much greater when readers can work with larger units of text, and as they become more efficient, readers' fluency and reading rate increase.

Studies of syntax have revealed that it is used more by older and better readers (Resnick,

1970). Young children with reading problems do not cluster words into phrases when they read (Clay & Imlach, 1971), and the mistakes they make indicate that they may not use context (including syntax) to help them with decoding (e.g., Pflaum & Bryan, 1981).

Semantics Semantics refers to the study of meaning in language. Because the reason for reading is to get meaning, semantics is very important. In reading, semantic cues are bits of ideas that help one to decode and to understand the meaning of what is being read. For example, consider the following sentence: *The student turned in her* _____. The meaning of the first part of the sentence helps reduce the number of possible words that could complete it. The missing word probably will not be *pajamas* or *car* because it almost has to be something having to do with school. It is not likely to be *classroom* because people do not turn in classrooms. It probably is not *grades* because even though grades have to do with school, they are something that would be turned in by a teacher, not a student. *Paper, books, homework*, and *test* are a few of the sensible possibilities. A reader finds them sensible because of the semantic cues in the remainder of the material being read.

Most of our knowledge about meaning in reading comes from studies about reading comprehension. Comprehension is greatly influenced by decoding skills; students with comprehension deficits have inferior performance on tasks requiring simple reading of words (Perfetti & Hogaboam, 1975). Importantly, poor comprehenders do not differ from good comprehenders in reading familiar words, but are much slower in reading unfamiliar words (Golinkoff & Rosinski, 1976). Also, the mistakes that learning-disabled students make in oral reading are more likely to change the meaning of what they are reading (Pflaum & Bryan, 1981). However, poor comprehenders do not have any more difficulty with determining the meaning of individual words than normal readers do (Rosinski, Golinkoff, & Kukish, 1975). Furthermore, when they hear a good reading of a story, poor comprehenders' scores are just as high as good comprehenders' scores; but when they hear a poor reading of a story, poor comprehenders' scores fall, while those of good comprehenders stay high (Oakan, Weiner, & Cromer, 1971). Considered together, these studies indicate that the reading comprehension deficits of poor readers are almost certainly rooted in but not simply a result of their difficulties with decoding.

In addition to having weak decoding skills, students with reading disabilities apparently do not monitor whether they are understanding what they are reading. Garner (1980) had good and poor readers examine stories as if they were editing them. For some of the original words in the stories, she had substituted others that did not make sense. The poor readers did not notice these changes in text, even though the changes made the passages nearly incomprehensible. Also, it appears that students with reading deficits have difficulty reasoning during comprehension. Kavale (1980) studied the kinds of statements made by normal and learning-disabled readers when they were asked to reason aloud while figuring out the answers to reading comprehension questions. Normally achieving students used efficient strategies while reasoning and often reached the correct solution to problems. Learning-disabled students, on the other hand, either used no recognizable plan or employed several different strategies haphazardly, and made nearly 50% errors. On further analysis, Kavale found that the kinds of thinking used by learning-disabled students were related to their inaccurate decoding of what they had read and their impoverished vocabularies. (See Box 7.2 for two views of the psychology of reading.)

Box 7.2

OPPOSING VIEWS ON THE PSYCHOLOGY OF READING

Conflicting theories about how reading should be taught have an interesting parallel in the theories of the psychology of reading. Psychologists have studied reading extensively and developed elaborate theories to explain the kind of thinking that goes on when a person reads. Rozin and Gleitman (1977) compared and contrasted two opposing views of the psychology of reading in this way:

At one pole stand those who claim that the reader is a plodder. He literally ploughs through text a letter at a time, building the words and sentences out of the individually identified phone-sized squiggles on the page; he converts the letters to sounds, which are then formed into phonological representations, which in turn contact the previously learned meanings. This plodder view is essentially a speeded-up, smoothed-out version of what the stumbling first-grader seems to do in "sounding out" the words of his primer. It is probably the common-sense view of any Phonecian on the Street. Because, on this account, meaning is derived through the systematic combination of minimal elements, the plodder view can be described as a "bottom up" approach. At the opposite extreme stand those romantics who view the reader as an explorer of the printed page. They suppose the fluent reader (including the average reader . . .) looks at the printed page as he does at other aspects of the visual world, sampling selectively from among many available cues, developing expectations for words or meanings, seeking confirmation of these guesses and, in general, bringing to bear at all levels his considerable linguistic, intellectual, and perceptual skills. On this view, then, reading is more problem solving than plodding through phonology. Because the reader is here conceived as arriving at the details of the printed message after deriving its meaning, the explorer view can be characterized as a "top down" approach.

From P. Rozin and L. R. Gleitman (1977). The structure and acquisition of Reading II: The reading process and the acquisition of the alphabetic principle. In A. S. Reker and D. L. Scarborough (Eds.), *Toward a psychology of reading: The proceedings of the CUNY Conference.* Hillsdale, NJ: Eilbaum, p. 59. Reprinted with permission.

Other Achievement Problems Reading underachievement is related to problems in other academic areas. Of importance here are other areas of language arts, particularly oral language (see Chapter 6) and spelling.

Oral Language Difficulties in oral language are common among students with reading disabilities. Many studies have revealed that deficits in vocabulary are characteristic of pupils who do not read well (e.g., Ackerman, Peters, & Dykman, 1971). Vocabulary deficits make it hard for learners to understand what they are reading, even when they have learned

to decode well and have strategies for figuring out what they have read (Becker, 1977). For example, the sentence *The small girl smermelled the kendox* is difficult to comprehend for anyone who does not have *to smermell* and *kendox* in his or her vocabulary. Reid and Hresko (1980) administered tests of reading and oral-language skills to kindergartners, first-graders, and second-graders, some of whom were enrolled in special classes for the learning disabled and some of whom were considered normal. They found that learning-disabled students consistently scored lower than their normally achieving age-mates. It is interesting to note that when normally achieving students began to read better, the relationship between reading and oral language diminished.

Spelling Spelling requires many skills that are similar to those used in reading. Among these are letter-sound correspondences and blending. However, these skills are somewhat different for spelling. For example, the letter-sound skill used in reading requires pupils to see a letter and say a sound, but in spelling it requires them to hear a sound and write (or say) a letter. Nevertheless, spelling and reading are intimately connected and students who have difficulty with reading are likely to have problems with spelling. Carpenter and Miller (1982) compared LD students with reading disabilities to normally reading peers and found that the LD students had significantly poorer spelling skills. In another study examining the kinds of errors students made in spelling, Carpenter (1983) found that students with reading disabilities produced more spellings that were unrecognizable than did capable readers of the same age and younger readers of the same reading ability. This is further evidence that students with reading problems have not mastered the phonological representation of our written language.

ASSESSMENT

Assessment of reading takes many different forms, depending on the purpose of the assessment. Students who have been referred may go through a *screening* assessment in order to decide whether further assessment or remedial help is needed, and if it is, in what areas. Those who require further help may go through a *diagnostic* assessment in order to identify the specific areas in which they need help. Those who are already receiving help in specific areas should go through *progress monitoring* assessment in order to determine whether their skills in those areas are improving. Each of the three major types of assessment is discussed in the following sections; for further information about assessment and its purposes, see Ysseldyke and Shinn (1981).

Screening

Screening is conducted to determine whether students who have been referred are in need of further assessment or of special services. Thus a screening assessment is a formal step in determining whether a reading difficulty merits special educational assistance. In some cases, a noneducational difficulty may be discovered during the screening process; for example, it may be found that a student has abnormal vision and the appropriate remedy would be to refer him or her for eye testing.

When students are referred for screening, it is usually because of a very general complaint (e.g., "He just isn't doing well at all"). It is common for referred students to be administered an assessment device that measures their performance in many areas and that compares them to national samples of students of similar age; this assessment is designed to narrow the complaint to more specific areas of difficulty.

The assessment devices used for screening include many of the most common tests in education. The *Iowa Test of Basic Skills* (Hieronymus, Lindquist, & Hoover, 1978), the *California Achievement Test* (CTB/McGraw-Hill, 1977–1978), the *Stanford Achievement Test* (Madden, Gardner, Rudman, Karlsen, & Merwin, 1973), the *Peabody Individual Achievement Test* (Dunn & Markwardt, 1970), the *Wide Range Achievement Test* (Jastak & Jastak, 1976), and the *Woodcock-Johnson Psychoeducational Battery* (Woodcock & Johnson, 1977) are among those most frequently encountered.

In addition, many tests devoted entirely to reading may be used as screening instruments. Some examples of these devices are the *Gates-MacGinitie Reading Tests* (Gates & MacGinitie, 1978), the *Gilmore Oral Reading Test*

(Gilmore & Gilmore, 1968), and the *Gray Oral Reading Test* (Gray & Robinson, 1967). Some of the reading tests that are used for diagnosis and are discussed in the following section may also be used for screening.

Diagnosis

Diagnosis of reading problems is performed to identify an appropriate intervention. That is, diagnostic assessment should help teachers plan instructional programs. In some cases, diagnostic activities may be focused on finding causes of a problem with the hope that treating the causes will eliminate the problem. In other cases, diagnosis is undertaken to identify more precisely what reading skills students lack so that remedial efforts can be devoted to eliminating these specific problems.

Diagnostic assessment is accomplished by using formal or informal methods or, usually, a combination of the two.

Formal Methods   Formal diagnostic methods include the administration of standardized tests of reading skills. Formal diagnostic tests in reading are usually composed of several subtests that are designed to measure specific parts of general reading skill. For example, a diagnostic test may include subtests of letter recognition, word recognition, reading rate, and other skills. If a student has lower scores on some subtests than on others, he or she is judged to be weaker in those areas and remedial activities for them would be selected.

Diagnostic reading tests may be administered to several students at the same time or to only one student at a time. Selected group and individual diagnostic tests are listed in Table 7.1. Some tests of both types assess skills that are, at best, only indirectly related to reading. For example, many diagnostic reading tests have subtests of syllabication that require students to divide a word into its syllables by putting a line between the letters that end one syl-

lable and begin the next. As Carnine and Silbert (1979) have indicated, this skill will be useful to students when they are writing and do not have room at the end of a line to complete a multisyllable word, but it is essentially useless for decoding text. As another illustration, some diagnostic reading tests require students to listen to the tester say a sound for a letter and then to mark that letter; this test is not directly related to reading because in reading students have to see the letter and say the sound, not hear the sound and find the letter (Lloyd, Cameron, & Lloyd, 1984). Furthermore, the kinds of materials used and questions asked on tests may sample only part of the area of reading they are designed to test. For example, different passages and types of comprehension questions result in different scores on comprehension tests, indicating that most reading comprehension tests are testing only some comprehension skills (Kendall, Mason, & Hunter, 1980). These problems indicate that teachers should examine diagnostic and other tests carefully before accepting them as appropriate devices for assessing reading skills.

Diagnostic Tests Administered to Groups
Nearly all group diagnostic instruments are standardized so that teachers can compare the performance of one student to that of a larger group of selected students. If a student's score is unusually low on a subtest, it would indicate that the student has a specific reading disability in that area *in relation to other students' performance* on that subtest. Diagnostic tests administered to groups have the advantage of allowing a teacher to assess the skills of many students at one time, but these tests have the disadvantage of not allowing teachers to assess behaviors that are more directly related to reading (Lloyd et al., 1984). For example, despite their widely accepted importance in reading diagnosis, group diagnostic tests do not as-

Table 7.1 Selected Diagnostic Reading Tests

GROUP TESTS			
Name of Test	*Grades*	*Time (minutes)*	*Subareas*
McCullough Word-Analysis Tests (McCullough, 1963)	4–6	70	Blends Diagraphs Phoneme discrimination Letter sounds Word recognition Syllabication Root words Affixes Phonetic symbols
Stanford Diagnostic Reading Test (Karlsen et al., 1976)	1.5–13	90–145	Decoding Vocabulary Comprehension
Silent Reading Diagnostic Tests (Bond et al., 1970)	2–6	90–135	Word recognition Root words Syllabication Blending Word beginnings and endings Letter sounds
INDIVIDUAL TESTS			
Name of Test	*Grades*	*Time (minutes)*	*Subareas*
Diagnostic Reading Scales (Spache, 1972)	K–12	45	Phonics skills Word recognition Passage reading
Roswell-Chall Diagnostic Test of Word Analysis Skills—Revised and Extended (Roswell & Chall, 1978)	1–3	10–15	Words Decoding Letter names Encoding
Woodcock Reading Mastery Tests (Woodcock, 1973)	K–12	20–30	Letter identification Word identification Word attack Word comprehension Passage comprehension

sess oral reading skill (Bond, Tinker, & Wasson, 1979; Durkin, 1978).

Diagnostic Tests Administered to Individuals Many individually administered diagnostic tests of reading skill also are standardized. However, the quality of standardization for some of them is very weak. For example,

Spache (1976) examined many diagnostic tests and reported that their reliabilities for various subtests were too low to allow users to trust them; he also argued that some subtests were so highly related to one another that they might not be testing independent skills. On the other hand, individually administered tests have the advantage of allowing the teacher to judge a student's actual reading performance rather than basing diagnosis on answers to multiple-choice items.

Informal Methods   Informal methods of diagnosing reading problems are based less on scores on structured tests and more on classroom performance. Probably the most widely used instruments for informal assessment are *informal reading inventories.* Another informal method is diagnosis by teaching or *clinical teaching,* a method that involves trying procedures and making judgments based on experience and intuition. Both of these methods are discussed in the following material.

Clinical Teaching   Probably the most informal approach to assessment is to try alternative approaches with students and use those that seem successful. In the beginning, this was the most popular approach to teaching in the field of learning disabilities because there were few useful formal tests or carefully researched instructional methods. Experienced teachers who had demonstrated their skills with hard-to-teach students found themselves working almost exclusively with children who had acquired the new label *learning disabled.* In the absence of reliable instruments and procedures, many used whatever they could find that seemed to work. More structured versions of this eclectic approach are still in use in the field of learning disabilities. The crucial difference is that now teachers have the means for determining whether procedures are actually working rather than having to rely on hunches about their effectiveness. For example, a teacher may frequently collect data about a student's performance (see the following section on progress monitoring) and then try different instructional programs; when the student's performance on the frequently collected data indicate that he or she is learning more rapidly, the program that is causing that im-

provement may be adopted. Similarly, if a teacher has a carefully sequenced set of instructional lessons for teaching a specific skill, a method for determining where in the program a student should begin can be to teach trial lessons from the sequence. If the learner does well on the highest lessons, there is no need to work on that skill; if he or she does poorly on lessons from the middle of the program but does well on lessons from the beginning, instruction should begin somewhere between the trial lessons.

Informal Reading Inventories   An informal reading inventory (IRI) is a series of reading passages or word lists graded in order of difficulty. A student reads from the series of lists or passages, beginning with one that the teacher thinks is likely to be easy. As long as the reading does not become too difficult, the student continues to read from increasingly harder lists or passages. As the student reads, the teacher monitors performance and may record the kinds of reading errors a student makes (e.g., omitted word, mispronunciation, reversal). When an IRI is made up of passages, the teacher may ask questions after each one to help estimate the student's comprehension of the material. Depending on the student's accuracy in reading and answering questions, various levels of reading skill can be ascertained. Table 7.2 shows how these levels are assigned. In general, the kind of material that a student can read with a certain degree of ease is considered to be at his or her *independent, instructional,* or *frustration level.* For example, if a student reads selections from a particular book with 96% correct decoding and answers four out of five comprehension questions correctly, that book would be considered to be at the student's instructional reading level.

IRIs can be constructed by teachers to correspond to the basal reading books used in the

Table 7.2   Reading Levels According to Informal Reading Inventories

Level	Accuracy		Implications
	Decoding	Comprehension	
Independent	>97%	100%	Student may use this level of material during seatwork, homework, or other activities when no teacher help is available.
Instructional	≥95%	>75%	Student may work on this level of material to learn new reading skills during times when reading instruction is in progress.
Frustration	<95%	<75%	Material at this level is too difficult for the student and should be avoided until skills have been improved.

school district or to other series of books. When a teacher makes a decision about using a textbook with a certain student based on an IRI constructed from that textbook, this placement decision has considerable validity (Jenkins, 1979). Also, some IRIs are available commercially. Examples of these are the *Informal Reading Assessment* (Burns & Roe, 1980), *Ekwall Reading Inventory* (Ekwall, 1979), and *Classroom Reading Inventory* (Silvaroli, 1979). Each of these (and other available IRIs) is quite different and a teacher should select and use commercially available IRIs carefully (Anderson, 1977; Jongsma & Jongsma, 1981). For further information about IRIs, consult textbooks on reading instruction or specific articles listed in Johns, Garton, Schoenfelder, and Skriba (1977).

Lovitt and Hansen (1976a) demonstrated how IRI techniques can be used to make careful and useful placement decisions. They selected five passages from each of the readers in the Lippincott series (McCracken & Walcutt, 1970) and wrote comprehension questions for each passage. Students read passages at each level on several days. Each learner was placed in the reader from which she or he correctly read an average of 45 to 60 words per minute with 4 to 8 errors per minute and answered 50% to 75% of the comprehension questions

correctly. Lovitt and Hansen's approach to placement enhances the value of IRIs by using repeated assessments, which help to ensure that an unusually high or low performance on one day will not bias the teacher's placement decisions, and by not depending on analyses of students' error patterns.

Progress Monitoring

Monitoring students' progress is a very important part of the assessment of reading. Progress monitoring should provide teachers with dependable information about how well students are doing in the areas of reading that lead to reading success. It should allow teachers to make changes in instructional programs without wasting valuable time working on what students already know quite well or presenting activities that are not helping them to progress.

Often, however, progress monitoring is done only haphazardly, if at all. Monitoring should consist of more than teachers simply stating their opinions about their students' improvement. Traditionally, progress monitoring has been accomplished by administering formal screening or diagnostic tests in the fall and spring of each year, and then estimating the gain from one testing to the next. Besides the

Teachers can learn a great deal about students' reading skills by having them read aloud.

statistical problems with this method, it requires that teachers wait until the end of the school year to determine how well their programs have worked and if they need change.

Progress monitoring systems that overcome these problems have been designed. Commercially available systems and systems based on applied behavior analysis techniques represent the two major approaches to monitoring students' progress.

Commercial Systems   Some commercially available progress monitoring systems have been designed to work with particular reading instructional programs. Others are not directly tied to one published reading program but may be used with various different ones.

Program-Based Systems   The *Tests of Basic Reading Skills* (Brezeinski & Schoe-

phoerster, 1976) accompany the Houghton Mifflin Reading Series (Durr, Windley, & Yates, 1976). According to Brezeinski and Schoephoerster, one purpose of the system is "to give periodic indication of mastery and provide information the teacher must have in order to determine the need for remedial instruction" (1976, p. 3). Brief tests are presented in "magazines" after students complete each part of the basal reading program. A magazine test for a particular part is designed to assess the skills students are expected to have mastered up to that point in the program. Students who score below 80% correct are considered to need remedial work.

The Mastery Tests that accompany the *Corrective Reading Program* (e.g., Engelmann, Becker, Hanner, & Johnson, 1978) are another progress monitoring system that is related to a specific program. An example of these tests is shown in Figure 7.1. The Mastery Tests allow teachers to determine whether additional practice on certain skills is needed or whether parts of lessons may be skipped because the students have already mastered that material. Unlike the magazine tests, which are presented only several times a year, the Mastery Tests are administered after every 2 to 10 days of instruction. The progress monitoring tests for one of the sections of *Corrective Reading* are designed so that the program may range from about 30 lessons for students who are learning rapidly to about 70 lessons for those who require extensive extra practice.

Generic Systems The second kind of progress monitoring system available commercially is not tied to a specific reading program. Instead of testing what a certain program is supposed to teach, these systems of progress monitoring are designed to test reading skills that are presumed to be important regardless of the reading program used. One system of this type is called *diagnosis: an instructional aid—reading* (Science Research Associates, 1975) and includes kits for grades 1–4 and for grades 3–6. The appropriate starting point for each student in the various areas of reading skills is determined by administering a survey test. When broad areas of instructional need have been identified, a series of miniature tests or objective-based probes is used to monitor progress toward mastery of specific skill objectives.

Applied Behavior Analysis Many schools and special projects have developed systems for monitoring progress that are based on applied behavior analysis (ABA). The various reading skills that are to be assessed are identified; direct tests of them are selected; the tests are designed so that they can be given frequently, easily, and without requiring much more than a few minutes; and the resulting systems are often tested to determine how normally

---

Mastery test 5

Note: Test each student individually. Administer the test so that the other students do not overhear the student being tested.

me

Task A Vowel variations: ē
1. **First tell me the sound the letter makes in the word and then tell me the word.**
2. Point to e in **me**. **What sound?** Touch. ēēē.
3. (Test item.) Touch the ball of the arrow. **What word?** Slash right. *Me.*
4. Repeat steps 2 and 3 for **the, she**.

the

she

Task B Vowel variations: ĕ
1. Point to e in **me**. **This letter does not say ēēē in the words you're going to read now.**

met

2. Point to e in **met**. **This letter says ĕĕĕ. What sound?** Touch. ĕĕĕ.
3. (Test item.) Touch the ball of the arrow. **What word?** Slash right. *Met.*
4. Repeat steps 2 and 3 for **them, shed**.

them

shed

Evaluating test results
If at least three-quarters of the group responded correctly to all six words, skip to lesson 31.

If between half and three-quarters responded correctly to all six words, go to lesson 26.

If less than half responded correctly to all six words, repeat lessons 24 and 25. Then retest.

Figure 7.1 A sample mastery test from the *Corrective Reading Program.*
From CORRECTIVE READING: DECODING A/WORD-ATTACK BASICS Teacher's Book, by S. Engelman, L. Carnine and G. Johnson. © 1978, Science Research Associates, Inc. Reprinted by permission of the publisher.

achieving students would perform on them. The result is that teachers have a loosely sequenced series of miniature tests that can be used to determine whether their students are moving closer to mastery of the skills assessed by the instruments.

One system of this sort was developed by the staff of Project ExCEL (see Epstein & Cullinan, 1981). The broad skill of reading performance was analyzed into smaller skill areas on the basis of the spelling patterns of words, and many of these skill areas were further divided into narrower groups. For example, "Consonant-Vowel-Consonant (CVC) words" (such as *sit, map,* and *run*) were selected as one of the many reading skill areas. Other skill areas included CCVC, CVC-silent e, and irregularly pronounced words. Examples of each of these types of words were placed on sheets of paper called a *probe.* Some probes were composed of words drawn from several different types of words so that students could not read probes correctly simply by adhering to a pattern. Figure 7.2 shows examples of these probes or miniature tests. Students' performance in reading the probes was assessed by having them read aloud from a sheet for 1 minute. Students were required to read only from probes representing skill areas on which they needed work. Teachers recorded how many words were read per minute and how many errors were made, thus gaining measures of rate and accuracy. After several days of 1-minute tests on a probe, teachers had established a baseline level of performance. Then they tried different reading interventions and compared the students' performance after each one to see how rapidly and accurately they read compared to their baseline performance. Frequent administration of the probes allowed teachers to judge whether their students were making satisfactory progress toward mastery of the reading skill areas. Epstein and Cullinan (1979) administered the Project ExCEL probes to normally achieving students in order to develop socially valid and appropriate goals for their use with learning-disabled children of elementary-school age.

Because the Project ExCEL system was not designed to parallel a particular reading series or program, the skills areas it assessed were selected on the basis of what its authors considered to be important reading skills regardless of the reading series used. Many other systems have also been developed in this way and have been used at the University of Washington Experimental Education Unit, the University of Oregon Regional Resource Center, and other places. Other progress monitoring systems have been designed so that they can be readily adapted to different reading series. For example, the staff at Project SIMS in Minnesota devised a set of reading probes that could be used by teachers who preferred to teach all short vowels first before working on other sounds for the vowels, or by teachers who preferred to present all of the various sounds for one vowel before beginning work on anther vowel. Finally, there are systems that are composed of probes or minitests such as those described above, but the probes are based entirely on the sequence and vocabulary of a specific reading program. For example, District 4-J in Lane County, Oregon, developed a probe system that closely parallels the Merrill Linguistic Reading program (Otto, Rudolph, Smith, & Wilson, 1975). Further discussion of these reading assessment procedures may be found in Lloyd (1979), Starlin (1971), and other sources.

In three studies with learning-disabled pupils, Lovitt and his associates found that applied behavior analysis procedures compare favorably with traditional achievement tests in the reading area. Eaton and Lovitt (1972) compared direct, frequent use of brief oral reading samples to achievement tests; they found that two achievement tests did not agree with

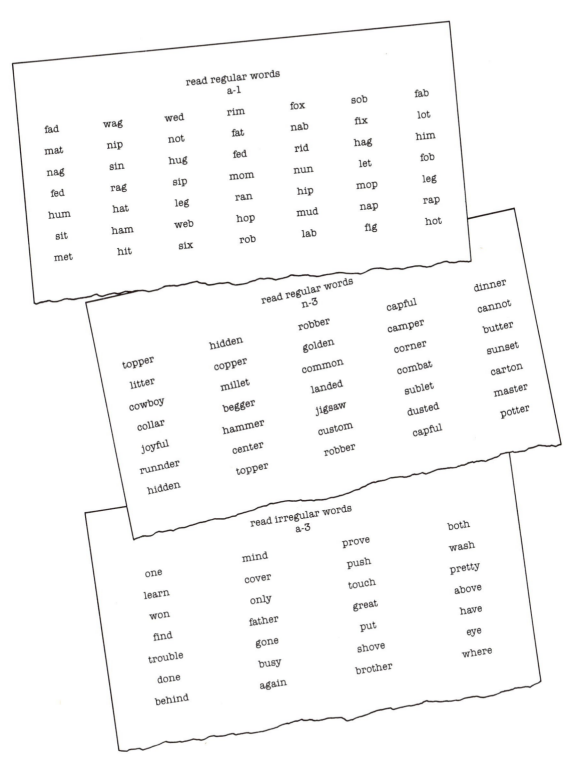

Figure 7.2 Samples of reading probes.

each other, that assignments of students to reading books made using the ABA approach were consistent with assignments based on tests, and that test scores obtained at the end of the year were quite different from one another and did not reflect how well students could read aloud. When Lovitt and Fantasia (1980) compared ABA procedures and achievement tests, they found that the two approaches agreed fairly well, but argued that the ABA approach provided more useful information. Lovitt and Hansen (1976a) used ABA procedures to assign pupils to reading textbooks. By combining the ABA techniques with an informal assessment similar to an IRI, they were able to make appropriate decisions about where instruction should begin for a student (see discussion in the previous section).

INTERVENTIONS

The most pressing problem for teachers of children and adolescents with reading disabilities is how to teach them. Without doubt, the best way to handle reading problems is to prevent them; ideally, appropriate beginning reading instruction should reduce the number of students with reading disabilities. However, there is no clear agreement on what is appropriate beginning reading instruction. Furthermore, although better beginning reading instruction would probably reduce the number of students who develop reading problems, some students would still fail, so there will always be a need for remedial approaches.

Both *remedial* (corrective) and *developmental* (beginning) approaches to reading instruction are particularly important in learning disabilities. In this section, both are discussed.

Developmental Approaches

Developmental approaches are designed for students who have had little formal exposure to reading instruction. They are first used at the kindergarten or first-grade level, and many of the developmental programs commercially available continue at least through the sixth grade. There has been great controversy about the relative value of various types of developmental reading approaches. Perhaps the greatest disagreement is over what aspect of reading should be emphasized with beginning readers. Some programs place greater emphasis on having students obtain meaning from what they read and lesser emphasis on the mechanics of converting printed language into its oral form; these are *meaning-emphasis* programs. A similar emphasis is made by advocates of *whole-language approaches*, who contend that meaning must come first and that children's own language must be used in instruction. Other programs emphasize teaching students to crack the written code that represents spoken language so that they can use what they know about oral language to determine the meaning of what is on the page; these are *code-emphasis* programs. Between the code- and meaning-emphasis approaches are others that adopt meaning-emphasis tactics but try to make code cracking easier by using words that have easy-to-read spelling patterns; these are *linguistic* programs.

Another major disagreement is about how *direct* beginning reading instruction should be. Direct instruction is led explicitly by the teacher, focused on specific measurable objectives, programmed in small learning steps, and so forth. Less direct instruction is discovery oriented; students are provided opportunities to help them learn but instruction is more child centered. Generally, code-emphasis programs are more direct and whole-language-emphasis programs are more discovery oriented.

Most published programs include some aspects of all of the above emphases. Programs that emphasize decoding during the early stages of instruction usually include work on

Table 7.3 Types of Approaches to Developmental Reading and Commercially Available Programs

Code Emphasis	Meaning Emphasis
Basic Reading (Lippincott)	
Open Court Basic Readers (Open Court)	Reading 720 (Ginn)
	Houghton Mifflin Reading Series (Houghton Mifflin)
Reading Mastery (Science Research Associates)	Basics in Reading (Scott Foresman)

Linguistic Emphasis	Whole-Language Emphasis
Merrill Linguistic Readers (Merrill)	Language Experiences in Reading (Encyclopaedia Britannica)
Programmed Reading (Webster/McGraw-Hill)	Chandler Reading Program (Noble & Noble)
SRA Basic Reading Series (Science Research Associates)	

comprehension, and programs that emphasize meaning at the beginning of formal instruction usually include some "word study" activities later. Publishers try to create reading series that will appeal to people who have many different opinions about reading instruction. Nevertheless, a program usually reflects some bias toward a type of approach. Table 7.3 identifies some of the major commercial reading programs and the type of approach that each favors. Each of the various types is discussed in the following sections.

Code Emphasis In a code-emphasis view, the major task during the early stages of developmental reading is to learn how to turn the squiggles on the page into spoken words. Code-emphasis programs are based on the idea that children who learn to decode (to convert printed language into oral language) fluently and accurately will have less trouble understanding what they read. Accordingly, students with good word-reading skills should have high reading comprehension; this is consistent with evidence about the relationship between decoding and comprehension (e.g., Dykstra, 1968b; Perfetti & Hogoboam, 1975). Also, when students have learned code-cracking skills, they should be able to read most words they have not previously seen. Because young children must read many words they never have seen previously, skill in figuring them out is very important to their reading progress. Those who cannot decode unknown words must depend on teachers, peers, parents, and others for help or must disregard the unknown words at the risk of not understanding what they are reading.

Code-emphasis programs teach students specific skills that are consistent with a task analysis of decoding. Bateman (1979), an advocate of code-emphasis instruction and task analysis, wrote:

> Task analysis of decoding reveals that it contains certain subskills: (1) responding to graphemes or grapheme clusters with appropriate phonemes or phoneme clusters; (2) responding in the appropriate temporal sequence, derived from the spatial order of the written symbols; and (3) blending the phonemes or phoneme clusters into words. (p. 248)

How these skills would be used in attacking a word is shown in Table 7.4. The first section of the table gives the instructional objective for decoding simple words. The section labeled "Strategy" shows the steps the learner would use in attacking each word. In Steps 1, 2, and 3, Bateman's phoneme-grapheme and temporal sequence subskills are required; Steps 2, 3, and 4 require Bateman's blending skills.

Although virtually all publishers and authors of commercial reading series claim that decoding skills are taught as a part of their pro-

Table 7.4　Task Analysis of Subskills for Word-Attack Strategy

---

Objective

Given a page of regularly pronounced real CVC words, the student will say each word aloud at a rate of 40 words per minute with no more than 2 errors per minute.

Examples

mat, fin, lop, dip, bet, can, rap

Strategy

Start at beginning of the word and, moving to the right, say the sound for each letter; slide from one sound to the next without stopping between sounds and then say the word.

Steps		Examples
1	Start saying sounds at the beginning:	*mmm*
2	Move toward the right and slide into the next sound:	*mmmaaa*
3	Slide into the next sound:	*mmmaaannn*
4	Say the word:	*man*

Objectives for Subskills Required for This Strategy

Given a list of words, the student will point to the beginning of each word and move his or her finger in the direction of reading (toward the right) with 100% accuracy.

Given a page with individual letters arranged in no particular order, the student will say the most common sound for each letter at a rate of 40 letters per minute with no more than 2 errors per minute.

Given printed words, the student will say the sounds for each letter in each word, sliding from sound to sound without pausing between them with 100% accuracy.

Given a stretched-out pronunciation of a word (e.g., *sssiiit*), the student will say the word at a normal rate of speech for 10 out of 10 trials correctly.

---

grams, code-emphasis programs can be discriminated from others by what they teach and how they teach it. Gurren and Hughes (1965) indicated that an approach emphasizes decoding skills if it provides "intensive teaching of all the main sound-symbol relationships, both vowel and consonant, from the start of formal reading instruction" (p. 340). However, some

code-emphasis programs go beyond teaching the main sound-symbol relationships and teach others as well. For example, Glass (1971) recommended teaching frequently occurring letter clusters such as *ab*.

Extensive evidence favors the code-emphasis approach to developmental reading. Some studies have been conducted in highly controlled laboratory settings. For example, Jeffrey and Samuels (1967) taught one group of kindergartners phoneme-grapheme relationships and another group whole words composed of those graphemes; the instruction received by the first group is similar to a code-emphasis approach and the instruction received by the second group is similar to a whole-word or meaning-emphasis approach. When the children had to learn a new list of words (a test of generalization), those who had received phoneme-grapheme training read more of the new words correctly on the first try and took fewer trials to learn all the words in the new list than did the students who had learned by the word method. Similar studies have shown that the same findings occur even when the words on the new list do not have regular pronunciations (Carnine, 1977) and when the students are handicapped (Vandever & Neville, 1976).

Additional supportive evidence has been reported in reviews of the research. Gurren and Hughes (1965) examined 18 studies and found 22 comparisons between code-emphasis and other approaches. Of the 22 comparisons, 3 were favorable to neither the code-emphasis approach nor the other approaches, none was favorable to the other approaches, and 19 were favorable to the code-emphasis approach. On measures of reading comprehension, they found that 22 of 24 comparisons were favorable to the code-emphasis programs. Chall (1983; originally published in 1967) provided a widely known and highly regarded review of much of the same evidence in a book called *Learning to Read: The Great Debate:*

Under a code emphasis, the child shows, from the very beginning, greater accuracy in word recognition and oral reading; this may or may not give him an immediate advantage on reading-for-meaning tests.... However, by the end of the first or sometime during the second grade the early advantage in word recognition produces better vocabulary and comprehension scores on silent reading tests. These advantages persist through about the third grade.... Under a meaning emphasis, the child has an early advantage ... on reading-for-meaning tests.... However, he has an early disadvantage in accuracy on oral word recognition (pronunciation) and connected oral reading tests ... which ultimately dissipates the early advantage on the standardized silent reading tests. At about the end of the first grade (or the beginning of the second grade), and continuing through about the third grade, meaning-emphasis programs tend to affect comprehension and vocabulary test scores adversely, mainly because the child does less well in word recognition. (p. 137)

Research reported after the publication of these reviews provides additional support for the superiority of code-emphasis programs. Bliesmer and Yarborough (1965) and Potts and Savino (1968) conducted direct comparisons among various published reading programs and found that the child in code-emphasis programs scored higher in decoding and understanding what they read. Dykstra (1968a, 1968b) reported that the outcomes of the Cooperative Research Program in First-Grade Reading Instruction (Bond & Dykstra, 1967) provided support for Chall's (1983) conclusion that code-emphasis programs lead to better overall achievement than meaning-emphasis programs.

Research conducted on the effectiveness of code-emphasis approaches with learning-disabled students has shown much the same results. Stein and Goldman (1980) found that DISTAR Reading (a code-emphasis program) was highly effective with learning-disabled children considered to have minimal brain dysfunction. Williams (1980) reported on a pro-

gram called the *ABDs of Reading* that includes many of the features of code-emphasis approaches; it was found to be effective in extensive evaluations with learning-disabled students. Wallach and Wallach (1976) described a code-emphasis approach for use with low-performing readers that virtually prevented reading failure in students with very low reading readiness skills. Carnine and Silbert (1979) provided a text on reading instruction that presents the code-emphasis approach in detail.

Linguistic Emphasis Linguistics is the study of human speech. Scholars who work in the field of linguistics have suggested that what has been learned in their discipline should be considered in planning reading programs for children (e.g., Fries, 1963). Linguistics scholars consider it essential that children learn the alphabetic nature of English; that is, they should be taught that the words *sand* and *stand* are spelled very much alike because they have many of the same sounds in them and that the difference they hear between the two words is represented by the presence or absence of the letter *t*. However, advocates of the linguistic approach to developmental reading do not think that words should be broken down into individual sounds (as in the code-emphasis approach) because sounds by themselves are meaningless, hard to produce, and unnatural.

In practice, students taught by linguistic approaches read lists and brief passages that are composed almost entirely of rhyming words. For example, a part of a lesson might be *A fat cat sat on a mat.* Words are carefully selected so that individual letters always have the same sound. All words are taught as rote associations between their printed and spoken forms (memorized). Skills for attacking new words are

... developed by linguistic groupings. If the child can recognize the spelling pattern in a word that he has never seen before, and if he can group it with words that have the same pattern of sound *and* spelling relationships, then he can read the never-before-encountered word. (Rasmussen & Goldberg, 1965, p. 5)

Though there are many testimonials about how helpful linguistic approaches are, there is little direct evidence about the effectiveness of linguistics-based programs. For example, Schneyer (1966) reported that the *Merrill Linguistic Readers* resulted in higher achievement for first-graders than did a meaning-emphasis program on some measures and lower achievement on others.

Meaning Emphasis   Approaches that emphasize reading for meaning during the developmental stages of reading instruction are based on the idea that students should not be diverted from the purpose of reading by word study activities. Instead, they should learn to read by reading. They should learn a vocabulary of words that will very quickly allow them to begin reading stories, and they should practice the words in these stories repeatedly. Because students are expected to learn these words as wholes, without building them up from the graphemes, this approach is also known as the "whole-word," "look-and-say," or "sight" approach.

The vocabulary of meaning-emphasis programs is usually limited to words that are necessary to create stories presumed to appeal to children. Lessons are structured around a set of words that will appear in a story read later in the lesson. Many of the words used are those that are common in the reading matter of children. For this reason, the vocabulary is fairly predictable; high-frequency sight words are used extensively, with the repetition expected to help students learn and remember them. Sight words are words that students should be able to read on sight, without having to use word-attack strategies. Lists of those words have been compiled (e.g., Dolch, 1948; Durr,

1973; D. D. Johnson, 1971) and are widely used in remedial programs.

Most basal reading programs of the past adopted a meaning-emphasis approach and many of these programs were compared to code-emphasis programs in the First-Grade Studies (Bond & Dykstra, 1967) and in Chall's (1983) "great debate." In Chall's review, meaning-emphasis programs were found to have some very early advantages over code-emphasis programs, but these disappeared by the end of the first grade, when children in code-emphasis programs excelled. In the First-Grade Studies (Dykstra, 1968a, 1968b), children in meaning-emphasis programs usually did not achieve as well as children in code-emphasis programs. As a consequence of the research and public clamor, basal programs have since included more work on "phonics." However, according to advocates of early intensive phonics instruction (e.g., Flesch, 1981), these changes have been relatively minor and insufficient.

Whole-Language Emphasis   Advocates of whole-language approaches to reading believe that learning to read is a natural part of normal language development. From their perspective, then, how children learn to read should be very similar to how they learned to use oral language. Developing beginning reading skills is viewed as a natural process of children actively inquiring about print and its meaning and gradually coming to use it just as they do spoken language. To some extent, whole-language approaches are similar to other meaning-emphasis approaches because they imply working first on teaching students to extract meaning from printed material rather than to convert it to oral-language equivalents.

Smith (1977), one of the champions of whole-language approaches to reading, suggested that children must realize that print is meaningful as a prerequisite to learning to read. He wrote that just as children develop spoken-language skills by learning that different sequences of sounds and words have different meanings,

> a similar insight—that differences on a printed page have a function, that they are meaningful—must also be the basis for learning written language. As long as children see print as purposeless or nonsensical, they will find attention to print aversive and will be bored. Children will not learn by trying to relate letters to sounds, partly because the task does not make sense to them and partly because written language does not work that way. In my view reading is not a matter of decoding letters to sound but of bringing meaning to print. (Smith, 1977, p. 387)

In practice, whole-language perspectives on reading usually translate into what is called a *language experience approach* (LEA). In LEA, the material to be read is based on students' experiences and the language they use to express these experiences. Often beginning reading students in an LEA program will have a group activity and then dictate a story about it to their teacher; each child may contribute one sentence, which the teacher writes on an "experience chart." Later the students may read and illustrate their story. Gradually, of course, the students will make more extensive contributions to their group stories and introduce more complex vocabulary and syntax. Eventually they will write and illustrate their own stories and read in textbooks. Texts about using LEA by Stauffer (1980) and M. Hall (1981) provide more detail about this approach.

Evidence about the effectiveness of LEA is discouraging. Bond and Dykstra (1967) reported that in several studies scores favored LEA in comparison to traditional basal reader approaches. But, they noted, these differences were also present in pretest measures of performance—students in the LEA programs had significantly higher scores before teaching

began. When the pretest scores were taken into account, the differences favoring LEA programs disappeared. In other words, the reason students in LEA achieved better reading scores after the first grade was that they had already achieved better scores before entering the LEA program. Results at the end of the second grade also revealed no significant differences favoring the LEA approaches (Dykstra, 1968b). Thus LEA was not found to be any better than traditional meaning-emphasis basal programs. Similarly, the Tucson Early Education Model in Project Follow Through, which emphasized an experience-based approach to language and reading (Maccoby & Zellner, 1970), failed to produce favorable effects; it actually resulted in worse achievement scores than the comparison programs (Abt Associates, 1976–1977).

Some sources do cite evidence that supports the effectiveness of LEA. For example, M. Hall wrote that "Research confirms this method's effectiveness in teaching beginning reading. In a review of thirteen research studies on the language experience approach from 1926 to 1965, Hildreth reports positive results for this approach in eleven instances" (Hall, 1981, p. 14; citation refers to Hildreth, 1965). However, what Hildreth actually wrote was, "The following are references to comparison studies of teaching initial reading through experience-related material in contrast to the use of standard traditional textbook methods: [here are listed thirteen citations].... In only two cases were the results negative for the [LEA] group" (Hildreth, 1965, pp. 293–294). Thus there were not 11 favorable studies, as Hall implied, but rather 11 studies that did not favor either LEA or the approach to which it was compared, 2 that favored an approach other than LEA, and none that favored LEA.

Specialized Approaches   Several beginning reading approaches have such unique charac-

teristics that discussing them in one of the preceding sections would be inaccurate classification. Particularly important among these are
the *Initial Teaching Alphabet* and *Peabody
Rebus Reading* programs.

Peabody Rebus Reading This program
shares many important features with the meaning-emphasis and whole-language approaches.
In particular, the rationale for the Rebus program is that students should first learn to treat
reading as a meaning-getting process. The
unique aspect of the Rebus approach is that
students are not exposed to words during beginning reading instruction. Instead, stories are
printed with rebuses (symbols or pictures). For
example, *the* is indicated by a hand with the
index finger pointing toward the right, *dog* by a
picture of a dog, and *under* by a drawing of a
square with a dot beneath it.

Initial Teaching Alphabet The *Initial
Teaching Alphabet* or i/t/a was designed to facilitate students' mastery of the decoding aspect of reading, and therefore it is similar to
other code-emphasis approaches. The unique
aspect of i/t/a is that it includes one grapheme
for each phoneme usually found in English.
For example, the letters *s* and *h* usually have a
unique sound when they occur together (*sh* as
in *hush*) and that sound has a unique symbol in
i/t/a. In fact, there are 40 different symbols in
the i/t/a alphabet. Thus the spelling for the
word *read* would be rɛɛd in the present tense
and ᴚɛd in the past tense. The rationale for
modifying the spelling system of English in this
manner is that it will make the task of learning
the alphabetic principle easier for children.
Evidence about the effects of i/t/a are mixed
(e.g., Downing, 1964; Dykstra, 1968a).

Other systems for simplifying the spelling
system of English include UNIFON (Whitman Publishing Company), *Words in Color*
(Gattegno, 1963), and the *Diacritical Marking
System* (Fry, 1964).

Remedial Approaches

Remedial interventions are at least as varied
as developmental interventions and many of
the same controversies boil in both areas. Historically, *multisensory* approaches have been
very popular methods for individualizing instruction in learning disabilities. During the
1960s and 1970s, some methods for individual-
ization attempted to capitalize on learners'
characteristics by *matching instruction to modality strengths*. During the same period, behaviorally based approaches were developed
and became more sophisticated (e.g., teaching
reading skills as cognitive operations). These
approaches, and additional techniques and
methods, are discussed in this section.

Many programs of reading instruction
emphasize the relationships among reading,
writing, and speaking.

Multisensory Two of the most widely known and long-standing approaches to teaching reading to children with learning disabilities include the recommendation to use several sensory modalities. The various modalities—visual (seeing), auditory (hearing), kinesthetic (body or muscle feeling), and tactile (touch feeling)—were all discussed and employed in the approaches of Grace Fernald and of Samuel T. Orton and Anna Gillingham. Despite this similarity, the Fernald and the Orton-Gillingham techniques are different in other ways.

Fernald Grace Fernald (1943) is probably the figure most readily associated with the visual-auditory-kinesthetic-tactile or VAKT approach. The rationale for the Fernald Word Learning Approach, which is usually known as the VAKT approach, is that by being taught to use as many senses as possible, the child comes to use additional experiences or cues in learning to read. If the child is weak in any one modality, the others will help to convey the information. In practice, the VAKT approach is not confined to reading; it is also used in spelling and writing instruction. It is essentially a language experience and whole-word approach. Fernald believed that overcoming the emotional problems failing students have with reading would be easier if their reading material was of interest to them. Therefore stories are written down as suggested by the students, with as much help from the teacher as needed, and then read. Also, a student selects words that he or she wishes to learn and works on them, repeatedly tracing and saying a word until it can be written from memory. Words that have been mastered are kept in a file so that a student may refer back to them as needed. Fernald was opposed to having students "sound out" words; she emphasized the reading and writing of words as wholes. Although there are strong advocates of the Fernald approach who can provide case studies of its successful use, research evidence does not reveal that it has been particularly successful (Myers, 1978).

Orton-Gillingham Another multisensory approach to reading has been advocated by Gillingham and Stillman (1965). The method is based on work the authors did with Orton in the 1930s and it is often known as the Orton-Gillingham approach. Orton, who was a neurologist, theorized that the brain stored information in both hemispheres and that the information stored in each was a mirror image of what was stored in the other. Thus, in one hemisphere, the printed word *was* would be represented in its usual form, while in the other hemisphere, it would be represented as *saw*. Children who had not completely developed lateral dominance (meaning one side of their brains had not grown dominant over the other, as usually happens) would be confused about which image was the correct one when reading. This theory accounted for reversals in reading and writing that Orton (1937) had observed. Orton suggested that the "whole-word" or "sight" approach to instruction only made these children's problems worse and that they should be taught reading and spelling according to a phonics approach.

Gillingham and Stillman (1965) made Orton's recommendations into a practical procedure. They created a program that was designed to remediate not only problems in reading but also related problems in spelling and handwriting. They recommended that students learn associations between letters and their sounds in all of the modalities required by the reading, spelling, and handwriting tasks. Thus students are taught to see a letter (visual) and say its sound (auditory), hear a sound (auditory) and write it (kinesthetic), and so forth. Initially, instruction is based on 5 letters.

When they have been practiced until they are mastered, 5 more letters are introduced and practiced, until all 10 have been mastered. More letters are then introduced one at a time. Additionally, when the first 10 letter associations have been mastered, work on blending letters into words is begun. Spelling and story reading are gradually introduced as the student develops facility with the vocabulary that can be built from the mastered grapheme-phoneme associations.

Beyond the case study reports of Orton (1937), there is no readily available reliable research evidence about the effectiveness of this approach to instruction. Some of the method's features are consistent with other effective approaches—for example, a code-emphasis approach in beginning reading is well supported; but other aspects of this approach do not receive the same strong support—for example, returning to rudimentary grapheme-phoneme work with remedial readers.

Hegge, Kirk, and Kirk Although not usually considered a multisensory approach, the *Remedial Reading Drills* of Hegge, S. Kirk, and W. Kirk (1970) emphasize use of multiple modalities during reading instruction. S. A. Kirk (1976) became interested in reading during his work with Monroe (1932). At the Wayne County Training School (see Chapter 1), he studied psychological research related to learning and applied it to these instructional programs. The *Remedial Reading Drills* are designed to help students remember phoneme-grapheme relationships by providing extensive practice and by simplifying the relationships between letters and their sounds (e.g., using only one sound for a letter until it has been thoroughly mastered; see research by Carnine, 1976, discussed in Chapter 2). In the program, students are taught to (1) say sounds for individual letters, (2) blend combinations of sounds, (3) write letters for sounds from memory, and (4) practice reading words aloud from prescribed word lists. Practice in reading from connected prose has to be provided by the teacher because the program is limited to reading letters and words in isolation.

Modality Matching Another way in which modalities have played a part in reading is the matching of types of learners with types of instructional programs. Children who have different "learning styles" are given instruction that matches their styles so that learning should be easier for them (see Lloyd, 1984, for a general critique of this idea). In earlier chapters, approaches to remediation that attempted to "patch up" weaknesses in auditory or visual perceptual skills were discussed. But, according to the modality-matching perspective, teachers should take advantage of students' strengths rather than remediate their weaknesses.

Although there are many types of learning styles (see, e.g., Chapter 3 on cognitive styles), the most popular ones considered in the area of learning disabilities have been visual and auditory learning styles. Visual learners are considered to have strong skills in visual areas of information processing; that is, they should score higher on tests that measure visual skills (e.g., the visual-manual channel of the *Illinois Test of Psycholinguistic Abilities*) than on tests that measure auditory abilities (e.g., the auditory-vocal channel of the *Illinois Test of Psycholinguistic Abilities*). Auditory learners would have just the opposite profiles.

Approaches to reading instruction can also be characterized as visual or auditory. Programs that require students to learn specific discriminations between words on the basis of their shapes (⌐⌐ versus ⌐⌐ for *dog* and *cat*) would be consistent with a "sight" approach; these programs would be considered visual. In contrast, programs that require students to use sounds and to blend words from smaller parts would be considered "auditory" programs.

These approaches are parallel to the meaning-emphasis and code-emphasis approaches to beginning reading.

According to the theory, different strokes are better for different folks. Advocates of this idea (e.g., D. J. Johnson & Myklebust, 1967; Lerner, 1971; Wepman, 1964) believe that when instruction requires use of learners' stronger modalities, better learning will result; but when instruction does not match with learners' styles, progress will be minimal. Thus auditory learners should be given auditory programs and visual learners visual programs.

The idea of individualizing instruction in this way was appealing in the 1970s; nearly 100% of teachers reported that they thought consideration of modalities was an important aspect of planning instructional programs, and well over 90% believed that there was research evidence supporting it (Arter & Jenkins, 1977). As appealing as the idea may be, however, there is little evidence that higher reading achievement results for students taught according to their modality strengths and weaknesses. Many studies of matching reading instruction to learning styles have been conducted, but the results have rarely favored this approach (see Arter & Jenkins, 1977; Bateman, 1979; Tarver & Dawson, 1978; Ysseldyke, 1973).

Behavioral Behavioral approaches to reading instruction have been developing rapidly in the field of learning disabilities. Two major forms of behavioral intervention, *Applied Behavior Analysis* (ABA) and *Direct Instruction,* have emerged as the major models in this area. Both approaches emphasize (1) reinforcement of correct responses, (2) correction of errors, (3) monitoring of progress, and (4) high structuring of the educational environment. In reading, the principal difference between the ABA and Direct Instruction approaches is that although Direct Instruction programs are designed to teach students "general case strategies" for attacking and solving decoding and comprehension problems, many (but not all) ABA approaches have placed greater emphasis on learning specific isolated skills.

Applied Behavior Analysis Some research with applied behavior analysis has examined comprehensive classroom programs for improving reading performance (e.g., Haring & Hauck, 1969), but most studies of reading problems using ABA procedures have provided information about specific intervention techniques. For example, there have been many demonstrations that learning-disabled students' reading accuracy can be improved by providing reinforcement for reading more words correctly and for reading with fewer errors (e.g., Jenkins, Barksdale, & Clinton, 1978; Roberts & Smith, 1980; Swanson, 1981).

Simply reinforcing more accurate oral reading, however, may not be a sufficient intervention. Even though oral reading and reading comprehension are intimately related, it is often the case that improvement in oral reading accuracy does not lead to improvement in answering comprehension questions correctly (Jenkins, et al., 1978; Roberts & Smith, 1980; Swanson, 1981). When the desired outcome of a reading intervention is greater accuracy in answering comprehension questions, interventions that are directly focused on that behavior are more desirable. For example, when Lahey, McNees, and Brown (1973) rewarded students with pennies for correct answers to comprehension questions, they found substantial increases in how well the children did. As another example, Knapczyk and Livingston (1974) prompted students to raise their hands and ask questions when they did not understand what they were to do or how to do it; they found that this simple procedure caused much better accuracy on reading comprehension tasks.

A more complete intervention would focus

on *both* oral reading accuracy and comprehension. Lovitt and Hansen (1976b) described a reinforcement-based intervention procedure for improving learning-disabled students' oral reading and comprehension. After identifying reading books at appropriate levels for each student (Lovitt & Hansen, 1976a; see previous discussion in section on diagnosis), a special procedure called "contingent skipping and drilling" was used. When students read from their readers and answered comprehension questions quickly and accurately, they were allowed to skip parts of the text that would usually be assigned for the next few lessons. However, when they did not meet the criteria for speed and accuracy, they were required to practice skills until they could do so. Over the course of a school year, the contingent skipping and drilling procedure resulted in great improvement in the students' reading performance.

Other studies have examined the contribution of various programming strategies for teaching reading. For example, Fleisher and Jenkins (1978) found that supplementary instruction in reading words from lists helped students on reading from lists but did not have much effect on their reading in context. In a study on how to introduce new words, Neef, Iwata, and Page (1977) found that new words were learned better when they were mixed in with words the students already knew.

Direct Instruction   The Direct Instruction approach to remedial reading includes many techniques similar to those described in the section on ABA, but also has some unique features. The major special feature is that Direct Instruction procedures are designed to teach students "general case" strategies for attacking and solving types of reading tasks. A sound-it-out strategy is a general case procedure for decoding; this approach is similar to the one described in Table 7.4. However, in Direct Instruction programs for remediating reading

problems, there is less emphasis on teaching the basics of this strategy (e.g., the sounds for letters) and more emphasis on teaching skills used during the oral reading of passages.

General case strategies are also taught for comprehension skills. For example, Carnine, Prill, and Armstrong (1978) designed a procedure for students to use to answer questions about the sequence of events in stories they read. Sequence questions require readers to indicate which event happened first, next, and last in the story. Many students have difficulty with this type of task. In the Carnine et al. study, the children were taught to locate each part of the possible answer in the story and mark it; then they learned to determine the order of those parts and use that order to answer the question. As another example, Kameenui, Carnine, and Maggs (1980) taught learning-disabled students to use a series of steps to answer questions that required understanding of sentences with clauses that often cause confusion; a sentence of this type is "Henry, who kissed Joan, ran home crying." The students were taught to restate the original sentence as two separate sentences so that they could answer questions about it (e.g., "Who did the kissing?"). Studies of both of these procedures and others similar to them have revealed that they have resulted in immediate and marked improvement in students' reading (Lloyd, Kosiewicz, & Hallahan, 1982).

The most widely known program for using Direct Instruction procedures with students who have reading difficulties is *Corrective Reading* (Engelmann et al., 1978). *Corrective Reading* includes scripted daily lessons designed to teach the component skills needed for fluent, accurate decoding; students read from carefully structured word lists and then participate in group and individual reading of stories. Research with *Corrective Reading* has revealed that it improves the reading of pupils with learning disabilities (Lloyd, Epstein, & Cullinan, 1981; Maggs & Maggs, 1979) and may be particularly valuable with students who have relatively greater deficits in reading (Pflaum & Pascarella, 1980).

Specific Techniques   In addition to the major approaches to remediation just discussed, various people interested in reading and learning disabilities have recommended highly specific techniques for use in reading instruction. Some of these techniques are described in the following paragraphs.

Neurological Impress Method   The Neurological Impress Method is a procedure for helping students acquire reading skills in which both teacher and student read aloud in unison. It has been recommended for use with students who have reading problems (Bos, 1982; Heckelman, 1969). The main purpose of the lessons is for the teacher and student to cover a great deal of material in much the same way that most competent readers would, without slow, laborious attention to detail. Virtually any material that the student chooses may be used for the lessons because it is believed that it is more important for these children to read a book or story that appeals to them than one that is appropriate for their reading level. Reports of informal studies using this approach (e.g., Heckelman, 1969) have described gains by students with reading problems, but results from more carefully controlled research studies (Hollingsworth 1970; Lorenz & Vockell, 1979) have not been favorable. For example, when Lorenz and Vockell (1979) compared the word reading and reading comprehension of two groups of learning-disabled elementary-grade students, one of which had received Neurological Impress Method training for a term and one of which had received the usual instruction, they found no differences.

Repeated Readings   Another procedure for improving reading performance is the method of repeated readings (Samuels, 1979). This method is based on the idea that in order to

become fluent readers, students must get extensive practice in reading; the result of this practice will be fluent decoding, which will free the students from concentrating on reading words and allow them to devote their attention to comprehending what they read. Samuels (1981) noted that many special education students do not have enough opportunity to practice reading:

> This is not done in training athletes and musicians. Basketball players practice jump shots over and over again; musicians practice short musical selections repeatedly. Their goal is to develop skills to a level of fluid accuracy. With enough practice, they do not have to devote much attention to the mechanics of their skills. With enough practice, readers will not have to devote much attention to the mechanics of decoding. (pp. 23–24)

The repeated readings procedure is quite simple: Students simply read and reread a passage of written material aloud until they can read it at a prespecified rate with accuracy. Some research indicates that the method is a valuable addition to a general reading program, both for normal (e.g., Dahl, 1979) and atypical learners (e.g., Samuels, 1979).

Context Training   Some evidence about how learning-disabled students read indicates that they may benefit from using context clues to help them decode (Pflaum & Bryan, 1981). Training procedures for helping them develop this skill have been investigated by Pflaum and Pascarella. In one study, they found that children with more severe reading deficits benefited from Direct Instruction, but children with less severe problems benefited from training that showed them how to monitor their own reading performance for errors and correct only those that seemed to change the meaning of what they were reading (Pflaum & Pascarella, 1980). In a second study (Pascarella & Pflaum, 1981), they found that children with a more external locus of control benefited from a more teacher-directed instructional program for learning context usage, but that children with a more internal locus of control benefited from a more student-directed program for learning the same skills.

Supplementary Materials   Many teachers build their remedial reading programs for learning-disabled students from a variety of instructional procedures, materials, and kits. Usually the teacher will retain the basal reading program used in the local school, but assign supplementary materials according to individual students' needs. Although there is no evidence that this is any more effective than—or even *as* effective as—a more systematic approach, the eclectic method is quite popular. Among the commercially available materials used are some devoted to *decoding* skills and some devoted to *comprehension* skills.

Decoding   Materials for work on decoding skills usually emphasize improving phonics skills or sight vocabulary. The *Dolch Sight Vocabulary* (published by Garrard) includes common words printed on cards and, for more difficult work, phrases composed of common words and printed on cards. These are used as flashcards during drill activities. Commercial series such as *Phonics We Use* (Lyons and Carnahan) and *Phonics Skill Builders* (McCormick-Mathers) are designed to aid in the development of word-analysis and word-attack skills.

Comprehension   Series of tasks requiring students to comprehend what they have read are available from many publishers. Examples of these are *Reading Laboratories* (Science Research Associates), *Reading for Understanding* (Webster/McGraw-Hill), and *Specific Skills Series* (Barnell-Loft). Each of these series uses brief passages and questions based on the passage, arranged in order of increasing difficulty.

SUMMARY

Pupils with reading disabilities have severe, persistent deficits that impair their progress in school. They may also be called dyslexics, corrective readers, or remedial readers. They have difficulty with the phonological, syntactic, or semantic aspects of reading—or a combination of them—and, thus, do not integrate skills in these areas into the smooth, fluent reading of their peers. As a consequence, their reading is often stumbling and confused. Their problems in reading are often associated with problems in spoken language and aspects of written language, particularly spelling.

Tools developed to assess reading performance include those designed for screening, diagnosis, and progress monitoring. Screening tests, which are usually measures of very general reading skill such as included in most standardized achievement tests, allow educators to identify students who may need further help. Diagnostic reading assessments may be accomplished using either formal (standardized reading tests) or informal means (clinical teaching or informal reading inventories); the purpose of diagnostic reading assessment is to ascertain where instruction should begin. Progress monitoring systems, which allow a teacher to revise a pupil's instructional program based on how the student is performing, often include series of miniature reading tests that can be given repeatedly and that have been found to compare favorably to traditional assessment approaches.

Educators hope to prevent reading disabilities by using effective developmental reading programs, but developmental programs are not always successful; thus, remedial or corrective programs are also needed.

Developmental programs usually emphasize one of four instructional approaches. They may choose a *code-emphasis* approach which focuses on mastery of skills that allow pupils to convert print into its spoken language equivalents. They may choose a *linguistic* approach which does not advocate the breaking of words into the underlying alphabetic code, but suggests the teaching of words according to spelling patterns so that pupils can discover the code. They may choose a *meaning-emphasis* approach which focuses on having pupils master a rote set of words that will allow them to begin reading stories very early in their school years. Or they may choose a *whole-language* approach which emphasizes the inter-relatedness of spoken and written language and seeks to teach reading by capitalizing on pupils' own experiences.

Interventions designed to serve a remedial rather than a developmental function have been just as diverse. Multisensory programs such as those of Fernald and Orton and Gillingham have been popular in the field of learning disabilities throughout its history. Matching pupil's modality preferences with types of instructional programs was championed by learning disabilities specialists, but has not been found to be effective. Several behavioral interventions, including very specific techniques and comprehensive remedial programs, have been recommended by other authorities in the field.

REFERENCES

Abt Associates. (1976–1977). *Education as experimentation: A planned variation model* (Vols. 3A and 4). Cambridge, MA: Author.

ACKERMAN, P. T., PETERS, J. E., & DYKMAN, R. A. (1971). Children with specific learning disabilities: WISC profiles. *Journal of Learning Disabilities, 4,* 150–166.

ANDERSON, W. W. (1977). Focus on measurement and evaluation—commercial informal reading inventories: A comparative review. *Reading World, 17,* 99–103.

ARTER, J. A., & JENKINS, J. R. (1977). Examining the benefits and prevalence of modality considerations in special education. *Journal of Special Education, 11,* 281–298.

BATEMAN, B. (1979). Teaching reading to learning disabled and other hard-to-teach children. In L. Resnick & P. Weaver (Eds.), *Theory and practice of early reading,* (Vol. 1, pp. 227–259). Hillsdale, NJ: Erlbaum.

BECKER, W. C. (1977). Teaching reading and language to the disadvantaged—what we have learned from field research. *Harvard Educational Review, 47,* 518–543.

BLIESMER, E. P., & YARBOROUGH, B. H. (1965). A comparison of ten different beginning reading programs in first grade. *Phi Delta Kappan, 46,* 500–504.

BOND, G. L., CLYMER, T., & HOYT, C. (1970). *Silent Reading Diagnostic Tests* (Rev. ed.). Chicago: Lyons and Carnahan.

BOND, G. L., & DYKSTRA, R. (1967). The cooperative research program in first-grade reading instruction. *Reading Research Quarterly, 2*(4), 5–142.

BOND, G. L., TINKER, M. A., & WASSON, B. B. (1979). *Reading difficulties* (4th ed.). Englewood Cliffs, NJ: Prentice-Hall.

BOS, C. (1982). Getting past decoding: Assisted and repeated readings as remedial methods for learning disabled students. *Topics in Learning and Learning Disabilities, 1*(4), 51–57.

BREZEINSKI, J., & SCHOEPHOERSTER, H. (1976). *Test manual: Tests of basic reading skills.* Boston: Houghton Mifflin.

BURNS, P. C., & ROE, B. D. (1980). *Informal Reading Assessment.* Chicago: Rand McNally.

CARNINE, D. (1976). Similar sound separation and cumulative introduction in learning letter-sound correspondences. *Journal of Educational Research, 69,* 368–372.

CARNINE, D. (1977). Phonics versus look-say: Transfer to new words. *Reading Teacher, 30,* 636–640.

CARNINE, D. W., PRILL, N., & ARMSTRONG, J. (1978). *Teaching slower performing students general case strategies for solving comprehension items.* Eugene, OR: University of Oregon Follow Through Project.

CARNINE, D., & SILBERT, J. (1979). *Direct instruction reading.* Columbus, OH: Charles Merrill.

CARPENTER, D. (1983). Spelling error profiles of able and disabled readers. *Journal of Learning Disabilities, 16,* 102–104.

CARPENTER, D., & MILLER, L. J. (1982). Spelling ability of reading disabled LD students and able readers. *Learning Disability Quarterly, 5,* 65–70.

CHALL, J. (1983). *Learning to read: The great debate* (rev. ed.). San Francisco: McGraw-Hill.

CHALL, J., ROSWELL, F. F., & BLUMENTHAL, S. H. (1963). Auditory blending ability: A factor in success in beginning reading. *Reading Teacher, 17,* 113–118.

CLAY, M. M., & IMLACH, R. H. (1971). Juncture, pitch and stress as reading behavior variables. *Journal of Verbal Learning and Verbal Behavior, 10,* 133–139.

CRITCHLEY, M. D. (1970). *The dyslexic child.* Springfield, IL: Charles C. Thomas.

CTB/MCGRAW-HILL. (1977–1978). *California Achievement Test.* Monterey, CA: Author.

DAHL, P. R. (1979). An experimental program for teaching high-speed word recognition and comprehension skills. In J. E. Button, T. C. Lovitt, & T. D. Rowland (Eds.), *Communications research in learning disabilities and mental retardation* (pp. 33–65). Baltimore, MD: University Park Press.

DOLCH, E. (1948). *Problems in reading.* Champaign, IL: Garrard.

DOWNING, J. A. (1964). The i/t/a (Initial Teaching Alphabet) reading experiments. *Reading Teacher, 18,* 105–110.

DUNN, L. M., & MARKWARDT, F. C., JR. (1970). *Peabody Individual Achievement Test.* Circle Pines, MN: American Guidance Service.

DURKIN, D. (1978). *Teaching them to read* (3rd ed.). Boston: Allyn & Bacon.

DURR, W. K. (1973). Computer study of high frequency words in popular trade juveniles. *Reading Teacher, 27,* 37–42.

DURR, W. K., WINDLEY, V. O., & YATES, M. C. (1976). *Houghton Mifflin reading series.* Boston: Houghton Mifflin.

DYKSTRA, R. (1968a). The effectiveness of code- and meaning-emphasis beginning reading programs. *Reading Teacher, 22,* 17–23.

DYKSTRA, R. (1968b). Summary of the second-grade phase of the Cooperative Research Program in primary reading instruction. *Reading Research Quarterly, 4,* 49–70.

EATON, M. D., & LOVITT, T. C. (1972). Achievement tests vs. direct and daily measurement. In G. Semb (Ed.), *Behavioral analysis and education* (pp. 78–87). Lawrence, KS: University of Kansas.

EKWALL, E. E. (1979). *Ekwall Reading Inventory.* Boston: Allyn & Bacon.

ENGELMANN, S., BECKER, W. C., HANNER, S., & JOHNSON, G. (1978). *Corrective reading* (series guide). Chicago: Science Research Associates.

EPSTEIN, M. H., & CULLINAN, D. (1979). Social vali-

dation: Use of normative peer data to evaluate LD interventions. *Learning Disability Quarterly, 2*(4), 93–98.

EPSTEIN, M. H., & CULLINAN, D. (1981). Project ExCEL: A behaviorally-oriented educational program for learning disabled pupils. *Education and Treatment of Children, 4,* 357–373.

FLEISHER, L. S., & JENKINS, J. R. (1978). Effects of contextualized and decontextualized practice conditions on word recognition. *Learning Disability Quarterly, 1*(3), 39–47.

FLESCH, R. (1981). *Why Johnny still can't read: A new look at the scandal of our schools.* New York: Harper & Row.

FERNALD, G. (1943). *Remedial techniques in basic school subjects.* New York: McGraw-Hill.

FRIES, C. C. (1963). *Linguistics and reading.* New York: Holt, Rinehart & Winston.

FRY, E. (1964). A diacritical marking system to aid beginning reading instruction. *Elementary English, 41,* 526–529.

GARNER, R. (1980). Monitoring of understanding: An investigation of good and poor readers' awareness of induced miscomprehension of text. *Journal of Reading Behavior, 12,* 55–63.

GATES, A. I., & MACGINITIE, W. H. (1972). *Gates-MacGinitie Reading Tests.* New York: Teachers College Press.

GATTEGNO, C. (1963). *Words in color.* Chicago: Learning Materials.

GILLINGHAM, A., & STILLMAN, B. (1965). *Remedial training for children with specific disability in reading, spelling and penmanship* (7th ed.). Cambridge, MA: Educators Publishing Service.

GILMORE, J. V., & GILMORE, E. C. (1968). *Gilmore oral reading test.* New York: Harcourt Brace Jovanovich.

GLASS, G. G. (1971). Perceptual conditioning for decoding: Rationale and method. In B. Bateman (Ed.), *Learning disorders, Vol. 4: Reading* (pp. 75–108). Seattle, WA: Special Child.

GOLINKOFF, R. M., & ROSINSKI, R. R. (1976). Decoding, semantic processing, and reading comprehension skill. *Child Development, 47,* 252–258.

GRAY, W. S., & ROBINSON, H. M. (1967). *Gray Oral Reading Test.* Austin, TX: Pro-Ed.

GURREN, L., & HUGHES, A. (1965). Intensive phonics vs. gradual phonics in beginning reading: A review. *Journal of Educational Research, 58,* 339–346.

HALL, M. (1981). *Teaching reading as a language experience* (3rd ed.). Columbus, OH: Charles E. Merrill.

HARBER, J. R. (1980). Auditory perception and reading: Another look. *Learning Disability Quarterly,* 3(3), 19–29.

HARING, N. G., & HAUCK, M. (1969). Improved learning conditions in the establishment of reading skills with disabled readers. *Exceptional Children, 35,* 341–351.

HARRIS, A. J., & SIPAY, E. R. (1980). *How to increase reading ability: A guide to developmental and remedial methods* (7th ed.). New York: Longman.

HECKELMAN, R. G. (1969). A Neurological Impress Method of remedial reading. *Academic Therapy, 4,* 277–282.

HEGGE, T. G., KIRK, S. A., & KIRK, W. D. (1970). *Remedial reading drills.* Ann Arbor, MI: George Wahr.

HIERONYMUS, A. N., LINDQUIST, E. F, & HOOVER, H. D. (1978). *Iowa Tests of Basic Skills.* Lombard, IL: Riverside Publishing.

HILDRETH, G. H. (1965). Experience-related reading for school beginners. *Elementary English, 42,* 280–284, 298–297.

HINSHELWOOD, J. (1917). *Congenital word blindness.* London: Lewis.

HOLLINGSWORTH, P. M. (1970). An experiment with the impress method of teaching reading. *Reading Teacher, 24,* 112–114.

JASTAK, J. F., & JASTAK, S. R. (1976). *Wide Range Achievement Test.* Wilmington, DE: Guidance Associates.

JEFFREY, W. E., & SAMUELS, S. J. (1967). Effect of method of reading training on initial learning and transfer. *Journal of Verbal Learning and Verbal Behavior, 6,* 354–358.

JENKINS, J. R. (1979). Oral reading: Considerations for special and remedial education teachers. In J. E. Button, T. C. Lovitt, & T. D. Rowland (Eds.), *Communications research in learning disabilities and mental retardation* (pp. 67–91). Baltimore, MD: University Park Press.

JENKINS, J. R., BARKSDALE, A., & CLINTON, L. (1978). Improving reading comprehension and oral reading: Generalization across behaviors, settings, and time. *Journal of Learning Disabilities,* 1978, *11,* 607–617.

JOHNS, J. L., GARTON, S., SCHOENFELDER, P., & SKRIBA, P. (1977). *Assessing reading behavior: Informal reading inventories.* Newark, DE: International Reading Association.

JOHNSON, D. D. (1971). The Dolch list reexamined. *Reading Teacher, 24,* 455–456.

JOHNSON, D. J., & MYKLEBUST, H. R. (1967). *Learning disabilities: Educational principles and practices.* New York: Grune & Stratton.

JONGSMA, K. S., & JONGSMA, E. A. (1981). Test re-view: Commercial informal inventories. *Reading Teacher, 34,* 697–705.

KALUGER, G., & KOLSON, C. J. (1978). *Reading and learning disabilities* (2nd ed.). Columbus, OH: Charles E. Merrill.

KAMEENUI, E., CARNINE, D., & MAGGS, A. (1980). Instructional procedures for teaching reversible passive voice and clause constructions to three mildly handicapped children. *The Exceptional Child, 27*(1), 29–41.

KARLSEN, B., MADDEN, R., & GARDNER, E. F. (1976). *Stanford Diagnostic Reading Test* (rev. ed.). New York: Harcourt Brace Jovanovich.

KASS, C. E. (1966). Psycholinguistic disabilities of children with reading problems. *Exceptional Children, 32,* 533–539.

KAVALE, K. A. (1980). The reasoning abilities of normal and learning disabled readers on measures of reading comprehension. *Learning Disability Quarterly, 3*(4), 34–45.

KENDALL, J. R., MASON, J. M., & HUNTER, W. (1980). Which comprehension? Artifacts in the measurement of reading comprehension. *Journal of Educational Research, 73,* 233–236.

KIRK, S. A. (1976). S. A. Kirk. In J. M. Kauffman & D. P. Hallahan (Eds.), *Teaching children with learning disabilities: Personal perspectives* (pp. 238–269). Columbus, OH: Charles E. Merrill.

KIRK, S. A., & ELKINS, J. (1975). Characteristics of children enrolled in the child service demonstration centers. *Journal of Learning Disabilities, 8,* 630–637.

KNAPCZYK, D. R., & LIVINGSTON, G. (1974). The effects of prompting question-asking upon on-task and reading comprehension. *Journal of Applied Behavior Analysis, 7,* 115–121.

LAHEY, B. B., MCNEES, M. P., & BROWN, C. C. (1973). Modification of deficits in reading for comprehension. *Journal of Applied Behavior Analysis, 6,* 460–475.

LARSEN, S., ROGERS, D., & SOWELL, V. (1976). The use of selected perceptual tests in differentiating between normal and learning disabled children. *Journal of Learning Disabilities, 9,* 85–90.

LERNER, J. W. (1971). *Children with learning disabilities.* Boston: Houghton Mifflin.

LERNER, J. W. (1975). Remedial reading and learning disabilities: Are they the same or different? *Journal of Special Education, 9,* 119–132.

LIBERMAN, I. Y., SHANKWEILER, D., LIBERMAN, A. M., FOWLER, C., & FISCHER, F. W. (1977). Phonetic segmentation and recoding in the beginning reader. In A. S. Reber & D. L. Scarborough (Eds.), *Toward a psychology of reading: The proceedings of the CUNY Conference* (pp. 207–225). Hillsdale, NJ: Erlbaum.

LLOYD, J. (1979). Ascertaining the reading skills of atypical learners. In D. A. Sabatino & T. L. Miller (Eds.), *Describing learner characteristics for special education* (pp. 293–332). New York: Grune & Stratton.

LLOYD, J. W. (1984). How should we individualize instruction—or should we? *Remedial and Special Education, 5*(1), 7–16.

LLOYD, J. W., CAMERON, N. A., & LLOYD, P. A. (1984). Reading assessment. In R. Fox & A. Rototori (Eds.), *Assessment in regular and special education.* Austin, TX: Pro-Ed.

LLOYD, J., EPSTEIN, M. H., & CULLINAN, D. (1981). Direct teaching for learning disabilities. In J. Gottlieb & S. S. Strichart (Eds.), *Developmental theory and research in learning disabilities* (pp. 278–309). Baltimore, MD: Unversity Park Press.

LLOYD, J. W., KOSIEWICZ, M. M., & HALLAHAN, D. P. (1982). Reading comprehension: Cognitive training contributions. *School Psychology Review, 11,* 35–41.

LORENZ, L., & VOCKELL, E. (1979). Using the neurological impress method with learning disabled readers. *Journal of Learning Disabilities, 12,* 420–422.

LOVITT, T. C., & FANTASIA, K. (1980). Two approaches to reading program evaluation: A standardized test and direct assessment. *Learning Disability Quarterly, 3*(4), 77–87.

LOVITT, T. C., & HANSEN, C. (1976a). Round one: Placing the child in the right reader. *Journal of Learning Disabilities, 9,* 347–353.

LOVITT, T. C., & HANSEN, C. L. (1976b). The use of contingent skipping and drilling to improve oral reading and comprehension. *Journal of Learning Disabilities, 9,* 481–487.

MACCOBY, E. E., & ZELLNER, M. (1970). *Experiments in primary education: Aspects of Follow-Through.* New York: Harcourt Brace Jovanovich.

MADDEN, R., GARDNER, E. R., RUDMAN, H. C., KARLSEN, B., & MERWIN, J. C. (1973). *Stanford Achievement Test.* New York: Harcourt Brace Jovanovich.

MAGGS, A., & MAGGS, R. (1979). Review of direct instruction research in Australia. *Journal of Special Education Technology, 2*(3), 26–34.

MCCRACKEN, G., & WALCUTT, G. C. (1970). *Basic reading.* New York: J. B. Lippincott.

MCCULLOUGH, C. M. (1963). *McCullough Word Analysis Tests.* Princeton, NJ: Personal Press.

MONROE, M. (1932). *Children who cannot read.* Chicago: University of Chicago Press.

MORGAN, W. P. (1896). A case of congenital word blindness. *British Medical Journal, 2,* 1378.

MYERS, C. A. (1978). Reviewing the literature on Fernald's technique of remedial reading. *Reading Teacher, 31,* 614–619.

NEEF, N. A., IWATA, B. A., & PAGE, T. J. (1977). The effects of known-item interspersal on acquisition and retention of spelling and sight-reading words. *Journal of Applied Behavior Analysis, 10,* 738.

NORMAN, C., & ZIGMOND, N. (1980). Characteristics of children labeled and served as learning disabled in school systems affiliated with child service and demonstration centers. *Journal of Learning Disabilities, 13,* 542–547.

OAKAN, R., WEINER, M., & CROMER, W. (1971). Identification, organization, and reading comprehension for good and poor readers. *Journal of Educational Psychology, 62,* 71–78.

ORTON, S. T. (1929). The "sight reading" method of teaching reading, as a source of reading disability. *Journal of Educational Psychology, 30,* 135–143.

ORTON, S. T. (1937). *Reading, writing and speech problems in children.* London: Chapman and Hall.

OTTO. W., RUDOLPH, M., SMITH, R. J., & WILSON, R. (1975). *Merrill linguistic reading program.* Columbus, OH: Charles E. Merrill.

PASCARELLA, E. T., & PFLAUM, S. W. (1981). The interaction of children's attribution and level of control over error correction in reading instruction. *Journal of Educational Psychology, 73,* 533–540.

PERFETTI, C. A., & HOGOBOAM, T. (1975). Relationship between single word decoding and reading comprehension skill. *Journal of Educational Psychology, 67,* 461–469.

PFLAUM, S. W. (1980). The predictability of oral reading behaviors on comprehension in learning disabled and normal readers. *Journal of Reading Behavior, 12,* 231–236.

PFLAUM, S. W., & BRYAN, T. H. (1981). Oral reading behaviors in the learning disabled. *Journal of Educational Research, 73,* 252–258.

PFLAUM, S. W., & PASCARELLA, E. T. (1980). Interactive effects of prior reading achievement and training in context on the reading of learning disabled children. *Reading Research Quarterly, 16,* 138–158.

POTTS, M., & SAVINO, C. (1968). The relative achievement of first graders under three different reading programs. *Journal of Educational Research, 61,* 447–450.

RASMUSSEN, D., & GOLDBERG, L. (1965). *Basic reading series.* Chicago: Science Research Associates.

REID, D. K., & HRESKO, W. P. (1980) A developmental study of the relation between oral language and early reading in learning disabled and normally achieving children. *Learning Disability Quarterly, 3*(4), 54–61.

RESNICK, L. B. (1970). Relations between perceptual and syntactic control in oral reading. *Journal of Educational Psychology, 61,* 382–385.

ROBERTS, M., & SMITH, D. D. (1980). The relationship among correct and error oral reading rates and comprehension. *Learning Disability Quarterly, 3*(1), 54–64.

ROSWELL, F. G., & CHALL, J. C. (1978). *Rosewell-Chall Diagnostic Reading Test of Word Analysis Skills* (Rev. ed.). New York: Essay Press.

ROSINSKI, R. R., GOLINKOFF, R. M., & KUKISH, K. (1975). Automatic semantic processing in a picture-word interference task. *Child Development, 46,* 247–253.

ROZIN, P., BRESSMAN, B., & TAFT, M. (1974). Do children understand the basic relationship between speech and writing: The mownmotorcycle test. *Journal of Reading Behavior, 6,* 327–334.

ROZIN, P., & GLEITMAN, L. R. (1977). The structure and acquisition of Reading II: The reading process and the acquisition of the alphabetic principle. In A. S. Reber & D. L. Scarborough (Eds.), *Toward a psychology of reading: The proceedings of the CUNY Conferences* (pp. 55–141). Hillsdale, NJ: Erlbaum.

SAMUELS, S. J. (1979). The method of repeated readings. *Reading Teacher, 32,* 403–408.

SAMUELS, S. J. (1981). Some essentials of decoding. *Exceptional Education Quarterly, 2*(1), 11–25.

SCHNEYER, J. W. (1966). Reading achievement of first grade children taught by a linguistic approach and a basal reader approach. *Reading Teacher, 19,* 647–652.

SCIENCE RESEARCH ASSOCIATES. (1975). *Diagnosis: an instructional aid—reading.* Chicago: Author.

SHANKWEILER, D., LIBERMAN, I. Y., MARK, L. S., FOWLER, C. A., & FISCHER, F. W. (1979). The speech code and learning to read. *Journal of Experimental Psychology: Human Learning and Memory, 5,* 531–545.

SILVAROLI, N. J. (1979). *Classroom Reading Inventory* (3rd ed.). Dubuque, IA: Wm. C. Brown.

SMITH, F. (1977). Making sense of reading—and of reading instruction. *Harvard Educational Review, 47,* 386–395.

SPACHE, G. D. (1976). *Diagnosing and correcting reading disabilities.* Boston: Allyn & Bacon.

SPACHE, G. D. (1972). *Diagnostic Reading Scales* (rev. ed.). Monterey, CA: Test Bureau.

STARLIN, C. (1971). Evaluating progress toward reading proficiency. In B. Bateman (Ed.), *Learning disorders, Vol. 4: Reading* (pp. 389–465). Seattle, WA: Special Child.

STAUFFER, R. G. (1980). *The language-experience approach to the teaching of reading* (2nd ed.). New York: Harper & Row.

STEIN, C. L'E., & GOLDMAN, J. (1980). Beginning reading instruction for children with minimal brain dysfunction. *Journal of Learning Disabilities, 13,* 219–222.

SWANSON, L. (1981). Modification of comprehension deficits in learning disabled children. *Learning Disability Quarterly, 4,* 189–202.

TARVER, S. G., & DAWSON, M. M. (1978). Modality preference and the teaching of reading: A review. *Journal of Learning Disabilities, 11,* 17–29.

TARVER, S. G., & ELLSWORTH, P. S. (1981). Written and oral language for verbal children. In J. M. Kauffman & D. P. Hallahan (Eds.), *Handbook of special education* (pp. 491–511). Englewood Cliffs, NJ: Prentice-Hall.

VANDEVER, T. R., & NEVILLE, D. D. (1976). Transfer as a result of synthetic and analytic reading instruction. *American Journal of Mental Deficiency, 80,* 498–503.

VELLUTINO, F. R. (1977). Alternative conceptualizations of dyslexia: Evidence in support of a verbal-deficit hypothesis. *Harvard Educational Review, 47,* 334–354.

WALLACH, M. A., & WALLACH, L. (1976). *Teaching all children to read.* Chicago: University of Chicago Press.

WEPMAN, J. M. (1964). The perceptual basis for learning. In H. A. Robinson (Ed.), *Meeting individual differences in reading* (pp. 25–33). Chicago: University of Chicago Press.

WILLIAMS, J. P. (1980). Teaching decoding with an emphasis on phoneme analysis and phoneme blending. *Journal of Educational Psychology, 72,* 1–15.

WOODCOCK, R. W. (1973). *Woodcock Reading Mastery Tests.* Circle Pines, MN: American Guidance.

WOODCOCK, R. W., & JOHNSON, M. B. (1977). *Woodcock-Johnson Psychoeducational Battery.* Boston: Teaching Resources.

YSSELDYKE, J. E. (1973). Diagnostic-prescriptive teaching: The search for aptitude-treatment interactions. In L. Mann & D. A. Sabatino (Eds.), *First review of special education* (Vol. 1; pp. 5–32). Philadelphia: JSE Press.

YSSELDYKE, J. E., & SHINN, M. R. (1981). Psychoeducational evaluation. In J. M. Kauffman & D. P. Hallahan (Eds.), *Handbook of special education* (pp. 418–440). Englewood Cliffs, NJ: Prentice-Hall.

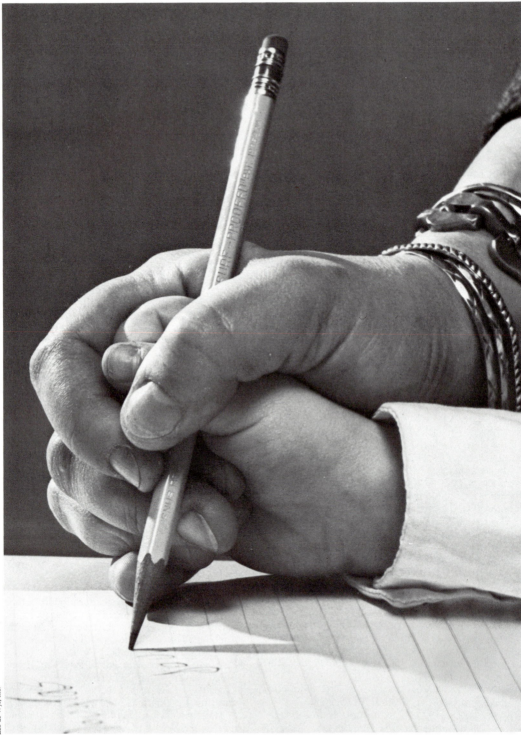

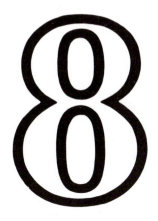

Writing Disabilities

Although learning to read is the first major step toward mastery of written language, learning to write is no less important to progress in school and life. Without written expression skills, students cannot do much more than answer orally or mark true-false and multiple-choice questions. Without written expression skills, it is hard to leave an understandable note, write a letter, answer employment ads, or create a poem or story.

Written expression requires skills in three major areas: handwriting, spelling, and composition. Although it is probably true that the expression of one's thoughts and feelings is more important than the mechanical aspects of writing, illegible handwriting, misspellings, and grammatical inaccuracies make it very difficult for a reader to understand the meaning of a written product. The effective writer commands enough skills in three major areas of written expression to get a message across without misunderstanding.

Aspects of writing disabilities have been discussed in previous chapters. Many of the difficulties learning-disabled students experience in handwriting (e.g., "reversals") were alluded to in Chapter 2 on "Perceptual Disabilities." Some of the difficulties students have with expressing themselves were discussed in Chapter 6 on "Spoken-Language Disabilities."

The three major aspects of written expression are considered in this chapter. The first section covers the topic of handwriting. It is followed by a discussion of problems in spelling. The chapter ends with a section on composition.

HANDWRITING

Handwriting is the most obvious feature of "the second R." Historically, much of the emphasis in handwriting instruction was on development of a stylish and rigidly uniform "hand." Over the years, teaching has changed substantially; compare, for example, the formation of the letter *s* and the general writing style of Thomas Jefferson's time with the formation of *s* and the style of today. With the expansion of electronic word-processing equipment, handwriting may change even more in the coming years.

Handwriting is a means to an end. Students who can write legibly and with reasonable speed are not deterred from expressing themselves by weak handwriting skills. Thus it is obvious that "handwriting is a tool skill which should become routine as rapidly and efficiently as possible" (Herrick, 1961, p. 264). It should not be stressed at the expense of more important skills, such as those necessary to speak, listen, read, spell, or compose well.

This section presents the characteristics of handwriting problems and methods of assessing and teaching handwriting.

Characteristics

Handwriting has long been an area of interest to those concerned about learning disabilities. Perhaps this is because pupils with writing disabilities produce clearly deviant writing—scrawling letter formation, for example—that is permanently available for study (unless the paper is thrown away). Perhaps, also, it reflects our fascination with a relatively good performance that is different in some strange way—mirror writing, for example.

Definitions and Terminology   A handwriting problem exists when a student writes illegibly or extremely slowly. Everyone occasionally produces some illegible letters, but some students do so frequently enough that understanding what they have written is difficult; at this point, the difficulty would be considered a problem. Also, most children write quite slowly when they are first learning to print or write in cursive; slow handwriting should be considered

a problem, however, when a student's writing speed interferes with his or her other work.

Problems with handwriting are also known as *dysgraphia*. Dysgraphia refers to "partial ability (or inability) to remember how to make certain alphabet or arithmetic symbols in handwriting" (Jordon, 1977, p. 189; see also, Cicci, 1983). Dysgraphia is usually associated with *dyslexia* in that both are medically oriented terms and those who use them usually consider the disorders to be the result of psychoneurological disturbance (e.g., McGrady, 1968).

Problems in Handwriting   Although children make many different mistakes in handwriting, most of their mistakes are made on a very few letters. The letters on which errors are most common are *a*, *e*, *r*, and *t* (Anderson, 1968). Students form these letters or the connecting strokes incorrectly, and as a result, the letters look like other letters. For example, if a cursive *d* is misformed in one way, it looks like *cl*. This and some other handwriting problems are shown in Figure 8.1.

Problems Related to Handwriting   Though IQ is not related to handwriting (Seifert, 1960), spelling apparently is. Students with poor handwriting are likely to have poor spelling skills. Two ways in which handwriting may contribute to misspellings are: (1) handwriting errors may make a word look like another word; and (2) slow, labored writing of letters may cause a student to forget the word he or she is trying to spell. The first problem is one of legibility and the second is one of speed.

Handwriting skill is also related to some perceptual and perceptual-motor skills. Wedell (Chapman & Wedell, 1972; Wedell & Horne, 1969) found that young students with handwriting problems had greater difficulties with position-in-space (on the Frostig test; see Chapter 2), drew poorly when drawing required crossing from one side of their bodies to the other, and did not benefit from practice on

Manuscript			Cursive		
g	written like oj		a	written like ci	
d	written like ol		g	written like cj	
n	written like r		d	written like cl	
k	written like ti		i	written like e	
r	written like v		t	written like l	

Figure 8.1 Samples of common handwriting problems.

handwritinglike tasks as much as other students.

Assessment

Screening Few of the general achievement tests commonly used in schools include assessment of handwriting. The *Test of Written Language* (Hammill & Larsen, 1983) does have a handwriting scale, and there are some formal devices that are designed specifically for evaluating handwriting, chief among them the *Ayers Scale* (Ayers, 1912) and the *Zaner-Bloser Evaluation Scale* (Freeman, 1979). On all these instruments, students copy written material and their written products are compared to samples of writing so that ratings of quality can be assigned.

Diagnosis Diagnostic efforts should be aimed at determining with which specific letters, types of letters, or letter combinations individual students have difficulty. One part of the *Basic School Skills Inventory—Diagnostic* (Hammill & Leigh, 1983) is a writing test that assesses many aspects of handwriting, including posture and holding a pencil as well as forming letters; the test is norm referenced and includes remedial recommendations.

However, formal diagnostic testing of hand-

writing is usually unnecessary. Teachers can simply examine samples of students' writing and identify those parts of writing that need further instructional work. To conduct a diagnostic evaluation, a teacher would first look at existing samples of a student's writing to judge whether there are general legibility problems (e.g., inconsistent spacing between letters or excessive erasures). Second, the teacher would determine whether the sample contains any of the more common types of handwriting errors (see Figure 8.1 for examples). Third, the teacher would ask the student to produce another handwriting sample (copying from prepared materials) that includes areas not assessed in the first sample or areas that the first assessment has revealed might be problems for the student.

Students' performance on various types of writing tasks may vary. For example, copying material from the chalkboard may be very difficult for a student who can write fairly well on other tasks. Diagnostic procedures and remedial recommendations for various types of writing tasks, as provided by Towle (1978), are shown in Table 8.1.

Progress Monitoring Collecting daily writing samples and scoring them carefully will suffice quite well for monitoring students'

Mirian Reinhart, Photo Researchers, Inc.

Handwriting performance can be assessed in many ways. A teacher may learn a great deal about this student's performance by evaluating both how he writes and how his written products look.

progress in developing handwriting skills. As already emphasized, the teacher's major concern should be that the students' handwriting is legible and not so slow that their production is impaired.

Progress monitoring can be used to evaluate both the legibility and the speed of handwriting. Brief time periods for assessment can be set aside each day. Students can be given probes (miniature tests) designed to assess the specific skill on which they need work, and then asked to write for a specified period of time (perhaps 1 minute). The resulting writing samples can be scored for the percent of letters written legibly (each letter to be judged as either legible or illegible), and the rate of letters written legibly (legible letters per minute). This information can be placed on graphs or charts to illustrate the progress of each student. If more precise scoring is needed for certain aspects of handwriting, each letter can be scored

as correct for (1) slant, (2) formation (shape), and (3) ending stroke (Haring, Lovitt, Eaton, & Hansen, 1978).

Students can be taught to evaluate their own progress. The accuracy of their judgments about the legibility of their writing can be enhanced by using plastic overlays showing correctly formed letters (Jones, Trap, & Cooper, 1977) or other self-correcting devices (Stowitschek & Stowitschek, 1979). Self-evaluation has been shown to improve LD students' handwriting (Kosiewicz, Hallahan, Lloyd, & Graves, 1982).

Interventions

One of the continuing controversies in handwriting instruction is whether to teach only printing or only cursive handwriting. Those who advocate teaching only printing (e.g., Herrick, 1960; Hildreth, 1960; Templin,

Table 8.1 Tasks and Guidelines for Handwriting Diagnosis and Remediation

Task	Stimuli	Administrative directive	Scoring
1 Writing letters	Blank lined paper.	Write the alphabet over and over Ready, begin. (At end of 1 minute say . . . stop please)	Count 1 for each letter legible. Total _____ Count 1 for each letter illegible. Total _____
2 Copying letters	Alphabet letters randomly presented (3 presentations of each letter) with line 3 spaces under each letter.	Copy these letters. Ready, begin. (1 minute) Stop please.	Count 1 for each letter legible. Total _____ Count 1 for each letter illegible. Total _____
3 Copying letters in sequence, near-point	Words in sentence with space to copy into below each word. Total of 60 letters or 10 words.	Copy these words in the space below. Ready, begin. (1 minute) Stop please.	Count 1 for each letter legible in sentence. Total _____ Count 1 for each letter illegible. Total _____ Count 1 for each letter out of sequence. Total _____
4 Farpoint copying	10 words in sentences written on chalkboard 3 yards from student. Line paper for students.	Copy these words onto your paper. Ready, begin. (1 minute) Stop please.	Count 1 for each letter in sequence. Total _____ Count 1 for each letter illegible. Total _____ Count 1 for each letter out of sequence. Total _____

[a] Compare score totals to criteria established by classroom performance.

[b] Design program based on child performance: criteria.

Performance criteria*	Interpretation†	
(Compare score totals to criteria—criteria are established by the teacher)	(Design program based on child performance: criteria. Choose type of program.)	
	Maintenance program	Instruction and/or practice program
50 legible letters per minute.	When performance is at or above criteria.	When performance is less than criteria.
2 or fewer illegible letters per minute.	When performance is at or below criteria.	When performance is greater than criteria.
50 legible letters per minute.	When performance is at or above criteria.	When performance is less than criteria.
2 or fewer illegible letters per minute.	When performance is at or below criteria.	When performance is greater than criteria.
40 legible letters in sequence per minute.	When performance is at or above criteria.	When performance is below criteria.
2 or fewer illegible letters per minute.	When performance is at or below criteria.	When performance is above criteria.
40 legible letters in sequence per minute.	When performance is at or above criteria.	When performance is below criteria.
2 or fewer illegible letters per minute.	When performance is at or below criteria.	When performance is above criteria.

Source: M. Towle (1978). "Assessment and Remediation of Handwriting Deficits for Children with Learning Disabilities," *Journal of Learning Disabilities,* 11(6), pp. 373–374.

1960; Western, 1977) argue that (1) printing is more similar to the kind of material students read, making it easier to generalize from one to the other; (2) printing is learned first and is therefore difficult to unlearn; (3) printing is more suited to the motor development of young children; (4) the printing of young children is more legible than their cursive; and (5) printing is preferred in business and industry.

Those who advocate teaching only cursive (e.g., Gillingham & Stillman, 1965; Larson, 1968; Strauss & Lehtinen, 1947) argue that (1) cursive letters are more difficult to write backward (i.e., reversed); (2) illegibilities because of poor letter or word spacing are eliminated by cursive; and (3) cursive is faster.

Research evidence does not show that either system is particularly easier to learn or that children write faster in either. Alphabets to replace both cursive and manuscript have been developed for handwriting, and some authors believe that these are particularly well suited for teaching the learning disabled (see, e.g., Joseph & Mullins, 1970).

Innumerable procedures for improving handwriting have been recommended. They include suggestions that learning-disabled students be given relaxation training (Carter & Synolds, 1974), that clay be molded to fit a student's pencil to encourage the correct grip, and that "flipbooks" that make moving models of the strokes for forming letters be used (Wright & Wright, 1980). Although some of these suggestions may be helpful, probably the most important interventions for handwriting are incorporated into comprehensive instructional programs.

Developmental Programs   Developmental handwriting instruction is dominated by two major programs, one marketed by Zaner-Bloser and the other by Barnes & Noble. These programs include teacher directions for demonstrating appropriate writing positions, letter formations, sequences of strokes for forming letters, pupil practice books, and other materials.

An interesting variation on handwriting instruction is marketed by Lyons and Carnahan under the name *Write and See*. The paper on which the workbooks are printed is treated with a chemical and the student uses a pen with special ink. When the student forms a letter correctly, the paper where he or she has written turns green. Initially students trace entire letters, but the cues are gradually *faded* (made less obvious) and the band within which they must write to make the paper turn green is narrowed so that better and better handwriting is shaped.

It is sometimes recommended that young children learning to write tell themselves the stroke sequences as they form letters. For example, while making the printed letter *m*, the child might say, "First, I make a short stick, then I make one hhhuuummmp, two hhhuuummmps. There, that's an 'm'." Preliminary research (Hayes, 1980; Robin, Armel, & O'Leary, 1975) has found some small beneficial effects of "verbal self-guidance," and according to Hallahan's theory about the passive learner (e.g., Hallahan & Reeve, 1980), this type of procedure may be particularly helpful to learning-disabled students.

Remedial Procedures   Handwriting problems have received considerable attention from behaviorally oriented special educators. Behavioral educators have been able to develop a "near-cure" for such handwriting problems as reversals while ignoring many of the psychological and physiological explanations.

The procedure used is quite simple: First, when the student writes a target letter, numeral, or word correctly, the teacher provides reinforcement (e.g., praise). Second, when the student writes an item incorrectly, the teacher requires him or her to correct it. At least six studies have been reported in which this type of procedure or one very similar to it has been used successfully (Fauke, Burnett, Powers, & Sulzer-Azaroff, 1973; Hasazi & Hasazi, 1972; Lahey, Busemeyer, O'Hara, & Beggs, 1977; Smith & Lovitt, 1973; Stromer, 1975, 1977).

SPELLING

Learning-disabled students often have more severe deficits in spelling than in reading. In reading, context and other cues help one to decode a word, but in spelling, one must produce the word after hearing or thinking it. As a consequence of their difficulties with spelling, LD students find writing tasks both laborious and aversive.

There is usually just one correct way to spell any particular word with a given meaning (homonyms—words that sound alike but are spelled differently, such as *here* and *hear*— have different meanings; and some words have "British" and "American" spellings—*behaviour* and *behavior*). Thus spelling does not allow any room for "creative" answers or "style"; a word is either spelled correctly or it is misspelled. This makes it difficult to give learning-disabled students "the benefit of the doubt," as teachers are often tempted to do in other areas.

In the following parts of this section, the characteristics of spelling problems, methods of assessing spelling skills, and instructional procedures for teaching spelling are discussed.

Characteristics

English is difficult to learn to spell. It would be much easier if each phoneme of our language had one and only one grapheme. But that is not the case. There are 251 different spellings for the 44 sounds of English (Hull, 1976) and the language contains many irregularly spelled words.

Definitions and Terminology   Spelling requires that a person *produce in written or oral form the correct sequence of letters that form a particular word.* To do this, a person converts *phonemes* (sounds) into *graphemes* (written letters). The phonemes may actually have been heard—as happens when a spelling word is dictated by a teacher; or they may have been covertly produced—as happens when one spells while writing a letter. Also, spellings may be produced by naming the letters in the correct order.

The formal name for the system of representing spoken language in a written form is *orthography.* Orthography comes from Greek *ortho*, meaning correct, and *graphy*, meaning writing. Thus when students learn the orthography of English, they are learning the system for the correct spelling of English.

Unlike the areas of reading and handwriting, there are not many different terms used to label students with difficulties in spelling. Some authors (e.g., Jordon, 1977) include spelling problems in their use of the terms *dyslexia* and *dysgraphia.* But there are no labels such as "misorthographers" to remember.

Problems in Spelling   Students who have difficulty with the orthography of English differ from other students in some important ways. Obviously one difference is in the way they spell, but some of the differences have to do with these students' performance in other areas.

Most of our knowledge about spelling problems comes from studies of the kinds of errors made by people when they spell. According to Graham and Miller (1979), analyses of misspellings reveal that most errors are (1) phonetically acceptable, (2) made in the middle of words, and (3) alterations of a single phoneme.

As children grow older, their approaches to the task of spelling words changes. Marsh, Friedman, Welch, and Desberg (1980) reported that 7-year-old normally achieving children simply write the most common graphemes for the phonemes in words; this strategy works well as long as the words are regularly pronounced consonant-vowel-consonant words. By the time they have reached the fifth grade, however, students have added other, slightly different strategies to the way they attack spelling. They have learned to use additional letters to indicate the pronunciation of parts of words; for example, they use the "silent *e*" rule. They appear to work by analogy; for example, in trying to spell the word *criticize*, they might realize that it has a second *c* because they know the word *critic* has a second *c*.

Similar evidence about changes in the development of spelling skill comes from studies by Beers (1974) and Gentry (1977) of the spelling errors of normally achieving students. Initially children spell words quite simply—for example, the word *type* might be spelled "TP." Later, however, they represent all of the phonemes of the word, though they might do so incorrectly; for example, *type* might be spelled "TIP," a spelling that reads correctly if the letter *I* is given its name. Still later, students may represent all of the sounds and employ some of the conventions of orthography, although they still may not spell correctly; for example, *type* might be spelled "TIPE." Ultimately, correct spellings emerge.

The most consistent finding about children with learning disabilities comes from studies comparing normally achieving students with those who have reading problems (Barron, 1980; Carpenter, 1983; Carpenter & Miller, 1982; Gerber & Hall, 1981). Learning-disabled students spell fewer words correctly than do their normally achieving age-mates, even when differences in IQ are taken into account (Carpenter & Miller, 1982). These studies also show that although reading-disabled pupils produce spellings that have some phonetic features of the correct spellings, their spellings do not include the special markings that show how to pronounce some parts of words (Gerber & Hall, 1981). Furthermore, in comparison with good readers who do not spell well, poor readers are more likely to produce unrecog-

nizable spellings (Carpenter, 1983; Frith, 1980).

Problems Related to Spelling   Obviously students who have difficulty spelling words will be hindered in their writing. They will produce misspellings that make it difficult for their readers to understand what they mean, and their writing vocabulary may be limited because they will try to use only words they are sure they can spell correctly.

Additionally, the close relationship between spelling and reading indicates that students with spelling problems are very likely to have reading problems. Frith (1980) studied the rare students who read well but spell poorly; she found that they may depend very heavily on the syntactic and semantic aspects of print to help them read, but that they have problems using phonology.

Assessment

Screening   Most standardized achievement batteries include measures of spelling skills—for example, the *California Achievement Tests* (Tiegs & Clark, 1977–1978), the *Peabody Individual Achievement Test* (Dunn & Markwardt, 1970), and the *SRA Achievement Series* (Thorpe, LaFever, & Haslund, 1963). Because pupils who have problems with spelling will very likely score low on any of these tests, using them makes it possible to identify students with spelling deficits. However, many major achievement tests assess spelling skills by having students select the correct spelling from several choices or indicate whether a spelling is correct or incorrect. Because students' performance on this type of task may differ from their performance on a task that requires them to produce the correct spellings of words themselves, further testing for spelling skills is usually well advised.

Other achievement batteries require that students write the spellings for words as they are dictated by the examiner. Examples are the

Metropolitan Achievement Tests (Durost, Bixler, Wrightstone, Prescott, & Balow, 1971), the *Wide Range Achievement Test* (Jastak & Jastak, 1978), and the *Woodcock-Johnson Psychoeducational Battery* (Woodcock & Johnson, 1977). Tests that require students to write spellings are more difficult but they test skills that are closer to those required in actual schoolwork.

Some tests that are designed specifically to measure spelling skill may also be useful for screening. For example, the *Test of Written Spelling* (Larsen & Hammill, 1976) provides several scores that allow comparison to norm groups so that a teacher can determine whether and to what extent a student is behind his or her peers.

Diagnosis Diagnostic methods should provide direction about teaching students: where to begin instruction, what areas of skill need teaching, and so forth. For the purpose of placement, probably the most useful diagnostic tests are those that accompany the spelling program being used. Other methods for diagnosis of spelling problems are *formal tests, analysis of spelling errors,* and *informal spelling inventories.* Each of these is described in the following paragraphs. (See also Box 8.1.)

Formal Tests Several formal tests assess different aspects of spelling skill. For example, the *Test of Written Spelling* (Larsen & Hammill, 1976) is composed of two types of words: those that follow regular spelling patterns (are spelled the way they sound) and those that have irregular spellings. Presumably, if students do well on the regularly spelled words but poorly on the irregularly spelled words, instruction in how to remember some words as wholes would be appropriate. Similarly, the *Gates-Russell Spelling Diagnostic Test* (Gates & Russell, 1940) assesses different parts of spelling skill (sound-symbol relationships, pronouncing words, and so forth) as well as

word-spelling ability. For students who have difficulty with certain of the subtests but not with others, an instructional plan would be prepared that emphasizes the subareas on which they need to work. Other tests such as the *Brigance Diagnostic Inventory of Basic Skills* (Brigance, 1977) also include spelling assessment sections.

Error Analysis Several methods of analyzing spelling errors have been proposed. Probably the most widely known of these is Boder's (1971a, 1971b) approach to classifying students with reading problems according to their spelling errors. Students whose misspellings were quite different from correct spellings were considered "diseidetic," meaning that they depended on visual information to produce their spellings. In contrast, other students' misspellings were classified as "dysphonetic," meaning that they used sound-system information to generate their spellings. In practice, dysphonetic misspellings were closer to correct than were diseidetic spellings. Holmes and Peper (1977), however, have shown the unreliability of these diagnostic categories. Other approaches to analysis of errors include recommendations about recording types of errors, such as where in the word the mistake occurs (Cartwright, 1969; Edgington, 1967).

Informal Spelling Inventories An informal spelling inventory may be constructed by selecting a sample of words from each level of an available spelling program. Students can be tested on their spelling of the words from the sample lists, and the level at which they make 20% or more mistakes may be considered their instructional spelling level. However, those who use this approach to diagnosis must be aware that some students may happen to know (or not know) how to spell only those words on the given lists. When placement decisions are made on the basis of an informal spelling in-

---

Box 8.1
SPELLING PROBLEMS OF AN LD STUDENT

Many tests—both formal achievement tests and informal weekly tests—require that students write the spellings for words their teachers dictate. An example of a pupil's spelling is shown in the following material. The girl who wrote these spellings was 8 years old. The words are those that are administered as a routine part of the *Wide Range Achievement Test* (Jastak & Jastak, 1978). According to the test manual, this student's spelling skill is at the 6*th* month of the first grade, or the 10*th* percentile. For her age, this represents a severe deficit in spelling. The correct words are (1) go; (2) cat; (3) in; (4) boy; (5) and; (6) will; (7) make; (8) him; (9) say; (10) cut; (11) cook; (12) light; (13) must; (14) dress; (15) reach; (16) order; (17) watch; and (18) enter.

1. goy	16. unin
2. cat	17. us
3. in	18. intn
4. bubu	19.
5. bna	20.
6. will	21.
7. mac	22.
8. Him	23.
9. Sa	24.
10. cot	25.
11. coc	26.
12. Hat	27.
13. most	28.
14. nos	29.
15. nis	30.

---

ventory, teachers should be certain to use the information gained from progress monitoring tests to adjust the placements as the year progresses.

Progress Monitoring Spelling is the area in which the usual teaching methods come closest to incorporating progress monitoring. Recording of weekly spelling test scores provides teachers with regularly collected data about how well their students are doing in spelling. However because the list of words on which the students are tested usually changes each week, scores may be at least partially influenced by the difficulty of a particular list. Also, students may be tested on words they already know and not get enough practice on words they do not know. Haring et al. (1978) described a procedure called "flow lists" for testing spelling that overcomes these difficulties and still provides the opportunity to monitor progress. A flow list is a spelling list made up of words that an individual student has not mastered; when he or she shows mastery of a word on the list, it is dropped and a new word is substituted. McGuigan (cited in Haring et al., 1978) found that spelling flow lists on which children spelled at least 50% of the words correctly led to success.

Because not all words are equally difficult to spell, simply counting the number of words students spell correctly is not an appropriate measure of their spelling skills. Instead, Haring et al. (1978) suggested that the number of letters spelled correctly in a word be counted. Deno, Mirkin, Lowry, and Kuehnle (1980) examined different means of measuring spelling performance and found that counting the number of correct two-letter sequences in a word was a trustworthy and valuable method.

Interventions

So many interventions have been recommended for teaching spelling that it is almost impossible to count them. Fortunately many of the interventions have been tested for effectiveness and research has revealed which ones are useful. Graham and Miller (1979) examined the evidence and indicated which procedures

Tom Bross, Stock Boston

Although it may seem commonsensical, it is important to have students actually write when assessing and teaching written language skills.

were supported by research and which were not. A summary of their report is given in Table 8.2.

Programs for teaching spelling can be divided into those that are developmental and those that are remedial. *Developmental* programs are designed to promote the spelling progress of normally achieving students, and *remedial* programs are designed to help poor spellers catch up with their peers or at least to improve their weak spelling skills.

Developmental Programs   A major controversy in spelling is how much instruction should be devoted to teaching students the regularities of English orthography. Some people believe that instruction should not emphasize

Table 8.2   Effective and Ineffective Practices in Spelling Instruction

1   Using a *synthetic* approach (one in which students learn to build up correct spellings from letter-sound correspondences and generalizations) is superior to a syllable approach.
2   Using the *test-study-test* method (giving a test, requiring students to study any misspelled words, and then giving another test) is better than using the study-test method.
3   Presenting words for study in list form is better than presenting them in sentences or paragraphs.
4   Requiring students to correct their own tests and practice on the words they misspelled is very beneficial.
5   Practicing words by writing them in the air is *not* beneficial.
6   Using spelling games encourages student practice.
7   Rewarding achievement in spelling is more beneficial than simply encouraging interest.
8   Alloting at least 65 minutes per week to spelling is important for successful learning.
9   Having students devise their own methods of studying is *not* valuable.
10 Requiring students to copy words repeatedly will *not* guarantee retention of the correct spellings.

Note: Adapted from Graham & Miller, 1979.

the relationships between spoken and written English because the English language is so irregular in its spellings. For example, *cough, plough, rough, though,* and *through* all end with the same four letters but have different ending pronunciations. Also, there are too many rules about converting speech to print for children to learn them all. Furthermore, the words that students would be taught in learning to relate spoken language to written language would not be those that are most useful to them; children rarely use many different words in their writing, and spelling instruction should cover those words that they do use.

On the other hand, some authors (e.g., Groff, 1979; Hodges, 1982) argue against the notion that students should be taught a core of known words as rote items, even if those words may be the ones most frequently used in students' writing:

> One of the central issues concerning how spelling should be taught involves the vehicle by which we spell—the writing system. For if, on the one hand, the orthography is regarded as an erratic artifact of its historical development, then the conclusion must inevitably be reached that learning to spell is dependent upon learning the spellings of independent words. On the other hand, if the orthography is regarded as being systematic, then it can be concluded that learning to spell involves learning characteristics of the system which can be generalized to words sharing those characteristics. (Hodges, 1982, p. 285)

Despite the apparent irregularity of the spellings of English words, there is a great amount of consistency. The word *cough,* although it is irregular, is not spelled *kromp!* Depending upon which "experts" one consults, there may be as much as or more than 90% regularity in English spellings (e.g., Deverell, 1971; Hanna, Hanna, Hodges, & Erwin, 1966).

Several of the major developmental programs are described in the following paragraphs.

Basic Goals in Spelling (Kottmeyer & Claus, 1976) is a popular series designed for use in grades 1–8. It has several emphases, including learning of sound-symbol associations, structural patterns, and orthographic generalizations. Word lists are arranged according to spelling patterns so that generalizations may be discovered by students; exceptions to spelling patterns are presented along with the regularly spelled words.

Spell Correctly (Benthul, Anderson, Utech, Biggy, & Bailey, 1974) is a very widely used program that is arranged according to spelling patterns and meaning patterns. The words in the word lists were selected to reflect those that students use in their own compositions. *Spell Correctly* also includes activities for learning other skills (e.g., finding words in a dictionary) and for enrichment.

Spelling (Buchanan, 1967) is a programmed series of nearly 500 lessons spread over eight workbooks and designed for use in the first four grades. The approach is synthetic; that is, pupils learn sound-symbol relationships and then learn to build spellings from the letters. In the course of the program, students learn over 1,300 words and enough about English orthography to allow them to generalize what they know to many other words. *Spelling* is sometimes used as a remedial program with older learning-disabled students who have severe deficits in spelling.

Spelling Mastery (Dixon, Engelmann, Meier, Steely, & Wells, 1980) is another programmed series of lessons designed to be used with second- through sixth-graders. It is a highly structured program that begins with an emphasis on a synthetic approach. Gradually, however, the program takes on a *morphographic* approach in which students learn to combine meaningful word parts (called morphographs) into words. Because students can recombine morphographs into other words, they develop a very large spelling vocabulary

(well over 10,000 words) from this program. *Spelling Mastery* is also sometimes used with remedial students whose skills are too low for them to be placed in the companion remedial program, *Morphographic Spelling* (see subsequent discussion of *Morphographic Spelling* in this section).

Other developmental spelling programs include *Basic Spelling* (Glim & Manchester, 1977), *Harbrace Spelling Program* (Madden & Carlson, 1974), and *Word Book* (Ort & Wallace, 1976).

Hammill, Larsen, and McNutt (1977) evaluated the effectiveness of several different commercially available spelling instructional programs, including some of those mentioned above, relative to other programs and to informal spelling programs. Students were tested at several different grade levels; the results revealed that some programs were more effective at certain grade levels, while others were more effective at other grade levels. For example, although the *Spell Correctly* program resulted in low achievement at the third- and fourth-grade level, it was effective at later grade levels.

There were two interesting findings in this study. First, the mean differences in spelling scores between groups of students, although statistically significant, were not great; only 2.6 correct spellings separated programs that were significantly different according to the statistical tests. Thus, although a program might lead to slightly higher scores on the criterion measure, the difference might not be very significant educationally. Second, after the fourth grade, spelling instruction using one of the commercial programs was no more effective than no formal spelling instruction. It may be that the spelling skills learned by the fourth grade—the basic strategy skills—are the ones that make a difference in achievement; after students have acquired fourth-grade-level skills, they may no longer need formal instruction.

Remedial Methods Some common practices in spelling instruction may be unwise for use with students who have learning disabilities. Kerr and Lambert (1982), for example, noted that using spelling lists composed of words a student has misspelled in his or her own compositions doesn't do much to improve spelling because when students write, they generally choose words they already know how to spell. Thus this kind of list would not really reflect the student's spelling problems. Lists made up of words that many students misspell will be little better because students, especially older ones, vary so much in the words they use. Finally, specially selected word lists probably would not include words that lend themselves to illustrating spelling patterns, and without sufficient examples of spelling patterns, students are unlikely to learn generalized spelling skills.

Other practices have empirical support. Chief among these are the ones described by Graham and Miller (1979) and summarized in Table 8.2. In addition, practices that have been found to be helpful with the learning-disabled (Anderson-Inman, 1981; Bryant, Drabin, & Gettinger, 1981; Gettinger, Bryant, & Fayne, 1982) include:

> Present only a few spelling words on each day of instruction.
>
> Provide *distributed* practice (repeat words at different times).
>
> Teach for generalization by focusing on phonemic spelling patterns.
>
> Maximize the effects of training in one setting in order to induce transfer to other settings.

Some valuable recommendations about remedial spelling are included in *multisensory* and *behavior analysis* techniques.

Multisensory Two of the traditional interventions for children with learning disabilities, the VAKT (Fernald, 1943) and Orton-Gil-

lingham (Gillingham & Stillman, 1965) approaches, include spelling as a part of their reading instruction. Another intervention, *The Writing Road to Reading* (Spalding & Spalding, 1962), is closely related to the Orton-Gillingham approach and also emphasizes spelling. In all of these approaches, students practice producing the spellings of words as part of the connection between the auditory and tactile-kinesthetic modalities. In the VAKT approach, extensive practice is devoted to spelling entire words from memory. In the Orton-Gillingham and Spalding and Spalding programs, a more synthetic approach is taken, so that students learn sound-symbol relationships and build up the spellings of words from their knowledge of these correspondences. A potentially important aspect of the multisensory approach is the kinesthetic feedback provided during repeated practice. Massad and Etzel (1972) found that children learned sound-symbol relationships more rapidly and with fewer errors when they practiced tracing sandpaper letters.

Applied Behavior Analysis Behavior analysts have examined several aspects of spelling instruction. Their studies revealed that many interventions have positive effects on spelling performance. These include: reinforcing improved spelling with free time (Lovitt, Guppy, & Blattner, 1969); imitating pupils' errors and then requiring the students to write the words correctly (Kauffman, Hallahan, Haas, Brame, & Boren, 1978); presenting daily practice tests on parts of a weekly spelling test before presenting the weekly test itself (Reith et al., 1974); requiring students to rewrite several times those words they missed on practice tests (Foxx & Jones, 1978; Matson, Esveldt-Dawson, & Kazdin, 1982; Ollendick, Matson, Esveldt-Dawson, & Shapiro, 1980); presenting a few unknown words in a list of known spelling words (Neef, Iwata, & Bailey, 1977); and arranging for tutoring by parents or peers (Broden, Beasely, & Hall, 1978; Harris, Sherman, Henderson, & Harris, 1972). (See Kerr & Lambert, 1982, for a more extensive discussion of some of these studies.) Several remedial spelling programs that use behavioral principles are described in the following paragraphs.

Morphographic Spelling (Dixon, 1976) is an intensive, highly structured, teacher-directed remedial spelling program for use with fourth- through twelfth-graders and adults. It is assumed that students placed in the program know the basic spelling skills (sound-symbol relationships, etc.), so the program begins instruction with "morphographs," small units of meaningful writing. Students are taught to spell morphographs and to use five rules for combining them. After about a year of 20-minute lessons five times a week, they are capable of spelling over 12,000 words. Maggs, McMillan, Patching, and Hawke (1981) reported on a study of the program that indicated it was quite effective with a large group of students, many of whom had been well below their expected level of spelling skills.

Add-a-Word is a spelling procedure in which flow lists are used (Haring et al., 1978; see discussion in the section on assessing spelling skills). In this approach, individualized lists are created and students are tested on their own lists each day. When a student demonstrates mastery of a word on the list, it is removed and another one is substituted. McGuigan (cited in Haring et al., 1978) found that this type of procedure aided in the remediation of spelling problems. Lovitt (1978) reported that although *Add-a-Word* was not as effective as *Morphographic Spelling*, it may be more effective than many other approaches.

Speed Spelling (Proff, 1978) is designed to build fluent, accurate spelling by drill and practice. Words are arranged in groups according to spelling patterns and are dictated to students. When students demonstrate mastery of a particular unit, they progress to the next unit. Timing and graphing of student performance are built into the program.

COMPOSITION

Even if they have adequate handwriting and spelling skills, students may still find it hard to use writing to communicate. Although it is unusual to encounter a student report that is neatly penned, correctly spelled, and still incomprehensible, obviously there is more to written expression than spelling and handwriting. Students must also learn to write sensible and orderly prose that is consistent with grammatical conventions.

Characteristics

Development Bereiter (1980) examined evidence about changes in children's written language and suggested a model of development for writing. In his view, the writer's focus progressively shifts from the process of writing (writing in the sense of handwriting and spelling) to the written product (writing in the sense of having written something) to communication with readers (writing in the sense of getting across one's message). At the third and most sophisticated level of writing, however, the writer's focus may return to the process; for example, the writer of poems labors to make meter or rhyme work. The goal of teachers should be to help their students reach a level of development that allows them to communicate what they want to say in writing.

As students get older, their writing changes. Clear indications of this developmental change can be seen when *T-units* are measured at different ages. A T-unit is a single main clause and the subordinate clauses that accompany it (Hunt, 1977). "The movie we saw" is not a T-unit; "I like the movie we saw" is a T-unit; "I like the movie we saw about Moby Dick, the white whale" is a longer T-unit; "We saw about Moby Dick, the white whale" is not a T-unit. T-units may be very brief (e.g., "Birds fly") or longer (e.g., "Flying continuously for many months, the swallows eat and mate in midair while circumnavigating the globe"). Hunt (1977) described the results of many comparisons of students' writing at various ages:

> Older students use longer T-units.
>
> Older students are likely to pack more ideas into each T-unit.
>
> Older students combine T-units by changing the part of speech of words, but younger students combine them by simply adding *and*.

This last point is important because it turns out that certain instructional activities can help students use the more mature means of combining sentences (see the discussion under "Interventions").

Another factor of writing that reflects change in skill is the *type-token* ratio. *Token* refers to the total number of words in a writing sample, and *type* refers to the number of different words. For example, the sentence, "The girl gave the other girl a smile," has eight tokens and six types. In general, as students get older, the ratio between types and tokens (the number of types divided by the number of tokens) increases, indicating that students are using proportionally more different words.

Problems in Composition   Few studies of the characteristics of learning-disabled students' writing have been reported. Myklebust (1965, 1973) conducted the most extensive early analyses. He had pupils write stories about a picture of a little boy playing with dolls and reported (Myklebust, 1973) that, relative to normally achieving pupils, students identified as learning disabled scored lower on measures of number of words, words per sentence,

syntactic accuracy, and abstraction. Students who were only moderately learning disabled did not differ from their normally achieving peers on gross writing production (numbers of words and sentences), but those who were severely learning disabled did.

More recently, the composition skills of learning-disabled and normally achieving students were compared by Poplin, Gray, Larsen, Banikowski, and Mehring (1980). At the third- and fourth-grade levels, the learning-disabled students scored significantly lower than their peers in word usage, style, and overall writing skill. At the fifth- and sixth-grade levels, they scored lower in vocabulary and thematic maturity as well as in word usage, style, and overall writing skill. At the seventh and eighth grades, the learning-disabled students continued to have significantly lower scores in all of these areas. There is some indication that learning-disabled students fall further behind as they get older, particularly in the mechanical aspects of written language.

Morris and Crump (1982) also studied the written-language performance of learning-disabled and normally achieving students at different ages. They found that older students used more complex syntax and vocabulary than younger students, regardless of whether they were learning disabled or normally achieving, but the writing samples of the two groups differed in two important ways. First, the learning-disabled students used less complex sentence structures, and second, they used fewer types of words in their writing than did the normally achieving pupils. Morris and Crump found no strong indication that the learning-disabled students fell further behind their peers as they grew older.

The overall picture derived from these studies is that learning-disabled pupils lag behind their normally achieving classmates in many aspects of written expression. The differences are not always consistent, but it appears that students with learning disabilities are likely to be weak in both the mechanical (e.g., grammar) and the more meaningful aspects of composition.

Assessment

Screening   Screening for the presence of writing disabilities is difficult because many students other than the learning disabled write poorly.

Standardized tests often measure only editorial or mechanical skills. For example, the *Metropolitan Achievement Tests* (Durost et al., 1971) have sections on punctuation, capitalization, and word usage, but do not include measures of writing performance. To be sure, facility in editing material is an important aspect of composition, but it should not be confused with skill in composing material spontaneously. Better tests of composition require that students provide a sample of their writing.

The main reason that most widely used general achievement batteries do not require writing samples is that scoring them is far too time-consuming and unreliable. Thus there is little hope that general achievement instruments will ever be adequate for screening for writing disabilities. Teachers will have to form an initial judgment of their students' writing, and formal identification of writing disabilities may have to be made by administering one of the instruments designed as a diagnostic device.

Diagnosis   The *Sequential Tests of Educational Progress* (STEP; Educational Testing Service, 1972) and the written expression section of the *Tests of Achievement and Proficiency* (Scannell, Haugh, Schild, & Ulmer, 1978) both assess writing skills. They require students to answer multiple-choice and true-false questions, most of which have to do with "mechanics" (e.g., punctuation and capitalization) rather than expression. On the STEP,

however, some questions are designed to assess organization and other nonmechanical composition skills.

The *Picture Story Language Test* (PSLT; Myklebust, 1965) and the *Test of Written Language* (TOWL; Hammill & Larsen, 1983) are two norm-referenced instruments that require students to compose writing samples. On the PSLT, students write a story about a picture of a boy playing. Aspects of the sample (number of words, average number of words per sentence, syntactic correctness, and degree of abstractness) are judged and compared with norms. On the TOWL, some subtests measure correct word usage and style, and students are asked to compose a writing sample about three cartoon panels showing a space adventure. Assessments of the writing sample provide scores for vocabulary, T-units, and maturity of theme (paragraphing, characterization, beginning-middle-ending structure, etc.). Presumably students with unusually low scores in any of these areas on either the PSLT or the TOWL should receive remedial instruction in the relevant skills.

Two other models for diagnosis were provided by Poteet (1980) and Weiner (1980a, 1980b). These assessment approaches are designed to evaluate students' writing samples in both mechanics (e.g., grammar) and composition (e.g., meaning). Both systems provide checklists that help the teacher or other evaluator describe the strengths and weaknesses of writing samples. Because they are not based on norms, Poteet's and Weiner's approaches are less formal and depend upon careful teacher scrutiny of the samples.

Progress Monitoring   Evaluating progress in composition skills can be easily accomplished by having students compose a sample of their writing on a regular basis. The samples can then be judged to determine whether they represent improvement.

Deno, Marston, and Mirkin (1982) studied several different procedures for evaluating writing samples. Their purpose was to determine what writing behaviors could be used by teachers to monitor progress. For composition, they compared length of T-units, number of "mature" words (Finn, 1977), total number of words, and length of words. They found that the total number of words and the number of mature words used in essays were closely related to students' scores on achievement tests and other measures of writing.

To monitor students' progress in writing, some authorities recommend having them write sample essays regularly. One can then count (1) the number of words in each essay and (2) the number of words not on Finn's (1977) list of common words. The results of these counts can be plotted on graphs. Interestingly, when students receive feedback about these and other features of their compositions, their writing often improves dramatically (Van Houten, Morrison, Jarvis, & McDonald, 1974), particularly when they evaluate their writing themselves (Ballard & Glynn, 1975).

Interventions

It is sometimes argued that instruction on the mechanical aspects of writing should be eliminated because such teaching may harm students' creativity. Teachers must be cautious about accepting this idea too readily. Certainly the teaching of writing should be realistic and geared to the kind of thinking that people normally engage in when they are writing. But the fundamental aspects of writing must not be disregarded, for they are essential to competence. Too often we fail to realize the importance of formal work as a prerequisite to creative products. Surely "gifted" jazz pianists know how to play simple scales and other exer-

cises. And the poems of E. E. Cummings were "creative" in part because he knew enough about the conventions of capitalization and punctuation to mock them.

In such popular books as *Hooked on Books* (Fader & McNeil, 1968) and *Balance the Basics: Let them Write* (Graves, 1978), it has been recommended that teachers encourage students to write nearly anything (poems, plays, entries in diaries, etc.) and not try to teach them *how* to write compositions. The main advantage of this approach is that it provides students with extensive practice opportunities, and practice probably helps them to move from Bereiter's (1980) beginning stage of written expression—in which they are concerned with the process of writing—toward the second stage—in which the product of writing is important. However, more specific instruction is probably needed to help learning-disabled students overcome their deficits in written expression.

This does not necessarily mean that instruction should be restricted to simple drill on grammatical "rules." Among others, Fadiman and Howard (1979) have commented on the unimportance of teaching grammar in the abstract. Although the authors are associated with the "back-to-basics" orientation, they see little reason to teach many rules. Of course, programs must include work on certain traditional aspects of grammar (nouns, verbs, etc.) because they are useful terms when talking with students about editing, but that work should not overshadow instruction in writing itself.

Programs   Many basal English textbooks include writing exercises among the exercises designed to teach correct grammar, and there are idea books for teachers (e.g., *Slithery Snakes and Other Aids to Children's Writing*, Petty & Bowen, 1967), but few programs have been explicitly designed to teach students writing skills.

Books are available that provide general directions to teachers about developing composition skills. For example, Sealey, Sealey, and Millmore (1979) describe a program for young children in which they create individual books. The approach begins by having the pupils write labels and captions for pictures they have drawn or cut out of magazines and put in their books. Later the teacher leads them into writing one-sentence descriptions for the pictures or drawings. At the third stage, the children are required to write two-sentence descriptions; here the conventions of punctuation and capitalization are introduced. In the fourth stage, the students write three-sentence or longer descriptions of the pictures; the sentences do not have to relate to one another. At the fifth stage, the children are asked to write thematically. Sealey and colleagues provide numerous activities to aid implementation of their approach.

More explicit directions about instruction are provided by other programs. For example, in *Expressive Writing* (Engelmann & Silbert, 1983), students are taught how to indent at the beginning of paragraphs, use topic sentences, describe a temporal series of events, and evaluate their own written products for a variety of features (run-on sentences, capitalization, punctuation, topic relevance). The daily lessons of this program, although very structured and directive, are focused on the specific skills that make up coherent written communication.

Several broad recommendations about instruction can be made on the basis of the research on writing (see Graham, 1982; Hayes & Flower, 1980; Petty, 1978; Silverman, Zigmond, Zimmerman, & Vallecorsa, 1981):

Have the students *plan* what they will write. Planning may range from simply making notes to preparing outlines.

Have the students *translate* their plans into a written product. Translating should focus mostly on getting a written product, a rough draft.

Have the students *edit* what they have written. Editing should include reading the product, to evaluate whether it communicates what one wants to say, and improving it. During editing, students might follow a checklist to make certain that the conventions of punctuation, capitalization, and grammar have been followed.

Techniques In some cases, simply having students write more will be sufficient to improve their compositional skills (Kraetsch, 1981). However, additional direction is often needed. Several instructional techniques are discussed in the following paragraphs.

Sentence Combining Sentence-combining exercises require students to take two related sentences and rewrite them as one. Examples of several sentence-combining tasks are shown in Table 8.3. Sentence combining has been found to be an effective means of improving students' written compositions (e.g., O'Hare, 1973). There is also evidence that work on sentence combining may benefit students' reading and listening comprehension (Straw & Schreiner, 1982). Perhaps the reason sentence-combining exercises have been found to improve writing is that they help students to produce sentences more "automatically," thus freeing them to focus on substance rather than mechanics (Flower & Hayes, 1980). However, as Smith (1981) cautioned, sentence combining should not become a decontextualized ritual; rather, it should be taught as a means of composing products that communicate what the writer wants them to communicate. A good use of sentence combining, when students have received sufficient training, is to have students use this skill to rewrite and improve their own writing samples.

Reinforcement Rewards for performance on various parts of composition have been studied repeatedly with young students

Table 8.3   Examples of Sentence-Combining Tasks

Combine Subjects:	

The woman ran the race.
The man ran the race.   >   The woman and man ran the race.

Jack went up the hill.
Jill went up the hill.   >   Jack and Jill went up the hill.

Combine Predicates:

The dog dug a hole.
The dog hid the bone.   >   The dog dug a hole and hid the bone.

The kids played basketball.
The kids jumped rope.   >   The kids played basketball and jumped rope.

Combine with "Who" or "Which":

Jim looked at the cat.
The cat was asleep.   >   Jim looked at the cat, which was asleep.

The cat looked at Jim.
Jim was asleep.   >   The cat looked at Jim, who was asleep.

(Brigham, Graubard, & Stans, 1972; Maloney & Hopkins, 1973; Maloney, Jacobson, & Hopkins, 1975). When teachers make reinforcement contingent on writing more words, students write more words. When using more "action verbs" is rewarded, students use more action verbs in their compositions ("run," "swing," and "throw" are action verbs, but "think," "are," and "want" are not). When use of different words was required for reinforcement, students wrote essays that included a wider vocabulary. It was found, however, that rewarding performance on a certain part of composition usually did not affect performance on the other parts. Thus it is necessary to design a reward system that will result in improvement in many different aspects of composition. Moreover, as effective as reinforcement has been shown to be, it is not a complete teaching program. Learning-disabled students still have to be shown a great deal about *how* to write communicatively.

Peer- and Self-evaluation   Peer editing and self-evaluation are other techniques that have proved effective in teaching composition. Secondary-school students with low achievement scores learned to use an editing and rating system for evaluating their peers' essays. These students scored higher on a posttest than students whose essays had been edited and rated by teachers (Karegianes, Pascarella, & Pflaum, 1980). Also, third-graders learned to check their own writing assignments according to guidelines (Ballard & Glynn, 1975). The self-evaluation procedure required them to count the number of sentences written, words written, and various types of words used, and to take other simple measures of their writing. According to these measures, the students assigned themselves points in a reward system. Ballard and Glynn found that this combination of self-evaluation and self-reward had positive effects on the students' writing. Self-evaluation was also an important part of an effective pro-

Many composition skills can be improved by having students evaluate their own writing or that of their peers.

gram described by K. Harris and Graham (in press) for improving the compositions of two learning-disabled children.

SUMMARY

Writing disabilities may include problems in handwriting, spelling, and composition or written expression. Although disabilities in writing did not receive as much attention as disabilities in reading, it is now recognized that they are an important part of the problems that many learning-disabled students experience.

Learning-disabled pupils' writing performance has characteristics that mark it as different from normal. Handwriting problems, sometimes referred to as dysgraphia, include misformation of letters, poor spacing between letters, and extremely slow writing; all of these problems may interfere with other aspects of writing performance. The misspellings of learning-disabled students usually are readable although they usually include mistakes involving a single phoneme and occur in the middle of words; generally, they are similar to the spellings of younger students. The compositions of learning-disabled students usually are shorter, include fewer different types of words, are composed of less-complex sentences, and have other characteristics that mark them as less mature than those of their peers.

The usual steps in assessment—screening, diagnosis, and progress monitoring—are followed with writing disabilities. Screening for handwriting problems can be easily accomplished by examining samples of a student's writing; screening for problems in spelling can be done by using widely-available achievement batteries; screening for problems in written expression is more difficult because it is not a routine part of school testing programs. Diagnosis of handwriting problems can also be accomplished by examining writing samples and identifying specific letters, letter combinations, or other features of handwriting that require intervention. However, diagnosis of spelling and written expression problems is more problematic; although some useful instruments are available, teachers' clinical judgments and more informal assessments are needed to make program-placement decisions. Monitoring progress in handwriting, spelling, and composition skills can be readily accomplished by collecting frequent samples of performance and counting discrete parts of them.

Developmental and remedial instruction in writing has received little attention and, thus, only general guidelines can be provided. In the area of handwriting, performance can be enhanced by extensive practice and feedback. In the area of spelling, it is important that students learn underlying skills (e.g., phoneme-grapheme relationships), some rote items (e.g., how to spell irregular words), and higher-order skills that will allow them to spell words that they rarely encounter (e.g., how to combine root words and affixes in order to write new words).

REFERENCES

ANDERSON, D. W. (1968). *Teaching handwriting.* Washington, DC: National Education Association.

ANDERSON-INMAN, L. (1981). Transenvironmental programming: Promoting success in the regular classroom by maximizing effect of resource room instruction. *Journal of Special Education Technology, 4*(4), 3–12.

AYERS, L. P. (1912). *A scale for measuring the quality of handwriting of school children.* New York: Division of Education, Russell Sage Foundation.

BALLARD, K. D., & GLYNN, T. (1975). Behavioral self-management in story writing with elementary school children. *Journal of Applied Behavior Analysis, 8,* 387–398.

BARRON, R. W. (1980). Visual and phonological strategies in reading and spelling. In U. Frith (Ed.), *Cognitive processes in spelling* (pp. 195–213). New York: Academic Press.

BEERS, J. W. (1974). First-grade and second-grade children's developing orthographic concepts of tense and lax vowels (Doctoral dissertation, University of Virginia, 1974). *Dissertation Abstracts International, 35,* 49708A.

BENTHUL, H. F., ANDERSON, E. A., UTECH, A. M., BIGGY, M. V., & BAILEY, B. L. (1974). *Spell correctly.* Morristown, NJ: Silver Burdett.

BEREITER, C. (1980). Development in writing. In L. W. Gregg & E. R. Steinberg (Eds.), *Cognitive processes in writing* (pp. 73–93). Hillsdale, NJ: Erlbaum.

BODER, E. (1971a). Developmental dyslexia: A diagnostic screening procedure based on three characteristic patterns of reading and spelling. In B. Bateman (Ed.), *Learning disorders: Reading* (Vol. 4, pp. 297–342). Seattle, WA: Special Child.

BODER, E. (1971b). Developmental dyslexia: Prevailing diagnostic concepts and a new diagnostic approach. In H. R. Myklebust (Ed.), *Progress in learning disabilities* (Vol. 2, pp. 293–321). New York: Grune & Stratton.

BRIGANCE, A. H. (1977). *Brigance Diagnostic Inventory of Basic Skills* (2nd ed.). North Billerica, MA: Curriculum Associates.

BRIGHAM, T. H., GRAUBARD, P. S., & STANS, A. (1972). Analysis of the effects of sequential reinforcement contingencies on aspects of composition. *Journal of Applied Behavior Analysis, 5,* 421–429.

BRODEN, M., BEASLEY, A., & HALL, R. V. (1978). In class spelling performance: Effects of home tutoring by a parent. *Behavior Modification, 2,* 511–530.

BRYANT, N. D., DRABIN, I. R., & GETTINGER, M. (1981). Effects of varying unit size on spelling achievement in learning disabled children. *Journal of Learning Disabilities, 14,* 200–203.

BUCHANAN, C. (1967). *Spelling.* Palo Alto, CA: Behavioral Research Laboratories.

CARPENTER, D. (1983). Spelling error profiles of able and disabled readers. *Journal of Learning Disabilities, 16,* 102–104.

CARPENTER, D., & MILLER, L. J. (1982). Spelling

ability of reading disabled LD students and able readers. *Learning Disability Quarterly, 5,* 65–70.

CARTER, J. L., & SYNOLDS, D. (1974). Effects of relaxation training upon handwriting quality. *Journal of Learning Disabilities, 7,* 236–238.

CARTWRIGHT, G. P. (1969). Written expression and spelling. In R. M. Smith (Ed.), *Teacher diagnosis of educational difficulties* (pp. 95–117). Columbus, OH: Charles E. Merrill.

CHAPMAN, L. J., & WEDELL, K. (1972). Perceptual-motor abilities and reversal errors in children's handwriting. *Journal of Learning Disabilities, 5,* 321–325.

CICCI, R. (1983). Disorders of written language. In H. R. Myklebust (Ed.), *Progress in learning disabilities* (Vol. 5, pp. 207–232). New York: Grune & Stratton.

DENO, S. L., MARSTON, D., & MIRKIN, P. K. (1982). Valid measurement procedures for continuous evaluation of written expression. *Exceptional Children, 48,* 368–371.

DENO, S. L., MIRKIN, P. K., LOWRY, L., & KUEHNLE, K. (1980). Relationships among simple measures of spelling and performance on standardized achievement tests (Research Report No. 21). University of Minnesota Institute for Research on Learning Disabilities.

DEVERELL, A. F. (1971). The learnable features of English orthography. In B. Bateman (Ed.), *Learning disorders: Reading* (Vol. 4, pp. 129–160). Seattle, WA: Special Child.

DIXON, R. (1976). *Morphographic spelling.* Chicago: Science Research Associates.

DIXON, R., ENGELMANN, S., MEIER, M., STEELY, D., & WELLS, C. (1980). *Spelling mastery* (Levels A–E). Chicago: Science Research Associates.

DUNN, L. M., & MARKWARDT, F. C., JR. (1970). *Peabody Individual Achievement Test.* Circle Pines, MN: American Guidance Service.

DUROST, W. N., BIXLER, H. H., WRIGHTSTONE, J. W., PRESCOTT, G. A., & BALOW, I. H. (1971). *Metropolitan Achievement Tests.* New York: Harcourt Brace Jovanovich.

EDGINGTON, R. (1967). But he spelled them right this morning. *Academic Therapy, 3,* 58–61.

Educational Testing Service. (1972). *Sequential Tests of Educational Progress.* Princeton, NJ: Author.

ENGELMANN, S., & SILBERT, J. (1983). *Expressive writing.* Tigard, OR: C. C. Publications.

FADER, D. N., & MCNEIL, E. B. (1968). *Hooked on books: Program and proof.* New York: Putnam.

FADIMAN, C. A., & HOWARD, T. (1979). *Empty pages.* Belmont, CA: Fearon Pitman.

FAUKE, J., BURNETT, J., POWERS, M. A., & SULZER-AZAROFF, B. (1973). Improvement of handwriting and letter recognition skills: A behavior modification procedure. *Journal of Learning Disabilities, 6,* 296–300.

FERNALD, G. M. (1943). *Remedial techniques in basic school subjects.* New York: McGraw-Hill.

FINN, P. J. (1977). Computer-aided description of mature word choices in writing. In C. R. Cooper & L. Odell (Eds.), *Evaluating writing: Describing, measuring, judging* (pp. 68–89). Urbana, IL: National Council of Teachers of English.

FLOWER, L. S., & HAYES, J. R. (1980). The dynamics of composing: Making plans and juggling constraints. In L. W. Gregg & E. R. Steinberg (Eds.), *Cognitive processes in writing* (pp. 31–50). Hillsdale, NJ: Erlbaum.

FOXX, R. M., & JONES, J. R. (1978). A remediation program for increasing the spelling achievement of elementary and junior high school students. *Behavior Modification, 2,* 211–230.

FREEMAN, F. N. (1979). *Handwriting measuring scale.* Columbus, OH: Zaner-Bloser.

FRITH, U. (1980). Unexpected spelling problems. In U. Frith (Ed.), *Cognitive processes in spelling* (pp. 495–515). New York: Academic Press.

GATES, A. I., & RUSSELL, D. (1940). *Gates-Russell Spelling Diagnostic Test.* New York: Columbia University Press.

GENTRY, J. R. (1977). A study of the orthographic strategies of beginning readers (Doctoral dissertation, University of Virginia, 1977). *Dissertation Abstracts International, 39/07A,* 4017.

GERBER, M. M., & HALL, R. J. (1981). Development of spelling in learning disabled and normally-achieving children. Unpublished manuscript, University of Virginia Learning Disabilities Research Institute.

GETTINGER, M., BRYANT, N. D., & FAYNE, H. R. (1982). Designing spelling instruction for learning-disabled children: An emphasis on unit size, distributed practice, and training for transfer. *Journal of Special Education, 16,* 439–448.

GILLINGHAM, A., & STILLMAN, B. (1965). *Remedial training for children with specific disability in reading, spelling and penmanship* (7th ed.). Cambridge, MA: Educators Publishing Service.

GLIM, T. E., & MANCHESTER, R. S. (1977). *Basic spelling* (rev. ed.). Philadelphia: Lippincott.

GRAHAM, S. (1982). Composition research and practice: A unified approach. *Focus on Exceptional Children, 14*(8), 1–16.

GRAHAM, S., & MILLER, L. (1979). Spelling research and practice: A unified approach. *Focus on Exceptional Children, 12*(2), 1–16.

GRAVES, D. (1978). *Balance the basics: Let them write.* New York: Ford Foundation.

GROFF, P. (1979). Phonics for spelling? *Elementary School Journal, 79,* 269–275.

HALLAHAN, D. P., & REEVE, R. E. (1980). Selective attention and distractibility. In B. K. Keogh (Ed.), *Advances in special education. Vol. 1: Basic constructs and theoretical orientations* (pp. 141–181). Greenwich, CT: JAI Press.

HAMMILL, D. D., & LARSEN, S. C. (1983). *Test of Written Language* (Rev. Ed.). Austin, TX: Pro-Ed.

HAMMILL, D. D., LARSEN, S., & MCNUTT, G. (1977). The effects of spelling instruction: A preliminary study. *Elementary School Journal, 78,* 67–72.

HAMMILL, D. D., & LEIGH, J. E. (1983). *Basic School Skills Inventory—Diagnostic.* Austin, TX: Pro-Ed.

HANNA, P., HANNA, J., HODGES, R., & ERWIN, R., JR. (1966). *Phoneme-grapheme correspondences as cues to spelling improvement.* Washington, DC: U.S. Government Printing Office.

HARING, N. G., LOVITT, T. C., EATON, M. D., & HANSEN, C. L. (1978). *The fourth R: Research in the classroom.* Columbus, OH: Charles E. Merrill.

HARRIS, K. R., & GRAHAM, S. (In press). Improving learning disabled students' composition skills: A self-control strategy training approach. *Learning Disability Quarterly.*

HARRIS, V. W., SHERMAN, J. A., HENDERSON, D. G., & HARRIS, M. S. (1972). Effects of peer tutoring on the spelling performance of elementary classroom students. In G. Semb (Ed.), *Behavior analysis & education—1972* (pp. 222–231). Lawrence, KS: University of Kansas Department of Human Development.

HASAZI, J. E., & HASAZI, S. E. (1972). Effects of teacher attention on digit-reversal behavior in an elementary school child. *Journal of Applied Behavior Analysis, 5,* 157–162.

HAYES, D. J. (1980). The effect of guiding six-year-old kindergarten and nine-year-old third grade children to verbalize formational strokes upon their ability to reproduce letterlike forms (Doctoral dissertation, University of Virginia, 1980). *Dissertation Abstracts International, 41,* 1234A.

HAYES, J. R., & FLOWER, L. S. (1980). Identifying the organization of writing processes. In L. W. Gregg & E. R. Steinberg (Eds.), *Cognitive processes in writing* (pp. 3–30). Hillsdale, NJ: Erlbaum.

HERRICK, V. E. (1960). Handwriting and children's writing. *Elementary English, 37,* 248–258.

HERRICK, V. E. (1961). Manuscript and cursive writing. *Childhood Education, 37,* 264–267.

HILDRETH, G. (1960). Manuscript writing after 60 years. *Elementary English, 37,* 3–13.

HODGES, R. E. (1982). Research update on the development of spelling ability. *Language Arts, 59,* 284–290.

HOLMES, D. L., & PEPER, R. J. (1977). An evaluation of the use of spelling error analysis in the diagnosis of reading disabilities. *Child Development, 48,* 1708–1711.

HULL, M. (1976). *Phonics for teachers* (2nd ed.). Columbus, OH: Charles E. Merrill.

HUNT, K. W. (1977). Early blooming and late blooming syntactic structures. In C. R. Cooper & L. Odell (Eds.), *Evaluating writing: Describing, measuring, judging* (pp. 91–104). Urbana, IL: National Council of Teachers of English.

JASTAK, J. F., & JASTAK, S. (1978). *Wide Range Achievement Test.* Wilmington, DE: Jastak Associates.

JONES, J. C., TRAP, J., & COOPER, J. O. (1977). Technical report: Students' self-recording of manuscript letter strokes. *Journal of Applied Behavior Analysis, 10,* 509–514.

JORDON, D. R. (1977). *Dyslexia in the classroom* (2nd. ed.). Columbus, OH: Charles E. Merrill.

JOSEPH, F., & MULLINS, J. (1970). A script to supplant cursive writing or printing. *Teaching Exceptional Children, 3*(1), 23–32.

KAREGIANES, M. L., PASCARELLA, E. T., & PFLAUM, S. W. (1980). The effects of peer editing on the writing proficiency of low-achieving tenth grade students. *Journal of Educational Research, 73,* 203–207.

KAUFFMAN, J. M., HALLAHAN, D. P., HAAS, K., BRAME, T., & BOREN, R. (1978). Imitating children's errors to improve their spelling performance. *Journal of Learning Disabilities, 11,* 217–222.

KERR, M. M., & LAMBERT, D. L. (1982). Behavior modification of children's written language. In M. Hersen, R. M. Eisler, & P. M. Miller (Eds.), *Progress in behavior modification* (Vol. 13, pp. 79–108). New York: Academic Press.

KOSIEWICZ, M. M., HALLAHAN, D. P., LLOYD, J., & GRAVES, A. W. (1982). Effects of self-instruction and self-correction procedures on handwriting performance. *Learning Disability Quarterly, 5,* 71–78.

KOTTMEYER, W., & CLAUS, A. (1976). *Basic goals in spelling* (5th ed.). New York: McGraw-Hill.

KRAETSCH, G. A. (1981). The effects of oral instructions and training on the expansion of written language. *Learning Disability Quarterly, 4,* 82–90.

LAHEY, B. B., BUSEMEYER, M. K., O'HARA, C., & BEGGS, V. E. (1977). Treatment of severe perceptual-motor disorders in children diagnosed as learning disabled. *Behavior Modification, 1,* 123–140.

LARSEN, S., & HAMMILL, D. D. (1976). *Test of Written Spelling.* Austin, TX: Pro-Ed.

LARSON, C. E. (1968). Teaching beginning writing. *Academic Therapy, 4*(1), 61–66.

LOVITT, T. C. (1978). New applications and new techniques in behavior modification. *Journal of Special Education, 12,* 89–93.

LOVITT, T. C., GUPPY, T. E., & BLATTNER, J. E. (1969). The use of a free time contingency with fourth graders to increase spelling accuracy. *Behavior Research and Therapy, 7,* 151–156.

MADDEN, R., & CARLSON, T. (1974). *Harbrace spelling program.* New York: Harcourt Brace Jovanovich.

MAGGS, A., MCMILLAN, K., PATCHING, W., & HAWKE, H. (1981). Accelerating spelling skills using morphographs. *Educational Psychology, 1,* 49–56.

MALONEY, K. B., & HOPKINS, B. L. (1973). The modification of sentence structure and its relationship to subjective judgment of creativity in writing. *Journal of Applied Behavior Analysis, 6,* 425–433.

MALONEY, K. B., JACOBSON, C. R., & HOPKINS, B. L. (1975). An analysis of the effects of lectures, requests, teacher praise, and free time on the creative writing behaviors of third-grade children. In E. Ramp & G. Semb (Eds.), *Behavior analysis: Areas of research and application* (pp. 244–260). Englewood Cliffs, N.J.: Prentice-Hall.

MARSH, G., FRIEDMAN, M., WELCH, V., & DESBERG, P. (1980). The development of strategies in spelling. In U. Frith (Ed.), *Cognitive processes in spelling* (pp. 339–353). New York: Academic Press.

MASSAD, V. I., & ETZEL, B. C. (1972). Acquisition of phonetic sounds by preschool children. I: Effects of response and reinforcement frequency. II: Effects of tactile differences in discriminative stimuli. In G. Semb (Ed.), *Behavior analysis & edu-*

cation—1972 (pp. 88–111). Lawrence, KS: University of Kansas Department of Human Development.

MATSON, J., ESVELDT-DAWSON, K., & KAZDIN, A. E. (1982). Treatment of spelling deficits in mentally retarded children. *Mental Retardation, 20,* 76–81.

MCGRADY, H. J., JR. (1968). Language pathology and learning disabilities. In H. R. Myklebust (Ed.), *Progress in learning disabilities* (Vol. 1, pp. 199–233). New York: Grune & Stratton.

MORRIS, N. T., & CRUMP, W. D. (1982). Syntactic and vocabulary development in the written language of learning disabled and non-learning disabled students at four age levels. *Learning Disability Quarterly, 5,* 163–172.

MYKLEBUST, H. R. (1965). *Development and disorders of written language.* Vol. 1: *Picture story language test.* New York: Grune & Stratton.

MYKLEBUST, H. R. (1973). *Development and disorders of written language.* Vol. 2: *Studies of normal and exceptional children.* New York: Grune & Stratton.

NEEF, N., IWATA, B., & BAILEY, J. (1977). The effects of known-item interspersal on acquisition and retention of spelling and sightreading words. *Journal of Applied Behavior Analysis, 10,* 738.

O'HARE, F. (1973). *Sentence-combining: Improving student writing without formal grammar instruction.* Urbana, IL: National Council of Teachers of English.

OLLENDICK, T., MATSON, J., ESVELDT-DAWSON, K., & SHAPIRO, T. (1980). Increasing spelling achievement: An analysis of treatment procedures utilizing an alternating treatments design. *Journal of Applied Behavior Analysis, 13,* 645–654.

ORT, L. L., & WALLACE, E. E. (1976). *Word book.* Chicago: Rand McNally.

PETTY, W. T. (1978). The writing of young children. In C. R. Cooper & L. Odell (Eds.), *Research on composing: Points of departure* (pp. 73–83). Urbana, IL: National Council of Teachers of English.

PETTY, W. T., & BOWEN, M. E. (1967). *Slithery snakes and other aids to children's writing.* New York: Appleton-Century-Crofts.

POPLIN, M. S., GRAY, R., LARSEN, S., BANIKOWSKI, A., & MEHRING, R. (1980). A comparison of components of written expression abilities in learning disabled and non-learning disabled students at three grade levels. *Learning Disability Quarterly, 3*(4), 46–53.

POTEET, J. A. (1980). Informal assessment of written expression. *Learning Disability Quarterly*, 3(4), 88–98.

PROFF, J. (1978). *Speed spelling.* Tigard, OR: C. C. Publications.

REITH, H. J., AXELROD, J., ANDERSON, R., HATHAWAY, F., WOOD, K., & FITZGERALD, C. (1974). Influence of distributed practice and daily testing on weekly spelling tests. *Journal of Educational Research*, 68(2), 73–77.

ROBIN, A. L., ARMEL, S., & O'LEARY, K. D. (1975). The effects of self-instruction on writing deficiencies. *Behavior Therapy*, 6, 178–197.

SCANNELL, D. P., HAUGH, O. M., SCHILD, A. H., & ULMER, G. (1978). *Tests of Achievement and Proficiency.* Boston: Houghton Mifflin.

SEALEY, L., SEALEY, N., & MILLMORE, M. (1979). *Children's writing: An approach for the primary grades.* Newark, DE: International Reading Association.

SEIFERT, E. P. (1960). Personal styles of handwriting in grades 6, 7, 8, and 9. *Dissertation Abstracts International*, 20(9), 3581–3582, (59-06594).

SILVERMAN, R., ZIGMOND, N., ZIMMERMAN, J. M., & VALLECORSA, A. (1981). Improving written expression in learning disabled students. *Topics in Language Disorders*, 1(2), 91–99.

SMITH, D. D., & LOVITT, T. C. (1973). The educational diagnosis and remediation of written b and d reversal problems: A case study. *Journal of Learning Disabilities*, 6, 356–363.

SMITH, W. (1981). The potential and problems of sentence combining. *English Journal*, 70(6), 79–81.

SPALDING, R. B., & SPALDING, W. (1962). *The writing road to reading.* New York: Morrow.

STOWITSCHEK, C. E., & STOWITSCHEK, J. J. (1979). Evaluating handwriting performance: The student helps the teacher. *Journal of Learning Disabilities*, 12, 203–206.

STRAUSS, A. A., & LEHTINEN, L. (1947). *Psychopathology and education of the brain-injured child.* New York: Grune & Stratton.

STRAW, S. B., & SCHREINER, R. (1982). The effect of sentence manipulation on subsequent measures of reading and listening comprehension. *Reading Research Quarterly*, 17, 339–352.

STROMER, R. (1975). Modifying letter and number reversals in elementary school children. *Journal of Applied Behavior Analysis*, 8, 211.

STROMER, R. (1977). Remediating academic deficiencies in learning disabled children. *Exceptional Children*, 43, 432–440.

TEMPLIN, E. M. (1960). Research and comment: Handwriting, the neglected R. *Elementary English*, 37, 386–389.

THORPE, L., LAFEVER, D., & HASLUND, R. (1963). *SRA Achievement Series.* Chicago: Science Research Associates.

TIEGS, E. W., & CLARK, W. W. (1977–1978). *California Achievement Tests.* Monterey, CA: CTB/McGraw-Hill.

TOWLE, M. (1978). Assessment and remediation of handwriting deficits for children with learning disabilities. *Journal of Learning Disabilities*, 11, 370–377.

VAN HOUTEN, R., MORRISON, E., JARVIS, R., & MCDONALD, M. (1974). The effects of explicit timing and feedback on compositional response rate in elementary school children. *Journal of Applied Behavior Analysis*, 7, 547–555.

WEDELL, K., & HORNE, I. E. (1969). Some aspects of perceptuo-motor disability in 5½-year-old children. *British Journal of Educational Psychology*, 39, 174–182.

WEINER, E. S. (1980a). Diagnostic evaluation of writing skills. *Journal of Learning Disabilities*, 13, 43–48.

WEINER, E. S. (1980b). The Diagnostic Evaluation of Writing Skills (DEWS): Application of DEWS criteria to writing samples. *Learning Disability Quarterly*, 3(2), 54–59.

WESTERN, R. D. (1977). The case against cursive script. *Elementary School Journal*, 78, 1–3.

WOODCOCK, R. W., & JOHNSON, M. B. (1977). *Woodcock-Johnson Psychoeducational Battery.* Boston: Teaching Resources.

WRIGHT, C. D., & WRIGHT, J. P. (1980). Handwriting: The effectiveness of copying from moving versus still models. *Journal of Educational Research*, 74, 95–98.

Arithmetic and Mathematics Disabilities

The areas of arithmetic and mathematics include the skills and knowledge used in computing answers to written problems and a great deal more. Understanding many concepts, including union of sets, proportionality, and equality, is also an important mark of achievement. Familiar skills such as managing money, telling time, and measuring volume are included in arithmetic and mathematics, and skills related to understanding and using computers are likely to become so.

Disabilities in reading and writing are often accompanied by disabilities in arithmetic and mathematics. During the first 20 years of the field of learning disabilities, there was little focus on problems with arithmetic computation and the learning of mathematical concepts. More recently, however, there has been increased emphasis on these areas.

One reason for the increased emphasis on arithmetic and mathematics disabilities is that both practitioners and researchers have realized there are many students with learning disabilities who have severe underachievement in these areas. Another reason for the increased emphasis is that psychologists have become interested in how people think when they work on arithmetic or mathematical problems and therefore have begun to study normal and abnormal learning in these areas. A third reason is that arithmetic and mathematics are very consistent or regular. Unlike the letter o, which has several possible sounds, the numeral 4 is always called "four," and although the word *run* may have many different meanings, the numeral 9 always has the same meaning. This consistency makes arithmetic and mathematics ideal for studying remedial teaching techniques.

CHARACTERISTICS

Many different terms have been used to describe students who do not develop the skills in arithmetic and mathematics that most students develop, and the problems that these students experience have been described in various ways. In this section, terms used to identify students who have disabilities in arithmetic and mathematics are discussed, the path of normal development is described, and the types of problems students experience are presented.

Terminology and Prevalence

Terminology *Dyscalculia* is the most widely used term for disabilities in arithmetic and mathematics. In general, dyscalculia means *inability to calculate*. Sometimes the term *acalculia* is used to refer to complete inability to use mathematical symbols and perform arithmetic computations and the term *dyscalculia* is reserved for less severe problems in these areas. *Developmental dyscalculia* may be used to distinguish the problem in children and youth from similar problems experienced by adults after severe head injuries.

Kosc (1974) suggested that there are "basic forms" (special types) of dyscalculia. On the basis of his experience with arithmetic learning problems, he described these types:

Verbal dyscalculia, which refers to problems in naming the amount of things.

Practognostic dyscalculia, which refers to problems in manipulating things mathematically—for example, comparing objects to determine which is larger.

Lexical dyscalculia, which refers to problems in reading mathematical symbols, including operation signs (+, −) and numerals.

Graphical dyscalculia, which refers to problems in writing mathematical symbols and numerals.

Ideognostical dyscalculia, which refers to problems in understanding mathematical concepts and relationships.

Operational dyscalculia, which refers to problems in performing arithmetic operations.

These types of dyscalculia have not been independently verified—the data Kosc reported about students in Czechoslovakia were not directly supportive of the categories—and they are quite difficult to differentiate in students who have arithmetic learning disabilities. Nevertheless, Kosc's discussion of so many types of dyscalculia illustrates the many problems students may have in arithmetic and mathematics.

Prevalence The commonly held assumption that disorders of arithmetic and mathematics learning are not as prevalent as disorders of reading and writing began to be empirically tested in the 1970s and 80s and is being shown to be misleading, if not completely false.

Several interested authorities (e.g., Dunlap & House, 1976) have suggested that there are many students with learning disabilities in arithmetic. Kosc (1974), for example, indicated that he suspected as much as 6% of the school-age population had these difficulties. Examinations of the pupils served by child service and demonstration centers (Kirk & Elkins, 1975; Norman & Zigmond, 1980) have revealed that many students have achievement deficits in arithmetic and mathematics. Norman and Zigmond (1980) reported that the average mathematics achievement of students in their study was about 75% of what would be expected on the basis of IQ. Although this level of learning efficiency is higher than that for reading and higher than the 50% criterion Norman and Zigmond used for comparison, such inefficiency in learning of mathematical skills indicates that the students studied certainly could benefit from remedial instruction. When McLeod and Armstrong (1982) questioned learning disabilities teachers about the reasons their students were receiving services, they found that nearly two out of three were getting help in arithmetic and mathematics, and that more than one in four had been assigned to special education primarily because

Many LD pupils have difficulty in arithmetic. Sometimes they continue to use the strategies of younger children, such as counting on their fingers.

of learning disabilities in arithmetic and mathematics.

As a result of these studies, we can reasonably assume that many students referred for services in a program for the learning disabled will need instructional help in mastering arithmetic and mathematics. These problems should be considered no less important than those associated with using spoken and written language (both reading and writing). They indicate a need for even more intensive and extensive educational intervention for students with learning disabilities.

Development

Changes in how students approach arithmetic problems reflect increasing sophistication in their thinking about arithmetic and mathematics. Many authors have discussed these changes

and presented developmental theories of the understanding of mathematical concepts (Carpenter & Moser, 1982; Piaget, 1941/1952).

Resnick (Resnick, 1983; Resnick & Ford, 1981) offered a clear and empirically supported view of development. She suggested that normally developing preschool children have learned several skills, including how to count and to compare quantities, and that they can use these skills to solve simple arithmetic problems (see also Siegler & Shrager, in press). Resnick thought that these skills were based on a rudimentary understanding of a number line. The number line concept is illustrated in Figure 9.1. Each number in the number line is linked to the next higher one in the way that it might be after extensive practice with counting. Also, each number is linked to a concept of the number of "things" that it represents (the drawings of dots). The number line represents

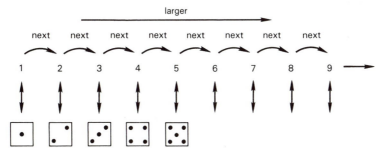

Figure 9.1   The mental number line thought to be representative of children's basic understanding of number concepts during the preschool years.
Source: L. B. Resnick, "A Developmental Theory of Number Understanding," in H. Ginsberg (Ed.), *The Development of Mathematical Thinking,* New York: Academic Press, 1983, p. 110.

children's understanding that numbers occur in order and that numeral names can be used to represent numbers of objects.

During the primary-school years, children learn to think about numbers as wholes that are composed of parts; for example, the number 7 may also be thought of as being composed of the numbers 4 and 3 or the numbers 5 and 2. Understanding of the part-whole concept of numbers allows school-age children to interpret and solve more sophisticated problems than when they were preschoolers. Also, during the primary years, children gradually develop greater competence in solving arithmetic problems "in their heads." A description of the changes in strategies that children use to solve simple addition problems appears in Box 9.1 on pp. 270–271.

The next major development in understanding numbers is learning the working of the decimal or base 10 system. At first, children learn to treat two-digit numbers (e.g., 17) in the part-whole manner, with the requirement that one of the parts must be a multiple of 10 (e.g., 43 is 40 and 3). Handling numbers in this manner is later extended to 100s, 1000s, and so forth, and is sometimes called the concept of "place value." Development of this concept allows students to perform more complex computations "in their heads," using strategies similar to those illustrated in Box 9.1.

Little work has been done on the normal development of arithmetic and mathematics knowledge in adolescent students. Some evidence about adult performance indicates that simple retrieval of facts and more rapid performance of mental computation strategies occur (e.g., Ashcraft, 1982; Groen & Parkman, 1972). Cawley and his associates (e.g., Cawley, Fitzmaurice, Shaw, Kahn, & Bates, 1979) have reported extensively on the problems of secondary-school students with learning disabilities, but it is not possible to infer how skills and concepts develop normally from their studies.

Related Problems

Children and adolescents who have arithmetic disorders have not yet been found to have a specific cluster of characteristics that students without arithmetic disabilities do not have. However, authorities in learning disabilities have suggested many different types of problems that may be associated with disabil-

---

Box 9.1
DIFFERENT STRATEGIES FOR SOLVING ADDITION PROBLEMS

Studies by cognitive psychologists have examined the strategies people use in solving arithmetic problems. Individuals have been observed as they worked and their behaviors noted; younger children have been found to be more dependent on counting aides such as their fingers. The amount of time that passes between when a problem is presented and when an individual gives an answer has been measured; individuals take longer to answer problems that call for strategies that require more counting. In general, as they get older, children use successively more sophisticated strategies to solve arithmetic problems. The more sophisticated strategies are usually more efficient.

Some of the strategies for simple addition that have been discussed by cognitive psychologists are shown here with the problem of 3 + 4 = ? used as an example.

Steps in the Strategy		*What Might Be Said*
1	Count out counters (e.g., fingers, blocks) for one addend into one pile.	1 "One, two, three."
2	Count out counters for the other addend into another pile.	2 "One, two, three, four."
3	Count all the counters together.	3 "One, two, three, four, five, six, seven."
4	Announce the last number name said in the counting sequence as the sum.	4 "Seven."
1	Count out counters for the second addend.	1 "One, two, three, four."
2	Begin counting with the name of the first addend.	2 "Three . . ."
3	Count on once for each of the counters put out in the first step.	3 ". . . Four, five, six, seven."
4	Announce the last number name said in the counting sequence as the sum.	4 "Seven."
1	Choose the larger of the two addends and name it.	1 "Four . . ."
2	Count on the number of times indicated by the other addend.	2 ". . . Five, six, seven."
3	Announce the last number name said in the counting sequence as the sum.	3 "Seven."
1	Choose a similar problem that is known by recall.	1 "Three plus three equals six."

2	Decide how much to adjust the answer.	2	"Four is one more than three."
3	Adjust the answer from the first step the amount indicated by the second step.	3	"Six, seven."
4	Announce the last number name said as the sum.	4	"Seven."

ities in arithmetic learning. Some of these suspected problems are general in nature, others are more specific, and the most valuable appear to be those that describe the kinds of mistakes students make on arithmetic tasks.

Indirectly Related Problems Many of the difficulties that have been discussed (e.g., Chalfant & Shefflin, 1969; Glennon & Cruickshank, 1981; Kaliski, 1967) are not directly related to arithmetic performance but fall into the categories of developmental problems and information-processing disorders. For example, general developmental lags (e.g., difficulty in ordering things by length, weight, size, or time of occurrence, or difficulty in outgrowing immature behaviors), perceptual disorders (e.g., difficulties with figure-ground, spatial, temporal, or eye-hand relationships), behavior problems (e.g., perseveration, inattention, "drivenness,"), and other quite general characteristics have been attributed to students with arithmetic learning disabilities.

Directly Related Problems Some of the difficulties identified by authorities as indicative of arithmetic learning disabilities are more directly associated with performance of arithmetic tasks. For example, in their list of behaviors considered characteristic of developmental dyscalculia, Glennon and Cruickshank (1981) included problems with such skills as (1) writing numerals and mathematical symbols correctly, (2) recalling the meanings of symbols and the answers to basic facts, (3) counting, and (4) following the steps in a strategy for solving multistep problems. Of course, difficulties such

as these are obviously associated with problems in developing competence in arithmetic.

Certain aspects of story problems make them difficult for many students. For example, Rosenthal and Resnick (1974) found that story problems given in reverse order and beginning with the missing number (e.g., ones for which an equation might be written in this way: $? = 5 + 3$) were considerably more difficult than other arrangements. Learning-disabled students' difficulties unique to the solving of "story problems" have also been investigated (Blankenship & Lovitt, 1976; Trenholme, Larsen, & Parker, 1978). These studies have revealed that learning-disabled students' performance was adversely affected by such features of story problems as (1) presence of extraneous information, (2) use of complex syntactic structures, (3) change of number and type of noun used, and (4) use of verbs such as "purchased" or "bought" rather than "was given." The implication of these findings is not that teachers of students with learning disabilities should avoid assigning problems with these features, but rather that they should teach their students how to solve them.

Problems Revealed by Error Analyses The most obvious characteristic of pupils with arithmetic and mathematics learning disabilities is that they make mistakes on problems. In fact, perhaps the most extensive study in the area of arithmetic and mathematics has been focused on the erroneous answers students give.

Mistakes made by students in answering

arithmetic problems are rarely random. Usually the errors are systematic and indicate that students are consistently applying a mistaken strategy to solve the problems (Cox, 1975; Ginsberg, 1977; Lankford, 1972). Extensive analyses of "bugs" or errors in computation have also been made recently by psychologists interested in children's thinking during solution of arithmetic problems (Brown & Burton, 1978; Young & O'Shea, 1981). Figure 9.2 shows some bugs that might be found in stu-dents' answers for various subtraction problems.

The analysis of computational errors has a history going back as far as the work of Buswell and John (1926). Ashlock (1976), a major contemporary advocate of error analysis, suggested that the errors made by individual students can be examined for patterns. These patterns are thought to allow insight into the mistaken strategies that students are using and therefore to provide direction for remedial instruction.

Figure 9.2 Mistaken answers to subtraction problems showing some common error patterns and the strategies they represent.

Problem	Mistaken Strategy
A. $\quad$ 73 $\quad$ − 44 $\quad$ 31	Simply subtract the smaller from the larger number in each column.
B. $\quad$ 93 $\quad$ − 44 $\quad$ 50	If the difference is less than zero, write 0 and continue.
C. $\quad$ 8̸1̸6 $\quad$ 1̸9̸6̸ $\quad$ − 42 $\quad$ 1414	Borrow in all cases and write the two-digit difference as if it went in the units place.
D. $\quad$ 236 $\quad$ − 144 $\quad$ 112	If the problem does not require borrowing in the first column, do not borrow in any column.
E. $\quad$ 7 $\quad$ 13 $\quad$ 8̸0̸3̸ $\quad$ − 127 $\quad$ 626	Borrow across a 0, without changing it, and subtract zero from the other digit in the column.
F. $\quad$ 7 $\quad$ 10 $\quad$ 13 $\quad$ 8̸0̸3̸ $\quad$ − 127 $\quad$ 686	When borrowing across a 0, do not borrow from it in turn.

This approach is discussed in greater detail in the section on "Diagnosis."

ASSESSMENT

Assessment of arithmetic and mathematics learning problems follows much the same course as assessment in the other areas of academic learning. Teachers may make referrals because students appear to be having difficulties, and students may be administered *screening* tests to determine whether further assessment is needed. If further assessment is needed, *diagnostic* testing will be done; this form of assessment is designed to help determine what specific arithmetic learning problems students may have and what kind of educational program will be needed to remedy these problems. When remediation is under way, assessment continues in the form of *progress monitoring.*

An unfortunate aspect of most of the work

on assessment in this area is that it has focused almost exclusively on computation. Very little work has been done on the assessment of mathematical concepts. Because knowledge of underlying concepts may facilitate mastery of arithmetic computation, students' understanding of concepts is an appropriate area for assessment.

Screening

Screening in arithmetic is conducted in order to identify students who are in need of further assessment or remedial services. Administration of a screening test helps educators to determine whether there is an arithmetic learning problem, or if one is suspected, to confirm it.

Screening usually consists of administering a norm-referenced test that makes it possible to compare the referred student to others of his or her age and grade. When a student is greatly behind age- or grade-mates on arithmetic

Hays, Monkmeyer

Standardized assessment of arithmetic test is a major part of screening and diagnosis.

screening tests, an arithmetic learning disability is suspected. Tests commonly used in screening include most of the general achievement batteries—the *California Achievement Test* (Teigs & Clark, 1977–1978); the *Iowa Test of Basic Skills* (Hieronymus, Lindquist, & Hoover, 1978); the *Metropolitan Achievement Test* (Durost, Bixler, Wrightstone, Prescot, & Balow, 1971); the *Stanford Achievement Test* (Madden, Gardner, Rudman, Karlsen, & Merwin, 1973); the *Peabody Individual Achievement Test* (Dunn & Markwardt, 1970); and the *Woodcock-Johnson Psychoeducational Battery* (Woodcock & Johnson, 1977)—as well as some tests devoted specifically to diagnosing arithmetic and mathematics (discussed in the next section).

Some instruments used for screening may provide preliminary diagnostic information. For example, the *Metropolitan Achievement Test* (Durost et al., 1971) contains two subtests related to arithmetic and mathematics; one that assesses computation skills and one that assesses knowledge of concepts. If a student performs poorly on one of these but not on the other, the difference probably reflects something about his or her difficulties with arithmetic and mathematics. Other suggestions about programming based on common achievement tests such as the PIAT and *Wide Range Achievement Test* (Jastak & Jastak, 1978) have been provided to learning disabilities teachers (e.g., Trembley, Caponiqro, & Gaffrey, 1980).

Diagnosis

Diagnostic procedures for identifying specific arithmetic and mathematics learning difficulties should help teachers by providing a means of assessing students' knowledge and use of different types of arithmetic skills and mathematical concepts. One approach to diagnosis is use of formal tests. Another is use of informal methods such as informal inventories and error analysis.

Formal Testing Formal diagnostic tests should allow the teacher to determine in which of the many areas of arithmetic and mathematics a student is having difficulties. Some of these areas are shown in Table 9.1. Diagnostic tests sample from some or all of these areas.

The *Key-Math Diagnostic Arithmetic Test* (Connolly, Nachtman, & Pritchett, 1971), is a very widely used diagnostic instrument for grades kindergarten through 8. The 14 subtests in the Key-Math are arranged into three general areas: (1) content, (2) operations, and (3) applications. The test covers most of the areas of knowledge and skill listed in Table 9.1 and provides different types of scores, ranging from a norm-referenced total test score to scores on individual items that can be used as program-planning aides. An extensive list of instructional objectives keyed to the items on the test accompanies it, making it easy to program in-

Table 9.1 Areas of Arithmetic and Mathematics Learning

Area	Examples
Basic information	Number-numeral relationships, counting, equality, symbol names
Computation skills	Addition, subtraction, multiplication, division
Problem solving	Writing algorithms for "story problems"
Fractions	Regular, decimals, percentages, renaming, computation using fractions, ratios, proportions, probability
Measurement	Meters and derivatives; inches, feet, miles, etc.; grams and derivatives; ounces, pounds, bushels, pecks, etc.; seconds, minutes
Money	Coin values, equivalencies
Algebra	Linear and quadratic equations
Geometry	Shape names, theorems

struction according to a student's performance on the test.

The *Stanford Diagnostic Mathematics Test* (Beatty, Madden, Gardner, & Karlsen, 1976) is another widely used diagnostic instrument. It includes four levels, each designed for administration to a different age group, ranging from first grade through high school. Three general areas of skill and knowledge—number system and numeration, computation, and applications—are assessed at each level (these include most of the areas shown in Table 9.1). Because the *Stanford Diagnostic Mathematics Test* can be administered to groups of students, it may also be used as a screening instrument.

Several other commercially available instruments may be used to diagnose problems in arithmetic and mathematics. *Diagnosis: an instructional aid in mathematics* (Guzaitis, Carlin, & Juda, 1972) is a system of probes for use with primary- and elementary-school students; items on the probes are based on instructional objectives and are keyed to sections of instructional materials for teachers to use in remediating problems. The *Buswell-John* (see Buswell & John, 1926) is a test of computation on which students write the answers to many items representing differing levels of difficulty for each of the computational operations. The *Diagnostic Mathematics Inventory* (Gessell, 1977) is a test based on instructional objectives in the arithmetic and mathematics areas; detailed information is provided about mistaken answers for each item and specific recommendations are made for remedial activities and appropriate instructional materials.

Informal Methods Informal methods of diagnosis should also assist the teacher in identifying specific areas of deficit and in making placement decisions. Informal diagnostic procedures are usually intended to assess more specific skills than formal diagnostic tests. Consequently they may be used in conjunction with formal methods in order to focus remedial efforts on highly specific targets. Informal arithmetic inventories and identification of patterns in errors are two of the most widely used informal diagnostic methods.

Informal Inventories Informal inventories of arithmetic computational skills can be very useful to the teacher of students with learning disabilities. Most teachers have students with widely differing skill levels in their classes and must assign and teach each one how to solve quite different types of problems. Determining which kinds of problems are appropriate for each student can be accomplished by using informal inventories.

Informal inventories are created by testing students on representative examples of different kinds of problems. Many of the diagnostic tests described above do this (e.g., the *Buswell-John*) in a broad way. Other informal inventories assess performance in a more detailed way and allow teachers to make more precise placement decisions. For example, placement tests at three grade levels are shown in Figure 9.3. Because these tests are designed to assess what a student can do, they are given without time limits or teacher assistance. They merely allow a teacher to determine what individual students have learned and what they should be taught next.

Error Analysis Analysis of students' mistaken answers has also been suggested as a method for determining what to teach students. Ashlock (1976), a major advocate of error analysis, provided extensive examples of students' mistaken answers, interpretations of them, and general suggestions for their remediation. For example, when a student's answers indicated that he or she failed to "carry," Ashlock suggested that the teacher use manipulative aids such as bundles of 10 and single sticks, draw boxes in the answer spaces for problems to prompt the student to write only one numeral in each column, and play games requiring the student to

Figure 9.3   Informal inventories of arithmetic and mathematics skills.
Source: J. Silbert, D. Carnine, & M. Stein, *Direct Instruction Mathematics,*
Columbus, OH: Charles E. Merrill, 1981 (pp. 27, 30, 32).

LEVEL B
For Beginning Second Graders

TESTER INSTRUCTIONS
  I. Symbol Skills
    1. Symbol Identification—Teens and Tens
    Point to each numeral below and ask,
    "WHAT NUMBER?"

    14 17 13 15 12 11
    26 48 35 52
    50 30 21 41

    Recording
    Write + next to each numeral identified correctly.
    Write the number said for each numeral identified incorrectly.
    (Stop testing when student misses three in a row and go to II.)

 II. Counting Skills

    Instructions
    1. "I'LL SAY A NUMBER. YOU SAY THE NUMBER THAT COMES NEXT; 39. WHAT
    COMES NEXT?"
    Repeat step 1 with 69, 49.

    Recording
    Write a + next to each numeral for which student responds correctly.
    Write the number said for each incorrect response.

    Recording for III, IV
    Write + if correct; write student's response if incorrect.
    Stop testing in a section when student misses two problems in a row.
    Proceed to next section.

III. Operations

    Written Presentation of Operations
    1. Give students pencil and point to problems on record form.
    "WORK THESE PROBLEMS AND WRITE THE ANSWERS."

IV. Story Problems

    1. "LISTEN. SAM HAD 3 HATS (pause 1 second).
    HE GOT 2 MORE HATS. HOW MANY HATS DID HE END WITH? LISTEN AGAIN.
    SAM HAD 3 HATS (pause 1 second).
    HE GOT 2 MORE HATS.
    HOW MANY HATS DID HE END WITH?"
    2. "NEW PROBLEM: ANN HAD 5 TOYS (pause 1 second).
    SHE GAVE AWAY 2 OF THE TOYS.
    HOW MANY TOYS DID SHE END WITH?"
    (Repeat story one time.)

Figure 9.3 (Continued)

3. "NEW PROBLEM: JACK HAS 4 EGGS (pause 1 second).
HE BUYS 3 MORE EGGS. HOW MANY EGGS DOES HE END WITH? LISTEN AGAIN.
JACK HAS 4 EGGS (pause 1 second). HE BUYS 3 MORE EGGS. HOW MANY EGGS DOES
HE END WITH?"

LEVEL D
For Beginning Fourth Graders

1. 374
   $+261$

2. $3{,}761$
   $+1{,}854$

3. $342 + 7 + 14 = \square$

4. 423
   -17

5. $3{,}529$
   $-1{,}872$

6. $203 \div 84$

7. 35
   $\times\ 4$

8. 47
   -3

9. $5 \times 24 = \square$

10. $\dfrac{4}{7} - \dfrac{2}{7} = \square$

11. How many inches in 2 feet? $\square$ inches

12. Bill had 15 apples, 3 bananas, and 27 oranges. How many pieces of fruit did Bill have? $\square$ pieces

13. Sam had 423 apples. He sold 58 apples. How many apples does he have left? $\square$ apples.

14. Jim had a quarter. He spent 17 cents. How many cents does he have left? $\square$ cents

15. Jack is 25 years old. His uncle is 8 years younger than Jack. How old is Jack's uncle? $\square$ years old

16. Circle five thousand and six.
    5,060   506   5,600   5,006

17. Circle four thousand and twenty.
    4,200   420   4,020   4,002

18. What time is it?
    __ half past 4
    __ a quarter to 4
    __ a quarter to 5
    __ a quarter after 4

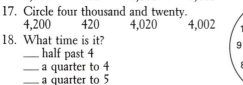

19. Jim has a quarter, a dime and 4 pennies. How many cents does Jim have? $\square$ cents

20. Jill has 5 cans of worms. There are 4 worms in each can. How many worms does Jill have? $\square$ worms

21. $4 \times \square = 24$

22. $3\overline{)18}$

23. $9\overline{)36}$

24. $5\overline{)19}$

25. $4\overline{)15}$

LEVEL F
For Beginning Sixth Graders or Junior High Students

1. Write this number:
   Six million four hundred thousand _____

2. Write this number:
   Eight hundred thirty thousand _____

3. 2.14
   $\times\ \ .7$

4. Round off this number to the nearest whole number:
   7.83 _____

5. Round off this number to the nearest tenth:
   8.693 _____

6. $7\overline{)2835}$

7. Work this problem: convert your answer to a mixed number.
   $\dfrac{4}{5} + \dfrac{3}{5} =$

Figure 9.3   (Continued)

8.   284   9. $7\overline{)42.91}$ 10.   3869   11. $47\overline{)1325}$
      ×346   1868
                                      +4285

12. $35\overline{)714}$ 13. $7.1 - 3.45$ 14. $9\overline{).36}$ 15. $8 + .34 + 7.02 =$
16. ¾ of 12 =   17. ¾ − ⅔ =   18. $8 - 3½ =$
19. Jill is a carpenter. She makes $8.75 every hour she works. She works 45 hours. How much does she earn? _____
20. Bill bought a piece of material which was 1 yard long. He cut off 1 foot and 3 inches. How much material does he have left? _____
21. Mrs. Adams is going to take a trip to see her daughter who lives 2,000 miles away. If Mrs. Adams drives 50 miles an hour, how many hours will she have to drive? _____
22. Jack weighs 38¾ pounds. He is 7¼ pounds lighter than his brother. How much does Jack's brother weigh? _____
23. James had 10 dollars. He bought a pen for $3.46 and a book for $1.83. How much does he have left? _____
24. There are 26 phones on each floor of an office building which is 48 floors high. How many phones are there altogether in the building? _____
25. Jack worked 3 hours and 40 minutes on Monday and 4 hours and 25 minutes on Tuesday. How many more minutes did he work on Tuesday than on Monday? _____

trade many smaller-valued chips for one more valuable chip.

Progress Monitoring

Some of the assessment instruments described in the preceding section may be readministered to determine if a student is making progress. For example, an achievement test may be given in the fall of each year in order to assess how much progress students are making.

Most formal, standardized instruments, however, are not designed to be readministered much more frequently than once a year. Also, their analyses are not fine-grained enough to be sensitive to small amounts of progress. Some of the diagnostic instruments allow more fine-grained estimates of progress, but do not have enough test items at each level to be readministered frequently. If students take the same tests over and over again, they may answer items correctly on the second or third try, not because they have learned the skills the items

require, but because they have become familiar with the particular items. Furthermore, a formal test often takes over 30 minutes, making frequent testing excessively time-consuming.

The most appropriate means of overcoming the difficulties with readministering tests is to adopt or create a set of miniature tests. These miniature tests or *probes* should include many examples of problems that require the same skills and should be constructed so that they can be readministered repeatedly and quickly. Several probe sheets for each type of problem should be created so that different ones can be used rather than repeatedly using the same one; this practice avoids the problem of students learning the answers to only those problems used on a probe. Examples of some probes are shown in Figure 9.4.

INTERVENTIONS

Arithmetic and mathematics instruction is influenced by decisions about the general princi-

```
  83        6        42        36         9
+  7      +65       +  8      +  7       +27


  57       39         5        29        45
+  4      +  3       +78       +  1      +  6


  76        5        51        27        32
+  9      +88       +  9       +  6      +  9


  63        9        58         7        45
+  9      +18       +  6       +68       +  9


   3       26        14         8         4
+87       +  8       +  7       +18       +49
```

```
                     66        70        90
                    ×60       ×44       ×79



                     34        50        20
                    ×80       ×55       ×63



                     37        30        72
                    ×60       ×48       ×40
```

Figure 9.4 Examples of probes used
in monitoring student progress.
From Precision Teaching Project. *Material
Directory*. Great Falls, MT: U.S. Dept of
Education, pp. M-3, M-6, M-7. Reprinted
with permission.

ples of instruction and by selections from the available instructional programs and techniques. These are the topics of this section.

General Principles of Instruction

Two questions about arithmetic and mathematics instruction provide the general basis for teaching. One question is, What should be taught? and the other is How should it be taught? These questions are not completely separate—a person's answer to one of them often implies an answer to the other—but they serve to structure the following discussion about general principles of instruction.

Content A major source of disagreement among mathematics educators is how much relative emphasis should be placed on developing an understanding of the structure of mathematics and how much should be placed on developing mastery of arithmetic skills. Earlier in this century, a rote-memorization or drill-and-practice approach was sometimes recommended, but it has few supporters in contemporary arithmetic and mathematics instruction.

Structural Resnick and Ford (1981) described the meaning of structure in this way:

> Structure in mathematics can be thought of as the structure of the subject matter itself, that is, the way the body of mathematical knowledge is internally organized and interrelated. The structure of a domain of knowledge is more or less objectively verifiable; expert mathematicians could probably come to some kind of consensus about the basic structure and content of the field. (p. 98)

The structural position is based in large part on the theories of Bruner (e.g., 1964), Piaget (e.g., 1941/1952), and others. In the structuralist approach, emphasis is placed on learners discovering principles of mathematics through experimentation. According to those who favor a

structuralist view, it is valuable because it allows learners to (1) grasp the general nature of mathematics, not just isolated arithmetic facts; (2) derive solutions to problems without extreme dependence on simple recall; (3) enjoy the excitement of achievement; and (4) receive credit for their ability to discover and invent understanding of mathematical relationships.

Fundamental The fundamentalist position is often erroneously associated with rote drill and practice alone. Actually, it is more consistent with an approach that recommends task analyses of cognitive operations and systematic teaching of concepts and operations. Instead of depending on students discovering principles, instruction is designed so that students are directly taught the principles and then given repeated opportunities to use them. Fundamental approaches are based on theories of learning such as those offered by Gagné (1970). According to those who favor a fundamentalist approach, it is valuable because it allows learners to (1) apprehend basic facts successfully; (2) develop the "automaticity" (rapid, accurate responding) necessary for solving real-world problems; and (3) benefit from carefully sequenced instruction.

These approaches to arithmetic and mathematics instruction are so general that it is nearly impossible to test them experimentally. As a consequence, there is no clear-cut evidence that favors either approach over the other. On some measures, specific procedures associated with one approach may be superior, but on other measures the reverse may be true.

Instructional Methods On the other hand, several aspects of instruction have been demonstrated to have beneficial effects on arithmetic learning. Rosenshine (1976) summarized the observational research on effective instruction and concluded that it represented what he called "direct instruction." Stevens and Rosenshine (1981) characterized effective instruction in this way: "(a) It takes place in groups, (b) it is teacher directed, (c) it is academically focused, and (d) it is individualized" (p. 1). Good and Grouws (1979; Good, Grouws, & Ebmeier, 1983) designed an instructional program in mathematics based, in part, on observational research. They devoted nearly the entire arithmetic period to working on arithmetic, provided a daily review for the group, demonstrated new skills for students, and gave them extended opportunities to practice the new skills under individualized teacher supervision and correction. They found that students learned significantly more in their experimental program than in traditional programs.

Silbert, Carnine, and Stein (1981) presented a similar view of effective arithmetic and mathematics instruction. They described not only the direct instruction teaching behaviors (e.g., scheduling plenty of time for arithmetic lessons) but also instructional programming techniques (e.g., sequencing of lessons) that result in improved chances of mastering arithmetic skills and mathematical concepts.

Programs

The most common form of instruction in arithmetic is the developmental approach. Developmental approaches usually include the familiar *basal programs* that are designed to be used with most students in regular classrooms. Most basal programs emphasize a structural approach but include activities consistent with a fundamental approach, too. Sometimes teachers of students who have difficulties learning arithmetic skills and concepts use basal programs and supplement them with *specific skills programs* in order to remedy the problems their students experience. In other cases, *specialized programs* designed for teaching slow or atypical learners are used. In virtually all cases, teachers must adopt *specialized*

teaching techniques in order to help their students master arithmetic and mathematics skills. This section includes descriptions of basal programs, specialized programs, specific skills programs, and special instructional techniques.

Basal Programs Basal (or "developmental") arithmetic and mathematics programs are offered by many major publishing houses. Among the most widely used are Holt's *Holt School Mathematics*; Scott, Foresman's *Mathematics Around Us*; Houghton Mifflin's *Modern School Mathematics*; Addison-Wesley's *Elementary School Mathematics*; and Laidlaw's *The Understanding Mathematics Program.*

Every basal program introduces basic skills such as addition, subtraction, multiplication, and division. Most also introduce other important content such as place value, measurement, geometry, and fractions. Despite the many similarities in what they cover, however, basal programs differ markedly in when they present material. For example, during the first grade, the programs published by Holt and by Heath devote a unit to presentations of fractions, but the program published by Macmillan does not.

Specialized Instructional Programs Specialized instructional programs are designed to correct for some of the problems their authors have discerned in other programs. In the following paragraphs, several specialized instructional programs are described.

The *Structural Arithmetic* program (Stern & Stern, 1971) is designed to develop students' understanding of arithmetic principles by giving them extensive experience with manipulating objects. The program is designed for use with kindergarten through third-grade students and includes different colored blocks and sticks that represent numbers from 1 to 10. The "1" block is a cube, the "3" stick is the equivalent of laying three "1s" in a line, and the 10 is the equivalent of laying ten "1s" (or two "5s") in a line. Thus numerical relationships are represented by different lengths. (Similar blocks are used in other approaches, particularly the Cuisenaire rods advocated by Gattegno, 1963.) Children are encouraged to work with the blocks and discover relationships among numbers; for example, exercises are designed to help them understand that the "7" can be matched by a "6" and a "1," a "4" and a "3," or in several other ways. Although experimental evidence about the effectiveness of *Structural Arithmetic* is not available, many teachers working with learning-disabled students use it.

Project MATH (Cawley et al., 1976) was designed as a comprehensive instructional program for students whose development is slower than normal. It is arranged in four levels and covers arithmetic instruction from prekindergarten through approximately sixth grade. The purpose of the program is to help students discover meaningful principles underlying mathematics. *Project MATH* emphasizes acquisition of arithmetic and mathematics skills and concepts through a curriculum that integrates arithmetic with students' daily experiences and individualizes instruction. The program is composed of six "strands" (patterns, sets, numbers, fractions, geometry, and measurement) that teachers can use as specific remedial materials. Additionally, extensive lists of objectives, materials, and activities are provided for each of the many lessons. Although the effectiveness of *Project MATH* has not been shown experimentally, reports during field tests of the program were positive (Cawley, Fitzmaurice, Shaw, Kahn, & Bates, 1978).

DISTAR Arithmetic I and *II* (Engelmann & Carnine, 1975, 1976) is a program designed for use with primary-aged pupils and is based on the Direct Instruction Model. In highly structured lessons involving frequent teacher questions and student answers, children learn (1) counting (forward, backward, from one number to another number, by numbers); (2) symbol identification (naming numerals and arithmetic signs); (3) equality; (4) strategies for solving equations; (5) basic facts in addition, subtraction, and beginning multiplication; and (6) related skills (e.g., time telling). *DISTAR Arithmetic* was the arithmetic program used in the Direct Instruction Model evaluated as a part of Project Follow-Through (Abt Associates, 1976, 1977). Students in the classrooms using the Direct Instruction Model had higher levels of achievement in arithmetic than did students in any of the eight other model programs evaluated. Although the DISTAR approach has been criticized as emphasizing rote learning at the expense of conceptual understanding, students taught with this program scored higher on tests of mathematical concepts and problem solving, too.

Specific Skills Programs Programs designed to help teach students specific skills differ from basal programs in that they are less comprehensive. Basal programs cover many—if not all—of the major areas of arithmetic and mathematics, while specific skills programs focus on only one area. For students who have mastered most of the skills covered in the basal curriculum used in their school but are having difficulty with a certain area, specific skills programs may be the most appropriate approach. However, teachers using specific skills programs must be very careful to integrate what students learn. Because specific skills programs are usually not coordinated with one another, they do not provide the systematic mixing and practicing of skills so important for learning the relationships among individual arithmetic and mathematics skills.

The *Computational Arithmetic Program* or CAP (Smith & Lovitt, 1982) is designed for use with students who need to learn basic addition, subtraction, multiplication, or division of whole numbers. The program includes directions for monitoring progress, suggestions and

Small group instruction and unison responding are common features of many direct instruction programs. Here, the teacher is signalling the student to answer a question about renaming fractions.

materials for reinforcing progress, and an extensive set of carefully sequenced worksheets. It is based on what Smith and Lovitt learned from their research with learning-disabled students (Lovitt & Smith, 1974; Smith & Lovitt, 1975; Smith & Lovitt, 1976; Smith, Lovitt, & Kidder, 1972).

The *Corrective Mathematics* program (Engelmann & Carnine, 1981) is composed of several modules, each of which covers a specific area of arithmetic or mathematics skill. These areas include (1) addition, (2) subtraction, (3) multiplication, (4) division, (5) money, and (6) measurement. Scripts for daily lessons are included, and accompanying workbooks provide students with extensive opportunities for practice. Similar programs are *Fractions* (Engelmann & Steely, 1980) and *Ratios and Equations* (Engelmann & Steely, 1981).

Techniques

Too many of the techniques recommended for teaching arithmetic and mathematics have little experimental support. However, several teaching techniques that do have research support are *modeling*, explicitly teaching students to use *strategies, reinforcing responses*, and *self-instruction*. These techniques are discussed in the following paragraphs.

Modeling Modeling has been and is a mainstay in teaching. It may be used in any of several ways:

The teacher may demonstrate for the student (e.g., "Watch me; here's how I do a division problem").

The teacher may have another student demonstrate (e.g., "Watch Judy; she's going to bisect that line").

The teacher may simply tell students a factual answer (e.g., "Nine plus five equals fourteen"). The teacher may use or construct materials that include demonstrations.

Smith and Lovitt (1975) reported a series of studies in which they investigated modeling as a technique for teaching learning-disabled boys arithmetic skills. They found that providing a demonstration and a permanent model (a problem with a written solution on the students' arithmetic sheets) resulted in greatly improved performance. Moreover, the students' performance improvements generalized to other problems for which they had received no demonstrations.

Strategy Training   In order to teach students new skills, teachers may model the steps involved in attacking a specific type of arithmetic problem. Lloyd (Cullinan, Lloyd, & Epstein, 1981; Lloyd, 1980; Lloyd & deBettencourt, 1982) described this approach as "academic strategy training." In strategy training, a task analysis of a cognitive operation is performed so that the steps leading to solution can be identified. Then students are taught the skills required by each of the steps. When students have mastered the component skills, they are taught how to put them together in order to attack a given type of problem. Mastery of the component skills prior to introduction of the strategy leads to more rapid learning of the strategy and greater generalization of it to related problems (Carnine, 1980). Examples of the application of this type of approach to the teaching of arithmetic are common. For example, Grimm, Bijou, and Parsons (1973) taught a young handicapped student to use a strategy for answering problems about number-numeral equivalencies. Lloyd, Saltzman, and Kauffman (1981) used a strategy training approach to teach learning-disabled students basic multiplication and division skills. And Smith and Lovitt (1975) modeled the steps in

strategies for learning-disabled students that helped them to learn, for example, regrouping in subtraction.

Reinforcing Responses   Reinforcing responses involves providing reinforcement for correct answers. It is important to note that arranging reinforcement contingencies for learning-disabled students who do not know *how* to perform tasks is of little value, as Smith and Lovitt (1976) demonstrated. In other words, it does no good to use rewards to "motivate" students who do not have the skills required to answer arithmetic problems. However, when students do know how to answer problems but do so inaccurately or at too slow a pace, reinforcing accuracy or faster work is an effective way to improve performance (e.g., Hasazi & Hasazi, 1972; Smith et al., 1972). Reinforcement does not have to take the form of tangible rewards, however; Fink and Carnine (1975) found that having students maintain graphs showing their performance had beneficial effects on their arithmetic progress.

Self-Instruction Training   Self-instructional techniques are another potentially effective approach to teaching arithmetic and mathematics. Self-instructional programs have been reported to be successful with handicapped learners (e.g., Johnston, Whitman, & Johnson, 1981; Whitman & Johnston, 1983). Also, specific parts of self-instruction that have been tested have shown some promise. For example, when Lovitt and Curtiss (1968) required a learning-disabled boy to read number sentences aloud (self-verbalization) before writing his answers, they noticed a substantial improvement in his performance. Similarly, Parsons (1972) found that requiring a student both to circle the operation sign (e.g., +) and to name it before attempting to solve arithmetic problems produced much better performance than simply having the student circle the sign.

SUMMARY

Arithmetic and mathematics disabilities, which are sometimes called dyscalculia, are common among pupils labeled learning disabled. The problems these pupils experience include difficulties in skills such as counting, writing numerals, and learning basic associations (e.g., number-numeral relationships). Furthermore, they are easily misled by irrelevant aspects of problems and some of the vocabulary that is often used in arithmetic problems. Finally, they are likely to follow mistaken solution strategies when working problems.

Most major standardized achievement tests include arithmetic subtests that allow educators to identify those students who are in need of further assessment and several of them may also serve the purpose of diagnosis. Although it may be aided by studying the results of screening tests, many teachers elect to administer other formal and informal instruments in order to identify specific areas of difficulty. The inherent structure of mathematics makes it possible for specific areas of computation skill to be isolated readily. Therefore, methods for diagnosing specific skill deficits and for monitoring progress toward mastery of skill areas may be developed easily. However, perhaps because computation areas are easier to analyze, conceptual aspects of arithmetic are too often overlooked.

Instructional programs vary in how much attention they devote to the structure of mathematics and to the fundamentals of arithmetic; in general, however, developmental programs emphasize a mixture of structural and fundamental approaches. In contrast, however, some programs place far greater emphasis on direct instruction (academically focused, individualized, teacher-direct, group work which includes frequent opportunities to respond and extensive teacher feedback), a general model of instruction that has proven very effective, particularly in the teaching of arithmetic. Some instructional programs popular in learning disabilities include these features. Some programs also incorporate techniques such as modeling, strategy training, reinforcement, and self-instruction which have been found to be effective in arithmetic instruction.

REFERENCES

Abt Associates. (1976). *Education as experimentation: A planned variation model,* Vol. 3A. Cambridge, MA: Author.

Abt Associates. (1977). *Education as experimentation: A planned variation model,* Vol. 4. Cambridge, MA: Author.

ASHCRAFT, M. H. (1982). The development of mental arithmetic: A chronometric approach. *Developmental Review, 2,* 213–236.

ASHLOCK, R. B. (1976). *Error patterns in computation: A semi-programmed approach.* Columbus, OH: Charles E. Merrill.

BEATTY, L. S., MADDEN, R., GARDNER, E. G., & KARLSEN, B. (1976). *Stanford Diagnostic Mathematics Test.* New York: Harcourt Brace Jovanovich.

BLANKENSHIP, C., & LOVITT, T. C. (1976). Story problems: Merely confusing or downright befuddling? *Journal for Research in Mathematics Education, 7,* 290–298.

BROWN, J. S., & BURTON, R. B. (1978). Diagnostic models for procedural bugs in basic mathematical skills. *Cognitive Science, 2,* 155–192.

BRUNER, J. S. (1964). Some theorems on instruction illustrated with reference to mathematics. *Sixty-third Yearbook of the National Society for the Study of Education, 63* (Pt. 1), 306–335.

BUSWELL, G. T., & JOHN, L. (1926). *Diagnostic studies in arithmetic.* Chicago: University of Chicago Press.

CARNINE, D. W. (1980). Preteaching versus concurrent teaching of the component skills of a multiplication problem-solving strategy. *Journal for*

Research in Mathematics Education, 11, 375–379.

CARPENTER, T. P., & MOSER. J. M. (1982). The development of addition and subtraction problem-solving skills. In T. P. Carpenter, J. M. Moser, & T. A. Romberg (Eds.), *Addition and subtraction: A cognitive perspective* (pp. 9–24). Hillsdale, NJ: Erlbaum.

CAWLEY, J. F., FITZMAURICE, A. M., GOODSTEIN, H. A., LEPORE, A. V., SEDLAK, R., & ALTHAUS, V. (1976). *Project MATH.* Tulsa, OK: Educational Development Corporation.

CAWLEY, J. F., FITZMAURICE, A. M., SHAW, R., KAHN, H., & BATES, H., III. (1978). Mathematics and learning disabled youth: The upper grade levels. *Learning Disability Quarterly, 1*(4), 37–52.

CAWLEY, J. F., FITZMAURICE, A. M., SHAW, R., KAHN, H., & BATES, H., III. (1979). LD youth and mathematics: A review of characteristics. *Learning Disability Quarterly, 2*(1), 29–44.

CHALFANT, J. C., & SHEFFLIN, M. A. (1969). *Central processing dysfunctions in children: A review of research.* (NINDS Monograph No. 9, U.S. Public Health Service Publication No. PH 43-67-61). Washington, DC: U.S. Government Printing Office.

CONNOLLY, A., NACHTMAN, W., & PRITCHETT, E. (1971). *Key-Math Diagnostic Arithmetic Test.* Circle Pines, MN: American Guidance Service.

COX, L. S. (1975). Diagnosing and remediating systematic errors in addition and subtraction computations. *The Arithmetic Teacher, 22,* 151–157.

CULLINAN, D., LLOYD, J., & EPSTEIN, M. H. (1981). Strategy training: A structured approach to arithmetic instruction. *Exceptional Education Quarterly, 2*(1), 41–49.

DUNLAP, W. P., & HOUSE, A. D. (1976). Why can't Johnny compute? *Journal of Learning Disabilities, 4,* 210–214.

DUNN, L. M., & MARKWARDT, F. C. (1970). *Peabody Individual Achievement Test.* Circle Pines, MN: American Guidance Service.

DUROST, W. N., BIXLER, H. H., WRIGHTSTONE, J. W., PRESCOT, G. A., & BALOW, I. H. (1971). *Metropolitan Achievement Test.* New York: Harcourt Brace Jovanovich.

ENGELMANN, S., & CARNINE, D. W. (1975). *DISTAR Arithmetic I* (2nd ed). Chicago: Science Research Associates.

ENGELMANN, S., & CARNINE, D. W. (1976). *DISTAR Arithmetic II* (2nd. ed). Chicago: Science Research Associates.

ENGELMANN, S., & CARNINE, D. W. (1981). *Corrective Mathematics.* Chicago: Science Research Associates.

ENGELMANN, S., & STEELY, D. (1980). *Fractions I and II.* Chicago: Science Research Associates.

ENGELMANN, S., & STEELY, D. (1981). *Ratios and equations.* Chicago: Science Research Associates.

FINK, W. T., & CARNINE, D. W. (1975). Control of arithmetic errors using informational feedback and graphing. *Journal of Applied Behavior Analysis, 8,* 461. (Abstract)

GAGNÉ, R. M. (1970). *The conditions of learning* (2nd ed.). New York: Holt, Rinehart & Winston.

GATTEGNO, C. (1963). *For the teaching of elementary mathematics.* Mt. Vernon, NY: Cuisenaire Company of America.

GESSELL, J. (1977). *Diagnostic mathematics inventory.* Monterey. CA: CTB/McGraw-Hill.

GINSBERG, H. (1977). *Children's arithmetic: The learning process.* New York: D. Van Nostrand.

GLENNON, V. J., & CRUICKSHANK, W. M. (1981). Teaching mathematics to children and youth with perceptual and cognitive deficits. In V. J. Glennon (Ed.), *The mathematical education of exceptional children and youth: An interdisciplinary approach* (pp. 50–94). Reston, VA: National Council of Teachers of Mathematics.

GOOD, T. L., & GROUWS, D. A. (1979). The Missouri Mathematics Effectiveness Project: An experimental study in fourth-grade classrooms. *Journal of Educational Psychology, 71,* 355–362.

GOOD, T. L., GROUWS, D, A., & EBMEIER, H. (1983). *Active mathematics teaching.* New York: Longman.

GRIMM, J. A., BIJOU, S. W., & PARSONS, J. A. (1973). A problem solving model for teaching remedial arithmetic to handicapped young children. *Journal of Abnormal Child Psychology, 1,* 26–39.

GROEN, G. J., & PARKMAN, J. M. (1972). A chronometric analysis of simple addition. *Psychological Review, 79,* 329–343.

GUZAITIS, J., CARLIN, J. A., & JUDA, S. (1972). *Diagnosis: An instructional aid in mathematics.* Chicago: Science Research Associates.

HASAZI, J. E., & HASAZI, S. E. (1972). Effects of teacher attention on digit-reversal behavior in an elementary school child. *Journal of Applied Behavior Analysis, 5,* 157–162.

HIERONYMUS, A. N., LINDQUIST, E. F., & HOOVER, H. D. (1978). *Iowa Tests of Basic Skills.* Lombard, IL: Riverside.

JASTAK, J., & JASTAK, S. (1978). *The Wide Range Achievement Test.* Wilmington, DL: Guidance Associates.

JOHNSTON, M. B., WHITMAN, T. L., & JOHNSON, M. (1981). Teaching addition and subtraction to mentally retarded children: A self-instructional program. *Applied Research in Mental Retardation, 1,* 141–160.

KALISKI, L. (1967). Arithmetic and the brain-injured child. In E. C. Frierson & W. B. Barbe (Eds.), *Educating children with learning disabilities: Selected readings* (pp. 458–466). New York: Appleton Century Crofts.

KIRK, S. A., & ELKINS, J. (1975). Characteristics of children enrolled in the child service demonstration centers. *Journal of Learning Disabilities, 8,* 630–637.

KOSC, L. (1974). Developmental dyscalculia. *Journal of Learning Disabilities, 7,* 164–177.

LANKFORD, F. G., JR. (1972). *Some computational strategies of seventh grade pupils* (Final Report of Project No. 2-C-013, U.S. Department of Health, Education, and Welfare Grant No. OEG-3-72-0035). Charlottesville, VA: University of Virginia Center for Advanced Studies.

LLOYD, J. (1980). Academic instruction and cognitive-behavior modification: The need for attack strategy training. *Exceptional Education Quarterly, 1*(1), 53–63.

LLOYD, J. W., & DEBETTENCOURT, L. J. (1982). *Academic strategy training: A manual for teachers.* Charlottesville, VA: University of Virginia Learning Disabilities Research Institute.

LLOYD, J., SALTZMAN, N. J., & KAUFFMAN, J. M. (1981). Predictable generalization in academic learning as a result of preskills and strategy training. *Learning Disability Quarterly, 4,* 203–216.

LOVITT, T. C., & CURTISS, K. A. (1968). Effects of manipulating an antecedent event on mathematics response rate. *Journal of Applied Behavior Analysis, 1,* 329–333.

LOVITT, T. C., & SMITH, D. D. (1974). Using withdrawal of positive reinforcement to alter subtraction performance. *Exceptional Children, 40,* 357–358.

MADDEN, R., GARDNER, E. R., RUDMAN, H. C., KARLSEN, B., & MERWIN, J. C. (1973). *Stanford Achievement Test.* New York: Harcourt Brace Jovanovich.

MCLEOD, T. M., & ARMSTRONG, S. W. (1982). Learning disabilities in mathematics—skill deficits and remedial approaches at the intermediate and secondary level. *Learning Disability Quarterly, 5,* 305–311.

NORMAN, C., & ZIGMOND, N. (1980). Characteristics of children labeled and served as learning disabled in school systems affiliated with child service and demonstration centers. *Journal of Learning Disabilities, 13,* 542–547.

PARSONS, J. A. (1972). The reciprocal modification of arithmetic behavior and program development. In G. Semb (Ed.), *Behavior analysis and education—1972* (pp. 185–199). Lawrence, KS: University of Kansas Department of Human Development.

PIAGET, J. (1952). *The child's conception of number.* New York: Norton. (Original work published 1941.)

RESNICK, L. B. (1983). A developmental theory of number understanding. In H. P. Ginsburg (Ed.), *The development of mathematical thinking* (pp. 110–151). New York: Academic Press.

RESNICK, L. B., & FORD, W. W. (1981). *The psychology of mathematics for instruction.* Hillsdale, NJ: Erlbaum.

ROSENSHINE, B. (1976). Classroom instruction. In N. L. Gage (Ed.), *The psychology of teaching methods: The 75th yearbook of the National Society for the Study of Education* (pp. 335–371). Chicago: University of Chicago Press.

ROSENTHAL, D. J., & RESNICK, L. B. (1974). Children's solution processes in arithmetic word problems. *Journal of Educational Psychology, 66,* 817–825.

SIEGLER, R. S., & SHRAGER, J. (In press). Strategy choices in addition: How do children know what to do? In C. Sophian (Ed.), *Origins of cognitive skills.* Hillsdale, NJ: Erlbaum.

SILBERT, J., CARNINE, D., & STEIN, M. (1981). *Direct instruction mathematics.* Columbus, OH: Charles Merrill.

SMITH, D. D., & LOVITT, T. C. (1975). The use of modeling techniques to influence the acquisition of computational arithmetic skills in learning-disabled children. In E. Ramp & G. Semb (Eds.), *Behavior analysis: Areas of research and application* (pp. 283–308). Englewood Cliffs, NJ: Prentice-Hall.

SMITH, D. D., & LOVITT, T. C. (1976). The differential effects of reinforcement contingencies on arithmetic performance. *Journal of Learning Disabilities, 9,* 21–29.

SMITH, D. D., & LOVITT, T. C. (1982). *The computational arithmetic program.* Austin, TX: Pro-Ed.

SMITH, D. D., LOVITT, T. C., & KIDDER, J. D. (1972). Using reinforcement contingencies and teaching aids to alter subtraction performance of children with learning disabilities. In G. Semb (Ed.), *Be-

havior analysis and education—1972 (pp. 342–360). Lawrence, KS: University of Kansas Department of Human Development.

STEVENS, R., & ROSENSHINE, B. (1981). Advances in research on teaching. *Exceptional Education Quarterly, 2*(1), 1–9.

STERN, C. A., & STERN, M. B. (1971). *Children discover arithmetic: An introduction to Structural Arithmetic* (rev. ed.). New York: Harper & Row.

TEIGS, E. W., & CLARK, W. W. (1977–1978). *The California Achievement Test.* Monterey, CA: CTB/McGraw-Hill.

TREMBLEY, P., CAPONIGRO, J., & GAFFREY, V. (1980). Effects of programming from the WRAT and PIAT for students determined to have learning disabilities in arithmetic. *Journal of Learning Disabilities, 13,* 291–293.

TRENHOLME, B., LARSEN, S. C., & PARKER, R., (1978). The effects of syntactic complexity upon arithmetic performance. *Learning Disability Quarterly, 1*(4), 80–85.

WHITMAN, T., & JOHNSTON, M. B. (1983). Teaching addition and subtraction with regrouping to educable mentally retarded children: A group self-instructional training program. *Behavior Therapy, 14,* 127–143.

WOODCOCK, R. W., & JOHNSON, M. B. (1977). *Woodcock-Johnson Psychoeducational Battery.* Boston: Teaching Resources.

YOUNG, R. M., & O'SHEA, T. (1981). Errors in children's subtraction. *Cognitive Science, 5,* 153–177.

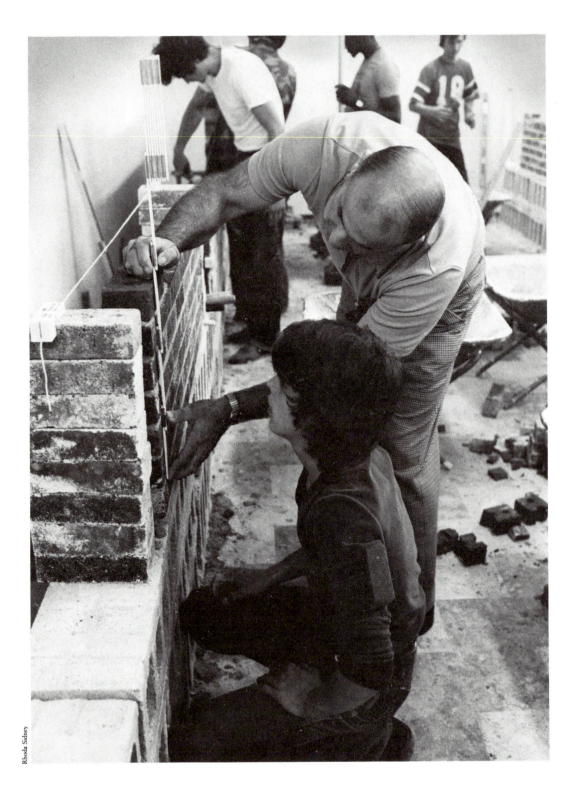

So What Is a Learning Disability?

We hope that, having read the first nine chapters of our book, you agree with us that we can make sense of the field of learning disabilities. We have tried to demonstrate that much is known about how to identify and remediate many specific learning problems. Research has yielded answers to a lot of the questions teachers and parents ask about how to assess whether a student needs special instruction and, when it is needed, how to teach the child effectively.

Nevertheless, many questions regarding the effective assessment and remediation of learning difficulties remain unanswered. As is the case in all professional fields, no sooner is one problem resolved than another becomes apparent. For example, teachers, psychologists, and researchers today are searching for answers to the question of appropriate education for learning-disabled adolescents and young adults and for solutions to the problem of LD students' lack of social skills. These areas of research have emerged only recently; for nearly two decades, researchers in the field have focused on assessment and remediation of the academic deficits of preadolescents.

In spite of remarkable progress in the field, some of the most basic issues still baffle us. What a learning disability is and how many children have such disabilities are two such issues that continue to perplex everyone who reads about or works with LD students. Learning disability is easy to define as an abstraction. When we consider flesh and blood children, however, our abstract definition that seemed so adequate, or even elegant, on paper becomes a house of cards. The moment we try to apply our neatly written criteria to an actual child, our definition collapses around us, a casualty of the child's living, breathing individuality. Naturally, if we have difficulty deciding that any given child fits our definition, then we have little basis for stating how many children are LD. Our estimation of the prevalence of learning disability often is based on a statistical probability that, like our definition, is attractive in the abstract but unworkable in practice.

Consider the dilemmas faced by the special education administrator described in Box 10.1. Then read our sketch of the controversies re-garding definition and prevalence. We hope that you will continue to study these basic issues and decide for yourself how you think they can best be resolved in practice.

Box 10.1
THE ADMINISTRATOR'S DILEMMA

Patrick Milton Wills frowned as he closed the file folders containing the information presented at the eligibility meeting for Edwin and J. C. Fifteen years ago, when he first became director of special education for the Marion County Schools, he had anticipated that his job would become easier as the years rolled by. Instead, it seemed to him that the decisions he faced were getting tougher all the time. True, the decisions about Edwin and J. C. were not his alone. He was only one member of the eligibility committee that was to decide whether these students were handi-capped under PL 94-142 and, therefore, eligible for special education. But that didn't make it any easier for him to decide how he felt about these boys' education. "Fact is," he thought to himself, "I have my hunches about them both. But if I were cross-examined in court, I'd have an awfully hard time defending any decision on either of them with hard facts and figures that make sense."

Mr. Wills let his mind drift back to the state's adoption of the LD definition under which Edwin and J. C. were being considered for special education. After seemingly interminable wrangling among state officials and LD experts, the state education de-partment decided that the proposed federal formula for defining LD was too com-plicated and unreliable. Learning disability, the state decided, meant a difference of 20 or more points between WISC-R Full-Scale IQ and standard scores for the Wood-cock-Johnson achievement test in written language or mathematics, or the Peabody Individual Achievement Test in math or reading. Seemed simple enough, he thought at the time. He remembered how the superintendent had slapped him on the back and said, "Well, P. M., I think we've finally got us a definition that'll cut out a lot of this needless haggling about who belongs in our LD classes."

Only it hadn't proved to be so simple. Take Edwin, for example. He was a third grader with a WISC-R Full-Scale IQ of 74. His W-J standard scores were lower than his IQ, 19 points in written language and 17 in mathematics. He didn't quite qualify for LD services under the definition, but he was certainly having lots of trouble in school. His teacher was at his wit's end to know what to do with Edwin. He was a constant behavior problem, according to the teacher—nearly always out of his seat, taunting and teasing his classmates, bullying smaller children on the playground, making life miserable for everyone. This was not a teacher whose class was generally disorderly or who had difficulty managing and teaching most children. Obviously, Edwin was not a bright child, though he didn't quite qualify as mentally retarded. And he was having more academic difficulty than one would expect based on his IQ.

A lot more difficulty, in fact. His parents were extremely concerned and wanted him placed in one of the county's self-contained LD classes. But the classes were already filled. Besides, nearly 4% of the county's students were already identified as LD, many of them with test score discrepancies smaller than Edwin's.

Then there was the case of J. C., a bright and talented sixth grader. J. C. had a Full-Scale WISC-R score of 129. Here was a highly motivated, well adjusted boy who was well liked by his peers, well liked by his teachers, and well-read on nearly every topic. But he had only third grade math skills. On all achievement tests, he scored about two standard deviations above the mean in written language; but his math scores were consistently 40 or more standard points below his IQ. He seemed not to care; his peers seemed not to notice; his parents were convinced that the problem was simply poor teaching and strongly resisted the notion of his being identified as LD. They gave permission for J. C.'s formal evaluation for special education only with great reluctance. And, to make matters worse, P. M. Wills knew that J. C.'s math instruction had been, for the past three years, anything but exemplary. "Perhaps," he thought, J. C. does not belong in an LD program even though he does technically fit the definition. I think his problems could quickly be resolved by a skilled tutor. And if he were my son, I don't think I'd want him in special education either."

P. M. Wills sighed. "Where are all those nice, neat cases I was taught about in graduate school?" he asked himself.

ISSUES REGARDING DEFINITION

Three central questions regarding the definition of learning disability are frequently debated:

1 Can children with learning disabilities be clearly distinguished from children with learning problems, that is, are LD children clearly different from children who are emotionally disturbed, mentally retarded, or merely low achievers?

2 Should the cause(s) of learning disabilities be stated in the definition?

3 What are the results of using the current federal definition?

Learning Problems versus Learning Disabilities

The very existence of the field of learning disabilities and its inclusion in federal legislation suggest that the population of learning-disabled children is clearly defined, if not clearly definable. Nevertheless, some leading researchers in the field argue that in practice the students classified as LD are not clearly different from students who are given other labels or are not even referred for possible placement in special education (Algozzine & Ysseldyke, 1983; Epps, Ysseldyke, & Algozzine, 1983; Glass, 1981; Shepard, Smith, & Vojir, 1983; Ysseldyke, 1983; Ysseldyke, Algozzine, & Epps, 1983; Ysseldyke, Algozzine, & Thurlow, 1983; Ysseldyke, Thurlow, Graden, Wesson, Algozzine, & Deno, 1983).

An example of the kind of research that leads some authorities to question whether children are being legitimately classified as LD is provided by Ysseldyke, Algozzine, and Epps (1983). In one of their studies they obtained psychometric test data on 248 3rd, 5th, and 12th graders who were classified as normal (i.e., had not been referred for evaluation for special education). Using tests and criteria commonly employed to determine eligibility for classification as learning disabled, they calculated the percentage of the sample of the children from regular education who would be classified as LD according to 17 different definitions. Table 10.1 contains the 17 definitions. Note that the definitions are grouped into those based on discrepancy between ability and achievement, those based on low achievement per se, and those based on test score scatter (i.e., differences between or among scores on subtests, a popular practice among some school psychologists). Table 10.2 shows the number and percentage of regular classroom students (who were not actually identified as LD) who would have been identified by each of the definitions had it been the criterion for determining that a child has a learning disability. The percentage of the total group of normal students who would have been identified ranged from 2% to 65%. The average percentage identified was 16% at the 3rd grade level, 18% at the 5th grade level, 28% at the 12th grade level, and 21% for the total sample of normal students. Of the 248 normal students, 211 (85%) met one or more of the criteria for being labeled LD; 68% met the criteria of two or more definitions; and 3.6% met the criteria of 10 or more.

Other analyses of trends in the data presented in Table 10.2 are possible. For example, Ysseldyke, Algozzine, and Epps (1983) point out that definitions based on ability-achievement discrepancies generally result in increasing percentages of children being identified at higher grade levels. The major conclusion suggested by the data presented in Table 10.2, however, is that many current definitions of learning disability will result in the identification of a surprisingly high percentage of the normal child population if the definitions' criteria are simply applied to children's test scores

without any additional considerations. That is, the objective criteria contained in current operational definitions of learning disability apparently would include many children who are not now identified as LD.

Given the foregoing conclusion, one might ask how well students who are identified as LD or low achievers fit these same definitions of learning disability. Ysseldyke, Algozzine, and Epps (1983) also obtained test data for 50 fourth-grade children who had been identified by their school districts as LD (although these school districts' criteria for identification were not available) and 49 fourth-graders in the same school districts who were classified simply as low achievers (i.e., scored at or below the 25th percentile on a standard achievement test). Table 10.3 shows the number and percentage of the low achieving and LD students who met the criteria for each of the 17 definitions of learning disability included in Table 10-1. The percentage of low achieving students meeting the criteria for identification ranged from 0% to 71%; the percentage of LD students ranged from 1% to 78%. Of the low achieving children, 88% could have been classified as LD by at least 1 of the 17 definitions; 4% of the learning-disabled sample did not meet the criteria for identification under any of the 17 definitions. The conclusion suggested by these data is that low achieving children and children identified as LD were about the same in terms of how well they fit the criteria included in current definitions. Particularly noteworthy is the percentage of children identified by their school districts as LD who did not fit many (or any!) of the definitions.

Other researchers (e.g., Epps et al., 1983; Shepard et al., 1983) also have gathered data indicating that many children identified as LD do not meet the usual definitional criteria. Shepard et al. (1983), for example, found that slightly more than half of a sample of 800 children identified as LD did not match conven-

Table 10.1 Criteria Used to Determine Eligibility for Learning Disabilities Classification

Definition	*Criteria*
Ability-Achievement Discrepancy	
1. 1976 Federal formula	Achievement in one or more areas below "severe discrepancy level" defined by 1976 federal formula: SDL = [CA × IQ/300 + 0.17] − 2.5. WISC-R Full-Scale IQ was used as a measure of IQ. Grade-equivalent scores for W-J Written Language, W-J Mathematics, PIAT Mathematics, PIAT Reading, and PIAT Spelling were used as indices of achievement.
2. Statistical discrepancy	Difference of 10 or more points between WISC-R Full-Scale IQ and standard scores for W-J Written Language Achievement, W-J Mathematics Achievement, PIAT Mathematics, and PIAT Reading.
3. Statistical discrepancy	Difference of 20 or more points between WISC-R Full-Scale IQ and standard scores for W-J Written Language Achievement, W-J Mathematics Achievement, PIAT Mathematics, and PIAT Reading.
4. Statistical discrepancy	Difference of 30 or more points between WISC-R Full-Scale IQ and standard scores for W-J Written Language Achievement, W-J Mathematics Achievement, PIAT Mathematics, and PIAT Reading.
5. Alternative federal formula	Achievement in one or more areas below "severe discrepancy level" defined by alternative to 1976 Federal Formula: SDL-5[IQ/100 × (CA − 5.2)]. Grade-equivalent achievement scores for W-J Written Language, W-J Mathematics, PIAT Mathematics, and PIAT Reading were evaluated.
6. Myklebust Learning Quotient	Learning Quotient in one or more areas at or below 89: LQ = actual achievement/expected achievement. Actual achievement, as measured by W-J Written Language, W-J Mathematics, PIAT Mathematics, and PIAT Reading, was compared to expected achievement based on the average of the student's chronological age, mental age, and grade-placement age.
7. Woodcock-Johnson severe deficit	Scholastic aptitude and achievement scores from the Woodcock-Johnson Psycho-Educational Battery were used to determine the student's functioning level (i.e., degree of discrepancy).
Low Achievement	
8. Standard score cutoff	Achievement in one or more areas at or below cutoff criterion of 85. Standard scores for W-J Reading, W-J Mathematics, and W-J Written Language Achievement as well as PIAT Mathematics and PIAT Reading were evaluated.
Low Achievement	
9. Standard score cutoff	Achievement in one or more areas at or below cutoff criterion of 77. Standard scores for W-J Reading, W-J Mathematics, and W-J Written Language Achievement as well as PIAT Mathematics and PIAT Reading were evaluated.
10. Standard score cutoff	Achievement in one or more areas at or below cutoff criterion of 70. Standard scores for W-J Reading, W-J Mathematics, and W-J Written Language Achievement as well as PIAT Mathematics and PIAT Reading were evaluated.

Table 10.1   (Continued)

Definition	Criteria
11. Standard score cutoff	Achievement in one or more areas at or below cutoff criterion of 85. Standard scores for W-J Written Language and W-J Mathematics as well as PIAT Mathematics and PIAT Reading were compared. The definition is identical to No. 8, except that W-J Reading was not included in this definition.
Scatter	
12. Verbal-Performance discrepancy	Difference of 9 or more points between WISC-R Verbal and Performance standard scores.
13. Verbal-Performance discrepancy	Difference of 12 or more points between WISC-R Verbal and Performance standard scores.
14. Verbal-Performance discrepancy	Difference of 15 or more points between WISC-R Verbal and Performance standard scores.
15. Subtest scatter	Difference of 10 or more points between scaled scores on highest and lowest WISC-R subtests.
16. Subtest scatter	Bannatyne's (1979) recategorization of WISC-R was used, in which the Spatial category (Picture Completion, Block Design, and Object Assembly) was greater than the Conceptualizing category (Similarities, Vocabulary, and Comprehension), which in turn was greater than the Sequencing category (Arithmetic, Coding, and Digit Span).
17. Subtest scatter	Significant differences between Bannatyne's (1979) categories, in which the Spatial category score was at least 7 points greater than the Conceptualizing category score, which in turn was at least 7 points greater than the Sequencing category score.

Source: J. Ysseldyke, B. Algozzine, & S. Epps, "A Logical and Empirical Analysis of Current Practice in Classifying Students as Handicapped," *Exceptional Children*, 1983, 50, 160–165.

tional definitions of learning disability but exhibited learning problems such as emotional disturbance or mild mental retardation. Ysseldyke, Algozzine, and Epps (1983) concluded that no reliable definitional criteria exist: "millions of children . . . perform poorly in reading, writing, mathematics, listening, speaking, and other academic areas; significant numbers of students are failing to profit from their educational experiences . . . No defendable system exists for classifying or categorizing these students; there are no defendable inclusionary and exclusionary principles to guide our efforts to classify them" (p. 165).

Not everyone would agree that recent research has shown that LD and low achieving children are very similar, or that the differences between children who are identified as learning disabled and those who are not are undetectable. McKinney (1983), for example, argues that Ysseldyke and his colleagues have examined only psychometric differences and that these do not reflect the very real and important distinguishing features of learning-disabled children. He points out that several of the five Learning Disabilities Research Institutes funded by the federal government for 6 years did find that LD children have specific deficits in information processing and adaptive behavior (see Kneedler & Hallahan, 1983). These

Table 10.2 Frequencies and Percentages of Regular Classroom Students Classified by Each of 17 Operational Definitions, Study 1

Defini-tion	3rd Grade	5th Grade	12th Grade	Total
1	3(4)*	1(1)	17(25)	21(10)
2	30(46)	43(63)	54(84)	127(65)
3	9(14)	14(21)	27(42)	50(25)
4	2(3)	0(0)	6(9)	8(4)
5	2(3)	0(0)	13(19)	15(7)
6	18(23)	28(39)	52(75)	98(45)
7	4(5)	2(3)	8(11)	14(6)
8	14(17)	15(19)	27(37)	56(25)
9	3(4)	5(6)	9(12)	17(7)
10	1(1)	1(1)	7(10)	9(4)
11	13(16)	11(14)	23(31)	47(20)
12	42(51)	42(52)	34(41)	118(48)
13	33(40)	32(40)	27(32)	92(37)
14	19(23)	20(25)	15(18)	54(22)
15	9(11)	12(15)	7(9)	28(12)
16	14(17)	12(15)	16(20)	42(17)
17	1(1)	1(1)	3(4)	5(2)

* Numbers in parentheses are percentages adjusted for cases missing information.
Source: J. Ysseldyke, B. Algozzine, & S. Epps, "A Logical and Empirical Analysis of Current Practice in Classifying Students as Handicapped," *Exceptional Children*, 1983, 50, 160–166.

deficits of LD children would not be reflected in the standardized test scores that were the basis for the criteria used in research by Ysseldyke and his research group.

Whatever the distinguishing characteristics of LD children may be, they clearly are not the kinds of test score criteria listed in Table 10.1. Current practices have led some commentators to label the situation a "diagnostic scandal" (Scriven, 1981). If the confusion about definition is to be cleared up, some authorities believe that criteria other than psychometric data will have to be established for identification of learning-disabled children.

Definition Based on Causal Factors

The two currently popular definitions of learning disability—the one in PL 94-142 and that of the National Joint Committee for Learning Disabilities (Hammill, Leigh, McNutt, & Larsen, 1981)—include statements

Table 10.3 Frequencies and Percentages of Low-Achieving and School-Identified LD Students Classified as LD by 17 Operational Definitions

Definition	Low-Achieving Sample	LD Sample	Total
1	2(02)*	9(09)	11(11)
2	30(71)	32(78)	62(73)
3	17(40)	19(45)	36(42)
4	2(03)	5(05)	7(08)
5	1(01)	3(03)	4(04)
6	25(25)	43(44)	68(69)
7	5(05)	7(07)	12(12)
8	21(21)	36(37)	57(58)
9	3(03)	13(13)	16(16)
10	0(0)	2(02)	2(02)
11	19(20)	33(33)	52(53)
12	19(48)	25(62)	44(55)
13	13(13)	16(16)	29(29)
14	6(06)	15(16)	21(21)
15	14(14)	7(07)	21(21)
16	8(08)	12(12)	20(20)
17	2(02)	1(01)	3(03)

* Numbers in parentheses are percentages adjusted for cases of missing information.
Source: J. Ysseldyke, B. Algozzine, & S. Epps, "A Logical and Empirical Analysis of Current Practice in Classifying Students as Handicapped," *Exceptional Children*, 1983, 50, 160–166.

regarding known or presumed causes of the disorder. The PL 94-142 definition hints that the cause of learning disability *may* be a neurological dysfunction, because it includes "such conditions as perceptual handicaps, brain injury, minimal brain dysfunction, dyslexia, and developmental aphasia." It specifically excludes problems that are "primarily the result of visual, hearing, or motor handicaps, of mental retardation, of emotional disturbance, or environmental, cultural, or economic disadvantage." The NJCLD definition specifically states that learning disability is "presumed to be due to central nervous system dysfunction;" and like the PL 94-142 definition, it excludes other handicapping conditions and environmental influences as direct causes of learning disabilities.

Obviously, the drafters of current definitions felt that the inclusion of direct or indirect statements about *presumed* causes, and particularly the *exclusion* of certain causes, would be helpful in clarifying what a learning disability is and is not. Although these inclusions and exclusions may be consistent with the history of the field of learning disabilities (see Chapter 1), some believe the empirical foundation for them is weak. Some speculate, therefore, that the inclusionary and exclusionary phrases in the definitions serve merely to give school personnel plausible reasons for exercising their clinical judgment that one child is learning disabled and another is not.

It is logical to assume that learning is neurologically based. The empirical evidence, however, is overwhelming that, given the state of the art in neurological testing, neurological problems *cannot* be reliably connected causally to most of the problems LD children typically have (Kauffman & Hallahan, 1979; Hallahan & Bryan, 1981; Whalen, 1983). Why, then, could one argue that a presumption of neurological dysfunction should be included in the definition? Brain research does offer tantalizing suggestions that some disorders of learning may be the result of pathology or immaturity of the central nervous system, but most of the work in this area is inconclusive regarding the influence of brain mechanisms on behavior and offers little, if any, guidance for teaching the learning-disabled child (cf. Kinsbourne, 1983). Some authorities note that including the presumption of neurological dysfunction can be used to exclude children from the category of learning disability. Neurological dysfunction is the presumed cause of behavioral and learning problems only after other possible causes have been eliminated. That is, when other plausible causes (e.g., inadequate instruction, emotional disturbance, cultural disadvantage) are ruled out, then neurological dysfunction is ruled in.

Can one logically and reliably determine that learning disability is *not* the result of sensory impairment, mental retardation, social or emotional disturbance, cultural differences, insufficient or inappropriate instruction, or psychogenic factors? The answer is: not always. A variety of intrinsic, extrinsic, and unknown factors contribute to learning disabilities, and these same factors are implicated in emotional disturbance and mental retardation (see Figure 1.2, Chapter 1). Moreover, some have pointed out that it is illogical to exclude social and cultural disadvantage as a primary factor in the causation of learning disabilities when research indicates so clearly that such factors often lead to learning problems (Hallahan & Cruickshank, 1973).

The inclusionary and exclusionary statements regarding causes that are found in current definitions of learning disabilities may serve a useful function—allowance for clinical judgment in deciding whether or not a child is LD. It must be remembered, however, that one must weigh the pros and cons of including statements regarding causes when those causes are in most cases unknown.

Results of the Current Federal Definition

Some authorites are of the opinion that the current federal definition is so unspecific, even with attempts to operationalize it by using various formulas and cut-off scores, that most children are likely to fit at least one diagnostician's interpretation of it. This has undoubtedly resulted in a great deal of confusion and has been a factor in the tremendous growth in the number of children considered learning disabled. To some extent, this looseness in definition has been beneficial, one might argue. Perhaps many children who otherwise would have been labeled mentally retarded, disadvantaged, or emotionally disturbed have been labeled LD—a more socially acceptable, less stigmatizing label that has allowed them to receive appropriate education and legal protections they otherwise would not have had. Henker and Whalen (1980) have discussed the advantages of PL 94-142 for hyperactive children, who often qualify for special education under the LD category even though hyperactivity is not mentioned in the federal definition.

On the other hand, one might argue that the current federal definition has had a pernicious effect on educational practice. Clearly it has left special educators open to the criticism that they do not know whom they are serving, or even which children they *should* be serving. Ysseldyke, Algozzine, and Epps (1983) stated bluntly, "Special educators face much embarrassment in attempts to defend current classification practices" (p. 165). Moreover, the federal Department of Education appears to be moving in the direction of placing a "cap" on the LD category in the face of the rapidly growing numbers of children who are being identified as learning disabled (*Report on Education Research*, 1983).

One way of viewing the current federal definition is to consider it a mixed blessing, then. It provided a legal starting point for the field of learning disabilities. It has allowed special education and related services to be delivered to many children who otherwise might not have received them. But it has encouraged conceptual confusion rather than conceptual clarity. And it has opened the floodgates of demand for special education services and contributed to the deteriorating credibility of special educators' diagnostic procedures.

ISSUES REGARDING PREVALENCE

The prevalence of learning disabilities seems to some observers and commentators to be on a runaway course. Learning disability has become the predominant category in special education. Ever higher prevalence figures are, some special educators feel, threatening a severe backlash in which the field will lose political and economic support because it has grown beyond reasonable proportions. Some federal officials now suggest, apparently in response to dramatic increases in the number of mildly handicapped children receiving special education services, that we must begin to consider more carefully how the children who qualify for special education differ from those who need remedial education of some type but are not handicapped (Sontag, Button, & Hagerty, 1982). Identifying the *truly* handicapped child would, presumably, save the learning disabilities category from being overrun and the Department of Education's budget from being broken. The suggestion of Sontag et al. is well taken, but it does not provide a solution to the problem of runaway prevalence. Learning problems exist on a continuum ranging from insignificant to profound, and one has difficulty determining precisely the point at which a problem of remedial education that can be handled by the regular classroom teacher becomes a learning disability that requires the services of a special educator. One is still left with the problem of setting an arbitrary cutoff point based on subjective criteria—the same problem one faces in determining who is LD and who is not.

Because prevalence is ultimately determined by the definition one uses, the problem of prevalence may seem to be secondary. McCarthy (1971) attributes the following statement to H. R. Myklebust, a pioneer in the development of learning disabilities: " 'Tell me how many [learning-disabled children] you want to find, and I'll write you a definition that will find that many' " (p. 15). The data presented by Ysseldyke, Algozzine, and Epps (1983) and other researchers demonstrate the feasibility of Myklebust's statement. The data also suggest that the difference between special and remedial education is arbitrary and that the remedial-versus-special-education distinction proposed by Sontag et al. (1982) will be no easier to make than the LD/not LD distinction.

Factors other than definition influence prevalence, however. The evidence suggests that current definitional criteria are not being applied consistently across the country. In some states and localities, many times more children are being identified as learning disabled than in others (General Accounting Office, 1981;

Glass, 1981). In all likelihood, the biases of diagnosticians, as well as political and economic forces, contribute to these differences in prevalence. Commentary on prevalence estimates and prevalence statistics must take into account the fact that the political forces of lobbying, legislation, litigation, and local school boards, as well as school finance at every level of government, greatly influence the number of children estimated to have learning disabilities and the number actually identified.

We have seen that the problem of definition, aside from the prevalence that a given definition will produce, seems irresolvable in the light of our current diagnostic methods. Reynolds and Wang (1981) and Ysseldyke, Algozzine, and Epps (1983) have suggested emphasizing educational services rather than identification and placement in special education categories. This alternative involves eliminating federal regulations regarding the identification and labeling of children but retaining the regulations requiring that children receive an appropriate education. Federal funding could be provided at higher levels for those school systems furnishing more comprehensive and effective services, thus giving an incentive for innovative service delivery. The focus then would not be on prevalence of handicapped children but prevalence of services.

REFERENCES

ALGOZZINE, B., & YSSELDYKE, J. (1983). Learning disabilities as a subset of school failure: The over-sophistication of a concept. *Exceptional Children, 50,* 242–246.

BANNATYNE, A. (1979). Spatial competence, learning disabilities, auditory-vocal deficits, and a WISC-R subtest recategorization. *Journal of Clinical Child Psychology, 8,* 194–200.

EPPS, S., YSSELDYKE, J. E., & ALGOZZINE, B. (1983). Impact of different definitions of learning disabilities on the number of students identified. *Jour-*
nal of Psychoeducational Assessment, 1, 341–352.

General Accounting Office (1981). *Disparities still exist in who gets special education.* Report to the Chairman, Subcommittee on Select Education, Committee on Education and Labor, House of Representatives of the United States. Gaithersburg, MD: GAO.

GLASS, G. V. (1981). *Effectiveness of special education.* Paper presented at the Wingspread National Invitational Conference on Public Policy and the Special Education Task of the 1980s. Racine, WI.

HALLAHAN, D. P., & BRYAN, T. H. (1981). Learning disabilities. In J. M. Kauffman & D. P. Hallahan (Eds.), *Handbook of special education* (pp. 141–164). Englewood Cliffs, NJ: Prentice-Hall.

HALLAHAN, D. P., & CRUICKSHANK, W. M. (1973). *Psychoeducational foundations of learning disabilities.* Englewood Cliffs, NJ: Prentice-Hall.

HAMMILL, D. D., LEIGH, J. E., MCNUTT, G., & LARSEN, S. C. (1981). A new definition of learning disabilities. *Learning Disability Quarterly, 4,* 336–342.

HENKER, B., & WHALEN, C. K. (1980). The changing faces of hyperactivity: retrospect and prospect. In C. K. Whalen & B. Henker (Eds.), *Hyperactive children: The social ecology of identification and treatment* (pp. 321–363). New York: Academic Press.

KAUFFMAN, J. M., & HALLAHAN, D. P. (1979). Learning disability and hyperactivity (with comments on minimal brain dysfunction). In B. B. Lahey & A. E. Kazdin (Eds.), *Advances in clinical child psychology* (Vol. 2, pp. 71–105). New York: Plenum.

KINSBOURNE, M. (Ed.) (1983). Brain basis of learning disabilities. *Topics in Learning and Learning Disabilities, 3*(1).

KNEEDLER, R. D., & HALLAHAN, D. P. (Eds.). (1983). Research in learning disabilities: Summaries of the institutes. *Exceptional Education Quarterly, 4*(1).

MCCARTHY, J. M. (1971). Learning disabilities: Where have we been? Where are we going? In D. D. Hammill & N. R. Bartel (Eds.), *Educational perspectives in learning disabilities* (pp. 10–19). New York: Wiley.

MCKINNEY, J. D. (1983). Contributions of the institutes for research on learning disabilities. *Exceptional Education Quarterly, 4*(1), 129–144.

Report on Education Research (July 6, 1983). July 6, 15(14), 5–6.

REYNOLDS, M. C., & WANG, M. C. (1981). Restructuring "special" school programs: a position paper. Paper presented at the Wingspread National Invitational Conference on Public Policy and the Special Education Task of the 1980s. Racine, WI.

SCRIVEN, M. (1981). Comments on Gene Glass. Paper presented at the Wingspread National Invitational Conference on Public Policy and the Special Education Task of the 1980s. Racine, WI.

SHEPARD, L. A., SMITH, M. L., & VOJIR, C. P. (1983). Characteristics of pupils identified as learning disabled. *American Educational Research Journal, 20,* 309–331.

SONTAG, E., BUTTON, J. E., & HAGERTY, G. (1982). Quality and leadership in special education personnel preparation. Paper presented at Invitational Meeting for Personnel Preparation, Washington, DC.

WHALEN, C. K. (1983). Hyperactivity, learning problems, and the attention deficit disorders. In T. H. Ollendick & M. Hersen (Eds.), *Handbook of child psychopathology* (pp. 151–199). New York: Plenum.

YSSELDYKE, J., ALGOZZINE, B., & EPPS, S. (1983). A logical and empirical analysis of current practice in classifying students as handicapped. *Exceptional Children, 50,* 160–166.

YSSELDYKE, J., ALGOZZINE, B., & THURLOW, M. (1983). On interpreting institute research: A response to McKinney. *Exceptional Education Quarterly, 4*(1), 145–147.

YSSELDYKE, J. E. (1983). Current practices in making psychoeducational decisions about learning disabled students. *Journal of Learning Disabilities, 16,* 226–233.

YSSELDYKE, J. E., THURLOW, M., GRADEN, J., WESSON, C., ALGOZZINE, B., & DENO, S. (1983). Generalizations from five years of research on assessment and decision making: The University of Minnesota Institute. *Exceptional Education Quarterly, 4*(1), 75–94.

Index